THE L]

Karen Harvey is Reader in Cultural History at the University of Sheffield. She specializes in the long eighteenth century, and has published widely on gender, sexuality, and material culture.

The Little Republic

*Masculinity and Domestic Authority
in Eighteenth-Century Britain*

KAREN HARVEY

OXFORD
UNIVERSITY PRESS

OXFORD
UNIVERSITY PRESS

Great Clarendon Street, Oxford, OX2 6DP,
United Kingdom

Oxford University Press is a department of the University of Oxford.
It furthers the University's objective of excellence in research, scholarship,
and education by publishing worldwide. Oxford is a registered trade mark of
Oxford University Press in the UK and in certain other countries

© Karen Harvey 2012

The moral rights of the author have been asserted

First Edition published in 2012
First published in paperback 2014

Published in the United States of America by Oxford University Press
198 Madison Avenue, New York, NY 10016, United States of America

British Library Cataloguing in Publication Data
Data available

Library of Congress Cataloging in Publication Data
Data available

ISBN 978–0–19–953384–8 (Hbk)
ISBN 978–0–19–968613–1 (Pbk)

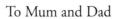

To Mum and Dad

Acknowledgements

This book would not have been completed without support from the following organizations: the Arts and Humanities Research Council for a Research Fellowship, the British Academy for a Small Research Grant and American Libraries Exchange Fellowships (at the Huntington Library), The William Andrews Clark Memorial Library and the 17th and 18th Century Studies University of California Los Angeles Center, the Andrew W. Mellon Foundation and the Henry E. Huntington Library, and finally the Department of History and Arts and Humanities Faculty at the University of Sheffield.

I thank the staff at Oxford University Press for their professionalism and continuing patience, and the anonymous readers for their constructive comments.

I have benefited from the comments of audiences at the universities of California State at Long Beach, Cambridge (Emmanuel College), Durham, Edinburgh, Exeter, Manchester, Newcastle, Oxford (Lincoln College), Princeton, Sheffield, and York, and at the Bard Graduate Centre, Institute of Historical Research, Victoria and Albert Museum, American Society for Eighteenth Century Studies, and the North American Conference on British Studies. Many individual colleagues have given information and advice during the project, for which I am grateful, including Patty Cleary, Flora Dennis, Clorinda Donato, Henry French, Stephen Hague, Tim Hitchcock, Julian Hoppit, Linda Kirk, Jennet Kirkpatrick, Ann Matchette, Michael McKeon, Alison Montgomery, Andrew Morrall, Craig Muldrew, Nicola Phillips, Carole Shammas, Norbert Schurer, Bob Shoemaker, John Smail, Tim Stretton, Claudia Tiersch, Susan Whyman, and Maria Zytaruk. For his support I thank John Tosh in particular. Several generous colleagues read late drafts of chapters and I have benefited from their expertise: I thank Matthew McCormack, Nicola Phillips, Alexandra Shepard, and especially Joanne Bailey and Helen Berry. Mike Braddick read (or listened to) everything and I thank him for his insightful comments.

I would also like to thank the many undergraduates at the University of Sheffield—too many to mention by name—who have discussed these ideas with me. Colleagues in the Department of History, and those several scattered throughout the University of Sheffield who work on the eighteenth century and material culture, have helped generate a creative environment in which to work. Several assistants and researchers have helped with tasks I was not able to do myself: Denzel Bath, Ros Buck, Alan Crosby, Kate Henderson, George Newberry, Matt Phillpott, Gary Rivett, Kathryn Stout, and Heather Swinsco. Staff at numerous libraries and local record offices have been very helpful, John Harnden at Herefordshire Record Office and Mary Robertson at the Huntington particularly so. For their generosity I would particularly like to extend my thanks to Elaine Hurst and Christine Jones at Astley Hall (Damhouse), Jonathan Kay, and Mr and Mrs Pickup.

Family has been dear to me during the later stages of this project; I am lucky that mine is Ken, Elaine, Mathew, Philip, Julie, Joanne, Charlotte, Max, and Sam Harvey. I could not have finished this without many wonderful friends, especially Helen Berry, Bec Christie, Eve Setch, Alex Shepard, and Maria Zytaruk. But for love, laughs, and joy, absolutely everything comes back to Mike, Cora, and Melissa. Let the good times roll!

Contents

List of Illustrations

1

Introduction

The little republic to which I gave laws, was regulated in the following manner: by sun-rise we all assembled in our common apartment; the fire being previously kindled by the servant.[1]

The family having suffered financial misfortunes, the vicar Charles Primrose brings his wife and children to a humble retreat. Primrose is given to lengthy speeches on proper governance in the state and it is also his wont to deliver solemn instructions to his children. Yet he does not govern over the family through abstract directives. The regulation of his 'little republic' is achieved not by 'laws' but out of both the habitual practices in which the family engage together and the physical nature of their house. 'Our little habitation' is snug at the base of a little hill, he explains, surrounded by neat hedges, marked by nice white-washed walls, filled with home-made pictures and well scoured dishes, and comprising just enough space—but no more—than will accommodate the family. Primrose's authority is grounded in his engagement with these material and social practices. His family will be pulled apart and his authority will come under threat; indeed, it will be the cause of some amusement. Yet even those who smile are acquainted with the kind of man they understand Primrose to be, and they recognize that his 'little republic' is the epicentre of his life.

In eighteenth-century British visual and written culture, the house became more visible than ever before. New genres exposed the domestic interior, which became increasingly a richly detailed setting for human dramas. Most notably, the domestic novel and the conversation piece imagined the activities of families in their homes. And men were present in these interiors, planted firmly next to wives in paintings and sometimes dominating the spaces of the home in novels.[2] Men's engagement with the domestic was a frequent subject of satire and humour, as it was almost certainly in *The Vicar of Wakefield* (1766), yet in many novels the nature

---

[1] Oliver Goldsmith, *The Vicar of Wakefield* (1766, Harmondsworth: Penguin, 1982, 1986), chapter 4, p. 50.

[2] See Michael McKeon, *The Secret History of Domesticity: Public, Private, and the Division of Knowledge* (London, Baltimore: Johns Hopkins University Press, 2005), pp. 672–717 on men in domestic novels; Hannah Greig, 'Eighteenth-Century English Interiors in Image and Text' in Jeremy Aynsley and Charlotte Grant (eds), *Imagined Interiors: Representing the Domestic Interior since the Renaissance* (London: V&A Publications, 2006), pp. 102–12.

of the authority that the father-patriarch wielded in the home featured as a source of some anxiety.[3] Nevertheless, the relationship between men and the domestic in the eighteenth century remains obscure.

Belied by representations of men in the domestic environment, this obscurity is the result of two very important and well-established historiographical narratives. The first charts changes in domestic patriarchy, founded on political patriarchalism in the early modern period and transformed during the eighteenth century by new types of family relationship rooted in contract theory. The second describes the emergence of a new kind of domestic interior during the long eighteenth century, a 'home' infused with a new culture of 'domesticity' primarily associated with women and femininity. In this book, I wish to shift the terms of these debates such that the engagement of men with the house is less obscure, and historians are better equipped to understand masculinity, the domestic environment, and domestic patriarchy. Let us now consider these two narratives in turn.

NEW-STYLED PATRIARCHY

It is well-established that before the mid-seventeenth century, the house and its social relationships were critical to men's wider social status. Political patriarchalism elevated the household as the key unit of social control, and the family was crucial in an analogy that aligned order in the household with order in the polity. In both practical and representational terms, a man's authority in the household was a central element in this political theory. Rapid social change in the seventeenth century put a premium on social order, found Susan Amussen, and the family was a key instrument in this.[4] The individual household was established as 'the primary unit of social control', and the householder's patriarchal control utilized for 'macrocosmic benefit'.[5] Printed sources on the household furnish plenty of supporting examples. As Dudley North wrote in 1669, 'All Power and Office is derived from the Sovereign in a State, and so is all from the Master in a Family. The Protection and Defence of a Kingdom belongs onely to the King, and so of a Family to the Master. All the People pay tribute to the Sovereign, and all work of Servants in a Family, whence profit may arise, is to the Masters use.'[6] Following the Restoration, however, the elite were more secure, discipline operated in more subtle ways, and the family was no longer required

---

[3] Brian McCrea, *Impotent Fathers: Patriarchy and Demographic Crisis in the Eighteenth-Century Novel* (Newark: University of Delaware Press, 1998), p. 28, *passim*. On *The Vicar of Wakefield*, see James P. Carson, '"The Little Republic" of the Family: Goldsmith's Politics of Nostalgia', *Eighteenth-Century Fiction*, 16, 2 (2004), pp. 173–96; Christopher Flint, '"The Family Piece": Oliver Goldsmith and the Politics of the Everyday in Eighteenth-Century Domestic Portraiture', *Eighteenth-Century Studies*, 29, 2 (1995–6), pp. 127–52.

[4] Susan Dwyer Amussen, *An Ordered Society: Gender and Class in Early Modern England* (New York: Columbia University Press, 1988).

[5] Lena Cowen Orlin, *Private Matters and Public Culture in Post-Reformation England* (Ithaca and London: Cornell University Press, 1994), p. 3.

[6] Dudley North, *Observations and Advices Oeconomical* (London, 1669), p. 33.

to sustain social order.[7] It was here, Amussen argued, that the roots of the private eighteenth-century family and the 'separate spheres' family of the nineteenth century were to be found.

Underpinning these findings are histories of political theory, notably Gordon J. Schochet's *The Authoritarian Family and Political Attitudes in 17th-Century England* (1975). Seeking first to restore patriarchalism to its rightful place in the history of political theory, this book then assessed changes in theories of political obligation. The book begins with Sir Robert Filmer's *Patriarcha* (written in *c*.1639, published in 1680)—invariably regarded as the exemplar of patriarchal political theory—in which magistrates gained their authority from and were due the same obedience as fathers, both divinely ordained. Schochet ends with John Locke's *Two Treatises of Government* (1690) which sought to distinguish between political and patriarchal authority and to craft a new basis for allegiance to a magistrate built upon the trust he inspired in operating for the common good. In this move from Filmer to Locke, Schochet tracked what he referred to as '[t]he disappearance of the family from Anglo-American political thought over two hundred years ago'.[8] It is this lifting of the political burden from the household in canonical political treatises that many subsequent histories reconstruct in practice; the absence of men in the eighteenth-century house mirrors this absence of the household from eighteenth-century theories of political obligation.

For all the rhetoric, patriarchalism as a model for the household was unstable in early-modern England. Lena Orlin's insightful work shows domestic patriarchy built upon this model as highly contested, 'irresolute in theory', and no doubt (she speculates) in social practice too.[9] Sure enough, a simple patriarchal model-in which men exercised unlimited control and women were submissive was not how lives were lived. Many women resisted ideals of female submissiveness.[10] Even when a powerful rhetoric of male power and female subordination circulated, women could soften and bypass male authority, without challenging it outright.[11] Outside the family, certainly, women could find areas outside male control, and even within the family, the wife was 'a subordinate magistrate within the miniature commonwealth of the family'.[12] As George Wheler put it in 1698, a wife in the family is 'acting by the joynt, tho not Independent Authority of her Husband'.[13]

---

[7] Amussen, *An Ordered Society*, pp. 31–2, 101–3, 186.

[8] Gordon J. Schochet, *The Authoritarian Family and Political Attitudes in 17th-Century England* (1975; New Brunswick, NJ: Transaction, 1988), p. xxv. See also Gordon J. Schochet, 'The Significant Sounds of Silence: The Absence of Women from the Political Thought of Sir Robert Filmer and John Locke (or, "Why can't a woman be more like a man?")', in Hilda Smith (ed.), *Women Writers and the Early Modern British Political Tradition* (Cambridge: Cambridge University Press, 1998), pp. 220–42.

[9] Orlin, *Private Matters and Public Culture*, p. 4.

[10] Laura Gowing, *Domestic Dangers: Women, Words and Sex in Early Modern London* (Oxford: Clarendon Press, 1996), pp. 185, 186.

[11] Bernard Capp, 'Separate Domains? Women and Authority in Early Modern England', in Paul Griffiths, Adam Fox and Steve Hindle (eds), *The Experience of Authority in Early Modern England* (Basingstoke: Macmillan, 1996), p. 125.

[12] Ibid. p. 130, quote at p. 127.

[13] George Wheler, *The Protestant Monastery: or, Christian Oeconomicks* (London, 1698), p. 50.

Men were to use both love and coercive power in the exercise of paternal authority, Wheler advised, while women should employ feminine wiles.[14] Wheler's Christian manifesto for the home reveals a complex understanding of what power was and how it might be exercised by the many different people in the house. There were gradations of power in the home, and authority was effected by different people in different ways.

The realities of early-modern households made men's fulfilment of patriarchy difficult.[15] And men's patriarchal authority was contested by other men as well as women; as Alexandra Shepard has shown, patriarchal authority was only one route to manliness.[16] Linda Pollock finds that family relationships—between siblings as well as between husbands and wives—experienced life cycles in which alliances and power relations changed over time.[17] The balance necessary for effective patriarchal authority was not simply that between husband and wife: patriarchy was more 'insecure and unsettled' than we once thought, Pollock believes, partly because of 'the constant threat of being undermined by other men, who had the power to cause harm'.[18] Power in the household was channelled through various routes, just as in this patriarchal society several hierarchies operated at any one time. Patriarchy was not a rigid system of male governance but a flexible 'grid of power' in which several different groups attained status and authority.[19] It is not surprising that, as Tim Meldrum has succinctly put it, households were characterized by a 'diversity of modes of authority'.[20] 'Patriarchy' as a term of description for the early-modern household should be used with care: it should not be understood to mean that only a male household head possessed authority and at the expense of others in the household. If patriarchy in general was a grid of relations, then domestic patriarchy was a system of order in the household in which different individuals may each have access to different kinds and levels of power. Thus, power in the household was not a zero sum game. Nevertheless, there is no dissent: men's governance in the household was deemed one important route to early-modern manly honour.[21] Men's domestic authority was the linchpin of domestic patriarchy as a system of order in the household, and this is why the figure

[14] Ibid. pp. 26, 45.
[15] One important example is Anthony Fletcher, *Gender, Sex and Subordination in England, 1500–1800* (New Haven; London: Yale University Press, 1995), pp. 230, 403–7.
[16] Alexandra Shepard, 'Manhood, Credit and Patriarchy in Early Modern England c. 1580–1640', *Past and Present*, 167 (2000), p. 106.
[17] Linda Pollock, 'Rethinking Patriarchy and the Family in Seventeenth-Century England', *Journal of Family History*, 23, 1 (1998), pp. 3–27, esp. pp. 4–5.
[18] Ibid. p. 22.
[19] Michael J. Braddick and John Walter, 'Introduction. Grids of Power: Order, Hierarchy and Subordination in Early Modern Society', in Michael J. Braddick and John Walter (eds), *Negotiating Power in Early Modern Society: Order, Hierarchy and Subordination in Britain and Ireland* (Cambridge: Cambridge University Press, 2001), pp. 1–42.
[20] Tim Meldrum, *Domestic Service and Gender, 1660–1750: Life and Work in the London House* (Harlow: Pearson, 2000), p. 37.
[21] Elizabeth Foyster, *Manhood in Early Modern England: Honour, Sex and Marriage* (Harlow: Addison, Wesley, Longman, 1999), *passim*.

of the household patriarch is well-developed in works on early-modern masculinity.[22]

Long-term continuity is suggested by John Tosh's study of men and the nineteenth-century home in *A Man's Place* (1999). Home was seen not only as a man's 'possession or fiefdom, but also as the place where his deepest needs were met'. Men were measured in part against their fulfilment of the roles of 'dutiful husbands and attentive fathers, devotees of hearth and home'.[23] Public standing flowed partly from domestic authority; '[d]omestic patriarchy' was crucial for masculinity.[24] Yet despite the apparent links between the seventeenth and nineteenth centuries, accounts of how domestic patriarchy transformed in the eighteenth century are quite distinct. Famously, Lawrence Stone's *Family, Sex and Marriage* (1977) replaced the patriarchal with the companionate family, tracing a shift from order and hierarchy to emotion and romantic love. These changes in domestic patriarchy were enabled partly by a process of consolidating individualism, which served to dismantle the authority of the domestic patriarch in the face of growing autonomy of other people in the household. As William James Booth explains, '[i]n place of the hierarchy of the household metaphor, liberal theory offered the concept of the juridical person, detached from a context of ruler and ruled, and equally endowed with the basic rights inherent in self-ownership or autonomy'.[25] Both political authority *and* household authority were made impersonal in contract theory.[26] One apparent result is a shift in the balance of power between husbands and wives.

A similar trajectory has been charted for early America. Mary Beth Norton's study, *Founding Mothers and Fathers* (1996) explores the day-to-day running of a patriarchal system in mid-seventeenth-century Anglo-America. Though challenged, the family was here dominated by the 'unified authority' of adult men as husband, preacher, and magistrate, a system which emphasized order, hierarchy, and paternal power in the family and the polity. By the mid-eighteenth century, an alternative view had taken hold: the family and polity were separated, the former made private and also closely related to women.[27] Carole Shammas has succinctly criticized this work: 'Notions about the antipatriarchal tendencies of republicanism become fused with modernization of the family arguments to produce one big theoretical stone of intergenerational affectivity rolling down a 1750–1850 hill and crushing the parental rod and patriarchal control over children's marriages and occupations.'[28]

[22] For a fuller discussion, see Karen Harvey, 'The History of Masculinity, circa 1650–1800', in Karen Harvey and Alexandra Shepard (eds), 'Special Feature on Masculinities' in *The Journal of British Studies*, 44, 2 (2005), pp. 298–300.

[23] John Tosh, *A Man's Place: Masculinity and the Middle-Class Home in Victorian England* (New Haven, Conn; London: Yale University Press, 1999), p. 1.

[24] Ibid. p. 4.

[25] William James Booth, *Households: On the Moral Architecture of the Economy* (Ithaca; London: Cornell University Press, 1993), pp. 174–5.

[26] Ibid. p. 144.

[27] Mary Beth Norton, *Founding Mothers and Fathers: Gendered Power and the Formation of American Society* (New York: Alfred A. Knopf, 1996), *passim*, esp. 404–5.

[28] Carole Shammas, *A History of Household Government in America* (Charlottesville; London: University of Virginia Press, 2002), p. 132.

Shammas's *A History of Household Government* (2002) argues that colonists in early America expanded the household head's jurisdiction to include some of the responsibilities of the state to a much greater degree and for much longer than in West Europe. The American Revolution (1775–83) and the rhetoric of libertinism had little impact on this. Instead, the father's powers were checked by legal rather than affective change, and only from around 1820. By 1880, 'separate spheres domesticity', with the paterfamilias offstage and remote, had been established.[29]

Very few scholars would now claim that domestic patriarchy collapsed in the eighteenth century. Women could be subjected as much by romantic ideals and language as they were by openly articulated rules of patriarchal authority and hierarchy.[30] The seminal work of Carole Pateman examined the apparent change marked by Locke, arguing that women remained subject to men as men but under different rules.[31] In the most important work on family and political thought, Rachel Weil disagrees with Pateman's reading of Filmer, but concurs that while Filmer used family relations as a metaphor for political relations, later Whig writers were concerned with the family itself.[32] For England, Anthony Fletcher's *Gender, Sex and Subordination* (1995) offers the most important sustained argument in this regard. Fletcher presents a sixteenth- and seventeenth-century world of subordination and discipline: 'Men wanted their wives to be both subordinate and competent.'[33] Subject to various challenges, patriarchy was subsequently revised and reinvigorated, and a new form of patriarchy emerged: a secular ideology based less on law, religion, and education through which men and women internalized the values that ensured their fulfilment of appropriate roles.[34] So fully did women internalize subordination, that men's use of violence to enforce obedience became less necessary.[35] Elizabeth Kowaleski-Wallace has also argued that family members' internalization of a father's rule characterized a 'new-style patriarchy'. As others have done, Kowaleski-Wallace draws on the work of Michel Foucault and Norbert Elias concerning the control of the individual through knowledge, culture, and manners in the eighteenth century. In this context the intense emotional relationships between fathers (or father-figures) and daughters depicted in eighteenth-century

---

[29] Ibid. *passim*, and p. 144.

[30] See, for example, Susan Moller Okin, 'Women and the Making of the Sentimental Family', *Philosophy and Public Affairs* (1982),11, 1, pp. 65–88.

[31] Pavla Miller, *Transformations of Patriarchy in the West: 1500–1900* (Bloomington: Indiana University Press, 1998), p. 67.

[32] Rachel Weil, *Political Passions: Gender, the Family and Political Argument in England, 1680–1714* (Manchester: Manchester University Press, 1999), p. 35.

[33] Fletcher, *Gender, Sex and Subordination*, p. 174.

[34] Fletcher's theory of the reinvigoration of patriarchy builds on earlier suggestions that men's power continued but changed in nature/justification during the eighteenth century. See, for example, Elizabeth Kowaleski-Wallace, who argues (against Stone and Trumbach) that with the influence of Locke there was not a decline of patriarchy, but rather an internalization of a father's rule over his children, and a 'new-style patriarchy': Elizabeth Kowaleski-Wallace (ed.), *Their Fathers' Daughters: Hannah More, Maria Edgeworth, and Patriarchal Complicity* (New York; Oxford: Oxford University Press, 1991), p. 17.

[35] Fletcher, *Gender, Sex and Subordination*, p. 203.

women's fiction confirmed that women were safely devotional.[36] For Pavla Miller this shift is less about love than self-control: '[a]s the patriarchalist social order began to falter, a number of thinkers speculated that peace, order, and prosperity could be secured if subjects as well as masters internalized a rigorous government of the self.'[37] The home may not have been integral to eighteenth-century theories of political obligation, nor even a mirror held up to the polity, but the connection between the home and the world had been reconceived rather than severed. The home was still required to stabilize and order the self, and was thus connected to the world (the 'public sphere') through subjectivity.[38]

Eighteenth-century domestic patriarchy appears to have operated in more subtle ways, though because these works rarely speak about the material practices of power it can be difficult to see quite how men maintained and exercised domestic authority in everyday life. Yet just as Tosh wishes to emphasize both 'domestic affections and domestic authority' in his study of the nineteenth-century home,[39] so some works insist on the continuing power of a more visible patriarchal model in the eighteenth century. Shawn Lisa Maurer's close study of early-eighteenth-century periodicals finds that 'ideas of companionship and complementarity served to reinscribe patriarchal attitudes, albeit in new forms. Men remained the intellectual, moral, and even, surprisingly, the emotional centers of the household, in addition to and as an important foundation of their work in the public realm.'[40] Sensitive to the nuances of power, and emphasizing how this 'simultaneously privileged and oppressed men', Maurer shows that it was 'as economic man—a position very different from the supposedly disinterested participant in the ancient *polis*, and a role mistakenly perceived as separate from private, domestic functions and relations—that the middle-class husband (and husbander) of the eighteenth century constructed himself as a familial patriarch'.[41] J. C. D. Clark's argument for the continuing efficacy of *ancien régime* structures of authority into the nineteenth century include a claim for the ongoing significance of political patriarchalism in the household.[42] Yet we do not need to accept the larger picture to recognize that for many groups—not just the traditional elite—a patriarchal model of family remained meaningful. Lisa Forman Cody's examination of images of fatherhood and of the King argues that a crisis in patriarchy/paternity in the second half of the eighteenth century was countered with efforts to reinstate men's authority over reproduction and the body. These efforts referenced a still viable patriarchal model of household.[43] Similarly, Matthew McCormack has

---

[36] Kowaleski-Wallace, *Their Fathers' Daughters*, p. 17; Eleanor Wikborg, *The Lover as Father Figure in Eighteenth-Century Women's Fiction* (Gainesville, FL: University Press of Florida, 2002), pp. 8–9.

[37] Miller, *Transformations of Patriarchy*, p. xvii.

[38] David Solkin, *Painting for Money: The Visual Arts and the Public Sphere in Eighteenth-Century England* (New Haven: Yale University Press, 1992), p. 86.

[39] Tosh, *Man's Place*, p. 1.

[40] Shawn Lisa Maurer, *Proposing Men: Dialectics of Gender and Class in the Eighteenth-Century English Periodical* (Stanford, CA: Stanford University Press, 1998), pp. 28–9.

[41] Ibid. pp. 29, 24.

[42] J. C. D. Clark, *English Society 1660–1832: Religion, Ideology and Politics during the Ancien Régime* (1985; Cambridge: Cambridge University Press, 2000), pp. 172–84.

[43] Lisa Forman Cody, *Birthing the Nation: Sex, Science, and the Conception of Eighteenth-Century Britons* (Oxford: Oxford University Press, 2005), p. 270.

carefully rehabilitated the patriarchal household as the linchpin of eighteenth-century political action.[44] Indeed, McCormack argues that it was changes in the eighteenth-century household itself that transformed the notions of electoral citizenship: 'an understanding of independent manliness predicated upon sentimental domesticity' shifted the focus from the markers of elite men (landed property and rank) to manly qualities and their expression through the roles of 'father, husband, breadwinner and householder'.[45] And while satire is a notoriously slippery historical source, the many jibes—often affectionate—made at the expense of men's attempts at exercising patriarchal authority in the home suggest some store set by these figures.[46] Order in the household more generally became a laughing matter in Swift's brutal *Directions to Servants* (1745), in which the stewards are instructed to 'Lend my Lord his own Money' and the house-keeper to ensure a favourite footman watches out while she and the steward 'may have a Tit-bit together'.[47]

A variety of sources suggest that the patriarchal household was a meaningful but also somewhat problematic concept in the eighteenth century. Tensions observable in sixteenth- and seventeenth-century families continued. The work of Joanne Bailey examines the conflicts that arose in marriage when the 'intrinsic ambivalence between the ideal of manhood and realities of marital material life could not be accommodated'.[48] The exigencies of married life necessarily involved an attenuation of the ideal of the male provisioner, in part through the expertise and authority held by women in the household. As Bailey puts it, 'co-dependency worked against male autonomy'.[49] Conflict arose because the expectations of female domestic expertise and male authority coincided. These are tantalizing glimpses of what would appear to be a culture in which the household remains central to the construction of culturally vaunted forms of masculinity. It is such a culture that this book sets out to reconstruct.

FROM HOME TO HOUSE

Yet how can there be such a culture to reconstruct if, as historical work on domesticity claims, the home was predicated on men's absence? Certainly, men's engagements with the eighteenth-century house are overshadowed in chronicles of the emergence of domesticity. Some recent works imply an inverse relation between domesticity and patriarchy during the eighteenth century. Created in new domestic architecture and decoration, embedded in modern concepts of the self through new forms of narrative, or performed through sociability using new items of

[44] Matthew McCormack, *The Independent Man: Citizenship and Gender Politics in Georgian England* (Manchester and New York: Manchester University Press, 2005), pp. 12–30.

[45] Ibid. 19, 18.

[46] In addition to Oliver Goldsmith, *The Vicar of Wakefield* (1766), with which this chapter began, for example, we must note Laurence Sterne's *The Life and Opinions of Tristram Shandy, Gentleman* (1759–67).

[47] Reverend Dr [Jonathan] Swift, *Directions to Servants in General* (London, 1745), pp. 73, 92.

[48] Joanne Bailey, *Unquiet Lives: Marriage and Marriage Breakdown in England, 1660–1800* (Cambridge: Cambridge University Press, 2003), p. 199.

[49] Ibid. p. 199.

material culture, eighteenth-century England is for many scholars *the* time and place where modern domesticity was invented, before coalescing into a more intense nineteenth-century domestic culture. Carole Shammas argues that the home became a centre for non-market-oriented sociability in the eighteenth century, a sociability orchestrated by women that stood opposed to the sociability outside the home engaged in by men.[50] A more broadly conceived domesticity is discussed in works on the eighteenth-century middling sort, notably those by Leonore Davidoff and Catherine Hall, and by John Smail, in which a feminine domestic ideology is one component of middle-class identity. As Margaret Ponsonby has summarized, '[t]he home was increasingly expected to be a haven of domesticity; in particular it should be the woman's role to create a home for her family'.[51] The separation of men and domesticity is now complete: eighteenth-century men were inducted into domesticity only by their wives, and otherwise unable to enter the domestic state.[52]

Through domesticity women gained power. In particular, through their responsibility for the fitting up and running of the home, women accrued status both within and without the home. Advice literature prepared gentry women for 'the exercise of power', and while a gendered hierarchy in the home was regarded as normal, the seemingly unending dramatic struggles between men and women dented patriarchal power and left space for 'female assertiveness'.[53] As Mary Beth Norton wrote of early American British colonies, paternal power was replaced by maternal care.[54] Taking histories of domestic patriarchy together with histories of domesticity, a remarkable shift appears to take place: if the seventeenth-century household was governed by men, the eighteenth-century home was a source of authority for women. From the perspective of the history of masculinity, but also gender history more widely, this body of work raises many questions. Did the culture of domesticity exclude men from the home? Undermine their engagements with it? Disqualify their claims to manly status through the household? As the 'home' took shape, how could men legitimately engage with the domestic?

Though rarely done, let us tease out what 'domesticity' means in historical work. For Carole Shammas, domesticity was created through specific social practices organized by women, notably those around new objects for hot drinks, taking place in an environment emptied of market-oriented activity. These components have been built upon by others: domesticity was constituted from a wide range of material objects used within an architectural space—the 'home'—that was not

---

[50] Carole Shammas, 'The Domestic Environment in Early Modern England and America', *Journal of Social History*, 14 (1980), pp. 3–24.

[51] Margaret Ponsonby, *Stories from Home: English Domestic Interiors, 1750–1850* (Aldershot: Ashgate, 2007), p. 13.

[52] Amanda Vickery, *Behind Closed Doors: At Home in Georgian England* (New Haven, Conn: Yale University Press, 2009), p. 88.

[53] Amanda Vickery, *The Gentleman's Daughter: Women's Lives in Georgian England* (New Haven, Conn: Yale University Press, 1998), p. 127; Vickery, *Behind Closed Doors*, p. 165. The degree of actual power women gleaned through this domestic role is a topic of some debate. See, for example, Kathryn Shevelow, *Women and Print Culture: the Construction of Femininity in the Early Periodical* (London: Routledge, 1989).

[54] Norton, *Founding Mothers and Fathers, passim*, esp. 404–5.

only spatially but increasingly ideologically separate from others, notably those for 'work' but also places for other forms of leisure and public activity. Whether or not the home is described as 'private', it is separated from other places and activities. John Tosh articulates this concept of domesticity when fully formed in the nineteenth century, identified by 'privacy and comfort, separation from the workplace, and the merging of domestic space and family members into a single commanding concept (in English, "home")'; significantly, domesticity had also by then acquired 'psychological and emotional dimensions'.[55] Rather than view the eighteenth century as a prequel to this nineteenth-century domestic culture, eighteenth-century domesticity displayed a distinctive nature and chronology. There were in fact two distinct stages. Prior to the 1740s, material changes transformed more homes into places of sociability and comfort; the domestic interior acquired greater material distinctiveness and was represented as an identifiable and separate place. It was at this point, in fact, that the domestic novel and conversation piece emerged. These genres register how in the second half of the eighteenth century, 'home' was given additional weight as an emotional and psychological category.[56]

Significantly, men were active in both stages of eighteenth-century domesticity. They consumed the objects from which domestic culture was crafted and were acknowledged to be essential figures in the emotionally laden place of home. Domesticity was gendered, but the home was not the preserve of women alone; 'whether constituted by authority, things, emotional or representational richness, men were implicated in, even necessary to, its constitution'.[57] In English domestic novels, certainly, 'domestic intimacy' could be founded in 'homosocial relationships'; men forged domesticity without women.[58] Margaret Hunt's *The Middling Sort: Commerce, Gender and the Family in England, 1680–1780* (1996) has made the most significant contribution to this subject. Hunt establishes that a 'middling moral discourse' was expressed in 'private domesticity', and that this served as a foundation for public virtue. Hunt is careful to show that this culture of home was created out of the different but equally significant contributions of both men and women, boys and girls. This middling-sort domesticity was as much about hard work and moral prudence, as it was about comfort, taste, and sociability.[59] Tosh makes the emphatic statement that '[t]he Victorian ideal of domesticity was in all respects the creation of men as much as women. "Woman's sphere" was a convenient shorthand, not a call to exclusivity'.[60] While there were tensions between masculinity and domesticity, historians of masculinity no longer regard

[55] Tosh, *Man's Place*, pp. 4, 30.

[56] Karen Harvey, 'Men Making Home in Eighteenth-Century Britain', *Gender & History*, 21, 3 (2009), pp. 527–8.

[57] Ibid. pp. 528–9.

[58] McKeon, *Secret History of Domesticity*, pp. 672, 673.

[59] Margaret Hunt, *The Middling Sort: Commerce, Gender and the Family in England, 1680–1780* (Berkeley: University of California Press, 1996), pp. 193–215. Quotes at pp. 199, 202.

[60] Tosh, *Man's Place*, p. 50. Deborah Cohen, *Household Gods: The British and their Possessions* (New Haven, Conn: Yale University Press, 2006) reinforces this. Her chapter 'In Possession', pp. 81–121, shows how only at the very end of the nineteenth century did men give up control of domestic culture.

men's activities in and valuing of the home as a transgression of a gendered private/public division. 'The point is rather', Tosh remarks, 'that men operated at will in *both* spheres; that was their privilege.'[61] There is as yet no study comparable to Tosh's for the eighteenth century, but it is evident that women were not the gatekeepers of the home.

It is also evident that 'domesticity' was not separate from the world outside the domestic, despite the impression (created in some sources and underlined in later studies) that 'true domesticity' was separate from business.[62] This is a profoundly important feature of Leonore Davidoff and Catherine Hall's *Family Fortunes* (1987).[63] It is also a central point of Hunt's work, which places domesticity alongside the public, political sphere within middling-sort family life.[64] Both studies also attend to both men's and women's role in domestic culture and the work undertaken by women in the domestic arena. Indeed, the home was created as a moral sphere, but this did not mean it was apolitical.[65] This view of domesticity has been furthered by Michael McKeon's *The Secret History of Domesticity: Public, Private, and the Division of Knowledge* (2005). McKeon examines the changing application of the concepts of 'public' and 'private', underlining the dominance of political patriarchalism until the late seventeenth century, and the subsequent separation of the home and polity in political theory.[66] A broader process of separation took place, however, in which an ever-increasing series of categories were divided as either public or private: family and state, home and public, men and women. It was this categorization or separation of knowledge that, for McKeon, constituted the transition to the modern world. Yet this modern separation of knowledge into 'public' and 'private' culminated in conflation. In modern societies, 'public' and 'private' are conflated in domesticity, argues McKeon, evident first in late-eighteenth-century domestic novels. McKeon has provided an intellectual history to complement the findings of women's and gender historians who emphasize that the domestic was emphatically not private, and that boundaries were blurred and porous.[67] Indeed, focusing on men's engagements with home shows how domesticity and home remained connected to the public, serving as implicit comments on the ethical and political. Armed with these insights about practice and language, we can move past arguments for the separation of public and private and expose

[61] John Tosh, 'The Old Adam and the New Man: Emerging Themes in the History of English Masculinities, 1750–1850', in Tim Hitchcock and Michelle Cohen (eds), *English Masculinities, 1660–1800* (London: Longman, 1999), p. 230.

[62] Elizabeth Kowaleski-Wallace, *Consuming Subjects. Women, Shopping, and Business in the Eighteenth Century* (New York: Columbia University Press, 1997), p. 121.

[63] Leonore Davidoff and Catherine Hall, *Family Fortunes: Men and Women of the English Middle Class, 1780–1850* (1987; Routledge, London, 1992).

[64] Hunt, *Middling Sort*, p. 9.

[65] Miller, *Transformations of Patriarchy*, pp. 125–6.

[66] McKeon, *The Secret History of Domesticity, passim*; Michael McKeon, 'Historicizing Patriarchy: The Emergence of Gender Difference in England, 1660–1760', *Eighteenth-Century Studies* 28, 3 (1995), pp. 296–8.

[67] For descriptions of space in seventeenth-century court cases, see Amanda Flather, *Gender and Space in Early Modern England* (Woodbridge: Boydell Press, 2007), *passim*, esp. pp. 43–4, 177. See also Orlin, *Private Matters and Public Culture, passim*.

the political and ethical issues that were embedded within the house. This study does so through a particular focus on masculinity.

An attention to 'home' is partly a manifestation of the more culturally inflected approaches to family life that have joined a long-standing historical interest in the early-modern family and household. Dominated in the early stages by demographic research, this area soon developed powerful chronologies of change in the composition of families, the role of wider kin, and the nature of hierarchy in the household.[68] These works examined the effect of demographic, economic and social factors on peoples' experiences of family. The word 'home' suggests something other than a collection of social relationships (family), an economic unit (household), or a physical construction (domestic interior). 'Home' encompasses all these meanings and more, notably the imaginative, emotional, or representational. 'Home' had certainly acquired new and rich meanings by the eighteenth century, and as I have discussed above, we can restore men's contributions to this domesticity.[69] This emphatically does not mean, however, that men and women shared the same attitudes towards the home, or performed the same roles. Gender should be central to a proper understanding of domestic life. The characterization of the home as a feminized space was an established trope well before the eighteenth century, with the result that men were imagined to have a problematical relationship with the home. In early modern drama, for example, the house was 'a symptom of the male subject . . . intimately connected with his political, social, and moral identities and functions'; but at the same time it was a source of some uneasiness, and never quite within a man's control.[70] This fraught issue of possession and authority is one that remained in the eighteenth century. An important claim of this study is that in transforming the eighteenth-century house into a home, we overemphasize just one of the rich meanings of the domestic interior possible during the eighteenth century. 'Home' is simply too narrow a concept for an understanding of eighteenth-century domestic experience, and it serves to overemphasize a particular formulation of 'domesticity'.

'Home' did not exhaust the meanings of the eighteenth-century house. Judith Lewis has found that aristocratic women used 'home' to refer to only those places of residence associated with 'emotional and physical comfort, family intimacy, and personal attachment'.[71] Not only did the aristocracy, as well as middling groups, invest in domesticity, but not all houses had been colonized by the home, at least for these women. It is the concept of 'house' that I will employ in this study.

---

[68] Peter Laslett, *The World We Have Lost* (London: Methuen, 1965); Peter Laslett, *Family Life and Illicit Love in Earlier Generations: Essays in Historical Sociology* (Cambridge: Cambridge University Press, 1977); Peter Laslett and Richard Wall (eds), *Household and Family in Past Time: Comparative Studies in the Size and Structure of the Domestic Group over the Last Three Centuries* (Cambridge: Cambridge University Press, 1972); Lawrence Stone, *The Family, Sex and Marriage in England, 1500–1800* (1977; Harmondsworth: Penguin, 1979).

[69] Harvey, 'Men Making Home', *passim*; Karen Harvey, 'Barbarity in a Teacup? Punch, Domesticity and Gender in the Eighteenth Century', *Journal of Design History*, 21, 3 (2008), pp. 205–21.

[70] Orlin, *Private Matters and Public Culture*, p. 268.

[71] Judith S. Lewis, 'When a House Is Not a Home: Elite English Women and the Eighteenth-Century Country House', *Journal of British Studies*, 48 (2009), p. 362.

Contemporary understandings of the house (or 'haus' in German) and household-family have been reconstructed by David Sabean and Naomi Tadmor respectively. They show the dividends of paying greater attention to the way contemporary meanings shaped experiences of the domestic, as well as pointing up the weight of the idea of 'house'. Tadmor's analysis of the concept of 'household-family' is highly significant to an understanding of men, as it has been to many other studies, though her work on the 'lineage-family' is just as important.[72] This study concurs with Sabean and Tadmor's examination of concepts as expressed through language. Men's writing is best understood with reference to this concept of 'house', which combined a configuration of space and gendered relationships of management. Having established that 'the good Management of an House' is a worthy occupation for men, the protagonists in the eighteenth-century translation of Xenophon's *The Science of Good Husbandry* debate the question, '[b]ut what do we mean by the Word *House?*'. The answer underlines the extent of men's management: 'a Man's Estate, whether it lies in or about the House, or remote from it, yet every Branch of that Estate may be said to belong to the House'.[73] 'House' was emphatically more than a physical shell or place of residence, and could itself be a repository of emotional and psychological meanings. Some of its meanings overlapped with 'home', but many were distinctive. Putting 'home' to one side liberates our analysis of the domestic from the connotations of a private and feminine space opposed to an 'outside' and public world; focusing on the 'house' foregrounds a different domestic culture, one centred on the household and its economic and political functions, and one in which men and masculinity were central.[74] This study is not an apology for the sometimes oppressive nature of men's authority; on the contrary, part of the ambition of this study is to reconstruct the force that this authority gleaned from some of the mundane and everyday practices that went on in households. Nevertheless, I seek to understand the men whose documents I have read. To understand what men thought and felt about their domestic life, rather than portray them as hapless victims or uncomfortable interlopers in the foreign land of the home, we need to employ their own concepts.

This project set out to answer the following questions: were men involved in domestic life? How did they legitimize their domestic engagement? How was men's domestic engagement represented by these and other men? What was the relationship between discourses of masculinity and domesticity? Was there a particularly manly attitude to the domestic realm and to engaging in domestic affairs? I have chosen to

[72] Naomi Tadmor, 'The Concept of the Household-Family in Eighteenth-Century England', *Past and Present*, 151 (1996), pp. 110–40; Naomi Tadmor, *Family and Friends in Eighteenth-Century England: Household, Kinship and Patronage* (Cambridge: Cambridge University Press, 2001), pp. 18–72; David Sabean, *Property, Production, and Family in Neckarhausen, 1700–1870* (Cambridge: Cambridge University Press, 1990), pp. 88–123.

[73] *The Science of Good Husbandry: or, The Oeocnomics of Xenophon*, trans. Richard Bradley (London, 1727), pp. 3, 4.

[74] Such an approach can take better account of the work of historian Jan de Vries, who insists on the household as an economic unit. See his *The Industrious Revolution: Consumer Behaviour and the Household Economy, 1650 to the Present* (Cambridge: Cambridge University Press, 2008).

answer these questions by examining public discourses, comparing these to the discourses drawn upon by men, and exploring in some detail the activities these men carried out. The result is a study that attempts to reconstruct the things that men actually did, but the main focus is to explore men's experiences of the house and domestic authority as shaped by their own and others' beliefs, assumptions, and expectations. These experiences were shaped by age, birth order, marital status, occupation, and region, though this social perspective gets us only so far. As Carole Shammas has said of work on early American families, some historians manage to 'omit the structure of household authority when they discuss the "much more" of fertility, household composition, family economy, intergenerational succession, and kinship'.[75] Only a cultural-historical approach can allow us to examine the structure and experience of household authority and the connections to male identity.

The Little Republic is a cultural history of social practice. The individual manuscript sources used in this book open up a world of men's daily domestic experiences. It is my aim to reconstruct the thought-world of this social practice, straddling to a degree the different historical approaches of studies of early modern manhood, on the one hand, and eighteenth-century masculinity on the other, approaches that have produced such different historiographies.[76] Such a work of cultural history confronts many issues, amongst them the reach or 'throw' of particular meanings, the relationships between what people thought and wrote and what they did, and finally change. In addressing the reach of meanings, historians need to make a professional judgment about the weight to give to particular sources or representations. To do so, argues Peter Mandler, they need to acquire 'a mental map of the *entire field of representation*', in which to judge the influence of their own objects of study.[77] Dror Wahrman has exhorted other cultural historians to develop a robust methodology 'for identifying a cultural pattern as dominant, residual, meaningful or adventitious, resonant or echoless'.[78] Wahrman's advice is particularly valuable to those who trace a discrete topic through the very broad field of an entire culture, such as the 'self' in eighteenth-century Britain (the subject of Wahrman's 2004 study).[79] *The Little Republic*, by contrast, begins with a relatively tightly defined intellectual history of the discourse of 'oeconomy' in printed books about the household. The weight given to the ideas about masculinity and the house within this are, I expect, palpable to anyone who reads them: this is the *raison d'être* of many of these sources. Yet the question of reach

---

[75] 'Carole Shammas Responds', *William and Mary Quarterly*, 52, 1, 1995, p. 165.

[76] See Karen Harvey and Alexandra Shepard, 'What Have Historians Done with Masculinity? Reflections on Five Centuries of British History, circa 1500–1950', *Journal of British Studies*, 44 (April 2005), pp. 274–80; Harvey, 'The History of Masculinity, circa 1650–1800', pp. 296–311; Alexandra Shepard, 'From Anxious Patriarchs to Refined Gentlemen? Manhood in Britain, circa 1500–1700', *The Journal of British Studies*, 44, 2 (2005), pp. 281–95.

[77] Peter Mandler, 'The Problem with Cultural History', *Cultural and Social History*, 1, 1 (2004), p. 97.

[78] Dror Wahrman, 'Change and the Corporeal in Seventeenth- and Eighteenth-Century Gender History: Or, Can Cultural History be Rigorous?', *Gender and History*, 20, 3 (2008), p. 591.

[79] Dror Wahrman, *The Making of the Modern Self: Identity and Culture in Eighteenth-Century England* (New Haven, Conn: Yale University Press, 2004).

remains a crucial one for me, because I try to demonstrate that this discourse of oeconomy was relevant to men. Rather than simply mapping out the culture field, then, my purpose is to show how a very specific discourse had significance to men's understanding of themselves and others. I do this in the only way I know how as an historian, and that is by showing how men's spoken and written words use this discourse.[80]

Yet I go further, and contend that the discourse of oeconomy was practised by men in their houses. Here, the issue becomes rather more about the relationship between words and practice. The personal domestic writings I explore from Chapter 3 are not used to show how 'practice' measured against the 'ideals' found in the printed public sources explored in Chapter 2. I describe oeconomy as a discourse rather than 'prescription', by which I mean (first) it was not a set of rules but a more flexible cultural resource, and (second) it was comprised of practices as much as words spoken or written. Oeconomy was an ideal model of living, certainly, and men's domestic practices generated documents that show that oeconomy was implemented; yet these manuscripts also constituted the discourse of oeconomy. Oeconomy was lived in material ways, rather than existing only in words on a page.[81] The third challenge is attending adequately to change over time. Continuity in the history of gender is undeniable and important, and while the work of women's and gender historians may be mistaken for presenting a static account, many attend to the subtle and shifting changes that affect men's and women's lives.[82] This book also argues for continuities—across the eighteenth century and indeed from the seventeenth into the nineteenth century; this would surprise few gender historians or historians of masculinity. Nevertheless, the history of masculinity (as in gender and women's history more widely) does need to re-engage with questions of chronology and periodization, and this book is framed by a detailed account of change, specifically concerning both the content and application of the discourse of oeconomy as examined in Chapter 2.[83]

This book is written as a contribution first and foremost to the history of masculinity and to gender history more widely. For some time the history of masculinity in the eighteenth century was dominated by work on social spaces and politeness. Another body of work addresses men's sexual or violent lives.[84] Some work has been done on men in domestic spaces.[85] David Hussey's assertion that 'the home formed one of the main arenas though which conceptions of polite masculine

---

[80] See Chapter 3, pp. 64–72.

[81] See Chapter 3, pp. 72–98, for a fuller discussion.

[82] A recent and critical discussion of these works can be found in Wahrman, 'Change and the Corporeal', esp. pp. 588–90.

[83] On the issue of gender and change, see the recent article, Alexandra Shepard and Garthine Walker, 'Gender, Change and Periodisation', *Gender & History*, 20, 3 (2008), pp. 453–62, and the other articles in this special issue.

[84] Bailey, *Unquiet Lives*; Philip Carter, *Men and the Emergence of Polite Society in Britain, 1660–1800* (Harlow: Longman, 2001); Elizabeth Foyster, *Manhood in Early Modern England* (Harlow: Longman, 1999).

[85] On periodicals, see Maurer, *Proposing Men, passim.*

gentility—mannered deference, restraint, sensibility of thought and action, decency and the civilizing action of mixed company—were encoded' is suggestive, though not sustained by any thoroughgoing study.[86] In contrast to this particular lens of new codes of manners, other work focuses on the equally important but much less mannered and glamorous side to men's engagement with household life.[87] Power, rather than politeness, is the key theme of this study. This book steps into the breach between work on seventeenth-century household patriarchs and nine-teenth-century domestic governors, encouraging a history of masculinity over the long durée. The sources I have used were not created to record the drama of family life, but rather its often unremarkable occurrences. Everyday, commonplace domestic activity was recorded in men's writing, and it is the very 'ordinariness' of these documents that allow historians to reconstruct the texture of men's past per-sonal lives.[88] These practices are not grandiose performances of strict discipline, but the often small yet articulate acts of household authority, underpinned by a widely circulating discourse of men's role as household managers. The notion of an inter-nalized 'new-style' patriarchy fails to capture the ways in which men's household authority was grounded in practical strategies of control, much like those adopted by middling-sort French men in the seventeenth century.[89] Regular practices of accounting, for example, brought together domestic housekeeping and govern-ance; such practices of oeconomy were the creation and enactment of men's domes-tic authority.

Little sense emerges from these records of domestic authority under continual threat, or of a furious 'patriarchal rage' arising from men's frustrated expectations of 'total control within the domestic environment'.[90] In eighteenth-century models of 'household government', men's domestic authority was invariably uncontested and unremarkable. Yet, reinstituting a focus on men's domestic authority and their practical engagement with the domestic does not imply downplaying the vital role that women played in that environment and the high status that accrued to women as a result.[91] Women were indispensable to men for the domestic tasks they pro-vided: 'I desire to know how the Gentleman can live in a House, without a

---

[86] David Hussey, 'Guns, Horses and Stylish Waistcoats? Male Consumer Activity and Domestic Shopping in Late-Eighteenth- and Early-Nineteenth-Century England', in David Hussey and Marga-ret Ponsonby (eds), *Buying for the Home: Shopping for the Domestic from the Seventeenth Century to the Present* (Aldershot: Ashgate, 2008), pp. 47–69.

[87] Hannah Barker, 'Soul, Purse and Family: Middling and Lower-Class Masculinity in Eighteenth-Century Manchester', *Social History*, 33, 1 (2008), pp. 12–35; Hannah Barker, 'A Grocer's Tale: Gen-der, Family and Class in Early Nineteenth-Century Manchester', *Gender & History*, 21, 2 (2009), pp. 340–57.

[88] Barker, 'A Grocer's Tale', p. 341.

[89] Julie Hardwick, *The Practice of Patriarchy: Gender and the Politics of Household Authority in Early Modern France* (Pennsylvania: Pennsylvania State University Press, 1998).

[90] Kenneth A. Lockridge, *On the Sources of Patriarchal Rage: The Commonplace Books of William Byrd and Thomas Jefferson and the Gendering of Power in the Eighteenth Century* (New York: New York University Press, 1992), p. 89.

[91] See, for example, Garthine Walker, 'Expanding the Boundaries of Female Honour in Early Mod-ern England', *Transactions of the Royal Historical Society*, 6th ser, 6 (1996), pp. 235–45, which argues that female honour stemmed from occupation and household activities as well as chastity.

Woman?', a juror pointedly asked during an Old Bailey trial of 1737.[92] Without women, men risked the loss of a range of domestic tasks and the status that came from a well-kept house. Yet a simple division of labour in the household did not exist, and men performed domestic tasks in households that were characterized by co-dependency.[93] Marriage marked men's rite of passage into adulthood, yet the significance of the house went much further than freeing men to undertake business elsewhere and providing comfort when this work was done.[94] Household management was a joint endeavour which prioritized the household as a communal unit; this book sets out to understand better the role of men in this unit.

This study of domestic lives draws on a range of different source types, general and specific, public and private. Public sources show how contemporaries imagined men's relationship to the house, and yielded templates available to men. Printed works of non-fiction, for example general household manuals, religious books and pamphlets, political treatises, dictionaries, encyclopedias, advice books to men, fathers, sons, women, and children, reveal a world in which the functioning of home depends on men's close involvement and investment. The use of these sources allows an engagement with some of the broader themes of historical work on gender and the home. Close readings of manuscript sources can produce rich and persuasive accounts, though.[95] This book is based on a close investigation of a series of middling-sort case studies, selected from a relatively small pool in order to give a range of occupations, wealth, region, and period. The study engages with work on the middling sort or the middle-class, and the sources were selected on this basis either by occupation or wealth.[96] There are over 25 case studies, ranging in date from 1665 to 1834, in occupation from mechanic to small shopkeeper, yeoman to rector, schoolmaster to lawyer. While a broadly middling group, these case studies include households of different sizes and wealth. They are also spread in terms of location, stretching from London to Cork and from North Devon to Fife; all but two are from England, however, and a majority are concentrated in the northern counties of Cumbria, Lancashire, Cheshire, and the East and West Ridings of Yorkshire.[97]

The middling sort is notoriously difficult to define, and while focused studies make convincing cases for coherent identities, broader studies must operate on the understanding that '[t]he middling sort was not a unified group'.[98] The case studies in this book align with the often precarious families in eighteenth-century London examined by Peter Earle, and the 'shopkeepers, manufacturers, better-off

---

[92] See Chapter 2, p. 65.   [93] Bailey, *Unquiet Lives, passim*, and pp. 203–4.

[94] Vickery, *Behind Closed Doors*, pp. 104–5.

[95] Lockridge's *On the Sources of Patriarchal Rage* is a superb example of this.

[96] Craig Muldrew 'Class and Credit: Social Identity, Wealth and the Life Course in Early Modern England', in Henry French and Jonathan Barry (eds), *Identity and Agency in England, 1500–1800* (Basingstoke: Palgrave Macmillan, 2004), pp. 147–77. On middle-sort values, Henry French, 'Social Status, Localism and the "Middle Sort of People" in England 1620–1750', *Past and Present*, 166 (2000), pp. 66–99.

[97] This provides a contrast to Margaret Ponsonby's focus on unremarkable middling sort homes from the West Midlands and West Sussex as a corrective to the published work on the landed and London. See, Ponsonby, *Stories from Home*.

[98] Hunt, *Middling Sort*, p. 14.

independent artisans, civil servants, professionals, lesser merchants, and the like' beneath the gentry but above the labouring studied by Margaret Hunt, rather than the large merchants of the 'middle-class' explored by John Smail.[99] A minimum income was £50 per annum, and while Hunt is comfortable describing as middling sort those whose income could reach £5,000, an upper limit of £2,000 is more typical.[100] When the bachelor Timothy Tyrell began his account book at around the age of 36, in 1729, he managed a modest building programme of three houses, paying bricklayers, labourers, painters, plasterers, and carpenters on a daily basis, and finally paying £11 to the builder in 1731.[101] Details of many houses let from the 1730s show that Tyrell received several hundred pounds a year from these rentals, and continued to receive rentals and pay taxes up to his death in April 1766.[102] Timothy junior was 11 at the time of his father's death, but went on to enjoy the fruits of his father's economic success. He married, had several children, became a 'remembrancer of the City of London', and a man of some wealth: the theft of his clothes in the winter of 1798 was deemed newsworthy, and reported in the press.[103] The goods and chattels of the Bury school usher Edmund Pilkington were appraised on 17 May 1755, valued at a total of £156 11s.[104] Pilkington describes himself as 'Yeoman' in his will of 1755, and left to his wife Margaret £20, his dwelling house, and her own cow—worth £5—to be kept with those of his eldest son, Edmund.[105] The Rector Daniel Renaud (1697–1770) had amassed considerably more wealth by the time of his death. His will, a modest document in extent and sentiment, beginning with the simple wish, 'I Give & Bequeath unto My Eldest Son David Renaud, All My Books, Manuscripts', shows he left property (bought for £174 in 1739) and land to his wife, and the considerable sum of £400 to each of his three daughters.[106] Renaud was not a very wealthy man, though he was a man of importance locally: his death was announced in the *General Evening Post* on Tuesday 30 June 1772.[107]

---

[99] Hunt, *Middling Sort*, p. 15. Peter Earle, *The Making of the English Middle Class: Business, Society and Family Life in London, 1660–1730* (London: Methuen, 1989).

[100] Hunt, *Middling Sort*, p. 15.

[101] [Timothy Tyrell, 1755–1832], 'Account book with mathematical exercises' (1725–1768), William Andrews Clark Memorial Library: MS. 1945.001, f. 156.

[102] Ibid. for example, ff. 79–84.

[103] *Old Bailey Proceedings Online* (<http://www.oldbaileyonline.org/>), December 1798, trial of John Newton and Mary Hawkins (t17981205-28). The case was reported in at least two papers, the *Oracle and Daily Advertiser*, Friday 7 December 1798, and *Bell's Weekly Messenger*, Sunday 9 December 1798. See *17th and 18th Burney Collection of Newspapers Online*, <http://find.galegroup.com.eresources.shef.ac.uk/bncn>, Gale Document Numbers: Z2001003428 and Z2000115489 (last accessed 9 September 2010).

[104] 'Will and inventory of Edmund Pilkington, Yeoman, 24th February 1755', Lancashire Record Office: WCW 1755. I thank Alan Crosby for his assistance.

[105] Pilkington's four cows are valued at £20 in total in the inventory. See 'Will and inventory of Edmund Pilkington'.

[106] 'The will of Daniel Renaud, 1770', Herefordshire Record Office: Probate series AA20, Box Number 334, June–September 1772. For details of the cost of property (Differnant's court), see Notebook of Revd Daniel Renaud, 1730–1769, Herefordshire Record Office: A98/1, ff.38–9. I thank John Harnden for his assistance.

[107] *General Evening Post*, Tuesday 30 June 1772, p. 3. See *17th and 18th Burney Collection of Newspapers Online*, <http://find.galegroup.com.eresources.shef.ac.uk/bncn>, Gale Document Number: Z2000444200 (last accessed 9 September 2010).

Higher up the social scale, the Cheshire solicitor Thomas Mort in 1732 bequeathed £1,085 in cash to friends and family, and his property placed in trust.[108] He was, as he stated in his will of 1737, a land-owning 'Esquire' and Lord of the Manor. This had been purchased by his great-grandfather in 1595, and by the time Mort's father died (in 1683) all four sons received small estates and subsequently entered the professions, commerce, and manufacturing.[109]

There are some significant differences between the case studies, then, and we can expect these various factors—occupation, wealth, region, as well as age and marital status—to affect considerably men's activities, or at least their written records. The account books of the bachelor solicitor Thomas Mort (d.1737) and William Parkinson of Derbyshire (*fl.* 1740s) include proportionately fewer smaller, lower value household items than the account book of Henry Richardson, 'clerk' and rector of Thornton-in-Craven in the West Riding from 1735.[110] We lack full biographical information about these men, but marital status seems to be an important factor in shaping their men's records. We can be certain that of the three only Richardson was married, and indeed his book is begun on the occasion of his marriage. Perhaps he had reason to be closely engaged with the house as he established this new household, or perhaps it was a small enough enterprise for him to be closely involved. In contrast, Mort had at least three servants at any one time. Parkinson inherited two-thirds of a house and land from the yeoman William Smedley in 1742; the other third was left to Smedley's wife Sarah. It was Smedley's wish that Parkinson (his nephew) ensure that Sarah 'be sufficiently and handsomely maintained with Meat Drink Washing and Lodging and all other necessaryes fit suitable and convenient for her from the time of my decease for and during the term of her natural life', and furthermore to assist in supporting 'the Maintenance and Education' of Smedley's fatherless grandchildren, offspring of Joseph Morley, managing the legacies to be given to the girls and the land left for the boys until the age of 21.[111] Given these extensive responsibilities, Parkinson was required to keep accounts for several households and made payments to many individuals for domestic services and housekeeping. Smaller items of expenditure are, not surprisingly, relatively uncommon in the volume. The level of men's engagement with everyday household consumption was partly determined by the size and wealth of the household, then, as well as life-course and marital status.

The geographical location of men also affected what they did and what they recorded. Despite the emphasis on the large town in most studies of the middling sort, the middling sort was a significant group in smaller provincial towns and rural areas. Henry French has established that this group is best demarcated by the

[108] 'Will of Thomas Mort of Damhouse 1736', Lancashire Record Office. I thank Alan Crosby for his assistance.

[109] John and Sylvia Tonge, *Astley Hall (Damhouse)* (John and Sylvia Tonge, 2002), pp. 7–10.

[110] Richardson was referred to as 'clerk' in the draft marriage settlement for Richard Richardson and Dorothy Smallshaw, 1750: WYAS Bradford, 68D82/14/47. Richardson was one party in this settlement.

[111] 'Will of William Smedley, 21 April 1742', Lichfield Record Office: B/C/11. Smedley administered Joseph Morley's estate. See Admon of Joseph Morley, 14 October 1740, Lichfield Record Office: B/C/11. I thank Kate Henderson for her assistance.

concept of 'gentility', a quality that connoted 'innate characteristics that ensured they, and only they, were fit to govern the rest of the social order'.[112] This book includes case studies of men in urban and rural areas, and the latter show a keen attention to the land and rentals. As lord of the manor Mort collected tithes and Parkinson was also engaged in large-scale farming. Daniel Renaud (b.1697) also collected land rents, though in capacity as rector of Whitchurch in Herefordshire. These men's records often situated them in the house. By contrast the Leeds merchant John Micklethwaite and York solicitor William Gray produced their writings in an urban context, and their occupations produced writing concerned to a large extent with commerce. Timothy Tyrell (b.1754), from a family of upholsterers in Reading and John Darracott in the busy port town of Bideford in North Devon were some distance from a large town, but situated in bustling places. While the occupations of Micklethwaite, Gray, Tyrell, and Darracott in some ways took them further from the house, we shall see that they nevertheless engaged closely with domestic activities and space. Given that attitudes to land were varied in rural communities, for some 'a long-term resource', for others 'a commodity to be assessed in terms of price and rent', divisions between the urban and rural middling sort should not be overdrawn.[113]

These case studies are supported by over 14 account books, 11 diaries, 9 commonplace books, bills and receipts, memoranda, letters, parish records, and probate material. Even within similar genres of writing, there is considerable variety between sources. For some of these men, their writing was profoundly confessional. John Darracott, John Stede, and Richard Kay, for example, were moved to write out of Christian devotion. They displayed a duty to both the family confessional community as well as the solitary reflection that was promoted in some Christian writing. Indeed, many of the documents were consonant with Christian ideals of manliness in which 'domesticity' was practically and metaphorically 'intimately connected with other aspects of a man's life'.[114] The priorities of these men were similar to those of the men examined by Hannah Barker for the same period: 'marital and familial relations, moral and spiritual development, and making a living'.[115] Not wishing to emphasize sex and shopping at the expense of religion, as some eighteenth-century historians have been accused, I will discuss this factor in the chapters that follow.[116] Some apparent omissions from these writings also require attention. For example, not all men wrote about the house extensively in their personal documents. The commonplace book of the Revd Joseph Wilson (c.1774–1821) is typical in its inclusion of a

---

[112] Henry French, *The Middle Sort of People in Provincial England, 1600–1750* (Oxford: Oxford University Press, 2007), p. 22, *passim*.

[113] H. R. French and R. W. Hoyle, *The Character of English Rural Society: Earls Colne, 1550–1750* (Manchester and New York: Manchester University Press, 2007), p. 300.

[114] William Van Reyk, 'Christian Ideals of Manliness During the Period of the Evangelical Revival, c.1730 to c.1840' (University of Oxford DPhil thesis, 2007), p. 80. Quote at p. 99. I am grateful to the author for sharing this work with me.

[115] Barker, 'Soul, Purse and Family', pp. 16–17.

[116] B. W. Young, 'Religious History and the Eighteenth-Century Historian', *The Historical Journal*, 43, 3 (2000), p. 859.

tremendous range of information. Wilson was Vicar of Hampsthwaite in the West Riding, from 1771–1790, when he resigned.[117] Land Tax returns for 1781–1790 show entries roughly averaging at £2 17s 4d, and being paid on several properties.[118] Wilson's volume contains notes on proceedings of the Skipton and Knaresborough Turnpike Commissioners between 1786 and 1807, demographic details of the local parishes, a set of 'Marriage Instructions', diary entries about farming, money, weather, and bees, and a letter from J. Browne dated 14 October 1737 from Queen's College. 'Home' is not very prominent, to be sure. And yet Wilson records '1796 The Loan to the Emperor of Germany for his Forces L4,600,000' alongside his payment for a pair of Sunday shoes and a painter's bill for his parlour.[119] The fact that these men did not record their innermost thoughts on soft furnishings is significant, certainly. Yet this does not necessarily mean that men did not engage with the domestic, but perhaps instead that they did so in ways that are not accounted for in existing work.

The mixed nature of these documents is itself suggestive. This applies to men's diaries, letters, and account books, as we shall see, but it is the commonplace book that exemplifies this best. Since the Renaissance, commonplace books had contained many different kinds of entry carefully ordered: important personal or family memoranda, others things of interest or note, and items intended to explicate general concepts. By the late seventeenth century this had become 'a rather lowly form of life', with volumes filled with unrelated items of often personal interest and what Ann Moss has described as 'scraps of uncoordinated trivia'.[120] The entries in the many eighteenth-century commonplace books kept by middling-sort men are indicative of this. Yet developments in the manner of commonplacing retained the cultural cachet of the practice. John Locke's new method of making commonplace books, published in French in 1686, ordered subject headings according to the first letter and first vowel. A central precept was that a range of different topics could be brought together within the same system, and this gained steadily in popularity during the eighteenth century. In this context, the ordering of written material was associated with 'the methodizing of one's thoughts, the pursuit of self-improvement, and the fashioning of the polite individual'.[121] The authors of the commonplace books used in this study failed to adhere closely to Locke's model, but their volumes that brought together different kinds of material were consonant with the notion of a self-improving and ordered person. In other words, the variety of material we find in individual men's writings, and the sometimes brief

[117] CCEd Record ID 283918, 51274, 51246, *The Clergy of the Church of England Database 1540–1835*, <http://www.theclergydatabase.org.uk>.

[118] Land Tax returns for Hampsthwaite, 1781–1832, West Yorkshire Archive Service, Wakefield: QE13/5/21. I thank Jennie Kiff for her assistance.

[119] 'Commonplace book of Revd Joseph Wilson c1774–1821', West Yorkshire Archive Service, Leeds: WYL753, Acc 1886, ff.17, 18, 25.

[120] Ann Moss, *Printed Commonplace-Books and the Structuring of Renaissance Thought* (Oxford: Clarendon Press, 1996), pp. 279, 280.

[121] Lucia Dacome, 'Noting the Mind: Commonplace Books and the Pursuit of the Self in Eighteenth-Century Britain', *Journal of the History of Ideas*, 65, 4 (October 2004), p. 615.

discussion of domestic activity, is not evidence of an absence of a particular engagement with the home, but evidence of a broad thought-world in which the domestic was just one integral part.

A wide-ranging history of eighteenth-century masculinity might explore a range of different 'styles' rather than forms: styles of good fellowship, for example, or politeness.[122] This study examines the style of men's domestic engagements in the eighteenth-century middling-sort house. *The Little Republic* argues that male authority in the household found continued expression during the eighteenth century, consolidated and embedded in the subtle but potent everyday material practices of the house. Men engaged with the house not simply as a unit of order, though. Like women, men bought an array of different kinds of goods for domestic consumption, and they used objects in the formation of relationships and the making of memory. Certain forms of domestic sociability, particularly those gathered around a table, succinctly captured men's authority and rootedness in the house, as well as their proprietorial engagement with domestic things. Men viewed and used domestic material in distinctive ways. In their careful management of property and their personal investment in meaningful domestic things, men of the middling sort grounded their identities in the material features and practices of their domestic lives. As do many of the works that explore women's paid employment outside the house, this study of men in the house confirms that a model of 'separate spheres' will no longer suffice.[123] Indeed, Chapter 5 discusses the degree to which the house—and all that it contained and symbolized—provided the grounding for these men's self-identities. Grounded in the skills and virtues associated with the good management of the house, these identities became increasingly important to the public identities of men and families. Middling-sort men worked hard to ensure that the esteemed practices of domestic authority were reproduced between men within their families, yet as I begin to explore in Chapter 6, oeconomical practices may also have been reproduced between men of different social ranks, such that we can identify a fraternity of oeconomy. This took place in the context of the intensification of a discourse of male domestic authority.

Men's domestic engagements and authority in the eighteenth century have remained obscure partly because when historians have looked for shaping ideas they have turned to canonical political theory. In contrast, this book begins with a study of what might be called 'lay political theory' in order to understand men's engagement with the domestic, their claims to domestic authority, and the cultural resources upon which these were founded. This writing foregrounded a general discourse of 'oeconomy'. Oeconomy was the practice of managing the economic and moral resources of the household for the maintenance of good order. Rather than 'domesticity', 'separate spheres', or 'political patriarchalism', it

---

[122] This idea of 'styles' is used by David Leverenz in *The Language of Puritan Feeling: An Exploration in Literature, Psychology, and Social History* (New Brunswick, NJ: Rutgers University Press, 1980), esp. pp. 162–206.

[123] Hannah Barker, *The Business of Women: Female Enterprise and Urban Development in Northern England, 1760–1830* (Oxford: Oxford University Press, 2006), pp. 170–3.

is oeconomy that is most useful in understanding men's (and arguably women's) engagements with the domestic. Oeconomy necessarily combined day-to-day management (housekeeping or domestic economy) and the macro- or global management of people and resources (governance or domestic patriarchy). If women were often presented as attending to the physical needs of the family, men were imagined to attend to the physical unit of the house and everything it encompassed; women attended to the bodies in the house, men attended to the body of the house.[124] Oeconomy was, first, a specific way of organizing the household. But, second, oeconomy was also a discourse that comprised values, structures, and practices. These could be adapted by people in differing circumstances and referred to or understood as 'oeconomical' and they shaped some of the ways in which men's actions in the domestic were understood. Oeconomy was emphatically not coterminous with masculinity in general, nor with a hegemonic 'patriarchal manhood' with which it shared some features.[125] It was not reliant on marriage or fatherhood, though it was most readily expressed through a paternal role. Oeconomy was a valued style of manliness and associated practices, rather than a life-stage or set of demographic factors. There was a close match between the positive qualities associated with manhood and the good management of a house, and oeconomy established the house as one component of a man's life that operated across the divide of 'inside' and 'outside' the house. Indeed, good oeconomy was proof-positive of the right to govern and be a citizen. Crucially, the discourse of oeconomy changed during the eighteenth century: as patriarchal theories of domestic authority were fused with a revived classical model, men's domestic identity was tied increasingly closely to ideas of political citizenship, the public good of society, and public-spirited contributions of the household to the national economy; this authoritative masculine identity rooted in the house became increasingly relevant to the developing social and political authority of the middling sort. Significantly for histories of the home which so often narrate a process of privatization and feminization, oeconomy brought together the house and the world, primarily through men's management of the resources of the household. It is to this discourse of oeconomy to which I will now turn.

---

[124] This does not mean that men did not undertake caring roles in practice. See Lisa Smith, 'The Relative Duties of a Man: Domestic Medicine in England and France, ca. 1685–1740', *Journal of Family History*, 31, 3 (2006), pp. 237–56, and also the discussion of medicine recipes in men's writing, Chapter 5, pp. 126–7.

[125] See Alexandra Shepard, *Meanings of Manhood in Early Modern England* (Oxford: Oxford University Press, 2003) for an account of relationships between patriarchal, anti-patriarchal, and alternative models of manhood, and the increasing importance of social status in the representation and application of these. See esp. pp. 70–89 and *passim*.

2

The Language of Oeconomy

A language of 'public' and 'private', juxtaposing the house against the outside worlds of work and politics, was a profoundly important and deeply gendered one in early-modern England. Historians have established the limitations of using this language as a guide to men's and women's experiences. Women's activities on the supposedly 'private' side of this dichotomy involved them in the 'public' and worldly arenas of economy and politics. More recently, historians have attended to men's domestic activities in the house.[1] No contemporary models or concepts can be easily reconciled with the realities of men's and women's activities, it seems; our knowledge of experiences has outstripped our understanding of representation. People can certainly say and believe one thing, and do quite another, yet language interacts with lives lived in complex and dynamic ways. Before considering how words connected to practices in Chapter 3, I will explore those concepts which shaped contemporaries' understanding of men's relationship with the house and household. This chapter takes as its focus a collection of printed works about the house, rather than a disparate set of cultural soundings, and is thereby able to reconstruct a coherent 'discourse' rather than diffuse cultural ideas. These written texts created not prescriptive normative ideals but a flexible discourse that was appropriated in whole or in part as a meaningful way of seeing, thinking, and living, and that operated materially in practice. These texts are the standing remains of the cultural architecture of men's domestic engagements.

It is the discourse of 'oeconomy',[2] rather than 'domesticity', 'separate spheres', or 'political patriarchalism', that holds the key to understanding men's (and women's) engagements with the domestic in this period. Oeconomy was the practice of managing the economic and moral resources of the household for the maintenance of good order. Derived from the classic Aristotelian model of *oikos*, the meaning

---

[1] For example, Joanne Bailey, *Unquiet Lives: Marriage and Marriage Breakdown in England, 1660–1800* (Cambridge: Cambridge University Press, 2003); Hannah Barker, 'Soul, Purse and Family: Middling and Lower-Class Masculinity in Eighteenth-Century Manchester', *Social History*, 33, 1, pp. 12–35.

[2] I have chosen not to use a dipthong in 'oeconomy'. Though sometimes the case in contemporary print (and where this is the case, I adhere to the original in quotations), generally the word was written without a diphthong. See, for example, Thomas Sheridan, *A General Dictionary of the English Language. One main Object of which, is, to establish a plain and permanent Standard of Pronunciation* (London, 1780), in which the following spelling and pronunciation is given: 'OECONOMICKS, e-ko-nom-miks. f. Management of household affairs.' (p. 4). This book does discuss diphthongs, but does not mention 'oe' (pp. 9–10). I thank Jane Hodson for discussing this with me.

of oeconomy changed over the seventeenth, eighteenth, and early nineteenth centuries. These changes affected not only how the household was seen, but also the wider significance that was attached to men's and women's domestic activities. One important point of change concerned the relationship of the household to the polity. Classical theory drew analogies between the *oikos* and the polity, yet saw them as separate; late-seventeenth-century English writers made the links concrete. While some historians have observed a subsequent splitting of household and polity later in the eighteenth century, this chapter insists instead that the eighteenth-century discourse of oeconomy attached the household firmly to the political arena. A second point of change concerned the economic activity of the household unit. Several historians have linked the divestment of the household's economic function in a period of nascent industrialization with the development of a discourse of 'the economy'. In contrast, this chapter examines the continuing emphasis placed on the economic role of households, a role that again underscored their importance to the nation. 'Oeconomy' changed in meaning over this period, but the emphasis on the wise management of the household resources in the original Greek *oikos* was always present. Given that '[m]anagement was a favourite eighteenth century term', informing all levels of the state and public activities, eighteenth-century English society was to prove particularly fertile ground for oeconomy.[3]

Oeconomy has received scant explicit treatment in historical studies of the family. Its relevance is palpable, though, in Margaret Hunt's important book, *The Middling Sort: Commerce, Gender and the Family in England, 1680–1780* (1996). This restored the work and agency of middling-sort women to the history of this rank, but Hunt demonstrated that the family was a joint venture of men and women. Men's contribution to the middling-sort family in particular united the moral and economic facets of oeconomy: the 'primary measures of middling male respectability' included securing credit, good written accounts, and sexual chastity through diligent work and self-control.[4] Another important element of the system of oeconomy was present in the form of the 'bourgeois patriarchalism' of this 'highly moral family order'.[5] Indeed, Hunt identified a need for future research to explore 'the linkages between hierarchical family structures and a larger polity that reproduced and extended male dominance even while much else was in flux'.[6]

These linkages were embodied and expressed in oeconomy. Contemporaries conceptualized the household and men's roles therein not through the theories of Filmer or Locke which dealt with high politics, but with a system that encompassed both moral philosophy and everyday household activities. Works on 'oeconomy'—particularly of the more philosophical kind—constituted a body of 'lay political theory', in contrast to these canonical works of 'high' political theory. This lay political theory was often written for a 'popular' audience, ostensibly dealing

---

[3] Paul Langford, 'The Management of the Eighteenth-Century State: Perceptions and Implications', *Journal of Historical Sociology*, 15, 1 (2002), p. 102, pp. 102–6.

[4] Margaret Hunt, *The Middling Sort: Commerce, Gender and the Family in England, 1680–1780* (Berkeley: University of California Press, 1996), p. 72.

[5] Ibid. p. 149.   [6] Ibid. p. 146.

with practical household provisioning, but also articulated to greater and lesser degrees the rules of a system of household management and governance.[7] As we will see in Chapter 3, this was an important cultural resource available to eighteenth-century men, and they drew on this when speaking of and imagining their role in the domestic in their own personal writings.

Despite arguments for the severance of the link between households and the polity and economy, oeconomy's *raison d'être* was to unite the moral and economic, and to situate the household in a wider economic and political environment. As Matthew McCormack's study of gender and later Georgian politics makes clear, the independence through which political action was legitimized was attainable only by those enjoying 'the stations of husband, father and householder'.[8] As Chapter 3 will demonstrate, the discourse of oeconomy valued household qualities as much as the social status of the householder. Focusing on how the unit of the house figured in the discourse of oeconomy, though, this chapter explores the changing connection between the household and the wider economy and polity. Over the century this connection became stronger and men's practices in the 'private' and 'public' arenas became increasingly—rather than less—equivalent.[9] As Hunt has shown, middling-sort 'prudential morality' underpinned ideas of political virtue. Middle-class writers targeted the upper-class family, replacing a classical model with a commercial one in which 'private domesticity' served as the foundation for public virtue.[10] This was not a gendered division between the spheres of home and work. Regardless of middling-sort domesticity, it was 'the market' that '*transcended* the so-called "public sphere" and went to the heart of family life'.[11]

This chapter similarly underlines the connections between the domestic and the public. In contrast, though, rather than the emergence of a new commercial middling-sort model, I argue that an older discourse of 'oeconomy' reoriented to serve as political legitimization for the middling sort. This chapter will discuss how the classical discourse of oeconomy linked household management to the civic sphere through specifically manly virtues. Indeed, though oeconomy encompassed women's housekeeping, as a model of household management oeconomy foregrounded men's engagement with the domestic. I will show that throughout the long eighteenth century, oeconomy was sustained by a more general republican tradition of civic virtue. In the two sub-genres of oeconomical writing—which dealt with the practice and theory of housekeeping respectively—men were expected to be closely engaged with the household, though writers established a gendered distinction

---

[7] I thank Jennet Kirkpatrick for sharing her idea of 'lay political theory' with me. This is deployed in Jennet Kirkpatrick, *Uncivil Disobedience: Studies in Violence and Democratic Politics* (New Brunswick, NJ: Princeton University Press, 2008), p. 7.

[8] Matthew McCormack, *The Independent Man: Citizenship and Gender Politics in Georgian England* (Manchester and New York: Manchester University Press, 2005), p. 27. See also Matthew McCormack, '"Married Men and the Fathers of Families": Fatherhood and Franchise Reform in Britain', in Trev Lynn Broughton and Helen Rogers (eds), *Gender and Fatherhood in the Nineteenth Century* (Basingstoke: Palgrave Macmillan, 2007), pp. 43–54.

[9] Shawn Lisa Maurer, *Proposing Men: Dialectics of Gender and Class in the Eighteenth-Century English Periodical* (Stanford, CA: Stanford University Press, 1998), pp. 24, 30, *passim*.

[10] Hunt, *Middling Sort*, pp. 193–215. Quotes at pp. 199, 202.   [11] Ibid. p. 9.

between levels of activity, allotting to men the task of overall management. Works published in the 1720s brought the theory of oeconomy to a new audience. Yet oeconomy had already been popularized to some degree, and fused with patriarchal theories of the polity. Together, these developments forged a powerful discourse that linked men's activities in the household to the wider economic and political world. No longer linked to the wider realm simply by manly virtues, the household became a constituent part of the national economy and the political order. And, as with the larger tradition of civic republicanism, this discourse of oeconomy transformed from a language of governance for the landed to a language of citizenship for the middling sort. By the 1770s, the language of oeconomy had changed to accommodate the middling sort and households no longer served a commonwealth of private families but were public-spirited contributors to the national economy. By the 1790s, oeconomy envisaged the household as the springboard for a more active citizenship and political engagement.

THE SHARED AND COMMON CULTURE OF THE HOUSE

Underpinning the discourse of oeconomy was the idea of the unity of the house. Any society that was to prove fertile ground for oeconomy depended upon this fundamental notion of the 'house'. In eighteenth-century England there was plentiful discussion of a gendered separation in which women were responsible for housewifery inside and men were responsible for husbandry outside. The popular works by Gervase Markham (1568?–1637)—republished several times throughout this period—are typical in this regard.[12] In Markham's *The English House-Wife* (1683), 'the perfect Husbandman, who is the Father and Master of the Family', is placed most assuredly 'for the most part abroad or removed from the house', while his 'English House-wife, who is the Mother and Mistress of the family . . . hath her most general imployments within the house'.[13] According to Richard Bradley, a later prolific writer of books on household and family, men undertook, 'the most dangerous and laborious Share of it in the Fields, and without doors, and the Women have the Care and Management of every Business within doors, and to see after the good ordering of whatever is belonging to the House'.[14] Yet a closer examination of printed works on the house, family, and household published between 1650 and 1820 shows that any gendered division of tasks was unstable, even in those books specifically intended for either male or female readers. On the female

---

[12] Markham's book on husbandry, first published in 1614, was published as late as 1707. Markham's book on housewifery, first published in *A Way to get Wealth* in 1625, was published as late as 1695. See Chapter 3, p. 70, for a brief discussion of Markham's life.

[13] Gervase Markham, *The English House-Wife, containing The inward and outward Vertues which ought to be in a Compleat Woman*, 9th edition (London, 1683), pp. 1–2.

[14] Richard Bradley, *The Country Housewife and Lady's Director, in the Management of a House, and the Delights and Profits of a Farm*, 6th edition (London, 1736), Part I, pp. vii–viii. For a discussion of Bradley's personal fortunes in the context of his own work, see Chapter 3 pp. 70–1.

'housewifery' side of the inside/outside separation, for example, cookery was particularly important. Cooking served the physical needs of the family through the
provision of both food and medicine, an important practical and symbolic household practice. Hannah Woolley's books were amongst the most reprinted during
the late seventeenth century, and her works were indicative of a sub-genre of
women's advice to women which paid considerable attention to cooking. Directed
specifically to gentlewomen in the title, to 'all other of the Female Sex' in the preface and poems at the beginning and end of the book, and with a frontispiece showing the different roles performed by female housekeepers and servants, Woolley's
Queen-like Closet (1670) presented women's hard domestic labour and management as a highly esteemed accomplishment conducted by women as a group
regardless of rank.[15] Many other works on cookery and housewifery by women for
women were published into the eighteenth century and beyond. Yet even within
this apparent beating heart of housewifery, gendered roles were not always prominent. The association between women, housewifery, and cookery was strong
enough to be used as a marketing strategy, but might go no further than the cover
of a book. Despite its title, *Cookery Reformed; or, the Ladies Assistant* (1755) failed
to discuss women's particular role in the kitchen or their duties in general, even
when it was republished the following year as *The Good Housewife; or, Cookery
Reformed* (1756).[16] Once past the title, this work was directed at a non-gendered
reader.

Men also wrote about cookery, admittedly adopting a candid tone with their
male readers, while demurring to their female readers: 'I pretend not to the least
Authority over my fair Scholars', apologized Thomas Edlin.[17] Regardless of their
apologies, men did not shy away from posturing as authoritative guides to women
in the kitchen. Richard Bradley apologized for publishing a book which 'falls
within the Ladies' Jurisdiction', excusing himself on the grounds that he was only
trying to 'assist, than to direct'.[18] Notwithstanding the apology, the second part of
Bradley's *The Country Housewife and Lady's Director* (originally published in 1732)
is dedicated to a man, 'Sir Hans Sloane, Bart. President of the Royal Society'.[19]
And no longer is the tone one of advising knowledgeable women. The first letter
in the book is from a man telling Bradley how he has directed his wife in the matter
of salting meat and then advising Bradley on how it should be done.[20] Indeed,
Bradley gives two reasons for writing the first part to *The Country Housewife and
Lady's Director* (originally published in 1727), both of which reveal his confidence
in matters culinary. First, he sought to rescue the many items found on farms and

---

[15] Hannah Woolley, *The Queen-like Closet: or, Rich Cabinet, stored with all manner of Rare Receipts
for Preserving, Candying and Cookery... to which is added A Supplement, presented to all Ingenious Ladies
and Gentlewomen*, 5th edition (1670; London, 1684), p. iii.

[16] *Cookery Reformed; or, the Ladies Assistant* (London, 1755); *The Good Housewife; or, Cookery
Reformed* (London, 1756).

[17] *The Oeconomist: or, Edlin's Weekly Journal*, 1 September 1733, p. 2, column 2.

[18] Bradley, *Country Housewife and Lady's Director*, Part I, p. viii. This edition combined books I
and II, originally published in 1727 and 1732 respectively.

[19] Ibid. Part II, p. iii.   [20] Ibid. Part II, pp. 2–3.

in gardens—such as 'Mushrooms, Lupines, Brocoly [*sic*], Morilles, Truffles, Skirrets [and] Scorzonera'[21]—that are regarded as 'incumbrances', and show his readers how to use them in cooking. 'The other Reason', he continues, 'is, the Difficulties I have undergone in my Travels, when I have met with good Provisions, in many Places in England, which have been murder'd in the dressing.'[22] Bradley knew his edible mushrooms from his poisonous fungi, and was able to identify a range of vegetables resembling parsnips. Indeed, of those for whom the sex is given, 30 of the recipes included in *The Country Housewife* were from women and 41 from men.[23] Men had intimate knowledge of—and strong opinions about—the minutiae of domestic life, even in the kitchen.

If tasks were not consistently gendered, a gendered separation of 'inside' and 'outside' was neither complete nor stable. The housewifery duties of women 'inside' sometimes overlapped with those intended for men. Markham's housewife is to possess inward virtues; she must be 'of chast *thoughts*, stout courage, patient, untired, watchful, diligent, witty, pleasant, constant in friendship, full of good Neighbour-hood, wise in discourse, but not frequent therein', for example, and be 'generally skilful in the worthy knowledges which do belong to her vocation'.[24] She also required outward skills for 'the preservation and care of the family touching their health and soundness of body', and the active knowledge of cookery, distillation, cloths, malting and oats.[25] Such skills required knowledge of events outside the house. For example, good cookery required knowledge of herbs and other plants predicated on the housewife's engagement in the garden.[26] As Nicola Verdon has written of eighteenth- and nineteenth-century farmers' wives, while the work performed by husbands and wives on farms was distinct, '[w]omen were not narrowly confined to the farmhouse'.[27] In many of these works—often directed at country readers—'inside' was a moveable feast.

The case was similar for the other side of the household venture, husbandry. In practice, husbandry—or skill in working the ground—took men (and, indeed, their wives) away from the house. Books on husbandry, unlike those on housewifery, were written by men and directed at male readers. Notably, Bradley's Preface to his *A Complete Body of Husbandry* (1727) presented the volume as a

---

[21] Lupines produce a pulse, morel is a type of edible fungi, skirret and scorzonera are vegetables akin to parsnips.

[22] Bradley, *Country Housewife*, Part I, pp. ix, x.

[23] Caroline Davidson, 'Editor's Introduction', in Richard Bradley, *The Country Housewife and Lady's Director*, ed. Caroline Davidson (London: Prospect Books, 1980), pp. 20, 43–7.

[24] Markham, *English House-Wife*, pp. 3–4.

[25] Ibid. *passim*; quote p. 4.

[26] Ibid. pp. 49–50; [William Lawson], *A New Orchard & Garden: Or, The best way for Planting, Graffing, and to make any ground good for a rich orchard* (London, 1683), containing *The Country House-wife's Garden: Containing Rules for Herbs and Seeds of common Use, with their Times and Seasons when to Set and Sow them. Together with the Husbandry of Bees, Published with Secrets very necessary for every Housewife: As also divers new Knots for Gardens* (London, 1684), pp. 60, 75.

[27] See Nicola Verdon, '… subjects deserving of the highest praise: Farmers' wives and the farm economy in England, c.1700–1850', *Agricultural History Review*, 51, 1 (2003), pp. 23–39; quote at p. 27.

contribution to 'so useful a science', marking it as a manly pursuit.[28] In these works, the spatial domain of the husbandman served the house but was demarcated as a different area.[29] Yet there was limited overlap between the roles of men and women. On malting, Markman stresses that while there are 'many excellent men-maulsters', this 'place of knowledge belongeth particularly to the House-wife'. Men are certainly involved in the malting activities taking place inside the household; a man 'ought to bring in, and to provide the Grain, and excuse her from portage or too heavy burthens', for example.[30] Here, husband and wife had shared responsibilities and there was some considerable flexibility in the tasks that they performed. But while separation was not complete, the emphasis was on interdependence rather than the equivalency of tasks.

Reading these books simply as 'prescriptive literature', practical guides to working the land or as 'sources' of information about who did what, occludes some of functions of these texts. Many of the books are concerned with recreation and leisure. Robert Brown's *The Compleat Farmer; or, the Whole Art of Husbandry* (1759) is illustrated with a title-page that smacks of eighteenth-century idealizations of the pastoral, and contains advertisements for books on letter writing, sport, jests, and wooing.[31] Husbandry in these works also figured as a site of fantasy. Gervase Markham's *Country Contentments* was subtitled *or the Husbandman's Recreations*, intended for *after the Toyl of more Serious Business*.[32] Richard Bradley situated husbandry within an idyll of pastoral pleasures: the best fowl, fish fruits, herbs, liquors, 'the pleasing Shade, the fairest Prospects, and the most harmless Mirth, and what Musick is there more ravishing to the Ear, then the Harmony of the Birds?' 'Nor is there any Sauces', he continues, 'which may not be gratified in the most delicious manner in the Country, and all these are the Joy, and in the Possession of the prudent Husbandman; for there is not any of the Delights here mention'd, that the Husbandman may not enjoy at his Pleasure.'[33] To his gentlemen readers, Thomas Edlin assured that his comments on household management were 'as capable of diverting the *Mind*, as a well disposed *Landskip* is of entertaining the *Sight*'.[34] As instruments of recreation and leisure, and surely consumed within the house, books about husbandry hardly made men's engagement with house remote.

Indeed, these books were domestic objects. John Flavell's *Husbandry Spiritualized* (1669) pictured his reader—a male husbandman—inside the house during

---

[28] Richard Bradley, *A Complete Body of Husbandry, Collected from the Practice and Experience of the most considerable Farmers in Britain* (London, 1727), p. i.

[29] See Karen Harvey, 'Men Making Home: Masculinity and Domesticity in Eighteenth-Century England', *Gender & History*, 21, 3 (2009), pp. 529–30.

[30] Markham, *English House-Wife*, p. 153.

[31] Robert Brown, *The Compleat Farmer; or, the Whole Art of Husbandry* (London, 1759).

[32] G[ervase] Markham, *Country Contentments; or the Husbandman's Recreations. Containing The Wholesome Experience, in which any ought to Recreate himself, after the Toyl of more Serious Business*, 11th edition (London, 1683).

[33] R[ichard] Bradley, *The Weekly Miscellany For the Improvement of Husbandry, Trade, Arts, and Sciences* (London), no 17, Tuesday 24 October 1727, p. 2.

[34] *Oeconomist: or, Edlin's Weekly Journal*, 1 September 1733, p. 2, column 1.

the evening.[35] The frontispiece to *Husbandry Moralized; or, Pleasant Sunday Reading for a Farmer's Kitchen* (1772, 1797?) seems to display its reader and his wife in a room, presumably the kitchen of the sub-title.[36] For readers in the house—rather than the field—many books on husbandry lack contents pages and/or indexes that would allow a reader to navigate the work for practical purposes. Instead, they are sometimes long, dense discussions about the idea of husbandry. Just as 'home' served representational functions, so husbandry was used to think with. These examples drew on biblical discussions of good stewardship and invested husbandry with spiritual meanings: Flavell's *Husbandry Spiritualized* begins, 'In the laborious Husbandman you see,/What all true Christians are, or ought to be.'[37] Whether spiritual aid or not, the content of these books cautions against seeing them as evidence for a masculine part of a gendered inside/outside dichotomy. Moreover, while invariably directed to male readers, they were surely used by both men and women: the 'husbandman' to which one copy of Flavell's book belonged, and who inscribed their name on its pages, was 'Phebe Chiselden'.[38] Reading books as objects rather than simply texts cautions that discussions of men's and women's activities in these works are no straightforward guide to practice.

The gendered inside and outside distinction was disrupted in several ways, then. Furthermore, it was positively disregarded in works that presented the family as a shared enterprise, one in which the aim was to consolidate and increase economic resources. One such manual—*England's Happiness Improved* (1697)—does not address itself to a specific reader, though one copy belonged to Robin Chown, Richard Wills, and Thomas White Chalfont during the eighteenth century.[39] The book takes the reader through distilling, pickling, confectionary, instructions for men and women buying goods at market, and finally rules for good house-keeping. As the title indicates, there is a patriotic theme to the book. Readers are exhorted not to buy foreign produce, in part because this has caused 'the great Exhausting of our Treasure, to the hindering the Circle of Inland Trade', but also because native produce is more agreeable to the English constitution.[40] But significantly, the riches, plenty, and pleasure resulting from the book's method accrue to the individual households not the nation, a situation that was to change: 'THE good Management of Houshold-Affairs is not only commendable, but turns to much Profit and Advantage;...So that some live more plentifully on a small Estate, or Income, by good Houswifery and Management, than others do on a much larger Competency.' Thus, 'Plenty may be had, and yet much saved at the Years end.'[41]

The shared and common culture of the house was suggested in the claims authors and publishers made to inclusivity and completeness: *The Universal*

[35] John Flavell, *Husbandry Spiritualized* (London, 1669), f. 15.

[36] *Husbandry Moralized; or, Pleasant Sunday Reading for a Farmer's Kitchen* (Dublin; [No date, 1772, 1797?]).

[37] Flavell, *Husbandry Spiritualized*, p. 17.

[38] Ibid. f. 11. British Library: shelfmark 4404.l.17.

[39] *England's Happiness Improved: or, an Infallible Way to get Riches, Encrease Plenty, and promote Pleasure* (London, 1697). William Andrews Clark Memorial Library: *TX154 E58.

[40] *England's Happiness Improved*, p. 2.   [41] Ibid. p. 157.

Family-Book (1703) is written 'for All Families, as well the Rich as those of the Lower Degree, Masters, Mistresses, and Servants';[42] *The Compete Family-Piece* (1736) is addressed to 'private Families'.[43] While certain sections were directed at men specifically (notably hunting), most were simply directed to the general and genderless reader. Amongst discussions of medicine, clothes, cleaning, cookery, brewing, and gardening in *The Universal Family-Book*, only the sections on pregnancy and labour, and on cosmetics and beauty, specify an 'especial' interest for female readers.[44] This is a manual aiming for the broadly conceived objective of 'the Public Benefit of Mankind', though this will be achieved through the generation of 'Knowledge, Profit, and considerable Advantage' and the achievement of 'plentiful Livelihoods' for individuals and their households.[45] *The Complete Family-Piece* (1736) is presented as the collaborative work of several gentlemen skilled in the areas it covers (including cookery, confectionary, physic, hunting, fishing, and husbandry). While sections on hunting, fishing, and husbandry are directed at gentlemen, the chapters on preserving, distilling, winemaking, and brewing are intended for the benefit of 'private Families'.[46] For the imagined non-gendered readers of such works, the household was very much a shared enterprise.

The image of the family as a shared enterprise reinforces Joanne Bailey's finding that in the seventeenth- and eighteenth-century household, 'co-dependency breaks down the crude assignment of differently gendered ideas and expectations to these activities'.[47] Uses of the term 'housekeeper' are revealing in this regard. The term applied to both men and women: Dudley North, the author of *Observations and Advices Oeconomical* (1669), proudly reassured his readers, 'I have been a Housekeeper a great part of my dayes'.[48] Markham refers to 'the general profit which accreweth and ariseth to the *Husband House wife*, and the whole Family' through malting,[49] and in a later discussion of oats explains, 'no *Husband Housewife*, or *House keeper*, whatsoever hath so true and worthy a friend, as his Oats are'.[50] The terms 'housewife' and 'housekeeper' were not reserved solely for women. Yet, while both men and women were expected to have a close and involved engagement with the domestic environment—both were housekeepers—the nature of that engagement was different. With regards to the house, the most significant gendered distinction was not between the 'inside' and the 'outside' or even between men's and women's specific household tasks; instead, the most significant gendered distinction existed within the house and between the nature of men's and women's engagement with different levels of task.

---

[42] *The Universal Family-Book: or, a Necessary and Profitable Companion for All Degrees of People of Either Sex* (London, 1703), p. ii.

[43] *The Complete Family-Piece: and, Country Gentleman, and Farmer's, Best Guide*, Second Edition (1736; London, 1737), p. x.

[44] *Universal Family-Book*, pp. iii, 78.

[45] Ibid. pp. i–ii.

[46] *Complete Family-Piece*, p. x.

[47] Bailey, *Unquiet Lives*, p. 203.

[48] Dudley North, *Observations and Advices Oeconomical* (London, 1669), f. 10. For a discussion of North's personal fortunes in the context of his own work, see Chapter 3 pp. 69–70.

[49] Markham, *English House-Wife*, p. 152.   [50] Ibid. p. 176.

A GENERAL SYSTEM OF MANAGEMENT

As the practice of managing the economic and moral resources of the household for the maintenance of good order, oeconomy combined both housekeeping and governance. As such, oeconomy was practised by both women and men, though their roles were not the same. Amanda Vickery has shown how the 'prudent economy' practised by provincial gentry women in their households between *c.*1750 and 1780 involved demanding administrative labour but also a broad range of practical skills. The power and status accessible to women who did this well is palpable in their own writings, as is the dividend to their frequently absent male relations thus freed to engage in other pursuits. Such gentry women had much in common with women of lower social status in the range of activities they supervised, yet the analogy of the 'museum curator administering her collection' will not suffice for middling-sort housewives.[51] Most women had a necessarily greater hand in the gritty everyday life of the household, as well as the more regular presence of husbands, both of which had consequences for the supervisory and managerial roles open to such women. For most women, 'oeconomy' would have meant engaging in housewifery and management at a more local level. Printed books on oeconomy for women are full of evidence of women's household labour, their resourcefulness, and their practical knowledge. They detail 'the quotidian actions of the hearth', and—as Sara Pennell has demonstrated—demand a 'reinstatement of female expertise to its place as an essential underpinning of economic survival and success'. Oeconomy, as Pennell rightly concludes, was often considered synonymous with 'good housekeeping', and thus a properly broadened history of the household economy which gives the 'encompassing ethic' of oeconomy its due should include these everyday kitchen activities of women.[52] And yet, as Pennell suggests, women's housekeeping does not account for oeconomy in its entirety. Housekeeping and family books geared to women were rooted firmly in a broader tradition of didactic literature, 'how-to' books that claimed to educate in practical knowledge.[53] For contemporaries, 'housekeeping' undertaken by women was imagined as day-to-day domestic tasks that serviced the bodily needs of family members. 'Housekeeping' undertaken by men was understood as overall management of the household at a global or overarching level. As in the case of the term 'housekeeping', 'oeconomy' had a level-specific meaning when used for non-elite women. In works such as William Ellis's *The Country Housewife's Family Companion* (1750), *The Good Housewife; or, Cookery Reformed* (1756), and Anne Battam's,

---

[51] Amanda Vickery, *The Gentleman's Daughter: Women's Lives in Georgian England* (New Haven, Conn: Yale University Press, 1998), pp. 127–60, esp. p. 147. On household management and elite women, also see Julie Day, 'Elite Women's Household Management: Yorkshire, 1680–1810' (Unpublished PhD thesis, University of Leeds, 2007).

[52] Sara Pennell, '"Pots and Pans History": The Material Culture of the Kitchen in Early Modern England', *Journal of Design History*, 11, 3 (1998), p. 214. See also Sara Pennell, 'The Material Culture of Food in Early Modern England, c.1650–1750', in Sarah Tarlow and Susie West (eds), *The Familiar Past? Archaeologies of later historical Britain* (London and New York: Routledge, 1999), pp. 35–50.

[53] Natasha Glaisyer and Sara Pennell, 'Introduction', *Didactic Literature in England, 1500–1800: Expertise Constructed* (Aldershot, Hampshire: Ashgate, 2003), pp. 2–3.

The Lady's Assistant in the Oeconomy of the Table (1759), 'oeconomy' referred to the material detail of everyday domestic life.[54] A specifically female 'oeconomy' constituted the mending of gloves and the choice of victuals for the table.[55] Women's housewifery was an important part of oeconomy, but it was only one part. As a practice of managing the household resources through a system of order, oeconomy required much more than the practical knowledge of housekeeping associated so closely with women. Indeed, for the middling ranks addressed in these works there was a clear distinction between 'good Housewives and Oeconomists'.[56] Operating at different levels, these housekeeping practices were nevertheless part of the same shared endeavour, and these differences and interconnections were articulated through the discourse of 'oeconomy'.

Practised by men and women but in different ways, oeconomy comprised a gendered distinction of level and was a system of household management built upon hierarchy. Whether on small or large estates, oeconomy involved a global manager and deputies. '*Oeconomy* is an Art and every Artist ought to be curious in the choyce of his Instruments', counselled Dudley North before giving his reader copious instructions on how to choose his wife and his servants.[57] As Edward Laurence later explained in his important book *The Duty of a Steward to His Lord* (1727), the landowner was the 'good *Oeconomist*' while his steward was the one who managed.[58] This same principle could of course be applied to the house, and this is important in understanding the seemingly conflicting roles encountered by women. Historians have noted the apparent tension in women's roles within the domestic environment between the demand for women's skill, expertise, and independence on the one hand, and expectations of submissiveness and obedience on the other, understood using concepts such as selective deference and the role of 'subordinate magistrate'.[59] In the context of oeconomy, though, a woman was a steward or deputy who related to a range of people in different ways, just one facet of a society with several different power hierarchies that made up a 'grid of power'.[60]

[54] William Ellis, *The country housewife's family companion: or profitable directions for whatever relates to the management and good oeconomy of the domestick concerns of a country life* (London, 1750); *The good housewife, or, Cookery reformed: containing a select number of the best receipts...from the papers of several gentlemen and ladies eminent for their good sense and oeconomy* (London, 1756); Anne Battam, *The lady's assistant in the oeconomy of the table: a collection of scarce and valuable receipts*, 2nd edition (London, 1759). William Ellis published a partner to his housewifery treatise in the same year, *The Modern Husbandman* (London, 1750).

[55] [Dorothy Kilner,] *Dialogues and Letters in Morality, Oeconomy, and Politeness, for the Improvement and Entertainment of Young Female Minds* (London, 1780), pp. 57, 76–7.

[56] *Complete Family-Piece*, p. v.

[57] North, *Observations and Advices Oeconomical*, p. 43.

[58] Edward Laurence, *The Duty of a Steward to His Lord* (London, 1727), p. 15.

[59] Linda Pollock, '"Teach her to Live under Obedience": The Making of Women in the Upper Ranks of Early Modern England', *Continuity and Change*, 4:2 (1989), pp. 231–58; Bernard Capp, 'Separate Domains? Women and Authority in Early Modern England', in Paul Griffiths, Adam Fox and Steve Hindle (eds), *The Experience of Authority in Early Modern England* (Basingstoke: Macmillan, 1996), pp. 117–45. Quote at p. 127.

[60] Michael J. Braddick and John Walter, 'Introduction. Grids of Power: Order, Hierarchy and Subordination in Early Modern Society', in Michael J. Braddick and John Walter (eds), *Negotiating Power in Early Modern Society: Order, Hierarchy and Subordination in Britain and Ireland* (Cambridge: Cambridge University Press, 2001), pp. 1–42.

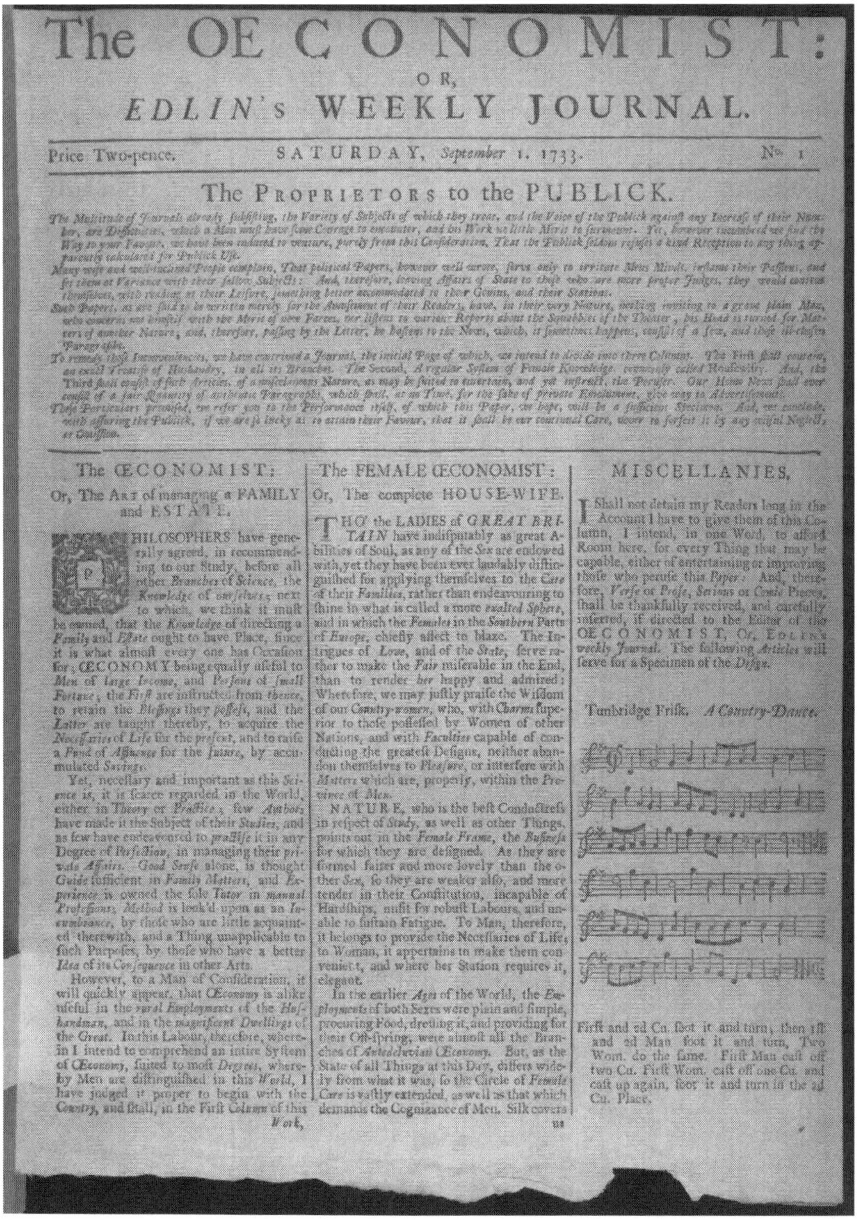

The OECONOMIST:

OR,

EDLIN's WEEKLY JOURNAL.

Price Two-pence. SATURDAY, *September* 1. 1733. No. 1

The PROPRIETORS to the PUBLICK.

The Multitude of Journals already subsisting, the Variety of Subjects of which they treat, and the Voice of the Publick against any Increase of their Number, are Difficulties, which a Man must have some Courage to encounter, and his Work no little Merit to surmount. Yet, however incumbered we find the Way to your Favour, we have been induced to venture, purely from this Consideration, That the Publick seldom refuses a kind Reception to any thing apparently calculated for Publick Use.

Many wise and well-inclined People complain, That political Papers, however well wrote, serve only to irritate Mens Minds, inflame their Passions, and set them at Variance with their fellow Subjects: And, therefore, leaving Affairs of State to those who are more proper Judges, they would content themselves, with reading at their Leisure, something better accommodated to their Genius, and their Stations.

Such Papers, as are said to be written merely for the Amusement of their Readers, have, in their very Nature, nothing inviting to a grave plain Man, who concerns not himself with the Merit of new Farces, nor listens to various Reports about the Squabbles of the Theater, his Head is turned for Matters of another Nature; and, therefore, passing by the Letter, he hastens to the News, which, it sometimes happens, consists of a few, and those ill-chosen Paragraphs.

To remedy these Inconveniencies, we have contrived a Journal, the initial Page of which, we intend to divide into three Columns. The First shall contain, an exact Treatise of Husbandry, in all its Branches. The Second, A regular System of Female Knowledge, commonly called Housewifry. And, the Third shall consist of such Articles, of a miscellaneous Nature, as may be suited to entertain, and yet instruct, the Peruser. Our Home News shall ever consist of a fair Quantity of authentic Paragraphs, which shall, at no Time, for the sake of private Emolument, give way to Advertisements.

These Particulars premised, we refer you to the Performance itself, of which this Paper, we hope, will be a sufficient Specimen. And, we conclude, with assuring the Publick, if we are so lucky as to attain their Favour, that it shall be our continual Care, never to forfeit it by any wilful Neglect, or Omission.

The ŒCONOMIST:

Or, The ART of managing a FAMILY and ESTATE.

PHILOSOPHERS have generally agreed, in recommending to our Study, before all other *Branches* of *Science*, the *Knowledge* of *ourselves*; next to which, we think it must be owned, that the *Knowledge* of directing a *Family* and *Estate* ought to have Place, since it is what almost every one has Occasion for; ŒCONOMY being equally useful to *Men* of *large Income*, and *Persons* of *small Fortune*; the *First* are instructed from *thence*, to retain the *Blessings* they *possess*, and the *Latter* are taught thereby, to acquire the *Necessaries* of *Life* for the *present*, and to raise a *Fund* of *Affluence* for the *future*, by accumulated *Savings*.

Yet, necessary and important as this *Science* is, it is scarce regarded in the World, either in *Theory* or *Practice*; few *Authors* have made it the Subject of their *Studies*, and as few have endeavoured to *practise* it in any Degree of *Perfection*, in managing their *private Affairs*. *Good Sense* alone, is thought *Guide* sufficient in *Family Matters*, and *Experience* is owned the sole *Tutor* in *manual Professions*; *Method* is look'd upon as an *Incumbrance*, by those who are little acquainted therewith, and a Thing unapplicable to such Purposes, by those who have a better *Idea* of its *Consequence* in other Arts.

However, to a Man of Consideration, it will quickly appear, that *Œconomy* is alike useful in the *rural Employments* of the *Husbandman*, and in the *magnificent Dwellings* of the *Great*. In this Labour, therefore, wherein I intend to comprehend an intire System of *Œconomy*, suited to most *Degrees*, whereby Men are distinguished in this *World*, I have judged it proper to begin with the *Country*, and shall, in the First *Column* of this *Work*,

The FEMALE ŒCONOMIST:

Or, The complete HOUSE-WIFE.

THO' the LADIES of *GREAT BRITAIN* have indisputably as great Abilities of Soul, as any of the *Sex* are endowed with, yet they have been ever laudably distinguished for applying themselves to the *Care* of their *Families*, rather than endeavouring to shine in what is called a more *exalted Sphere*, and in which the *Females* in the *Southern* Parts of *Europe*, chiefly affect to blaze. The Intrigues of *Love*, and of the *State*, serve rather to make the *Fair* miserable in the End, than to render *her* happy and admired: Wherefore, we may justly praise the Wisdom of our *Country-women*, who, with *Charms* superior to those possessed by Women of other Nations, and with *Faculties* capable of conducting the greatest Designs, neither abandon themselves to *Pleasure*, or interfere with *Matters* which are, properly, within the *Province* of *Men*.

NATURE, who is the best Conductress in respect of *Study*, as well as other Things, points out in the *Female Frame*, the *Business* for which they are designed. As they are formed fairer and more lovely than the other *Sex*, so they are weaker also, and more tender in their Constitution, incapable of Hardships, unfit for robust Labours, and unable to sustain Fatigue. To Man, therefore, it belongs to provide the Necessaries of Life, to Woman, it appertains to make them convenient, and where her Station requires it, elegant.

In the earlier *Ages* of the World, the *Employments* of both Sexes were plain and simple, procuring Food, dressing it, and providing for their Off-spring, were almost all the Branches of *Antediluvian Œconomy*. But, as the State of all Things at this Day, differs widely from what it was, so the Circle of *Female Care* is vastly extended, as well as that which demands the Cognizance of Men. Silk covers us

MISCELLANIES.

I Shall not detain my Readers long in the Account I have to give them of this Column, I intend, in one Word, to afford Room here, for every Thing that may be capable, either of entertaining or improving those who peruse this *Paper*: And, therefore, *Verse* or *Prose*, *Serious* or *Comic* Pieces, shall be thankfully received, and carefully inserted, if directed to the Editor of the OECONOMIST, Or, EDLIN's *weekly Journal*. The following *Articles* will serve for a Specimen of the *Design*.

Tunbridge Frisk. *A Country-Dance.*

First and 2d Cu. foot it and turn, then 1st and 2d Man foot it and turn, Two Wom. do the same. First Man cast off two Cu. First Wom. cast off one Cu. and cast up again, foot it and turn in the 2d Cu. Place.

Figure 1: *The Oeconomist: or, Edlin's Weekly Journal* (September 1733), p. 1. By kind permission of the Beinecke Rare Book and Manuscript Library, Yale University.

A neat illustration of men's and women's imagined engagements with different levels of task is the single extant issue of *The Oeconomist: or, Edlin's Weekly Journal*, published in September 1733. The two-page issue has three columns. First and on the left, 'The ŒCONOMIST: Or, the Art of managing a FAMILY and ESTATE', which summarizes neatly the comments of 'philosophers' on this 'science', but also promises detailed instruction on husbandry, gardening, and grazing. Second and in the centre, 'The FEMALE ŒCONOMIST: Or, The complete HOUSE-WIFE', which will include instructions for country and city housewives (with discussion of, for example, livestock and brewing, and cookery and confectionary respectively), a description of the female trades and their profits, and a final section for 'Persons of *Distinction*'. Placing these columns side by side was the prompt for the author's claim to originality: 'uniting *Theory* and *Practice*' in 'joining the Rules of *Morality* and *Prudence* to the Art of *conducting a Family*'.[61] The third column, on the right, consisted of 'Miscellanies' designed 'to entertain, and yet instruct'.[62] The division between husbandry—or the art or science of managing a family and estate—and housewifery was here conveyed by the design of the page. And this division was a gendered division of type of task, but particularly level of task. The layout visualized a distinction typical of English writing on household at this time. Importantly, though, oeconomy could only operate effectively within a coherent unit. The joint efforts of housewives and oeconomists would be 'beneficial to the Publick', assisting households to acquire what they needed but also to save for the future. *The Oeconomist: or, Edlin's Weekly Journal* is an extremely rare document and this suggests that it was not a long-lived or popular publication. Yet, targeted at gendered individuals of different ranks and different places, applying their theory and practice harmoniously within, and for the benefit of, distinct household units, it does provide a map of distinctions found in many other works.

Edlin's *Journal* is unusual because it brought together in a single publication two different sub-genres of writing on oeconomy: those which dealt with the practice of housekeeping on the one hand, and the art, science, or theory of household management on the other. Two publications by Richard Bradley from the 1720s will illustrate these sub-genres. Until he published these works, Richard Bradley had limited his extensive list of publications mainly to botany, as befitting the first Professor of Botany at Cambridge from 1724. But during the 1720s he began to publish a series of works on oeconomy. In 1725 he revised and translated Noel Chomel's *Dictionaire Oeconomique: or, The Family Dictionary*.[63] This monumental work brought together all the topics one might find scattered in a host of other family books: information on cattle and other livestock, human health, estate management, gardening and husbandry, small-scale domestic production (of soap and cotton, for example), weights and measures, and sports and recreation. As in the original, Bradley's two-volume work is organized alphabetically. There are entries on bread, brewing, and brick-making, on gout, grafting, and gravy, and on

---

[61] *Oeconomist: or, Edlin's Weekly Journal*, 1 September 1733, p. 2, column 2.   [62] Ibid. p. 1.
[63] N[oel] Chomel, *Dictionaire Oeconomique: or, The Family Dictionary*, Revised by Richard Bradley (London, 1725). The translation was also published in Dublin in 1727 and 1758.

lemonade, lettice, and 'loosness'. In its range, this work exemplified the didactic guidebooks on the practice of housekeeping.

Yet Bradley's revised translation of Chomel was altered for an English audience. He inserted new material, drawing on his own expertise as Fellow of the Royal Society and Professor of Botany. On husbandry and gardening he included information from Hartlib, Platt, Blyth, Markham, Evelyn—a canon of (male) writers in this field; while with regards to physic, cookery, and confectionary, he also inserted recipes on preparing cordial waters in order to replace paragraphs which displayed an 'Inconsistency with our Religion or Oeconomy'.[64] Most significantly, however, Bradley's preface imposes a spatial, rather than alphabetical, order on the work that follows: 'Having now instructed us in the Manner of improving Estates without Doors' Bradley says of Chomel, 'He then brings us home, and prescribes the best and cheapest Way of providing and managing all manner of Meats and Sauces in the Kitchen, even from the most ordinary kind of Diet, to the most elegant Service for a Prince's Table.'[65] In framing Chomel's dictionary with outside/inside distinctions, Bradley brought this work into line with the many English didactic works on the topic, several of which he was himself writing, and some of which have been discussed above. In 1726 he published *The Country Gentleman and Farmer's Monthly Director*. In the same year appeared *A Complete Body of Husbandry, Collected from the Practice and Experience of the most considerable Farmers in Britain*.[66] From 4 July of that year, Bradley, also produced the four-page *Weekly Miscellany For the Improvement of the Husbandry, Trade, Arts, and Sciences*. Somewhat mischievously, Bradley informed his readers that it was important to include the features on husbandry in this periodical because 'it will be a more speedy means of bringing them to practise, than if we were to wait their Publication in a larger Volume'.[67] Bradley's periodical may have provided the model for Edlin's *The Oeconomist*, though its content was different, focusing on 'the encrease of Riches' and 'the advancement of Natural Knowledge' through trade ('whether at Home or Abroad'), husbandry, new inventions, and antiquities.[68] The issues, which ran until 21 November 1727, included features on hurricanes, gardening, clay water pipes, lobsters, and shells. Bradley's publications in this year also attended to domestic oeconomy: the first part of *The Country Housewife and Lady's Director* was first published in Dublin and London in 1727; a second part was published in 1732; and combined editions appeared in 1736, 1753, and 1762.[69] As Bradley noted, the gendered 'without doors'/'within doors' separation embodied by the companion works on husbandry and housewifery came together in 'The Art of Oeconomy'.[70]

---

[64] Bradley, 'Preface', Chomel, *Dictionaire Oeconomique*, p. vi.   [65] Ibid. p. v.
[66] Richard Bradley, *A Complete Body of Husbandry, Collected from the Practice and Experience of the most considerable Farmers in Britain* (London, 1727). On Bradley's publications see, Bradley, *Country Housewife and Lady's Director*, ed. Davidson, pp. 35–41.
[67] Bradley, *Weekly Miscellany*, 1, Tuesday, 4 July 1727, p. 2. No issues have been reported after November 1727. See the entry in the English Short Title Catalogue, <http://estc.bl.uk/> (last accessed July 2010) (Hereafter 'ESTC').
[68] Bradley, *Weekly Miscellany*, pp. 1–2 (quote at p. 2).
[69] Richard Bradley, *The Country Housewife and Lady's Director* (Dublin, 1727).
[70] Bradley, *Country Housewife and Lady's Director* (1736), Part I, pp. vii–viii.

Bradley's *Dictionaire Oeconomique* was mainly a practical guide, but includes a comment on the theory of oeconomy. The definition provided underlines oeconomy's force as a general system of management and order, and one that extends through and out of the household:

> OECONOMY, a certain Order in the Management of a Family and domestick Affairs: Hence the Word Oeconomist, for a good Manager. But Oeconomy may be taken in a more extensive Sense, for a just, prudent, and regular Conduct in all the Parts of Life, and relative Capacities. But as for the Word Oeconomicus (Oeconomist) it was formerly used for the Executor of a Last Will and Testament, and the Person that had the Oeconomy and fiduciary Disposal of the Deceased's Goods.[71]

While the dictionary carved up practical knowledge into topics organized alphabetically, and Bradley's preface imposed an inside/outside distinction on the whole two-volume work, here readers saw how oeconomy was predicated precisely on relations between 'all the Parts of Life'.

In his own works and the translation of Chomel, Bradley focused primarily on the practical skills of housekeeping and husbandry. In contrast, he presented a fuller account of oeconomy as the art or science of management, and as having 'an extensive sense', in his 1727 translation of Xenophon's classical work on oeconomy, *The Science of Good Husbandry; or, the Oeconomics of Xeonophon* (London, 1727). Xenophon (*c*.430–356 BCE) produced a work that was unique in Greek literature, bringing together material on household management with material on agriculture or husbandry.[72] The work differed in some important aspects from Aristotle's comments on *oikos* in his *Politics*; notably, while for Aristotle the husband always holds complete authority, Xenophon granted women the potential for authority, once taught well by their husbands. In this way, Xenophon's ideas were 'radical' in a classical context.[73] More importantly, the *oikos* for Xenophon was not an analogy for, but a microcosm of, the *polis*.[74] As we will see, for eighteenth-century readers Xenophon's work represented the 'theory' for much of the didactic material on housewifery and husbandry. It exemplifies the second tradition of oeconomical writing: not the practical and didactic, but the moral and philosophical.

The two sub-genres of oeconomical writing had different foci, but they concurred in their definitions of oeconomy as 'the just and regular Distribution of a Man's Goods, or the wise Management of his Possessions, or of his Household'.[75] Emphasized in this theory was the overriding theme of order: the practice of oeconomy was simply 'the Ordering of a House'.[76] Rooted in a model of civic republicanism, this practice of ordering or managing within the household

---

[71] Chomel, *Dictionaire Oeconomique*, entry for 'Oeconomy'.

[72] Sarah B. Pomery, 'Preface', Xenophon, *Oeconomicus: A Social and Historical Commentary*, trans. Sarah B. Pomery (Oxford: Clarendon Press, 1994), p. vii.

[73] Ibid. pp. 34, 68.

[74] Jane Garnett, 'Political and Domestic Economy in Victorian Social Thought: Ruskin and Xenophon', in Stefan Collini, Richard Whatmore, and Brian Young (eds), *Economy, Polity, and Society: British Intellectual History 1750-1950* (Cambridge: Cambridge University Press, 2000), p. 207.

[75] *The Science of Good Husbandry: or, the Oeconomics of Xenophon* (trans. Richard Bradley, 1727), p. i.

[76] Ibid. p. 37.

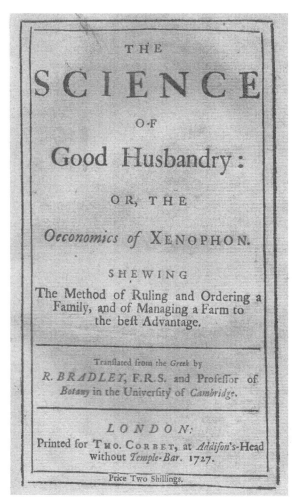

Figure 2: Title page of Xenophon, *The Science of Good Husbandry; or, the Oeconomics of Xenophon*, trans. Richard Bradley (1727). By kind permission of The William Andrews Clark Memorial Library, University of California, Los Angeles.

extended to the outside, because the well-ordered house was the training ground for skills that were at the heart of public manly behaviour. As Sarah Pomeroy has remarked of the *Oeconomicus*, Xenophon's original interest in the domestic economy reinforced civic values: 'The oikoi constituted the foundation of the polis and served to reproduce the citizen population; therefore strengthening the individual oikoi would result in a more stable and vigorous polis.'[77] This was also evident in Bradley's claim that oeconomy earned men 'Honour and Reputation' and taught

---

[77] Pomery, 'Preface', p. 46.

them self-governance, perhaps the key virtue of any man seeking masculine status.[78] In this vision, a man who could manage his household could command
kingdoms.[79] As a theory and as a style of masculinity, oeconomy extended much
further than the management of the household, then.

Bradley's translation of Xenophon provided a theoretical supplement to the
how-to guides, but it also overlapped with them. The preface to the 24 October
issue of *The Weekly Miscellany* proclaimed husbandry 'the Mother of all other Sciences'.[80] Bradley goes on to note that the husbandman is specifically a manager—
'the Ruler and Director of a Farm, whose Business is rather the Work of the Brain,
then [*sic*] of the Hands'—mentioning Xenophon's 'Œconomics' in this section.[81]
Indeed, the second issue of *The Weekly Miscellany* had carried an advert for Bradley's Xenophon.[82] By the same token, Bradley's translation of Xenophon attended
to some of the practical tasks involved in the system of management. In Xenophon, ordering the house required the husband to pay close attention to the items
bought for the house and the nature of interior decoration: the house should not,
Bradley explains, be filled with 'unnecessary Decorations', but be 'built with due
Consideration, and for the Conveniency of the Inhabitants'.[83] This practical
involvement facilitated men's engagement at a more general level, though: men
had to know the details of the working household so they were able to train, dele-
gate to, and supervise their wives and others. While men were participants in the
mundane and everyday in the didactic books, their roles as global managers or
instructors became pronounced in Xenophon.

Xenophon's ideas had circulated in European culture for some two centuries
prior to Bradley's translation. The *Oeconomicus*—and also a Pseudo-Aristotelian
version, the *Oeoconomica*—was translated and adapted in classical Greece and
Rome. Xenophon's work was first translated into manuscript Latin editions in the
*c.*1450s, but was cited in works on family and marriage by civic humanists as early
as 1416. Published commentaries appeared in 1564 and 1586, yet Xenophon's
ideas (particularly on the important role of women in the home) were popularized
in the translations of Juan Luis Vives' works from the 1520s, under the patronage
of Catherine of Aragon. The *Oeconomicus* was also used as a key text by English
humanists at Cambridge during the mid-1500s.[84] Pomeroy remarks that 'the
unique feature of the *Oeconomicus*—the possibility of governance by an educated,
well-qualified woman—became a reality' under Elizabeth I.[85] Xenophon's work
found a particularly receptive audience in England.

Bradley's claim to have produced the first English translation was inaccurate.[86]
Indeed, from the mid-sixteenth century, Xenophon had already served as a source
for vernacular household books.[87] The first English translation of Xenophon

---

[78] *Science of Good Husbandry*, p. 1–2.   [79] Ibid. pp. 87–8.
[80] Bradley, *Weekly Miscellany*, 17, Tuesday, 24 October 1727, p. 2.   [81] Ibid. p. 2.
[82] Ibid. 2, Tuesday, 11 July 1727, p. 4.   [83] *Science of Good Husbandry*, p. 61.
[84] Pomery, 'Preface', pp. 68–79.   [85] Ibid. p. 86.   [86] *Science of Good Husbandry*, p. v.
[87] Craig Muldrew, *The Economy of Obligation: The Culture of Credit and Social Relations in Early
Modern England* (Basingstoke: Macmillan, 1998), p. 159; Alexandra Shepard, *Meanings of Manhood
in Early Modern England* (Oxford: Oxford University Press, 2003), p. 77.

appeared in 1532, by Gentian Hervet. This was also the first dateable English translation of any Greek work and the first published translation of any of Xenophon's works.[88] While the book may have borne some resemblance to domestic books for women, Pomeroy noted that of the copies of Hervet's translation she consulted, all were autographed by men.[89] Whatever the readership, this was a popular work, reprinted five times before 1573. Greek editions with Latin translation were also published in 1693, 1703, and 1750. Assuming that Bradley's claim to originality was ingenuous, he may have worked from one of the early editions. Following Bradley's translation of 1727, a reprint of Hervet's earlier translation of 1532 was published in 1767.[90] This latter version was edited by Robert Vansittart as an antiquarian project.[91] But certainly in the first half of the eighteenth century, Xenophon was of more than antiquarian interest, as the inclusion of his ideas in several printed works attest.[92] His other works were appearing in several editions throughout this period, and the *Biographia classica* (1740) acknowledged the breadth of his corpus, taking in 'the Management of Family Affairs' and 'the more arduous Matters of State and Policy'.[93] And the kind of men who feature in later chapters of this book were readers of his works. The cousins of Richard Kay of Baldingstone, for example, experienced a week of intensive classical study, learning 'Socrates, Xenophon, ith' forenoon', with Horace and others studied in the afternoon.[94]

A comparison of the two English translations of the *Oeconomicus* from 1532 and 1727 shows that while the content remained largely stable, there were some clear differences. Bradley's translation was notable for its front matter: a three-page dedication and a four-page preface, in contrast to the brief *c.*15-line address to the reader in Hervet's version. These preliminaries positioned the work firmly in

---

[88] Pomery, 'Preface', p. 81.   [89] Ibid. pp. 85–6.

[90] Ludwig Wilhelm Brüggemann, *A view of the English editions, translations and illustrations of the ancient Greek and Latin authors* (Stettin, 1797), p. 141. Brüggemann also notes two Latin translations of 1695; 1705 and 1750. He dates the first English translation as 1534, although the ESTC reproduces a copy dating from 1532: <http://estc.bl.uk/> (last accessed July 2010).

[91] Vansittart was an unmarried member of the Hell-Fire Club and famous for 'debauchery'. Mrs Thrale commented that he needed a governess to keep him in tow. His editing of the volume seems not a little ironic. E. I. Carlyle, 'Vansittart, Robert (1728–1789)', rev Robert Brown, *Oxford Dictionary of National Biography*, Oxford University Press, 2004; online edn, October 2005 <http://www.oxforddnb.com/view/article/28106> (last accessed 13 July 2007).

[92] See Doohwan Ahn, 'Xenophon and the Greek Tradition in British Political Thought', in James Moore, Ian Macgregor Morris, and Andrew J. Bayliss (eds), *Reinventing History: The Enlightenment Origins of Ancient History* (London: Centre for Metropolitan History, Institute of Historical Research, School of Advanced Study, University of London, 2008), pp. 33–55.

[93] *Biographia classica: the lives and characters of all the classic authors, the Grecian and Roman poets, historians, orators, and biographers* (London, 1740), vol. 2, pp. 29, 32. On Xenophon see also John Adams, *The flowers of ancient history. Comprehending, on a new plan, the most remarkable and interesting events, as well as characters, of antiquity*, 3rd edition (London, 1796), pp. 144–5, where there is no mention of the domestic writings; Joseph Addison, *Interesting anecdotes, memoirs, allegories, essays, and poetical fragments, tending to amuse the fancy, and inculcate morality* (London, 1794), vol. 4 of 4, p. 271, refers briefly to the work on oeconomy.

[94] 2 April 1723, 'Extracts from the Journals of Mr Richd Kaye of Baldingstone & Chesham in the Par. of Bury Co. Lanc. now in the possn of Mrs Kay of Bury. Jan. 20. 1848. R.R.R.', Chetham's Library: C.6.34–77 Raines Collection, vol. 31, f. 440.

the present of eighteenth-century England. The treatise is dedicated to James Creed, a merchant who later became an alderman. Bradley flatters him as 'a Lover of Wisdom, good Order, and the Welfare of his Country', in stark contrast to the 'false Pretenders to Oeconomy' chastised at the close of the Preface.[95] Bradley also offered a useful taxonomy for the corpus of works on the household published under his own name, juxtaposing the practice of husbandry with the science of husbandry. The translation of Xenophon was a work of theory, he clarified, presented at a time when 'the Multitude [...] live without Rule', it would chime with contemporary concerns: 'Good Order, [...] is what every one talks of.'[96]

The main text of the two English editions differs in some small detail. While the sixteenth-century edition and its reprints are titled *Xenophon's Treatise of House-holde*, 'science' only appears in the main text, while the word 'oeconomy' is absent. There are some other minor omissions and differences. Describing his young wife's knowledge with regards to marriage and reproduction, the character Ischomachus comments in the 1532 edition that she had been brought up well 'as concerne the lower partes of the bely'; this comment was missing in the later translation.[97] The sixteenth-century references to 'almyghty god' have reverted back to 'the Gods' in 1727.[98] Finally, while Hervet's version presents a decidedly Christian threat to those who rule tyrannically against the will of others (and in keeping with Xenophon's threat of an eternity in hell in the original), Bradley's translation levels the decidedly more modest and secular warning that such a man 'can never hope for the least Ease or Comfort'.[99]

Bradley's 1727 edition of Xenophon did not, therefore, represent either the first English translation or a radical new interpretation. Classical notions of virtue were central to understandings of the social order and the working of credit throughout the early-modern period.[100] The ambition of these texts was

---

[95] *Science of Good Husbandry*, pp. iii, vii. Henry Kent, *The directory: containing an alphabetical list of the names and places of abode of the directors of companies persons in publick business* (London, 1736), p. 15, describes Creed as a 'lead merchant' in Southwark. See *Eighteenth Century Collections Online*, <http://find.galegroup.com.eresources.shef.ac.uk/ecco/>, Gale Document Number: CW124861477 (accessed 7 April 2009) (Hereafter, '*ECCO*').

[96] *Science of Good Husbandry*, p. v.

[97] Xenophon, *Xenophon's Treatise of Housholde*, trans. Gentian Hervet (London, 1532), facing p. 22; *Science of Good Husbandry*, p. 43. *Xenophon Memorabilia and Oeconomicus*, The Loeb Classical Library, trans. E. C. Marchant (London, 1923), translates the original as training 'in control of her appetite', p. 415. Pomeroy translates this as 'very well trained to control her appetites': Xenophon, *Oeconomicus*, trans. Pomery, p. 139.

[98] *Xenophon's Treatise of Housholde*, facing p. 32, p. 22, facing p. 64; *Science of Good Husbandry*, pp. 43–4, 62, 131. It is 'God' in *Xenophon Memorabilia and Oeconomicus*, trans. Marchant, p. 417, but 'the gods' in Xenophon, *Oeconomicus*, trans. Pomery, e.g. p. 139. For a comment on such anachronisms in earlier editions, see Xenophon, *Oeconomicus*, trans. Pomery, pp. 97–101.

[99] *Xenophon's Treatise of Housholde*, facing p. 64; *Science of Good Husbandry*, p. 131. *Xenophon Memorabilia and Oeconomicus*, trans. Marchant, p. 525. On the Christian setting of Hervet's translation, see Xenophon, *Oeconomicus*, trans. Pomery, pp. 81–2. In Pomeroy's edition, 'For ruling over willing subjects, in my view, is a gift not wholly human but divine, because it is a gift of the gods: and one that is obviously bestowed on those who have been initiated into self-control. The gods give tyranny over unwilling subjects, I think, to those who they believe deserve to live a life in Hades like Tantalus, who is said to spend the whole of eternity in fear of a second death.' Xenophon, *Oeconomicus*, trans. Pomery, pp. 209–11.

[100] Muldrew, *Economy of Obligation*, p. 136.

to increase the social and economic success of the household as a unit, indicated clearly in books such as Markham's collection *A Way to Get Wealth* (1625). This model of order with the objective of accumulating resources was a strategy particularly important for the middling sort. For this group, while financial distress and poor credit were seen as the result of the moral failings of the household, so 'the maintenance of virtue for those households which continued to prosper and grow wealthy, was used as a justification for their success, status and social and institutional power in an uncertain and competitive economic environment'. Craig Muldrew argues that, as a result 'the world view of the middling sort' was 'a constant vigilance to maintain their credit according to the expectations of public perception'.[101] Earlier household manuals were targeted at estates large and small, and this emphasis is retained in Bradley's faithful rendering of Xenophon's emphasis on good management to increase riches.[102] In this sense, Bradley's Xenophon is not a watershed in writing on oeconomy. And yet repackaged as a contemporary and socially-relevant theory or 'science', priced at two shillings, and published at the same time as a flurry of other works on household management, Bradley's Xenophon was the most thoroughgoing philosophical discussion of the classical model of oeconomy published in English for 154 years. In the fifty years following the Revolution of 1688, English male writers envisaged themselves as a 'civic individual through the use of Aristotelian and civic humanist categories, which required amongst other things that there be a material foundation, the equivalent of Aristotle's *oikos*, for his independence, leisure and virtue.'[103] Xenophon's work facilitated this independence by enabling the master to manage intermediaries who stood between him and the material increase in the wealth of the household.[104] Bradley's translation exemplified a long-standing form of didactic writing but offered a crystallized version of the classical model for a new civic readership, one which would prove receptive. Xenophon's work avowed that 'Empire and oikos, public and private, are organized according to the same principles'.[105] Civic humanism 'defined "man"...as a *political animal*'.[106] In eighteenth-century England, oeconomy offered an attractive theory linking men's household management to the wider economic and political spheres.

[101] Ibid. pp. 273–4. Quotes at p. 274.

[102] Bradley's other works were read by those with substantial families. The author of a letter published in the second part of his *Country Housewife* reported 'my Family' to consist of 'thirty Persons'. See Bradley, *Country Housewife*, Part II, p. 3. However, most of those whose recipes are published are 'commoners'. See Davidson, 'Editor's Introduction', Bradley, *Country Housewife*, pp. 19–20.

[103] J. G. A. Pocock, *The Machiavellian Moment: Florentine Political Thought and the Atlantic Republican Tradition* (1975; Princeton, NJ: Princeton University Press, 2003), p. 450.

[104] William James Booth, *Households: On the Moral Architecture of the Economy* (Ithaca and London: Cornell University Press, 1993), p. 85.

[105] Xenophon, *Oeconomicus*, trans. Pomery, p. 241. Here Pomeroy is commenting on the section in which Socrates tells Critobulus that he could model himself on the king of the Persians, who considers farming and the art of war both as essential bodies of knowledge and who governs accordingly.

[106] John Barrell, 'Foreword', *The Birth of Pandora and the Division of Knowledge* (Basingstoke: Palgrave Macmillan, 1992), p. xiv.

A LONG HISTORY OF PATRIARCHALISM

Alongside civic humanism, patriarchalism created a fertile environment for the popularization of classical oeconomy. Prior to 1727, works such as Dudley North's *Observations and Advices Oeconomical* (1669) and George Wheler's *The Protestant Monastery: or, Christian Oeconomicks* (1698) had discussed at length an oeconomical model of household order, but geared to the direct support of a patriarchal state. The respective office, authority, and duty of each household member were described, but with different emphases than in classical oeconomy. While the classical theory of oeconomy envisaged the *oikos* governed with two aims in mind—'securing and increasing the wealth of the household and the proper use of the wealth thereby created'—these seventeenth-century writers made the household instrumental to the wider society and polity.[107] For North, order resulted in good fortune and sound government, while for Wheler it transformed a house into 'a Heavenly Mansion' at a time of worrying decay in the English Church.[108] In classical thought, all human communities required 'rule and subjection': 'it is precisely the proper ranking of rulers over ruled that raises a composite, whether the soul, the household, or the city, above the level of a mere heap, an aggregate, and transforms it into an ordered whole.'[109] In this way, both ancient and early-modern patriarchal ideas of community were fundamentally hierarchical, but an Aristotelian vision in which the market was envisaged as a household was merged with patriarchalism's connection between the household and the body politic.[110]

In his work of 1669, for example, Dudley North certainly armed male household managers with a political role. The *Observations* was based on the *Propositioni, overo Considerationi in Materia di Cose di Stato*, a compilation of works by three Italian authors, which North describes as 'consisting of certain politick and prudential Considerations'.[111] North's rendering of this late-sixteenth-century Italian text sought to restore the household to discussions of government: 'the government of private Families may be considerable even with Princes', he writes in the Preface, 'because their Principalities are composed of Families, and they who are known to have well governed their private fortunes, are the rather judged fit for Publick Offices'.[112] He continued: 'Writers very considerable fetch their chief argument for Monarchy (as being the most natural and ancient Government) from its

---

[107] Booth, *Moral Households*, p. 39.
[108] George Wheler *The Protestant Monastery: or, Christian Oeconomicks* (London, 1698), p. 20.
[109] Booth, *Households*, p. 40.
[110] Ibid. pp. 96, 147. See Keith Tribe, 'The "Histories" of Economic Discourse', *Economy and Society*, 6 (1977), pp. 313–43. On an Aristotelian view of *oikos* in seventeenth-century political thought, see Pocock, *Machiavellian Moment*, p. 390. On early-modern political arithmetic as one way to achieve social and political order, see Peter Buck, 'Seventeenth-Century Political Arithmetic: Civil Strife and Vital Statistics', *Isis*, 68 (1977), pp. 67–84.
[111] North, *Observations and Advices Oeconomical*, A5v–A6r; Dale Randall, *Gentle Flame: The Life and Verse of Dudley, Fourth Lord North (1602–1677)* (Durham, NC: Duke University Press, 1983), p. 85.
[112] North, *Observations and Advices Oeconomical*, p. 8. See Lawrence Stone, *The Family, Sex and Marriage in England, 1500–1800* (1977; Harmondsworth: Penguin, 1979), p. 274.

Conformity with the Paternal.'[113] Though North worked with Parliament during the civil wars, he later proclaimed his loyalty to Charles I, and was pardoned by Charles II.[114] His comparison between household and monarchical government in the work accords with his royalist sympathies, yet North recognized that there were significant differences between family and state, particularly because the contrasting positions of servants and children relative to the father was not replicated in the state. Crucially, though, each realm requires a similar hierarchical model of management: 'neither of them can well subsist withont due subordinations, and good order'.[115] The relevance of 'Christian Oeconomicks' to English government is less plain in Wheler's account, yet there is concurrence (not just analogy) between the just, natural and divine power of the 'Chief Father' (God), the 'Publick Father of our Country' (the King), and 'a Private Father of a Family'.[116] The power of the paternal office is at the heart of Wheler's vision, as it was for North. There is a palpable echo here of Robert Filmer's argument that the authority of the prince in any kingdom or commonwealth 'is the only Right and Natural Authority of a Supreme Father'.[117]

Such books contain normative representations of men in the household, but they were also written by men who themselves had domestic lives which are discussed in their works. Sir Dudley North prefaced his text with a lengthy autobiographical account, and described how he was writing the book at the moment that he moved to the country and to 'the chief Mansion-house of our Family'.[118] The book was written not upon marriage, but at the end of his life, soon after the death of his own father in 1667, and at the moment of retirement. George Wheler, later knighted, also provided an autobiographical statement in his preface to *The Protestant Monastery: or, Christian Oeconomicks* (1698), informing the reader that the first section of the book was written twenty years before publication, 'penned soon after my entrance upon a Conjugal State; I suppose Seven Years before my entrance into Holy Orders'.[119] This would date the composition to 1677: he was married in September of that year, and ordained in about 1683.[120] Both these authors rooted their prescriptive works partly in their own domestic experience of the gentlemanly housekeeping of the landed elite. Indeed, uniting the person of the householder and politician in the real figure of the landed author gave a force to what would later become the standard model for the 'state's role in the management of the economy' in early political economy, 'the organisation of a royal household, where polity and economy are intricately linked'.[121] These late-seventeenth-century

---

[113] North, *Observations and Advices Oeconomical*, p. 32–3.
[114] Randall, *Gentle Flame*, pp. 59–73.
[115] North, *Observations and Advices Oeconomical*, Observation. XV. Also see XLV.
[116] Wheler, *Protestant Monastery*, pp. 24–5.
[117] Robert Filmer, *Patriarcha: or The Natural Power of Kings* (London, 1680), p. 23.
[118] North, *Observations and Advices Oeconomical*, Preface, unnumbered, f. 5. See chapter 3, p. 7.
[119] Wheler, *Protestant Monastery*, v3.
[120] N. G. Wilson, 'Wheler, Sir George (1651–1724)', *Oxford Dictionary of National Biography*, Oxford University Press, 2004; online edn, January 2008 <http://www.oxforddnb.com/view/article/29193> (accessed 15 October 2004).
[121] Keith Tribe, *Land, Labour and Economic Discourse* (London, Routledge, 1978), p. 81.

writers' emphases on hierarchy can be aligned with the Tory 'ideology of order' that lived on well after the Revolution of 1688. As Dickinson has pointed out, notable critiques of political patriarchalism notwithstanding, 'the social and economic realities of the post-Revolution period still made it possible to regard a system of rank, degree and order as natural, inevitable and beneficial. The real and pervasive influence of fathers, employers and the great landowners could not be gainsaid by any intellectual construct.'[122] Indeed, in lay political theory, late-seventeenth-century writers melded the discourse of oeconomy with political patriarchalism.

A transformed historical context limited the usefulness of these models, though. Many in those swelling groups who traded and exchanged lacked the foundation of land and wealth that allowed them the independence to act virtuously for the public good.[123] Increasingly, it appeared that in a commercial society the public good might be best served by those with experience of work and commerce.[124] This shift was profoundly gendered: men virtuously pursued profit and the household was proof of their civic-mindedness, independence, and good credit, while women conducted disciplined household consumption. 'Profits were now "honourable"', argues Howell, 'because they would be invested in the household that was the foundation of the good society'.[125] During the early eighteenth century, then, household manuals appeared that catered not to the landed gentleman but to smaller householders. Typical of oeconomy's usage in the many early-eighteenth-century manuals that later emerged was the discussion by Daniel Defoe in *The Family Instructor* (1715). Arranged in a series of instructive dialogues, Defoe's book narrativized the events of one family, taking the reader through a series of case studies through which he was able to delineate the appropriate and mutual duties of all family members. The first part concerned 'paternal Duty, such as Instruction, Reproof, Authority and Discipline in a Father'; the second part described 'the Duty of Heads of Families as Masters of Servants, and how Servants ought to submit to Instruction and Family Regulation'; while the final part attended to 'the Duty of Husbands and Wives to exhort and perswade, intreat, instruct, and *by all gentle Means* if possible, prevail and engage one another to a religious holy Life'.[126] While Defoe is clear that he wants his instruction to 'afford suitable Lessons to Fathers, Mothers, Master of Families, &c. in their Duty of Family-Instruction', the weight given to the head of household in this family system is palpable.

Defoe's work came from and spoke to a new audience; not landowners with stewards and a fleet of other servants, but smaller householders who nevertheless might occupy important positions of moral or social status. This was an example

---

[122] H. T. Dickinson, *Liberty and Property: Political Ideology in Eighteenth-Century Britain* (London: Weidenfeld and Nicolson, 1977), p. 51.

[123] Pocock, *Machiavellian Moment*, pp. 450, 464.

[124] Barrell, 'Foreword', *The Birth of Pandora*, p. xv.

[125] See Martha Howell, 'The Gender of Europe's Commercial Economy, 1200–1700', *Gender and History*, 20, 3 (2008), pp. 519–38. Quote at p. 532.

[126] Daniel Defoe, *The Family Instructor*, 2nd edition (London, 1715), pp. 296–7. See *ECCO*, Gale Document Number: CW3322894096 (accessed August 2007).

of a relatively secular manual about household order for the burgeoning upper-middling audience of Defoe's other works. Here, political patriarchalism is less pronounced, though the emphasis on order in the household, on discipline and subordination, remains explicit. Defoe continued the theme in his treatise on servants, *The Great Law of Subordination Consider'd* (1724), asserting that 'the Rule of Subordination [...] is essential to Family-Oeconomy'.[127] The emphasis was increasingly on the disciplining of middling-sort families, partly in order to maintain credit and achieve the social and economic success of a household. As Muldrew has demonstrated, 'personal order' was crucial if the household was to remain competitive, such was the connection between morals and creditworthiness.[128]

The third part of Defoe's *Family Instructor* is explicitly intended to foster a 'holy life', though.[129] Whether in the profoundly Christian treatise of Wheler, or the more diffuse religious language of North and Defoe, oeconomy supplemented and supported another vision of the house where the family was a religious assembly and in which paternal authority was central. The significance of religion for men's role in the household is notable in the earlier classically inflected versions of patriarchalism. Filmer's comments on paternal authority in *Patriarcha* (1680) famously begin with Adam, of course.[130] The paternal hierarchy of the family reflected and extended the paternal hierarchy of faith. Yet there was a continued integration of religion—if more generally expressed—in later works too. Josiah Woodward's *The Necessary Duty of Family Prayer* (first published in 1717 and running to at least 13 editions before 1800), though initially addressed to 'a pious Master or Mistress of a Family', is soon targeted at the 'good Housholder' and 'the little Assembly of his Family'.[131] Demonstrating the continuing public relevance of religion, Woodward connects the regulation of families with the condition of society: 'every Governour of a Family is either a Publick Benefactor or a Publick Grievance, according to the good or ill management of his Family'.[132] As with the spiritual meditations on husbandry discussed above, Woodward's book advocated 'Religious Government' in families as a method of 'National Reformation', through which the nation would become 'regular and religious'.[133] This pairing of order and faith, as too of family and the public, was a recurring theme in writings on oeconomy.[134] Several Evangelical writers created a particularly intense version of domestic ideology at the end of the eighteenth century, although the link between Evangelicalism and marriage,

---

[127] Daniel Defoe, *The great law of subordination consider'd; or, the insolence and unsufferable behaviour of servants in England duly enquir'd into* (London, 1724), p. 11. *ECCO*, Gale Document Number: CW112656736. Published later as Daniel Defoe, *The behaviour of servants in England inquired into* (London, [1726?]), p. 11. *ECCO*, Gale Document Number: CW104196855 (both accessed April 2008).

[128] Muldrew, *Economy of Obligation*, p. 298.   [129] Defoe, *Family Instructor*, p. 297.

[130] Filmer, *Patriarcha*, p. 57.

[131] Josiah Woodward, *The Necessary Duty of Family Prayer*, 6th edition (1722), pp. 7, 8.

[132] Ibid. p. 11.

[133] Ibid. pp. 6, 11. Not surprisingly, Woodward wrote about the Societies for the Reformation of Manners in the late 1690s.

[134] It can also be seen in the later important work of Sarah Trimmer, in which 'oeconomy' is a general term to mean order. Sarah Trimmer, *The oeconomy of charity; or, an address to ladies concerning Sunday-Schools* (London, 1787).

family and domesticity was not always so close.[135] For many Christian writers, marriage and family life could be a source of difficulty in a man's life.[136] Nevertheless, both Protestant religion and oeconomy were holistic guides for good or right living in England, with theoretical (theological) components that also gave meaning to the small, the mundane, and the everyday. Accordingly, most oeconomical works were underpinned by a diffuse religious language throughout.

Philippe Sylvestre Dufour's advice to his son, published in English 1742, is a good example of this feature of the theoretical writings on oeconomy. Sylvestre Dufour organized his instructions 'under three Heads, *Spiritual, Personal, Social or Civil*. By the *First*, I shall teach you what you owe to GOD; by the *Second*, what you owe to yourself, and by the *Third*, what you owe to your Neighbour'.[137] Order and regularity is essential to all areas: 'what you do, let it be done with Order'.[138] Other values connect not only the three areas of behaviour, but also the son's inner self with all encounters in the public. Justice, for example, should be exercised in the son's treatment of servants, but also in general conversation: 'especially remember, that a mixt Conversation is not a Monarchy State, where one alone has a Right to speak and pre-side; but rather a kind of Republick, where every Individual has a Right, in his Turn, to speak, and propose what he thinks fitting and reasonable'.[139] Similarly, prudence was more than a simply economic issue: if the son can learn to despise 'Pride, Covetousness, Gluttony, Idleness, Impurity, Anger and Envy', then he will easily 'be carried to the Love and Practice of Humility, of proper Œconomy, neither profuse, not sordid, of Sobriety, of Diligence, of Chastity, Moderation and Charity'. Prudence will be 'very Salutary and Advantageous' for both 'the Good of your Soul and Body'.[140] Works such as Dufour's advice book and Bradley's translation of Chomel's domestic dictionary were complementary texts that together facilitated an oeconomic way of life.

The house was never a secular space in oeconomical writing, though nor was it always obviously Christian. An important title in this regard is Robert Dodsley's popular *The Oeconomy of Human Life*. This book shows the continuing force of a discourse of specifically religious oeconomy. It also suggests the increasingly frequent use of the concept to mean a general system of order outside the house, beginning to appear in works such as *National Oeconomy Recommended* (1746) and *Miscellaneous Reflections upon the Peace, And... on a just, as well as real and national Oeconomy* (1749), both of which discuss national defence in the context of public finance and structures of governmental power.[141] *The Oeconomy of Human Life*

---

[135] William Van Reyk, 'Christian Ideals of Manliness During the Period of the Evangelical Revival, c.1730 to c.1840' (University of Oxford DPhil Thesis, 2007), chapter 2, pp. 71–109, esp. 73–8.

[136] Ibid. pp. 99–107.

[137] Philippe Sylvestre Dufour [pseud Jacob Spon], *Moral Instructions for Youth: Or, a Father's Advice to a Son. Translated from the French, At first only for particular, and now publish'd for general Use. Being an attempt to season the growing generation with Virtuous Principles* (London, 1742), p. 7.

[138] Ibid. p. 52.

[139] Ibid. pp. 54–5.

[140] Ibid. p. 42.

[141] *National Oeconomy Recommended, as the only means of retrieving our trade and securing our liberties* (London, 1746); *Miscellaneous Reflections upon the Peace, And its consequences. More especially on a just, as well as real and national Oeconomy* (London, 1749).

Figure 3: Frontispiece of Robert Dodsley, *The Oeconomy of Human Life* (1751). By kind permission of the Beinecke Rare Book and Manuscript Library, Yale University.

was first published in 1751, with 142 editions between 1750 and 1800, and 95 more from 1801. Produced as fine and richly illustrated volumes as well as small pocket-sized books, the substantive sections of the text remained stable through the many different editions.[142] This work repackaged a loosely Christian patriarchalism and oeconomic order for a new audience, wrapped in an indistinct religious language, and apparently originating from an Indian manuscript handed

---

[142] *The Oeconomy of Human Life. Translated from an Indian Manuscript. Written by an Ancient Bramin. To which is prefixed an account of the manner in which the said manuscript was discovered. In a Letter from an English Gentleman now Residing in China to the Earl of E***** (London, 1751).

to what the author described as a 'Chinese', rather than Tibetan, Lama.[143] This is no simple guide on how to institute order and management; rather, the book describes oeconomy as a system of morality built upon and exercised through ordered relationships that extend out of the household.[144] Part I of *The Oeconomy of Human Life* laid out guides for the conduct of men in a series of roles—husband, father, son, brother—and then in position to others outside the house—wise and ignorant, rich and poor, masters and servants, and magistrates and subjects. These relationships and their duties and responsibilities echo the earlier books which taxonomize the various household relationships in turn. Benevolence is an important theme, but strict obedience is also necessary. Describing the relationship between master and servant, there is little trace of reciprocity, but rather a taxonomy of the powers and responsibilities of the king: he who is 'clothed in purple', creates laws for his 'subjects', is merciful and punishes justly; 'His people therefore look up to him as a father', the author explains, 'with reverence and love'.[145]

The Oeconomy of Human Life inspired a handful of responses.[146] One of these— *The Oeconomy of Female Life* (1751)—claimed to provide a female-centred corrective. This responsive text is a satire, mocking the grave style and knowing maxims of the original, while undoing the moral order of the relations therein. The book has a narrower compass, focusing only on women's relationships with husbands. Advising female readers on the management of husbands, for example, *The Oeconomy of Female Life* invites women to enter repeated adulterous affairs: 'When thou hast given transport to one lover, spread thine arms unto another, wouldst thou be constant to him whom no ties have bound thee unto?' Imagining a reader might worry about being caught, the author bravely suggests, 'be generous to a thousand, and thou shalt be suspected with none of them'.[147] This satire provides one gauge of the tenor of early responses to Dodsley's work. But the many republications of *The Oeconomy of Human Life*, in which the substantive content remained unchanged, suggest that this general guide to oeconomical living was a tremendous success. Placed against the detailed didactic oeconomical works, though, the book reads less as a practical users' guide to living and more a remote and disengaged but religiously motivated treatise.

---

[143] Another writer pointed out that the author of the *Oeconomy of Human Life* had 'borrowed your *Indian* maxims from *Hebrew* and *Roman* moralists'. Lady, *Maxims and Cautions for the Ladies: Being a Complete Oeconomy for the Female Sex* (London, 1752), pv *ECCO*, Gale Document Number: CB129956850. I thank Sophie Daniels for this reference. These references suggest Eastern influences. There are certainly similarities between the *The Oeconomy of Human Life* and *The Morals of Confucius* (published in English editions in 1691, 1706, and 1724). See the ESTC, <http://estc.bl.uk/> (last accessed November 2011). See also, Edmund Leites, 'Confucianism in Eighteenth-Century England: Natural Morality and Social Reform', *Philosophy East and West*, 28, 2 (1978), pp. 143–59.

[144] On theft of this book see *Old Bailey Proceedings Online* (<http://www.oldbaileyonline.org/>, accessed 10 September 2010), 21 April 1773, trial of Robert Kippling, t17730421-12.

[145] *Oeconomy of Human Life*, pp. 71, 73, 74.

[146] Donald D. Eddy, 'Dodsley's "Oeconomy of Human Life," 1750–1751', *Modern Philology*, 85, 4 (1988), pp. 52–4.

[147] *The Oeconomy of Female Life. By a lady* (London, 1751), p. 31. *ECCO*, Gale Document Number: CW124613514.

NATIONAL OECONOMY

As we have seen, the discourse of 'oeconomy' changed, transformed by its fusion with patriarchalism and reworkings in a later civic republican context. Throughout, oeconomy theorized the connections of the household to the wider world, notably through the manly civic virtues inculcated in the house, in the system of order that the household established for the state, or in the religious morality instilled in household relationships. Over the course of the eighteenth century, another development took place. Whereas oeconomic writings had been concerned with the economic fortunes of individual households, these works increasingly placed the dividends of oeconomic management in the context of a national economy. Keith Tribe has noted that mid-century writings begin to position the husbandman or farmer in the larger frame of a national market or economy.[148] Jonathan White adds to this a parallel development in which oeconomy bifurcated into private and national forms, serving to orient the private interests of (in this case, labouring) families towards the national interest. Women were confined to 'manage the oeconomy of the domestic sphere', while male breadwinners were left to 'oversee their domestic order'.[149]

The practical household manuals of oeconomy had always positioned the involvement of men in the mundane and everyday domestic within a larger vision, one that stressed the increase of the household's riches. Some writers in the second half of the century continued to limit oeconomy to this domestic housekeeping. The essay 'Upon Œconomy' was published in a 1769 issue of the *Town and Country Magazine*, in response to what the author reported as a recent widespread interest in 'public as well as private œconomy'.[150] Oeconomy could mean '*good management*', but of economic resources: 'Œconomy hath ever been a testimony of prudence.' 'Real œconomy', the writer clarified, 'is the happy medium between prodigality and avarice.'[151] Similarly, echoing the earlier distinction between global management and day-to-day practice, but reversing the vocabulary, Trusler reduced both to financial management: 'frugality means balancing the books and is done by the husband. Oeconomy means management, includes making up for any imbalance, and is done by the wife', he wrote.[152] Titles on housekeeping for women continued to appear, devoid of the larger context of the household economy, yet providing detailed instructions on practice gleaned from years of experience that sought to 'join œconomy with neatness and elegance', or provide 'Curious Receipts' for 'an elegant Entertainment'.[153] In one of Dorothy Kilner's dialogues

---

[148] Tribe, *Land, Labour and Economic Discourse*, pp. 61–4.
[149] Jonathan White, 'Luxury and Labour: Ideas of Labouring-class Consumption in Eighteenth-century England' (Unpublished PhD thesis, University of Warwick, 2001), pp. 152–68. Quotes at p 164.
[150] 'Upon Œconomy', *Town and Country Magazine* (London, 1769), p. 119.
[151] Ibid. p. 120.
[152] John Trusler, *The distinction between words esteemed synonymous in the English language, pointed out, and the proper choice of them determined*, 2nd edition (London, 1783), p. 124.
[153] Elizabeth Raffald, *The Experienced Housekeeper, for the use of Ladies, Housekeepers, Cooks, &c.* (London, 1789), p. iii; Hannah Glasse, *The House-Keepers's Pocket Book, and Complete Family Cook* (London, 1783), title page.

for children, such oeconomy as practised by wives was mocked as insubstantial. A Mrs Collop was viciously taken to task by the narrator: 'And though every mistress of a house should endeavour to provide as genteelly as oeconomy will permit, yet, to spend the whole of her thought, and attention, and much of her time upon such a subject, shews that her mind must be very empty indeed. And she had much better apply to improving and cultivating that, than only preparing new dainties for her palate.'[154]

Other writers sought to retain the moral significance of the management of the household economy in a changing economic and social context, attending more extensively to the broader social value of the practical involvement of men in the household. Writers insisted on the import of household oeconomy to this larger system. In *Rural Oeconomy* (1770), Arthur Young insisted that his focus was not on oeconomy as 'frugality', but on 'the system of GENERAL MANAGEMENT, which embraces a variety of objects'.[155] In his later writings, following his shift to the political left, William Cobbett similarly made a passionate defence of what he called 'economy', in response to its denigration, 'as if it meant parsimony, stinginess, or niggardliness', practised by 'misers and close-fisted men'.[156] In this defence of the practices of the labouring poor, the word 'economy' had simply replaced 'oeconomy': 'ECONOMY means, management, and nothing more; and it is generally applied to the affairs of a house and family, which affairs are an object of the greatest importance, whether as relating to individuals or to a nation.'[157] As Raymond Williams has rightly identified, both Arthur Young and William Cobbett were writing about country life in a period of unprecedented social, economic, and technological change.[158] Their work covers some of the same ground of the earlier writing on husbandry, then, but has a new political charge. And it was during this period, from the 1770s to the 1820s, the two strains of oeconomic writing identified earlier in this chapter—the didactic and philosophical—began to come together in a new configuration.

Arthur Young's works are a good illustration of the development through which individual households were placed in a national context.[159] Young's book is also an example of the continuing resonance of oeconomy as a system of general household management with wider moral and political import. The work continued the emphasis on rural living observable in earlier works (from Markham to Bradley, for example), defining oeconomy as a 'system of GENERAL MANAGEMENT',[160] and appending a translation of a German text titled *The Rural Socrates*. Young commented that this book displayed an example, 'not only of oeconomy, industry, sobriety, and every domestick virtue, but also of most spirited

---

[154] [Dorothy Kilner], *Dialogues and Letters in Morality, Oeconomy, and Politeness, for the Improvement and Entertainment of Young Female Minds* (London, [1780]), p. 77.

[155] Arthur Young, *Rural Oeconomy: or, Essays on the Practical Parts of Husbandry* (London, 1770), p. 2.

[156] William Cobbett, *Cottage Economy* (London, 1822), p. 2.

[157] Ibid. pp. 1–2.

[158] Raymond Williams, *Cobbett* (Oxford: Oxford University Press, 1983), pp. 22–3.

[159] Tribe, *Land, Labour and Economic Discourse*, pp. 66–7.

[160] Young, *Rural Oeconomy*, p. 2.

husbandry'.[161] Yet the inclusion of the classical work allowed Young's book to go further than earlier treatises on husbandry. The translation begins by comparing the need for the regulation of a man's 'domestick affairs by the rules of a wise and prudent oeconomy', to that of 'the wisest systems of legislature, and the best political institutions' which also require 'a general scheme of oeconomy, sensibly executed'.[162] With this appendix, Young's work was both a practical guide to husbandry and a philosophy of right living in a house and society, the many detailed instructions on the well-proportioned and balanced farm set against 'the just and philosophic principles'.[163] Indeed, in critiquing other publications on rural oeconomy, Young's central point was that the practice must operate not for '*private* profit' but for '*public* good'.[164] Young's work is an early indication of how the emphasis on the accumulation of riches in a single household was shifting to a concern for right living in a national community.

Such changes parallel those taking place elsewhere. In French popular print as well as in the works of canonical authors during the 1750s and 1760s, 'economic activity was remade a quasi-patriotic pursuit', and a form of 'civic engagement'.[165] '[F]arming, trade, and industry were widely represented as fields for the pursuit of honor as much as arenas for the accumulation of profit.'[166] The civic republican tradition had been strong in England, as noted earlier.[167] Yet here too the value of civic republican aristocratic virtue to good governance in the public sphere was being challenged.[168] New ways of speaking about work developed in several genres, that served to naturalize work and 'show that middle-class workers were autonomous and politically responsible citizens—with no need of the inherited land that republican tradition had taken as a prerequisite of material independence and virtuous citizenship'.[169] Classical markers of manly independence shifted and became more 'inclusive'.[170]

In this changing context, the potential for oeconomy to become a language of political action was evident. A short-lived monthly published between January 1798 and December 1799, *The Oeconomist, or Englishman's Magazine*, provides a

---

[161] Ibid. pp. 375–6. Young does not discuss Xenophon, but we should note that Xenophon's work sets out to demonstrate that Socrates was a true oeconomist. Booth, *Households*, p. 92.

[162] Young, *Rural Oeconomy*, p. 360.

[163] Ibid. p. 175.

[164] Ibid. p. 369.

[165] John Shovlin, *The Political Economy of Virtue: Luxury, Patriotism, and the Origins of the French Revolution* (Ithaca, NY; London: Cornell University Press, 2006), p. 11.

[166] Ibid. p. 129.

[167] Caroline Robbins, *The Eighteenth-Century Commonwealthman: Studies in the Transmission, Development and Circumstance of English Liberal Thought from the Restoration of Charles II until the War with the Thirteen Colonies* (1959; New York: Athenaeum, 1968).

[168] Barrell, *Birth of Pandora*, p. xv, p. 53 and *passim*.

[169] Ted Underwood, *The Work of the Sun: Literature, Science, and Political Economy, 1760–1860* (Basingstoke: Palgrave Macmillan, 2005), p. 3.

[170] For a useful summary, see Matthew McCormack and Matthew Roberts, 'Conclusion: Chronologies in the History of British Political Masculinities, c. 1700–2000', in Matthew McCormack (ed.), *Public Men: Masculinity and Politics in Modern Britain* (Basingstoke: Palgrave Macmillan, 2007), pp. 188–91.

Figure 4: Title page of *The Oeconomist, or Englishman's Magazine*, 1 January 1798. By kind permission of Southern Regional Library Facility, University of California, Los Angeles.

neat illustration of this change. Published in Newcastle, the book was advertised in local newspapers: the first edition was advertised in the *Sheffield Iris*, for example, described as 'a collection of remarks on various subjects, relating to the common concerns, and adapted to the common sense of plain men'.[171] The frontispiece for the first year's issues features a pastoral scene, depicting a woman, seated under an ancient tree, with husbandry implements at her feet, and scenes of farming in the

---

[171] Advert for 'The Oeconomist', *Sheffield Iris* (Sheffield, 2nd February 1798), University of Sheffield Special Collection: RBR, 378206. I thank Anna Herniman for this reference.

fields behind her. Echoing this scene of honest plenty is the periodical's mix of essays and miscellanea with the recurring themes of the cottage, food, farming, poverty, and diet. The banner encircling the woman in the frontispiece reads 'Truth Liberty Virtue'. Morality and economy are bound together, as in traditional models of oeconomy. Thus, articles on the rights of men and their conduct in society are neighbours with those on feeding large groups of the poor in Newcastle soup kitchens.[172] While one major concern of the editors was understood to be the 'domestic œconomy' for the benefit of the 'lower classes', the essays assume a much broader compass.[173] The recurring concern with a specifically English history rendered the model of oeconomy patriotic.[174] A religious element is less pronounced, though readers are counselled to be frugal with their dress, diet, furniture, money, and time, all in imitation of 'our Saviour, and of God'.[175] But overall the engagement is political, and also radical. As the imaginary reader 'Miss Verjuice' reports on her reading the journal:

> I and some other prudent young ladies of my acquaintance, had expected, from the title, to be instructed in some improved modes of cooking, and told of means to set out three handsome courses, with as little expence as two.—Instead of which, we found nothing but receipts for pickling Mr Pitt, and preserving the constitution.[176]

The lady's expectation is understandable, replies one of her interlocutors, because '*Economist* is composed of two Greek words which signify *the regulation of a family*'. But the strongest proponent of the periodical, Mr Search, insists on the broader meaning: 'political measures do in their effects obtrude themselves with such imperious force into the most sacred recesses of domestic retirement, that for the regulation of a family it is absolutely necessary to be, alas, too intimately acquainted with the regulations of state'. As a result, Search argues that the magazine must, 'diffuse information among the people that will instruct them to employ their constitutional privileges for such regulations in the state as may have a happy influence on their domestic concerns'.[177] While in 1790s France, republicans had consolidated the notion of 'a commercial republicanism with the farmer as its archetypal citizen',[178] English radicalism insisted on the significance of the household to the economy and polity. The state's apparent intrusion in the domestic unit was politicizing it and requiring action on the part of householders. An oeconomy that encompassed the minutiae of domestic life, along with engagement with the market, became one form of political participation and citizenship. The publication conveys the older sentiments of progressive writers who sought to bring middling-sort values of industriousness and respectability to labouring families to enable their and the nation's progress. Now articulated in terms of resistance, these might perhaps be seen as a riposte to the conservatives who

---

[172] *The Oeconomist, or Englishman's Magazine* (Newcastle), 1 January 1798, pp. 2–4, 18–20, 73–5.
[173] Ibid. 1 January 1798, p. 18.
[174] Ibid. 1 January 1798, pp. 20–3; 5 May 1798, p. 132.
[175] Ibid. 5 May 1798, pp. 134–6. Quote at p. 135.   [176] Ibid. 5 May 1798, p. 129.
[177] Ibid. 5 May 1798, p. 130.   [178] Shovlin, *Political Economy of Virtue*, pp. 129, 207.

deployed some of the same ideas in attempts to discipline these families in rational budgeting for the public good.[179]

'In Georgian England', points out Matthew McCormack, 'the *household* and the *householder* were the basic units of social conceptualization.'[180] Oeconomy had transformed from the classical model of the patrician-householder exercising one's skills as a manager of the household's resources for the increase in wealth, to a vision of middling and labouring citizens practising domestic order and management in order to ensure prudence and cultivate a public-spirited, politically engaged virtue. A 1797 edition of Dodsley's *Oeconomy of Human Life*, published with Italian translation, advertised itself as a necessary guide to youth for the purposes of 'public utility', while the translator exhorts the young readers to 'Consider their dependence upon society...consider the many endearing connections resulting from it, with other infinite advantages both commercial and political'.[181] Some later authors consolidated this integration of oeconomy into a national vision. William Cobbett sought to include various social classes in his specifically 'Radical nation', an entity that incorporated both the private and public.[182] The framing of this within a long-standing language of rural England positioned Cobbett as both a radical and a reactionary.[183] In *Cottage Economy* (1822), for example, Cobbett envisaged the nation as composed of 'the *economy* of the several families', reasoning that the powerful and honoured nations in the world possess able families in which good economic management generates '*abundant living* amongst the people at large, which is the great test of good government, and the surest basis of national greatness and security'.[184] In this context, and echoing the practical advice of the Newcastle *Oeconomist*, Cobbett famously advised the labourer against tea-drinking, but also '*fine* and *flimsy* dress', and glass.[185] Cobbett's later *Advice to Young Men* (1829) bore the same dual-attention to the detailed practicalities of domestic life and its wider political context. Addressed to the middling- and upper-classes, the work consisted of letters to men at different life stages: youth, bachelor, lover, husband, father, citizen, or subject. The book was rooted in earlier works of advice, though lacked the overtly religious element of many earlier texts, and also presented citizenship as a more active, even aggressive, role.[186] Indeed, the outline of ordered roles represented by

---

[179] White, 'Luxury and Labour', *passim*, esp. pp. 132–67. See also Margaret Rose Hunt, 'English Urban Families in Trade, 1660–1800: The Culture of Early Modern Capitalism' (Unpublished PhD dissertation, New York University, 1986), pp. 299–302.

[180] Matthew McCormack, *The Independent Man: Citizenship and Gender Politics in Georgian England* (Manchester and New York: Manchester University Press, 2005), p. 25.

[181] Robert Dodsley, *L'Economia della Vita Umana Di Roberto Dodsley, In Inglese, con Traduzione in Lingua Italiana* (Leeds, 1797), f.1, p. 8.

[182] Leonora Nattrass, *William Cobbett: The Politics of Style* (Cambridge: Cambridge University Press, 1995), pp. 205–16. Quote at p. 216.

[183] Williams, *Cobbett*, pp. 56–7.

[184] Cobbett, *Cottage Economy*, pp. 3, 4. Advice to labouring men on oeconomy continued. A later example is J. A. Leatherland, 'The Household Economy of the Workman', *Essays and Poems, with a brief Autobiographical Memoir* (London, 1862), pp. 43–64. I thank Stuart Hogarth for this reference.

[185] Cobbett, *Cottage Economy*, pp. 19, 196, 198.

[186] Nattrass, *William Cobbett*, pp. 183–93.

the intended readers shared much with the framework of Dodsley's treatise. But whereas the earlier book presented the fulfilment of the roles of husband, father, son, brother, master, and magistrate from within, as duties that an individual performed in a broader but decontextualized web of management consisting of relationships, Cobbett situated these men in a carefully drawn and tangible civil society or community, where there is bad air, hard labour, and real poverty.[187] For the Radical politician Cobbett, the household was not a training ground for politics but was itself thoroughly politicized, as were men's roles within it.

Civic ideals had always been discernable in the continuing emphasis on oeconomical management to increase the wealth of individual households. The foregoing discussion has argued that they were further consolidated in the revival of Xenophon's work in the early decades of the eighteenth century, and furthermore fused with patriarchalism in ways which made the house newly politically relevant. Towards the end of the century, this oeconomical discourse of the economic and political significance of male domestic management was appropriated in a more explicitly national discourse. In France, political economy reconciled 'commercial modernity with the need to preserve and regenerate public virtue',[188] and by the 1820s individual economic activity was participation in a 'virtuous marketplace', serving the public good rather than self-interest.[189] The beneficiary of oeconomy also changed in English writing, with the emphasis shifting to the nation.[190] In these lay political works we also see another shift in which oeconomy transformed from a language of governance for the maintenance of order, to one of citizenship and political engagement.

POLITICAL ECONOMY

The consolidation of the public relevance of the household as a unit of economy runs against the grain of arguments for the emptying out of market-related activities from the domestic sphere, a process linked to the development of 'political economy'. First in France and Germany in the seventeenth century, and then later in Britain, political economy referred to the theories and practice of managing *the* economy by the state. The significance for the home is evident in Davidoff and Hall's comment that the home became 'the basis for a proper moral order in the amoral world of the market, [because] the new world of political economy necessitated a separate sphere of domestic economy'.[191] As William Booth puts it, '[t]he

---

[187] William Cobbett, *Advice to Young Men* (London, 1829). See pp. 284–5 for the duties of the citizen.

[188] Shovlin, *Political Economy of Virtue*, p. 207.

[189] Victoria Thompson, *The Virtuous Marketplace: Women and Men, Money and Politics in Paris, 1830–1870* (Baltimore, MD; London: Johns Hopkins University Press, 2000), pp. 3, 9; quoted in Shovlin, *Political Economy of Virtue*, pp. 219–22.

[190] A similar shift can be seen in men's personal writing on oeconomy. See in particular the uses of Robert Sharp, discussed in Chapter 3, pp. 71–2.

[191] Leonore Davidoff and Catherine Hall, *Family Fortunes: Men and women of the English middle class, 1780–1850* (1987; Routledge, London, 1992), p. 74.

economy is thus disembedded from the *oikos*.'[192] Carole Shammas has noted that the term 'oeconomy' was used by liberal theorists to discuss production, speculating that it was adapted from the household to give 'private activities primacy in the generation of wealth and downplaying the importance of government policies'.[193] Shammas argued that although earlier legal writers had drawn on the Greek tradition of oeconomy to categorize the rights and duties of household members, once liberal theorists adopted 'economic to refer to the production and distribution of goods and services', legal writers in the United States 'switched to the Latin root for household, *domus*, and grouped household dependencies under "domestic relations"'.[194] Michael McKeon has similarly argued that the management of household economy became the model for management of the larger economy through 'political economy', thus leaving 'the household divested of its economic function [which then] became the model for the "domestic sphere"'.[195] The household served as the model for *the* economy, but was left emptied of economic function. 'Political economy', it has been argued, clinched the linguistic separation necessary for gendered separate spheres.

This claim warrants further scrutiny, however. Careful attention to the usage of terms demonstrated that 'oeconomy' and 'economy' continued to refer to different but related arenas, and the notion of the household's economic function endured. Examples of 'economic' and 'economist', and which relate to the household in the *Oxford English Dictionary*, only switch from oeconomick/oeconomic and oeconomist in 1831 and 1857 respectively. Indeed, it is important that we resist reading every instance of 'oeconomy' as a traditional form of 'economy'. The seventeenth-century writer William Petty used the term 'oeconomy'—not, as one historian writes, 'economy'—to refer to production as well as household matters, for example.[196] In imposing a modernized spelling the erasure of the house from formal bodies of economic thought is apparently complete. Yet 'oeconomy' was not simply subsumed within 'economy'. In dictionaries after the mid-eighteenth century, oeconomics is still defined as 'management of household affairs' and 'the art of managing the affairs of a family, or community', though 'economy' earns more detailed explication and assumes the meanings relating to household, order, and frugality.[197] To some extent the words overlap and can be used interchangeably, but crucially the original Greek meaning of *oikos*—and Xenophon's version in

[192] Booth, *Households*, p. 10.

[193] Carole Shammas, 'Anglo-American Household Government in Comparative Perspective', *William and Mary Quarterly*, 52 (1995), p. 105, and note 6, p. 105.

[194] Ibid. p. 105.

[195] Michael McKeon, 'The Secret History of Domesticity: Private, Public, and the Division of Knowledge', in Colin Jones and Dror Wahrman (eds), *The Age of Cultural Revolutions: Britain and France, 1750–1820* (London; Berkeley: University of California Press, 2002), pp. 179–80.

[196] Tony Aspromourgos, 'The Mind of the Oeconomist: An Overview of the "Petty Papers" Archive', *History of Economic Ideas*, 9 (2001), 1, pp. 83–5.

[197] Samuel Johnson, *A Dictionary of the English Language*, 4th edition (London, 1777), vol. 1, for the first definition of oeconomics and economy; *Encyclopædia Britannica; or, a Dictionary of Arts and Sciences* (Edinburgh, 1771), vol. 3 for the second definition of oeconomics. I thank Mary Clayton for the latter reference.

particular—remained live in late-eighteenth-century uses: 'political oeconomy' was not an archaic version of 'economy', but integrated the household model.[198] In the *OED*, examples of 'economical' which concern specifically material resources and their development, or political economy, date only from 1781.

Indeed, at the very end of the century the two terms could be used interchangeably in a discussion that encompassed both domestic- and market-oriented activity. The article 'To the Editors of the Œconomist' which appeared in *The Oeconomist; or, Englishman's Magazine* in 1798 referred to the publication as 'the Economist', and the running header for the article was 'Dialogue on the Economist'.[199] Given the availability of the term 'economy', the choice to use 'oeconomy' in such works signalled precisely a discussion of economics stretching from the level of household to the level of the market. 'Economy' could include and refer to the household, while 'oeconomy' emphasized the wider relevance of the economic function of the household in particular.

There is little doubt that in the emerging canon of 'economic literature', 'economic' does come to exclude 'oeconomy'. In the middle decades of the eighteenth century, husbandry, housewifery, and household management are missing from the main sub-categories of this corpus, those of classes of people, Colonies, Commodities, Companies, Fisheries, Husbandry, Manufactures, Policy, Public Finance, Trade, and Miscellaneous.[200] The main authors of works of both strains of oeconomic writing listed by Richard Bradley are also missing from the short-list of important authors writing economic literature.[201] In what are now established as the canonical texts of political economy, a public and private separation came to the fore and household diverged from the economy and polity. Political economy should not be viewed simply as the antecedent of economics, yet one of its central components was the concept of a wider economy to be managed by the state. Jean-Jacques Rousseau's essay 'On Political Economy' (published in London in 1767) acknowledges the roots of 'economy' in 'oeconomy', and also the differing meanings:

> The word Economy, or Œconomy, is derived from *oikos, a house*, and *nomos, law*, originally signifying only the prudent and lawful government of an house, for the common good of the whole family. The meaning of the term hath been since extended to the government of the great family, the state. In distinguishing these two acceptations of the word, the latter is called *general* or *political* economy, and the other domestic or particular economy. It is the first only which is discussed in the present tract.[202]

---

[198] Tribe, *Land, Labour and Economic Discourse*, pp. 80–2.

[199] 'To the Editors of the Œconomist', *The Oeconomist, or Englishman's Magazine*, No. V, May 1798, pp. 127–32.

[200] Julian Hoppit, 'The Contexts and Contours of British Economic Literature, 1660–1760', *The Historical Journal*, 49, 1 (2006), p. 88. This study is based on Massie's library of 2418 titles collected between 1748 until *c.*1760.

[201] These were Hartlib, Platt, Blyth, Markham, and Evelyn. See Bradley, 'Preface', Chomel, *Dictionaire Oeconomique*, p. vi.

[202] J.-J. Rousseau, 'A Dissertation on Political Economy', *The Miscellaneous Works of Mr J. J. Rousseau*, vol. 2 (1755; London, 1767), p. 1. See *ECCO*, Gale Document Number: CW3324653279 (accessed 6 April 2009).

Oeconomy has bifurcated, but economic functions exist in both arenas. In the related matter of governance, Rousseau goes on to explain that the state and the family 'differ too much in magnitude and extent to be regulated in the same manner'.[203] 'Paternal authority' remains viable for household government in the family, if not in the state.

While Rousseau's emphasis was on government and order, Cæsar Beccaria discussed commerce and wealth. He wrote that 'the study of public oeconomy must necessarily enlarge and elevate the views of private oeconomy, by suggesting the means of uniting our own interest with that of the publick'.[204] There was interconnectedness between public and private, a 'mutual chain of reciprocal services', which would generate a sympathetic society.[205] Yet while Beccaria's 'private' realm encompassed workers, husbandmen, professionals, and occupations, families and households were not included. Nor were they present as anything more than sites of consumption in Adam Smith's *An Inquiry into the Nature and Causes of The Wealth of Nations* (1776). Inhabitants of households have needs and desires that require servicing—food, clothing, furniture, 'equipage'—but the regulation and order of households is not part of Smith's important account.[206] As Rousseau intimated, public and private require different models of governance or regulation; 'political economy' may have taken the household as a model, but expressly excluded households from regulation by the state.

It is worth noting, here, that feminist approaches to gender have reconsidered 'the assumptions on which the discipline of economics has been built', in part by recovering the continuing relevance of the household to economic theory.[207] Alongside the genre of political economy, then, a discourse of 'oeconomy' persisted. In his 1803 *Treatise on Political Economy*, Jean-Baptiste Say historicized political economy through its etymological roots from the Greek: 'economy, the law which regulates the household' and 'political, from...civitas, extending its application to society or the nation at large'.[208] He continued in terms redolent of earlier writings on oeconomy: 'A household, conducted without order', he wrote, 'is preyed upon by all the world...it is exposed to the perpetual recurrence of a variety of little outgoings, on every occasion, however trivial.*' Buried in Say's footnote is another example of this discourse:

> * I remember being once in the country a witness of the numberless minute losses that neglectful housekeeping entails. For want of a trumpery latch, the gate of the poultry-

[203] Ibid. p. 1.
[204] Cæsar Beccaria, *A Discourse on Public Oeconomy and Commerce* (London, 1769), p. 15. *ECCO*, Gale Document Number: CW3304376264 (accessed 6 April 2009).
[205] Ibid. p. 16.
[206] Adam Smith, *An Inquiry into the Nature and Causes of The Wealth of Nations* (London, 1776). See, for example, pp. 14–15, 205–6. Quote at p. 205 *ECCO*, Gale Document Number: CW3306157733 (accessed 6 April 2009).
[207] Garnett, 'Political and Domestic Economy', p. 206.
[208] Jean-Baptiste Say, *A Treatise on Political Economy* (1803; Philadelphia: Lippincott, Grambo & Co., 1855), 6th edition, trans. C. R. Prinsep, ed. Clement C. Biddle, footnote 2, Book I, chapter 4. See *Library of Economics and Liberty*, <http://www.econlib.org/library/Say/sayT.html> (accessed July 2009). Say's book was first published in France, and in London from 1821.

yard was forever open... One day a fine young porker made his escape into the woods, and the whole family, gardener, cook, milk-maid, &c., presently turned out in quest of the fugitive. The gardener was the first to discover the object of pursuit, and in leaping a ditch to cut off his further escape, got a sprain that confined him to his bed for the next fortnight: the cook found the linen burnt that she had left hung up before the fire to dry; and the milk-maid, having forgotten in her haste to tie up the cattle properly in the cow-house, one of the loose cows had broken the leg of a colt that happened to be kept in the same shed. The linen burnt and the gardener's work lost, were worth full twenty crowns; and the colt about as much more: so that here was a loss in a few minutes of forty crowns, purely for want of a latch that might have cost a few sous at the utmost; and this in a household where the strictest economy was necessary...[209]

Say's vision of the disorderly farm is not merely a residual trace of early-modern oeconomy. His comments chimed with the sentiments of the works on oeconomy written at the turn of the nineteenth century. Rather than 'political economy' supplanting 'oeconomy', then, there were two distinct but interlinked discourses. The former developed partly out of the latter, although emerged shorn of the household.

These discourses also shared other common features. Both displayed a focus on virtue and economy and a desire to—in the words of Dugald Stewart, a Professor of Moral Philosophy—present 'an ideal order of things'.[210] From the early decades of the nineteenth century, these works also shared the aim of establishing systems to improve the wealth of the 'nation' or 'society', rather than the wealth and morals of individuals and small collectives.[211] Finally, they displayed a de-Christianized (rather than secularized) tendency 'descended from a version of the philosophy of mind *that was conceptualized in theological terms*'.[212] Thus early-nineteenth-century political economy was de-Christianized rather than secularized. The roots of the theoretical discipline of political economy within this earlier theological moral philosophy are observable in some of the works discussed above, such as Sylvestre Dufour's advice and *The Oeconomy of Human Life*, again pointing to the shared underpinnings of works of oeconomy and political economy. The theory, practice, and sphere of 'oeconomy'—the household—remained somewhat distinct from economy and political economy, but retained its economic, political, and moral functions. Xenophon's legacy continued well into the nineteenth century.[213]

CONCLUSION

If more traditional divisions between 'public' and 'private' were breaking down over the eighteenth century, if 'public' and 'private' were ultimately conflated and

---

[209] Say, *Treatise on Political Economy*, book III, chapter V, paragraph 12.
[210] Dugald Stewart, *Elements of the Philosophy of the Human Mind* (Boston, 1847), p. 159; quoted in Mary Poovey, 'Between Political Arithmetic and Political Economy', in John Bender (ed.), *Regimes of Description: In the Archive of the Eighteenth Century* (Stanford, CA: Stanford University Press, 2005), p. 70.
[211] Poovey, 'Between Political Arithmetic and Political Economy', pp. 71–3.
[212] Ibid. p. 76. Italics in original.
[213] Garnett, 'Political and Domestic Economy', *passim*.

their shared ethical and political meanings brought together, then oeconomy was surely one instrument of this conflation. At the heart of this project was order. Household governance remained central, effected by oeconomical management. This account of the lay political theory of the household suggests an alternative to the step-change accounts of 'high' political theory which tend to trace the occlusion of classical and absolutist thought by 'that contractarianism which set the foundations for liberalism'.[214] In these other writings, models persist, overlap, and transform; at any one time we can observe dominant, residual, and emergent features of culture.[215] Robert Filmer's vision of fathers as absolute monarchs contrasts sharply with John Locke's 'very shattered and short Power' of the paterfamilias.[216] Yet despite this contrast, in popular writing on oeconomy aspects of Filmer's account remained conventional well into the eighteenth century. Indeed, patriarchalism, with a stress on order, remained secure as part of what one historian has described as 'a deep-rooted Toryism'.[217] Echoing J. C. D. Clark, Pavla Miller argues, 'patriarchalism was challenged on many fronts, but remained a viable and powerful system of rule' until the end of the eighteenth century.[218]

The argument here is not for tradition and continuity, however. The translation of Xenophon, and the more general deployment of classical ideas of oeconomy both before and after, is indicative of the continuing power of classical republican theories of household. These classical ideas were united with newer patriarchal themes during the seventeenth century to forge a potent language of strict order and deference. This combination of the classical and patriarchal was dominant throughout the long eighteenth century, transforming to become the language of the smaller householder rather than the large landowner. From the 1770s, this was blended with a model of national republicanism in ways that rendered oeconomic management no longer a language of political governance for the elite, but a language of citizenship for the middling sort. Explicit analogies between the household and polity faded, but this was replaced by an emphasis on the skills and virtues of the benevolent citizen. Subsequently, the discourse of oeconomy centred on frugality and honest virtue in a national community, becoming a potent language of political engagement. This connects with John Tosh's finding for the nineteenth century that manly values drawing on work and home were to become shared by the 'commercial, manufacturing, and professional classes', as well as 'the labour aristocracy'.[219] By the end of the century, the household was no longer a

---

[214] Booth, *Households*, p. 97, fn 3.

[215] The notion of the residual (to be studied alongside the dominant and emergent) in culture is from Raymond Williams, *The Sociology of Culture* (New York: Schocken, 1982), p. 204.

[216] John Locke, *Two Treatises of Government*, ed. Peter Laslett (1690; Cambridge: University of Cambridge Press, 1960), p. 341.

[217] R. R. Johnson, 'Politics Redefined', *William and Mary Quarterly*, 35, 4 (1978), p. 713. Quoted in Pavla Miller, *Transformations of Patriarchy in the West, 1500–1900* (Bloomington and Indianapolis: Indiana University Press, 1998), p. 290.

[218] Miller, *Transformations of Patriarchy in the West*, p. 75. See Chapter 1, p. 7.

[219] John Tosh, 'Masculinities in an Industrializing Society: Britain, 1800–1914', *Journal of British Studies*, 44 (2005), pp. 331, 332.

metaphor for politics but a practical component of it: the actions of men in the domestic environment had become an implicit comment on ethical and political topics. Significantly for histories of the home which often narrate increasing privatization and feminization, oeconomy brought together the house and the world, and it did so through men's activities as they managed the moral and economic resources of the household. 'Housekeeping' was important to manly status and oeconomy determined that men had considerable knowledge of the material aspects of the house, though it was a man's managerial engagement with the domestic environment that was emphasized. Oeconomy for men insisted on houses to keep and households to manage. Men's domestic management connected the most mundane domestic activity with governance within and without the house. Thus men's domestic authority remained significant, connecting the matters of the house with the national economy and polity.

3

Words into Practice

The discourse of oeconomy established firm connections between men and the house. The previous chapter exposed the cultural architecture of men's domestic engagements, paying particular attention to how this changed over time. This chapter shows how men inhabited that shifting cultural space. Rather than explore household government by distinguishing between 'prescription' and the 'ordinary social practice' that conformed or not to didactic ideals,[1] this study regards texts about oeconomy as one element of a discourse within which men gave meaning to their actions. Oeconomy served as an important cultural resource for men, a relevant language for middling-sort men used in their writing and speech. Yet different sources open up different access points of past experience. Printed works are carefully constructed for a public world of print, and were read as such. Texts created in other settings—in the court house, in the private closet—are also constructed for an audience, but they differ in the way they are made and the audience for whom they are made; quite simply, they provide more direct—though not unmediated—evidence of an individual's personal experience. Other writing shows that oeconomy was also practised by men in ways that legitimized and required their engagement with the household not just at the local but particularly at the global level. Many of the written works of accounting used in this chapter not only describe but also constituted domestic practices of oeconomy. These texts leave evidence of these practices, therefore, practices which in turn themselves held considerable rhetorical power. Men's engagement with the household encompassed housekeeping but also management and governance, and when aligned with a discourse of oeconomy that invested these practices with social authority and men's use of this language to judge manly characters, it is clear that these practices sustained men's domestic authority. The authority of this role as oeconomical manager fashioned a range of men's engagements with the domestic, but also invested men with wider social power. Most importantly, and as the later part of this chapter discusses, these records show how men *lived* oeconomically, as well as wrote about living oeconomically.

---

[1] Alexandra Shepard, 'Manhood, Credit and Patriarchy in Early Modern England *c.* 1580–1640', *Past and Present*, 167 (2000), p. 95. Also see Anthony Fletcher, *Gender, Sex and Subordination in England, 1500–1800* (New Haven; London: Yale University Press, 1995), pp. 214, 254; Joanne Bailey, *Unquiet Lives: Marriage and Marriage Breakdown in England, 1660–1800* (Cambridge: Cambridge University Press, 2003), p. 199.

DREAMS OF MY FATHER

Oeconomy was a yardstick of masculinity: for some it was internalized as a value, for others it was an ideal to attain. Some examples of uses of the word 'oeconomy' show its contemporary resonance. We know that men used the word when speaking in situations where it could make a material difference. Sometimes oeconomy was spoken of as housekeeping and management. In a trial at the Old Bailey in 1737, Constant Seers was accused of stealing a coat from the house of William Hookman. The defendant argued that she had bought shoes from a woman in the house, and merely picked up the coat when it had fallen to the ground. Hookman countered, 'I have not had a Woman Servant in my House these five Years. My Sister comes to make my Bed, when she's at Leisure; when she is not, my Man-servant does it.' This statement seemed to raise questions about Hookman's domestic situation because a member of the jury asked, 'I desire to know how the Gentleman can live in a House, without a Woman?' Hookman elaborated, 'Sir, If you desire to know the Oeconomy of my Family, I'll give it you in a few Words. My Sister, when she has Leisure, comes to make my Bed; when she has not, my Man does it.'[2] Oeconomy referred to who did what in the household: in this case, in a properly ordered household the making of a bed is properly a woman's—or at least a servant's—task, while this 'household-family' is managed by the household head.[3] In this context, the question 'how the Gentleman can live in a House, without a Woman?' concerns housekeeping and management. In this trial, the question helps assess Hookman's moral character versus that of the defendant and her witnesses. 'Oeconomy' in this instance related specifically to the house.

Some uses move past a focus on the management of household relations and referred to the 'extensive sense' of oeconomy discussed in Chapter 2.[4] At his trial for deception in 1747, some of the questioning naturally focused on Hugh Pelling's character. The witness John Thomson claimed he had long found Pelling 'a Man of great Probity and Honour', adding, 'I have had a Grandson of his under my Care, and I think him a Man of good Oeconomy.'[5] Other witnesses testified that Pelling had an honest character, and one reinforced Thomson's stress on probity by mentioning that he had passed several accounts for him. Pelling's financial probity was clearly central in the case, involving falsifying papers and receipts allegedly to defraud the Governor and Company of Merchants of Great-Britain, but it extended further to his capacity as a manager, here expressed in his care of a younger man. In another trial for forgery in 1775, a letter produced as evidence again referred to 'oeconomy' to indicate the good financial management of the defendant,

---

[2] *Old Bailey Proceedings Online* <http://www.oldbaileyonline.org/> (accessed September 2003), 20 April 1737, trial of Constant Seers (t17370420-64). Seers was found guilty.

[3] Naomi Tadmor, 'The Concept of the Household-Family in Eighteenth-Century England', *Past and Present*, 151 (1996), pp. 110–40; Naomi Tadmor, *Family and Friends in Eighteenth-Century England: Household, Kinship and Patronage* (Cambridge: Cambridge University Press, 2001), pp. 18–43.

[4] See Chapter 2, pp. 33–43.

[5] *Old Bailey Proceedings Online* <www.oldbaileyonline.org> (accessed August 2007), January 1747, trial of Hugh Pelling (t17470116-27).

the notorious swindler Daniel Perreau. Ironically, given Perreau's earlier extravagant lifestyle, the writer believed that his 'proper well-judged oeconomy' would enable Perreau to manage on a budget; this financial management was consonant with Perreau's character of an 'honest worthy gentleman', 'a man of very fair character', and 'a very fair dealing honest man'.[6] Perreau was executed at Tyburn less than a year later, but such evidence suggests the potential value of establishing a man's character and social reputation through recourse to the language of oeconomy.[7]

Practising oeconomy enabled a man to manage with order, integrity, and justice. With its centring on the house it also assisted middling-sort men to distance themselves from the corrupting arena of public politics; the devotion that a middling-sort man must show towards 'his estate and investments, his marriage, a well-run household, and bringing up virtuous children' were perfectly encapsulated in oeconomy.[8] Of course, the trope of virtue in private was very much a public statement. Oeconomy may have been centred on the house, but it was deployed in the crafting of men's public personae, and not just in the criminal courts. In a reflection on the character of his friend, the actor David Garrick in 1760, the novelist Lawrence Sterne praised his 'prudence' and 'honesty' in the face of 'the inconstancy of what is called the Public'. '[A]s every man of honour and discretion would', he continued, he has sought to 'regulate the taste' and 'reform the manners of the fashionable world', while with 'well judged œconomy' he has remained independent.[9] Garrick's manly identity was safeguarded from the follies of the world because he had, in effect, practised oeconomy on 'the Public'. Oeconomy was here a set of virtues.

As the concept of oeconomy became increasingly relevant for middling-sort men during the eighteenth century, as discussed in Chapter 2, so a shift can be detected in the uses of the word as men observed and commented on other men in the world around them. The 280-page manuscript commonplace book of R. Mathews, written during the 1780s, is typical of the varied nature of many men's personal writings at this time. Written in London, and containing excerpts on the history of England, current events, recipes, and other miscellaneous materials, Mathews was particularly concerned with events in America. Many of the disparate themes of the volume come together in Mathew's essay, 'General Washington's Economy'. The piece lays out Washington's management of political and military affairs, including his personal conduct, stressing his prudence. He is 'very Reserved

[6] *Old Bailey Proceedings Online* <www.oldbaileyonline.org> (accessed August 2007), 31 May 1775, trial of Daniel Perreau (t17750531-2).

[7] Donna T. Andrew, 'Perreau, Robert (c1734–1776)', *Oxford Dictionary of National Biography*, Oxford University Press, 2004 <http://www.oxforddnb.com/view/article/65813> (accessed 18 December 2010). See also Donna T. Andrew and Randall McGowen, *The Perreaus and Mrs Rudd: Forgery and Betrayal in Eighteenth-Century* (London and Berkeley: University of California Press, 2001).

[8] Margaret Hunt, 'English Urban Families in Trade, 1660–1800: The Culture of Early Modern Capitalism' (unpublished PhD thesis, New York University, 1986), p. 295.

[9] *Letters of the Late Rev. Mr Laurence Sterne, To his most intimate Friends…To which are prefix'd, Memoirs of his Life and Family*, 3 vols (London, 1775), pp. 103–4.

and Loves Retirement', makes important decisions with careful consultation, 'punishes neglect of Duty with great Severity, but is very tender and indulgent to recruits until they Learnt the Articles of war'; he is a tender man of faith, but it is in the art of war that he excels.[10] The echoes of *The Oeconomy of Human Life*, here, are striking.[11] Oscillating between his personal characteristics and his political and military role, the piece finally settles on the former. Washington's economy manifests itself in a temperate diet, which exemplifies the rational discipline he shows elsewhere: 'the only Luxury he indulges himself in is a few Glasses of Punch after Supper'.[12]

In conscious ways, then, the language of oeconomy was used to present men's moral character and public conduct. Men also internalized the values of oeconomy, and reflected critically on how they and others 'measured up', as examples of two men's dreams suggest. Richard Kay (1716–1751), unmarried and living with his parents, worked with his father as a doctor in Baldingstone, near Bury in Lancashire. The Kays operated from the family home, which Richard's father Robert had gained after his older brother had moved to 'the New House at Chesham', on '*fryday* 12th June 1713'.[13] Part of this well-established and prosperous yeoman family, Richard Kay assiduously kept a diary and other documents throughout his life. In August 1737, two months after the death of his cousin Robert Kay (two years his senior), and while his father was unwell with a painful thumb, Kay reported having a dream. He dreamt that his father had died, and though 'I do not remember I thought any Thing of his Sickness & Death, but I thought I was present at his Burial, & imagin'd several Instances relating thereto; I thought I must carry on my Father's Business.' Set against this feeling of responsibility, the scene is one of gathering pressure, and of Richard's inability to cope. First, patients come in a 'Throng', and he does not know which remedy to prescribe. Then, he and his mother receive from 'a Gentlewoman' on an adjoining estate, 'a sharp threatening Letter, demanding of us what was never neither known to be demanded or allowed on before'.[14] Though the letter was addressed to himself and his mother, Richard feels that it is his burden alone: she is, he explains, 'but a Woman, [and] full of her Cares & Concerns'. Kay seems to crumble beneath the duties of oeconomical manager: 'I imagined that I who was the Head & Hope of the Family, was one that she had great Dependance upon, & in the midst of all these my Cares & Concerns which had been upon me but for ten Days or a Fortnight I fancy'd myself to be

---

[10] 'General Washington's Economy', in 'R. Mathews Commonplace book' (c1780s), Henry E. Huntington Library: HM694, f 141.

[11] See the discussion in Chapter 2, pp. 48–50.

[12] 'General Washington's Economy', f. 142.

[13] 'Extracts from the Journals of M[r] Rich[d] Kaye of Baldingstone & Chesham in the Par. of Bury Co. Lanc. now in the poss[n] of M[rs] Kay of Bury. Jan. 20. 1848. R.R.R.', Chetham's Library: C.6.34–77 Raines Collection, vol. 31, f. 431.

[14] Diary of Richard Kay, Chetham's Library: A.7.76: 19 August 1737. Kay dreamt of his father's death on at least one other occasion: see 21 May 1748. The letter suggests that the dream was about more than Kay's anxiety about 'the burdens of medical practice'. See also Dorothy Porter and Roy Porter, *Patient's Progress: Doctors and Doctoring in Eighteenth-Century England* (Oxford: Polity, 1989), p. 117. Whatever the cause, Kay predeceased his father by three months.

alone weeping, bemoaning my Self in my present Condition & lamenting my Father's Death.' Richard Kay had started his diary just four months earlier, at his coming-of-age at 21. In his description of his dream we can observe the anxieties of a young man, acutely aware of the significance of this year in his own life-course, brought sharply home by the experience of illness and death in the family. He acknowledged that Christians should not be overly superstitious with regards to dreams, but admitted that previous dreams had 'deeply humbled me'; out of this dream, he confessed, 'tis my Desire O Lord that I may get much Good by it'.[15]

Related anxieties about a son's passage into a new life-stage of manhood were expressed in another dream, this time one experienced by a father and reported by the son. Much of the anonymous diary of a young bachelor in Bath from 1769 concerns the relationship between the diarist and his father. From the son's perspective, one central issue was obedience, and this manifested in the ongoing tension between father and son over the latter's choice of a bride. The son is suffering, rather badly, from unrequited love for Miss Dalby, but his father intervened to suggest Esther P as a bride instead. The son replied, he reports, that he would rather be hanged.[16] The response of the father to this, as reported by the son, is revealing. On 28 January 1769, the son made the following entry:

> My Father dreamt last night too—[…] he saw a Farm House and in the Farm Yard Miss D—he recollecting the affair between me and her, wou'd not speak to her—but pass'd on, […] altering his mind resolv'd to speak to Miss D—as he went by—he goes into the House—every thing in great confusion…some persons present told him how low and bad she had been and ask'd him if he wou'd take her home with him for his Son, my Father knowing my inclination for her readily agreed to it went up to her and kiss'd— but was surprized when he came near her to see her cheeks sunk in, her countenance pale, her head and other parts quite sluttish, and altogether disgusted him and made him repent of his engagement, but thinking he shou'd oblige me persisted in it—going into the yard to make water he saw M^r. Bigg …, says he M^r. B. how is this there seems to be great disorder here?—tis bad management replies he, there's no oeconomy in the House—the old Man's corpse was arrested for arrears…—but they have a good bottom but don't manage well—twas thro' this negligence that his Body was arrested…here in this confusion the dream ended—and tis time to end this days narrative.[17]

There are many important details in the son's report of his father's dream, not least the connection between the grotesque female body, sexual immorality, and disorder. The father's dream—or at least his report of it as glossed by his son—was clearly, I suggest, an expression of his anxiety about his son's future: his ambivalence to Miss D is plain, and so are his concerns about his son's failure to obey his wishes in the matter. Bad management, an absence of oeconomy—in the house of Miss D and her father, but also perhaps in the house of the diarist—is critical in moral, financial, and physical decay.

---

[15] Kay, 19 August 1737.
[16] 'Bath Diary for 1769', Henry E. Huntington Library: HM62593, 6 January 1769. Research has unfortunately not identified the author of this diary.
[17] Ibid. 28 January 1769.

There was little consensus about the cause of dreams in the eighteenth century. Nevertheless, there is evidence that distinctive sleep patterns made dreams particularly intense experiences.[18] These dreams fit neatly into Peter Burke's assessment that from the seventeenth century there was a transition in the West from an emphasis on 'public symbols to private ones' in dreams.[19] Dating a century later than Burke's examples, these dreams contain personal details, but their themes do not map neatly onto those isolated by Burke.[20] Instead, the dreams seem preoccupied with a locus of issues around masculinity, household, private personal qualities, and their public performance; masculinity and oeconomy are here, to use a phrase employed by Burke, 'emotionally relevant' themes. And as we saw for the example of printed works in Chapter 2, in neither case does oeconomy mean simply frugality or small-scale decisions about household economy. It is noteworthy that these are the dreams of non-conformist men, but in Methodist circles a female subculture of dreams emerged during the eighteenth century.[21] In these two households—first, a physician father and unmarried apprentice physician son, and second, a preacher father and unmarried teacher son—oeconomy framed the father–son relationship, but also linked effective household management with social reputation. Men worried about this and these worries turned in men's heads as they slept.

Men used the word 'oeconomy' to describe their lives and they also drew on the concept to make sense of manly identity. Yet arguing that oeconomy was meaningful for masculinity does not mean that it determined men's experiences. Indeed, we have plenty of evidence that men felt that they fell short of oeconomy. Interestingly, this was the case for three of the men whose works on oeconomy were discussed in Chapter 2: Dudley North, Gervase Markham, and Richard Bradley.[22] Author of *Advices and Observations Oeconomical* (1669), Dudley North was born in 1602.[23] He attended Cambridge, moved to Gray's Inn in 1619, and undertook a brief military expedition, but his revelling in idleness and bad company while living with his parents in London precluded a prudent and oeconomical life.[24] Following a move to the Inner Temple in 1622, further military expeditions, and indulgence in debauchery (as he describes it) in Holland, it was a short turn as an MP and experience with his father's estate management which slowly rendered

---

[18] A. Roger Ekirch, 'Sleep We Have Lost: Pre-industrial Slumber in the British Isles', *American Historical Review*, 106, 2 (2001), pp. 343–65.

[19] Peter Burke, 'The Cultural History of Dreams', in Peter Burke, *Varieties of Cultural History* (Cambridge: Polity Press, 1997), p. 42.

[20] These are death and burial, the church, kings, wars, politics, and injury to the dreamer or to something associated with the dreamer. See Burke, 'Cultural History of Dreams', p. 32.

[21] See Phyliss Mack, *Heart Religion in the British Enlightenment: Gender and Emotion in Early Methodism* (Cambridge: Cambridge University Press, 2008), pp. 219–60.

[22] See Chapter 2, pp. 27–30, 32, 36–45.

[23] Dale B. J. Randall, 'North, Dudley, fourth Baron North (1602–1677)', *Oxford Dictionary of National Biography*, Oxford University Press, 2004 <http://www.oxforddnb.com/view/article/20296> (accessed 15 October 2004). On North also see R. Grassby, *The English Gentleman in Trade* (Oxford: Oxford University Press, 1994).

[24] Dudley North, *Observations and Advices Oeconomical* (London, 1669), ff. i–iv (unnumbered).

him 'every inch the gentleman'.[25] Nevertheless, the life laid out in *Advices and Observations Oeconomical* continued to elude North. His domineering father began a 'great shedding of property' in 1631, at precisely the same time that his marriage to Anne Montagu was being planned.[26] This congruence of his father's ill financial fortunes and his own marriage must have brought oeconomy to the forefront of his mind. Living the first few years of their marriage at the family home of Kirtling, and often required to stay there with Lord North even after the purchase of their own home at Tostock, Dudley suffered 'not onely a doubling of charge, but a very great hinderance [*sic*] to me in my whole course'.[27] In this large household, several accounts were kept; as Anne wrote later, she had 'been faine to wright & cast account to help my lord'.[28] Nevertheless, the family experienced ongoing financial problems.[29] His comment in the *Observations* that 'All men know (and some of us by experience) the great charge of fitting a large House' was no doubt heartfelt.[30] In 1667, aged sixty-four, Dudley became fourth Lord North. As Dale Randall points out, it is no surprise that after the tumultuous years of the Civil War he should describe his turn to housekeeping in the manner that he does in the *Observations*: 'now at last I am come to reside in the chief Mansion-house of our Family, where I have no other ambition then to end my days with a peaceable and pious dissolution; So much of my self tyred and retired'.[31] *Advices and Observations Oeconomical* was the work of an old man describing the practices he mastered only late in life, and the solace he gained from the well-ordered household.[32]

For other writers on household, their works were in even greater tension with their own experiences. Gervase Markham's family was plagued with debt and his elder brother squandered the family estate. Markham himself, author of the guide to household profit-making *A Way to Get Wealth* (1625), died in poverty in 1637.[33] Richard Bradley's numerous works published during the 1720s belie the struggles he himself experienced. The Cambridge chair of Botany that he took up in 1724 was unpaid, though even before this Bradley experienced some form of crisis: an 'unfortunate affair at Kensington, whereby I lost all my substance, my expectations, and my friends'.[34] The crisis arose due to Bradley's struggles with oeconomy.

---

[25] Quoted in Dale B. J. Randall, *Gentle Flame: The Life and Verse of Dudley, Fourth Lord North (1602–1677)* (Durham, NC: Duke University Press, 1983), p. 46. See also pp. 34–46.

[26] Ibid. p. 19. See pp. 28–34 on North's father, and pp. 49–50 on his marriage of 24 April 1632.

[27] North, *Observations*, pp. 98–9. See also Randall, *Gentle Flame*, pp. 51–2.

[28] BL Add MS 32,500, 18*r*. Quoted in Randall, *Gentle Flame*, p. 91.

[29] Randall, *Gentle Flame*, pp. 76–8.　　[30] North, *Observations*, p. 90.

[31] Ibid. Preface, unnumbered f5.

[32] North published poems, claiming they were written 'to a domestique confinement'. Quoted in Michael McKeon, *The Secret History of Domesticity: Public, Private, and the Division of Knowledge* (Baltimore, Maryland: Johns Hopkins University Press, 2005), p. 56.

[33] Matthew Steggle, 'Gervase Markham (1568?–1637)', *Oxford Dictionary of National Biography*, Oxford University Press, 2004 <http://www.oxforddnb.com/view/article/18065> (accessed 15 October 2004).

[34] Caroline Davidson, 'Editor's Introduction', in Richard Bradley, *The Country Housewife and Lady's Director*, ed. Caroline Davidson (London: Prospect Books, 1980), pp. 13–14; British Library: Sloane MS 3322, fol. 50, quoted in Frank N. Egerton, 'Bradley, Richard (1688?–1732)', *Oxford Dictionary of National Biography*, Oxford University Press, 2004 <http://www.oxforddnb.com/view/article/3189> (accessed 3 August 2007).

Between 1717 and 1719 he had assisted with James Brydges' new garden at Cannons, supervising the planting, a physic garden, and hot house. But the finances for the project were poorly administered, and Brydges later accused Bradley of mismanaging £460.[35] It is not a little ironic that the failed botanical adviser on the estate should subsequently seek to solve his financial straights by writing a series of works on estate and household management. While living the oeconomical life may have been an ambition, this was not always attainable in practice.

It is clear that people do not always follow their own instructions. By the same token, individuals can acknowledge but engage reflectively with ideological precepts.[36] Later in the century, men from lower social groups reflected on their experiences of oeconomy critically. Benjamin Shaw (1772–1841), who worked in mills and machine shops as a mechanic, grappled with the disparity between how he believed husband and wife should practice oeconomy, and how in fact he and his wife Betty conducted their affairs. Married in 1793, Benjamin wrote later about the tensions in their early years of marriage: 'as my wife had never been shown the way to manage household affairs [*sic*] in the best way, our money did not do us the good it might had it been in some hands...I could not prevail with her either by fair, or fowl means, to change this plan. She began this way, & we have continued in this way, do all I could to prevet [*sic*] it.'[37] Benjamin had tried but failed to improve Betty's practices. As his narrative continues, Benjamin begins to render Betty culpable for the mismanagement of the household's financial resources: 'I never enquired what she did with the money', he explains of their practices in 1822, because 'if a man have Both to get money, & to trouble himself with the care of lying it out, what Better is he with a wife than a servant—or what woman would be content to have, no share in the management of the family'.[38] Benjamin believed a well-managed domestic economy was the work of the wife, though he was ultimately responsible for the family's financial straights and status.[39] Indeed, having earlier tried to reform Betty, Benjamin was later driven to intervene in domestic management, as discussed below. As D'Cruze remarks, Shaw struggled to maintain '[t]he father's social power [as] embedded in the relationships of the domestic economy'.[40] The struggle arose because of both their failings in oeconomy.

Shaw's vision of the domestic economy mirrored that of William Cobbett, excerpts of whose works appear in Shaw's unpublished collections of aphorisms and extracted writings. A rough contemporary of Shaw, Robert Sharp also held the

---

[35] Davidson, 'Editor's Introduction', pp. 12–13. See Egerton, 'Bradley, Richard (1688?–1732)', ibid.

[36] Lena Cowen Orlin, *Private Matters and Public Culture in Post-Reformation England* (Ithaca; London: Cornell University Press, 1994). Orlin undertakes a suggestive analysis of 'patriarchalism in practice', providing five instances where people engaged critically with these ideals.

[37] *The Family Records of Benjamin Shaw, mechanic of Dent, Dolphinholme and Preston, 1772–1841*, ed. Alan G. Crosby (Record Society of Lancashire and Cheshire, 1991), p. 32.

[38] Ibid. p. 61.

[39] Shani D'Cruze, 'Care, Diligence and "Usfull Pride": Gender, Industrialization and the Domestic Economy, *c*.1770 to *c*.1840', *Women's History Review*, 3 (1994) pp. 327, 336.

[40] Ibid. p. 339.

oeconomical model of Cobbett in high regard, having read Cobbett's *Cottage Economy* in 1821.[41] In Sharp's view, 'economy' was a practice to be carried out in the family and the nation. Writing in his diary in 1830, during an economic crisis, Sharp commented on both a neighbour's failure to use 'Economy' to set aside resources that would see him through the current situation, and an MP's speech for 'Economy and retrenchment'.[42] His lengthy diary is full with references to 'economy' practised in his own household, but also in the households of others. Yet oeconomy was sometimes frustrated, even within his own house. Desiring to be frugal, Sharp tipped some broken clay pipes with sealing wax, instead of discarding them. But he found it to be an exercise in false economy: 'I believe I used as much Wax as would have bought good pipes, but never mind, the Pipes were useful.—this is Domestic economy.'[43] Sharp's varying use of the term 'economy' to mean both practical domestic housekeeping and management of the nation's resources chimes with the changes observable in the printed materials.[44] Men drew on the language of oeconomy in different ways in different times and places, but this language was relevant for disparate experiences. From Baldingstone in Lancashire to the London court of the Old Bailey, and from polite Bath to industrializing Preston, the language and discourse of oeconomy was one that men employed as a personal ideal and a measure of social reputation. Yet the shift from Dudley North to Robert Sharp is a substantial one, both in the focus of oeconomy (from the household to the nation) and in the social group for whom it held meaning and social value.

OECONOMY MADE MANIFEST

The discourse of oeconomy was an important cultural resource for men, and as such was enacted as well as spoken and thought. Order and management of the household's resources was conducted in many ways, but written accounts—all that these written records contained and represented—were the spine of the oeconomic household. The everyday practices of accounting enabled the practical management of a household's resources, but these accounting practices also expressed the authority that men wielded over other members of the household. Significantly, household accounting was distinct from estate accounting as it developed in England: whereas the latter used a charge and discharge system, in which the steward managed the rent, cash, and goods of the estate and was himself held accountable for these, in the case of small-scale household accounts the householder was responsible for their accuracy and integrity.[45] Partly as a result and as discussed below,

---

[41] *The Diary of Robert Sharp of South Cave: Life in a Yorkshire Village, 1812–1837*, ed. Janice E. Crowther and Peter A. Crowther (Records of Social and Economic History, New Series 26, For the British Academy, by OUP, 1997), Letter to his son William, 25 December 1821, p. 8.

[42] Ibid. Tuesday 9 February 1830, p. 246; Thursday 18 February 1830, p. 247.

[43] Ibid. Tuesday 30 November 1830, p. 288.

[44] See discussion in Chapter 2, pp. 51–7.

[45] David Oldroyd, *Estates, Enterprise and Investment at the Dawn of the Industrial Revolution: Estate Management and Accounting in the North-East of England, c.1700–1780* (Aldershot: Ashgate, 2007), pp. 18–21.

middling-sort men's books of accounts were highly expressive material objects. Accounting unified both oeconomy as domestic housekeeping and oeconomy as governance, and it was through such practices of oeconomy that men's domestic patriarchy was concretized. These sources demonstrate that in ordering the financial affairs of the household, men controlled not only property but people.

Additionally, accounting shaped the way that men conducted other engagements with the domestic. Beverly Lemire has identified accounting as a 'mode of writing'—a 'transcendent method of expression'—that showed the 'impact of quantitative culture' on the household.[46] Certainly, and as I explore below, accounting records were literary works as much as documentary sources. The numeric form was not only combined with other types of writing, but to some extent shaped the form of many written family records. Significantly, this form of ordered record keeping is subtly different in form and more limited in extent—though related to—both the archiving by women in their early American homes and what Susan Stabile describes as a peculiarly 'feminine mode of memory', and also 'the systematic creation, collection and passing on of such an archive' by Quaker women in early nineteenth-century England studied by Sandra Stanley Holton.[47] Indeed, this chapter intends to demonstrate the rootedness of men's writing in their homes, and in situating men at the centre of this more modest domestic record-keeping offers a contrast to accounts of women's work of collecting domestic archives. Taking the records of men alongside those of women suggests that eighteenth-century houses may have been the setting for the creation of distinctively gendered forms of writing.

The different meanings of 'account'—including numerical counting, because of, estimation, and narration—were all established by the mid-seventeenth century, and indicate the range of values placed upon accounts.[48] Accounts were proof of good credit. Men used these records to satisfy themselves and others—to give a good account—of their dealings. As John Mair explained in *Book-Keeping Methodiz'd* (1751), these records were kept 'for the sake of his own Memory, or in order to give a satisfactory Account of his Conduct and Management to Persons concerned'.[49] Written accounts thus replaced memory as the record of many transactions in early-modern England.[50] In a still largely agrarian economy, with farm-

---

[46] Beverly Lemire, *The Business of Everyday Life: Gender, Practice and Social Politics in England, c.1600–1900* (Manchester and New York: Manchester University Press, 2005), pp. 195, 187, 188. See also Mary Poovery, *Genres of the Credit Economy: Mediating Value in Eighteenth- and Nineteenth-Century Britain* (Chicago: Chicago University Press, 2008).

[47] Susan M. Stabile, *Memory's Daughters: the Material Culture of Remembrance in Eighteenth-Century America* (Ithaca, NY; London: Cornell University Press, 2003), p. 14; Sandra Stanley Holton, *Quaker Women: Personal Life, Memory and Radicalism in the Lives of Women Friends, 1780–1930* (Abingdon: Routledge, 2007), p. 2.

[48] 'account, n.', OED Online, June 2011, Oxford University Press <http://www.oed.com.eresources.shef.ac.uk> (accessed March 2006).

[49] John Mair, *Book-Keeping Methodiz'd: or, A Methodical Treatise of Merchant-Accompts, according to the Italian Form*, 2nd edn (Edinburgh, 1751), p. 1.

[50] Craig Muldrew, *The Economy of Obligation: The Culture of Credit and Social Relations in Early Modern England* (Basingstoke: Macmillan, 1998), pp. 63–4.

ing 'the reigning taste of the present times', it is significant that husbandry, the practice so crucial to male oeconomy, had its 'foundation' in good accounts.[51] For the man in the country, writing good accounts swiftly was 'as requisite to his office, as the knowing wheat from barley'.[52] Writers were adamant that new methods of calculation were necessary in order that 'a right Understanding' of the value of things could be assessed, and 'ignorance', 'Fraud and Injustice' be thereby dispelled.[53] Accounts were valuable not because they enabled the accumulation of profit, but because they prevented families from living above their means, and especially because they provided a particularly robust kind of knowledge, '*true* experience, not the random notions that are carried in the memory'.[54] Accounts were authoritative objects, a true numerical record grounded in direct experience of the everyday.

We can gather a good sense of the social and cultural weight of accounts from their totemic status. Accounts operated as physical things of value that people needed to validate with sight. At Cannons, a house north-west of London, James Brydges, Duke of Chandos, instructed his principal secretary in dealings with tenants, instructing him, for example, to make entries into an account book but also to 'bring [the account book] down along with you', or to meet with a man requesting payment, '& then shew him [the] Accot & Receipt, that he may see I paid the money so many yeares ago'.[55] Men had to *see* the accounts. And the volumes of accounts were themselves items of value, the purchase of which was noted within their pages. Smedley paid 7s 6d 'for this Book & another' on 23 January 1742;[56] Francis Blake also paid the considerable 3s for 'The Price of this Book' in January 1765.[57] These valuable objects were carried around in men's pockets, no doubt for safekeeping and verification. Men's clothing was full of large pockets each big enough to take a book, and a single outfit might accommodate 6 or 8, ready for display at a moment's notice.[58]

Other men not only kept accounts to show associates, but also asked those associates to sign the document. For example, in the account book of the solicitor and Lord of the Manor Thomas Mort, the entry for 19 August 1721 details the purchase of stones and flags from John Leyland and John Ashall for £7 10s. Below the

---

[51] Arthur Young, *Rural Oeconomy* (1770), pp. 173, 206.

[52] Ibid. p. 215. The relationship between literary and numeracy can be seen in several manuscripts, where boys (and girls) practice and perfect both skills. Very good examples are [Timothy Tyrell, 1755–1832], 'Account book with mathematical exercises' (1725–1768), William Andrews Clark Memorial Library: MS 1945.001; and Account book of Rebecca Steel, William Andrews Clark Memorial Library: MS fS8135 M3 H531 1702.

[53] John Richards, *The Gentleman's Steward and Tenants of Manors Instructed* (London, 1760), *passim*, and pp. xx, xiv.

[54] Young, *Rural Oeconomy*, p. 205. See also p. 207. For more on accounts, see Natasha Glaisyer, *The Culture of Commerce in England, 1660–1720* (Woodbridge: The Boydell Press, 2006), pp. 100–42.

[55] Stowe Papers, Henry E. Huntington Library: STB Box 13 (3) 8 May 1730, (18) 8 July 1730.

[56] Account book of William Smedley, Henry E. Huntington Library: HM3119223, January 1742.

[57] Francis Blake, 'Acct Book from 1 January 1765 to 22 February 1766', William Andrews Clark Memorial Library: MS.1985.002, 1 January 1765.

[58] On women's pockets, and their relationship to women's domestic economy, see Barbara Burman and Jonathan White, 'Fanny's Pockets: Cotton, Consumption and Domestic Economy, 1780–1850', in Jennie Batchelor and Cora Kaplan (eds), *Women and Material Culture, 1660–1830* (Basingstoke: Palgrave Macmillan, 2007), pp. 31–51.

entry are four signed names, two of the vendors, and two witnesses, Samuel Stockton and William Heyes, confirming that Leyland and Ashall have received the money and that they will 'make satisfaction' to Mort by providing the correct amount of flags.[59] Though in English common law account books were not admissible evidence alone, witnesses had long been called upon to verify written transactions in the courtroom.[60] The legal significance of some of these entries might explain why these volumes were initially preserved. Signed records reinforced the publicity of an exchange for those involved and perhaps for the state; account books were also written family records as opposed to orally transmitted memories. It is partly in this context that the social value of the account book inscribed 'Timothy Tyrell' becomes legible. This was compiled by at least two generations of the Reading family of drapers. The bulk of the entries date from 1734–66, though the back inside cover shows various entries, including those dated 1724, 1729, 1759, and 1782.[61] Such tangible evidence of long-past events must have surely inflated the volume's status, a valued compendium of family information.

For the middling-sort men of central interest to this book, accounts can be contextualized in men's occupational and community tasks. Many authors of surviving account books collected rents or tithes, performed writing services for others, and were figures of some local repute. The Tyrell account book contains several entries for collections of rents. One section gives over a separate page for individual properties, and here the author lists the quarterly rents received over a period of many years during the 1730s, 40s, and 50s. Elsewhere, the author details the taxes paid. Daniel Renaud was a Rector, responsible for the administration of the church buildings and estate in Whitchurch for over forty years from 1728. Edmund Pilkington was schoolmaster in Bury from 1720 to 1755. He recorded his salary from Mr Unsworth and income from 'scholars', and also receives payments for additional writing services, including a 'first lay book', indentures, and a 'Second lay book' for Unsworth, and a lay book, poor notes, and indentures from 'Michael Bentley's Overseers'.[62] Pilkington also paid day labourers for agricultural work.[63] The account book of William Parkinson details the several properties and households that the author managed as executor of the yeoman William Smedley, Parkinson's uncle, who died in 1742. Parkinson had been left two-thirds of Smedley's

[59] Account book of Thomas Mort, 26 March 1703–13 September 1725. Henry E. Huntington Library: L3A1 [new location S10 K3]. On the volume and authorship, see Dorothy Bowen, 'Thomas Mort of Dam House', *Huntington Library Quarterly*, 8, 3 (May, 1945), pp. 323–34.

[60] Charles W. Wootton, 'The Legal Status of Account Books in Colonial America', *Accounting History*, 5, 33 (2000), pp. 39–40; Muldrew, *Economy of Obligation*, pp. 63–4. The status of written contracts was reinforced in 1677, when 'An Act for prevention of Frauds and Perjuryes' ensured that contracts for goods valued at £10 or more would be binding if 'some Note or Memorandum in writing of the said bargaine be made and signed by the partyes'. See 'Charles II, 1677: An Act for prevention of Frauds and Perjuryes', *Statutes of the Realm: volume 5: 1628–80* (1819), pp. 839–42, xvi. *British History Online*: <http://www.british-history.ac.uk/report.aspx?compid=47463> (accessed September 2010). I thank Craig Muldrew for his assistance.

[61] [Tyrell], 'Account book', back inside cover.

[62] [Edmund Pilkington] Account book, William Andrews Clark Memorial Library: MS1976.001, ff. 4, 38, 63, 66–9.

[63] Ibid. ff. 9–37.

house and several parcels of land—inherited from his father—and on the death of his aunt, Sarah Smedley, he was to receive the other third.[64] The account book centres on the activities of the farm in Borrowash, though rents were collected and King's, window, and land tax paid on several other properties. For example, in 1742, the lists of rents received names 13 different individuals.[65] In July 1747, a total of £3 13s and 2d was paid in King's and windows tax on five different properties.[66] The book also recorded payments of 12s 6d 'for Church & poor' and 2s 6d 'to Church warden's minister for planting Religion in far parts'.[67] As Lord of the Manor, Thomas Mort was certainly an important local figure with responsibilities to the local adjoining parishes of Ashley and Tildsley. Mort gave to the parishes on several occasions, for example in 1704 recording giving 10s 6d for the church at Ashley, £1 12s 3d for the poor at Ashley, and 3s 6d for the poor at Tildsley.[68] Some of the men who left these papers were 'chief inhabitants',[69] but all were significant figures in their local communities and active in civic and church administration. These men possessed the numerate and literate skills necessary for keeping accounts, but understood their economic and social value.

Publicly significant, these volumes were nevertheless completed in the house. In urban houses, purpose-built furniture, a partitioned space or even a separate room may have been used for hours a week, as amongst the merchant middling-sort in Sweden, where '[t]he husband's arena was the office with its accounts, correspondence and contact with important connections'.[70] Accounts were also important to the increasingly 'capitalist' rural economy, in which land was one source of livelihood in a diversified system of profit and loss, monitored by keeping accounts.[71] As such, farmhouses included a separate room for this kind of paperwork. The ground floor of John Plaw's design for a large farmhouse in his *Rural Architecture* (1794) is notable for the way each room has more than one entrance, thus enabling movement through all the rooms. The exceptions are the tiny pantry off the servants' kitchen, and the 'Account & Store Room' at the front of the house.[72] The setting apart of such spaces rooted and elevated the status of accounting deep within the house. The traffic of paper through which bills and receipts came into the house, were spiked at a desk, copied and re-copied into bound volumes, and

---

[64] Will of William Smedley, 21 April 1742. B/C/11, Lichfield Record Office. I thank Kate Henderson for her assistance.

[65] Account book of William Smedley, 'Money Received, 1742'.

[66] Ibid. 10 July 1747, 25 July 1747.

[67] Ibid. 6 March 1742, 26 October 1742.

[68] Account book of Thomas Mort, 10 August 1704, 11 August 1704. See also 'Townships: Astley', *A History of the County of Lancaster: Volume 3* (1907), pp. 445–9. *British History Online*: <http://www.british-history.ac.uk/report.aspx?compid=41365> (accessed 8 September 2010).

[69] This is the term used by Henry French in *The Middle Sort of People in Provincial England, 1600–1750* (Oxford: Oxford University Press, 2007).

[70] Quote from Ida Bull, 'Merchant Households and their Networks in Eighteenth-century Trondheim', *Change and Continuity*, 17 (2), 2002, pp. 216–17. See also Ann Smart Martin, *Buying into the World of Goods: Early Consumers in Backcountry Virginia* (Baltimore, Maryland: Johns Hopkins University Press, 2008), p. 69.

[71] H. R. French and R. W. Hoyle, *The Character of English Rural Society: Earls Colne, 1550–1750* (Manchester and New York: Manchester University Press, 2007), pp. 37–8. Quote at p. 38.

[72] 'Design for a Farm house', John Plaw, *Rural Architecture* (London, 1794).

then carried on a man's person to be offered as public statements of household credit, comprised practices that went to the heart of the house and out again. Time, space, objects, and skill were required. In this way, accounting records must be studied not simply for their numeric content, but also viewed as forms of writing that are the physical remnants of practices that articulated men's social and economic authority, within and without the house.

THE LABOUR OF GENDER

Merchant communities required the cooperation of all family members as well as gender differentiation, presenting a 'complicated mixture and coexistence of *both* patriarchal authority *and* equality'.[73] Accounts were tied to men's social authority in particular, but it is important to recognize that women also kept accounts. Amanda Vickery has reconstructed the hard work and social status of the management and 'daily governance' of the genteel female housekeeper, using the extensive manuscript records of Elizabeth Shackleton: reference books on keeping the 'provisions, property and personnel' of the house. These remarkable records demonstrate the extent to which some women ran the household, and recorded this in their own accounts.[74] Business women also kept accounts, though for lesser tradeswomen (as with men) memory was often used instead of written records.[75] In smaller households, too, women were likely to have kept accounts and certainly short-term records of expenditure. But while relatively few account books survive for middling-sort men, even fewer accounts remain from middling-sort women, whether because they were fewer in number, more ephemeral as objects, or considered less valuable. Literacy rates of women in some occupations were very high, and women were expected to contribute to the family economy by providing 'clerical assistance' to male relatives in supportive and facilitative roles.[76] Nevertheless, accounting required both literacy and numeracy: literacy rates were approximately 50 per cent higher for men than for women and there is no reason to suspect this was any different for numeracy.[77]

[73] Bull, 'Merchant Households', p. 217.

[74] Amanda Vickery, *The Gentleman's Daughter: Women's Lives in Georgian England* (New Haven, Conn: Yale University Press, 1998), pp. 141, 133. The subject of Vickery's primary case-study—Elizabeth Shackleton—left only records of expenditure, not income.

[75] Nicola Phillips, *Women in Business, 1700–1850* (Woodbridge: Boydell, 2006), pp. 97–8, 114–15. Muldrew says that accounts were very rare before the eighteenth century, giving several examples of tradesmen who kept poor accounts or none at all into the eighteenth century. See Muldrew, *Economy of Obligation*, pp. 61–4.

[76] Margaret Hunt, *The Middling Sort: Commerce, Gender and the Family in England, 1680–1780* (Berkeley: University of California Press, 1996), pp. 85–6. Quote at p. 86.

[77] On literacy rates from signing one's names, see Jonathan Barry, 'Literacy and Literature in Popular Culture', in Tim Harris (ed.), *Popular Culture in England, c. 1500–1850* (London: Macmillan, 1995), p. 76. Here they are put at 60% for men and 40% for women, though these are widely thought to be underestimates. Indeed, Keith Thomas has shown that it was harder to learn numeracy than to learn to read. See Keith Thomas, 'Numeracy in Early Modern England', *Transactions of the Royal Historical Society*, 5th ser, 37 (1987) pp. 103–32.

While girls were taught accounting, Hunt concludes, 'the skill was deemed more crucial for sons'.[78] Women made important contributions to the middling-sort family economy, to be sure, but these need to be set firmly within a hierarchical and unequal middling family culture.[79]

The strong association between men and accounting records was one expression of men's ownership of goods and property. This truism is crucial to an understanding of men's engagements with the domestic. Some historians have argued that the key to understanding legal inequities between men and women was coverture: a theory of common law traditionally seen as subsuming a married woman's legal identity (and therefore her ability to make contracts and purchase items on credit) under that of her husband. Susan Staves has argued that by the late eighteenth century the imposition of coverture was an expression of the 'deeper patriarchal structures' being imposed by the courts.[80] In contrast, Amy Erickson has demonstrated that common law operated alongside the law of equity, in which married women exercised a considerable degree of autonomy and control over their property.[81] Notably, wives could be granted property in a 'separate estate' usually awarded in trust outside the bounds of coverture, though even this form of female financial independence was contested.[82] Common law coverture itself had limits. Margot Finn sees it 'existing in a state of suspended animation'.[83] Within common law, the law of necessities sanctioned the making of contracts by women for necessaries, albeit as agents for their husbands.[84] Married women's 'economic authority' was sanctioned by the county courts in their dealings on debt and credit. Indeed, 'the imposition of middle-class conceptions of economic probity was achieved only at the price of attenuating parallel middle-class notions of gender difference'.[85] Married women were necessarily acknowledged to be economic agents in the home for the purposes of consumption. As histories of business women demonstrate, 'patriarchal power was less pervasive than has often been presumed'.[86]

---

[78] Hunt, *Middling Sort*, p. 59. See also Hunt, 'Time Management, Writing and Accounting in the Eighteenth Century English Trading Family: A Bourgeois Enlightenment', *Business and Economic History*, 2 series, 18 (1989), pp. 150–9.

[79] Hunt, *Middling Sort*, p. 100.

[80] Susan Staves, *Married Women's Separate Property in England, 1660–1833* (Cambridge, Mass: Harvard University Press, 1990), p. 4.

[81] Amy Erickson, *Women and Property in Early Modern England* (London: Routledge, 1993), p. 19.

[82] Hunt, *Middling Sort*, pp. 157–62.

[83] Margot Finn, 'Women, Consumption and Coverture in England, c.1760–1860', *Historical Journal*, 39, 3 (1996), p. 707. Joanne Bailey makes similar points about the law of agency in her 'Favoured or Oppressed? Married Women, Property and "Coverture" in England, 1660–1800', *Continuity and Change*, 17, 3 (2002), pp. 1–22.

[84] Finn, 'Women, Consumption and Coverture', p. 709. Finn's discussion of the representation of coverture and the law of necessities under common law in *The Law of Evidence* (1760) reflects perfectly the complex and long-standing vision of patriarchy outlined in many books on the household—men govern and hold power, but wives can exercise husband's powers on their behalf.

[85] Finn, 'Women, Consumption and Coverture', p. 721.

[86] Hannah Barker, *The Business of Women: Female Enterprise and Urban Development in Northern England, 1760–1830* (Oxford: Oxford University Press, 2006), p. 171. See pp. 134–51 for a useful discussion of the many different circumstances in which women could benefit from the law.

There thus appear to have been co-existing, seemingly contradictory, conceptions of women's position. Yet characterizing eighteenth-century law as 'patriarchal' is legitimate if we define patriarchy in a way that accommodates the exercise of often considerable authority on the part of women in the interests of the shared household unit. A woman's power was often legitimized by that of her husband, though exercised independently for the household. Significantly, as Nicola Phillips makes clear, the ability to trade was not contingent upon women's legal rights.[87] The complex nature of English law meant that there was space for even married women to trade, although 'the law could only imagine and define the family in one form with a nominal male head and with a common economic goal'.[88] Women's abilities in business were understood as taking place within a household economy, and thus common law envisaged them as agents of husbands or trustees of their separate estate.[89] Even in the case of equity, the law 'only conferred upon wives the ability to act *as if* they were individual agents'.[90] There was continuity in this regard across the seventeenth and eighteenth centuries, though coverture was to some extent revised. Tim Stretton has shown that the limits to married women's legal rights under coverture resulted from the customary power of men over women. The 'curious legal fiction' that women's legal identity was erased in unity of person for husband and wife emerged only gradually.[91] In his important comments on this matter, for example, William Blackstone shifted the explanation of coverture from male force to legal logic, presenting not a divestment of married women's legal independence, but the triumph of rational liberty in the figure of the husband: 'Coverture therefore represented the ultimate expression of the common law's benevolent paternalism.'[92] Men's absolute property rights—crystallized in coverture—were, therefore, an unworkable form of social imagining. '[T]he rhetoric of absolute property was politically important' to the eighteenth-century nation-state and empire, yet the same is true of households and gendered authority.[93] So, at the same time that (even married) women had ongoing room for manoeuvre on property and contracts at law, then, men's legal personae became more fully established; both were situated in the notion of a particular form of household government. Similarly, women's agency in the household was entirely compatible with the central tenet of the discourse of oeconomy that men had ultimate control over goods and property. This balance can be observed in middling-sort men's account books, documents which offer a fascinating insight into the household practices shaped by the domestic patriarchy of oeconomy.

---

[87] Phillips, *Women in Business*, p. 24.   [88] Ibid. p. 46.   [89] Ibid. p. 42.

[90] Ibid. p. 39. On women's property see also Amy Erickson, 'Common Law versus Common Practice: The Use of Marriage Settlements in Early Modern England', *Economic History Review*, 2nd ser, 43 (1990), pp. 21–39.

[91] Tim Stretton, 'Coverture and Unity of Person in Blackstone's *Commentaries*', in Wilfrid Prest (ed.), *Blackstone and His Commentaries: Biography, Law, History* (Oxford: Hart, 2009), p. 120 and *passim*. I thank the author for sending me an advance copy.

[92] Stretton, 'Coverture and Unity of Person', p. 124.

[93] John Brewer and Susan Staves, 'Introduction', in John Brewer and Susan Staves (eds), *Early Modern Conceptions of Property* (London and New York: Routledge, 1996), p. 18.

Men's accounts embodied men's global management but also show the involvement of both men and women in many levels of the household, especially with regards to consumption practices. Indeed, the subject of gendered practices of household consumption is one that has received considerable attention from historians. Lorna Weatherill's study of possession using probate inventories from 1660–1740 shows some limited differences between men's and women's property. Men possessed more tables and clocks; women possessed a relatively larger amount of table linen, looking glasses, and pictures, and (in middling-ranking social groups) more new, decorative goods. Men and women apparently consumed in equal measure books and utensils for hot drinks.[94] Social rank is an important factor, however. Amanda Vickery has found more startling differences for the gentry. Between 1751 and 1781, men of the gentry purchased higher status provisions (such as snuff, wine, and game) and their consumption tended to be intermittent, impulsive, expensive, and dynastic. Women, on the other hand, bought caps, ruffles, accoutrements: their consumption was regular, visible, mundane, and repetitive.[95] Using diaries, though, Finn has countered previous underestimations of the range of male consumption and demonstrated that middling-sort men were keen consumers with great personal investment in small things.[96] David Hussey has also shown that Vickery's findings do not hold for men of the 'lesser provincial elites and middle classes', who '[f]ar from being merely the agents of solid, substantial spending... navigated the embryonic consumer and retail markets with an easy, skilled familiarity'.[97] If men of the gentry took greater responsibility than their wives for the purchase of expensive items, middling-sort men seemed to share a greater range of consumption decisions with women.

This shared practice is significant in the light of Jan de Vries' argument for an 'industrious revolution' in north-west Europe between 1650 and 1850 consisting of changes in the production and consumption habits within the household, reinforcing his insistence on household-level decisions.[98] Indeed, household accounts were surely one of the household technologies facilitating these developments. Where gendered accounting practices have been studied, a complex picture emerges. Vickery's comparative study of consumption by husbands and wives in three gentry marriages shows a range of practice, albeit underpinned by some

---

[94] Lorna Weatherill, 'A Possession of One's Own: Women and Consumer Behaviour in England, 1660–1740', *Journal of British Studies*, 25 (1986), pp. 131–56.

[95] Amanda Vickery 'Women and the World of Goods: A Lancashire Consumer and her Possessions, 1751–81', in John Brewer and Roy Porter (eds), *Consumption and the World of Goods: Consumption and Society in the Seventeenth and Eighteenth Centuries* (London: Routledge, 1993), pp. 274–301.

[96] Margot Finn, 'Men's Things: Masculine Possession in the Consumer Revolution', *Social History*, 25, 2 (2000), pp. 133–54.

[97] David Hussey, 'Guns, Horses and Stylish Waistcoats? Male Consumer Activity and Domestic Shopping in Late-Eighteenth- and Early-Nineteenth-Century England', in David Hussey and Margaret Ponsonby (eds), *Buying for the Home: Shopping for the Domestic from the Seventeenth Century to the Present* (Aldershot: Ashgate, 2008), pp. 68, 56.

[98] Jan de Vries, *The Industrious Revolution: Consumer Behaviour and the Household Economy, 1650 to the Present* (Cambridge: Cambridge University Press, 2008).

'deeply held and consistent categorizations of material responsibility'.[99] The case studies reveal a practice of 'female domestic management within a framework of male superintendence and surveillance', a 'more restricted female financial mandate' within a 'patriarchal accounting system', and a system in which the husband pays for his personal items and larger purchases partly from money that enters the household through the wife's account book, a volume that records her expenditure on the household and children.[100] Practices varied but general patterns emerge; these studies underline Vickery's earlier finding that, 'the daily management of consumption fell to women' alongside husbands' general management.[101]

This pattern can be seen in the middling-sort accounts examined for this chapter. The account book of Henry Richardson, appointed rector of Thornton-in-Craven in North Yorkshire in 1735, underlines some of these findings.[102] Married some time into his term as Rector in 1748, the Richardsons clearly practised a gendered division of consumption. Mrs Richardson apparently undertook small levels of daily consumption; Mr Richardson carried out a larger extent of consumption—including some relatively low-value purchases for himself and the household—and all this consumption was funnelled through his own beautifully written volume. Richardson's account book covers the years 1748–53, from 'The first Year after I was Married', he writes. These accounts record his purchases of a range of items, including mustard, coffee, stockings, coat, servants' wages, post for letters, coal, threshing corn, turnpike, losing at cards, and his wife's clothes. Though the range of goods purchased was quite broad, there is little sign here of the new consumer goods that were appearing in increasing numbers in inventories. Richardson was a rural Rector who travelled to the Manchester assembly, but he was somewhat removed from the network of new commercial or merchant families for whom such goods were of growing importance.[103] Richardson buys oak furniture, the odd book or item of cutlery or flatware, and though he spends a considerable amount on clothes, these are simple shirts and outer garments of black and grey. A rare flash of colour appears in the form of 'two India Hankerchiefs [*sic*] narrow striped purple and white for 7 shillings'.[104] A 'consumer revolution', comprising new ways of learning about and buying goods, as well as substantive changes in the nature and quantity of those goods possessed, does not seem to hold much value in understanding this mid-century rural Rector.[105]

[99] Amanda Vickery, 'His and Hers: Gender, Consumption and Household Accounting in Eighteenth-Century England' in Ruth Harris, Lyndal Roper, Olwen Hufton (eds), *The Art of Survival: Gender and History in Europe, 1450–2000: Essays in Honour of Olwen Hufton, Past & Present*, Supplement 1 (2006), p. 36.

[100] Ibid. pp. 23, 24.

[101] Vickery, *Gentleman's Daughter*, p. 166.

[102] 'Henry Richardson' (CCEd Person ID 116903), *The Clergy of the Church of England Database 1540–1835* <http://www.theclergydatabase.org.uk> (accessed August 2008).

[103] Henry Richardson, 'A Diary of Disbursements since January ye first 1748 The First Year after I was Married', West Yorkshire Archive Service, Wakefield: C658, entry for 23 June 1748.

[104] Ibid. entry for 4 August 1748.

[105] The key volume on the consumer revolution of eighteenth-century Britain is Neil McKendrick, John Brewer and J. H. Plumb, *The Birth of a Consumer Society: The Commercialisation of Eighteenth-Century England* (Cambridge: Cambridge University Press, 1982). The notion of a 'consumer

Nevertheless, the gendered patterns of consumption suggested by Richardson's book echo with those found elsewhere. The bed, oak chest and table, and clock chime with Vickery's argument that men bought larger items, Weatherill's finding that clocks appear with greater frequency in men's inventories, and Donald's claim that clocks and watches were a key accessory of the gentleman. The soap, candles, and handkerchiefs reinforce Finn's emphasis on the smaller, regular, and rather mundane items of some men's consumption. Yet this account book is not a complete or sufficient record of the household economy, because within Henry's account book are hidden the many purchases made by his wife. Roughly every month Henry wrote in his accounts, 'Let my Wife have for House Use'. Numerous items of necessary domestic consumption are contained within these brief entries, reminding us of the essential participation of Mrs Richardson in household consumption. It was Henry who 'Let', 'Lent', or 'Paid' Mrs Richardson these monies. Only once did Henry 'give' his wife money, and this entry might suggest just how he rated the importance of her consumption: on 18 June 1748, Henry recorded 'Gave my Wife for Pockett Money—2 12–6'.[106] The money that Richardson 'paid' his wife totalled £19 4s 9d in 1748. This did not include money he paid direct to others for his wife's goods, such as the £2 16s he paid to a Mrs Phillips for making his wife's clothes on 20 January 1748. But it is a tiny fraction of the figure of £1185 1s 2d that Richardson apparently paid out during that year.[107] Discussing the similarly peremptory entries in which Abraham Grimes detailed the amounts given to Mrs Grimes in his account book of 1781–8, Vickery concludes that the volume 'constructs her more like an eldest daughter than a wife and mistress of the household'.[108] There is significant household labour hidden behind the entries for Mrs Richardson, and she must have surely kept some form of accounts herself. Mr Richardson's volume presents an inaccurately narrow picture of women's role in the household economy, and the volume cannot provide reliable data on the division of labour between this husband and wife, let alone show us how this was given meaning in the context of their personal relationship. But it does allow some general observations about the relative roles of the Richardson's that concur with other findings. First, any division of labour did not fall neatly either side of a domestic threshold; some domestic consumption of a fairly mundane type was shared. Second, the subsuming of Mrs Richardson's entries within the larger (global) account book also shows that while the wife undertook regular and mundane consumption, this consumption was managed by her husband alongside the much more substantial forms of consumption undertaken by him.

revolution' continues to hold sway despite criticisms. See, for example, Sara Pennell, 'Consumption and Consumerism in Early Modern England', *Historical Journal*, 42, 2 (1999), pp. 549–64.

[106] Richardson, 'A Diary of Disbursements', entry for 18 June 1748.

[107] This is based on data from the entries for the year 1748 in Richardson, 'A Diary of Disbursements'. This is an extremely high figure for annual expenditure. We might compare it to the annual expenditure calculated for Richard Latham—a small yeoman and tradesman—for the same year of £31 4s 51/2 d. See *The Account Book of Richard Latham, 1724–1767*, Records of Social and Economic History, New series; 15, ed. Lorna Weatherill (Oxford: Published for the British Academy by Oxford University Press, 1990) p. xxii.

[108] Vickery, 'His and Hers', p. 25.

Of similar social rank to Richardson, schoolmaster Edmund Pilkington also recorded catch-all payments to his mother and his wife.[109] Account books from households of much larger size and higher social rank suggest similar accounting practices between husbands and wives, however. The ledger that the York solicitor William Gray kept with his wife Faith for the years 1812 to 1844, though for a much more substantial household, shows the same pattern. The volume records the disbursements to the 'House Account' alongside payments for 'Mr Gray's Pocket expenses', with the 'House' payment being then recorded in the receipts of Faith Gray. In 1818, for example, a note of William's expenses of 7s 6d was recorded below £50 for the house disbursed from the joint accounts, the latter then recorded in Faith's receipts.[110] These transactions were all apparently kept by Faith, though they mirror the divisions observable elsewhere as payments for the 'house' were made from husband to wife. In the 1700s, the unmarried Thomas Mort used the same language when giving money to the servant Harry Whaley, 'for yᵉ use of yᵉ House'.[111] William Parkinson similarly records the £1 1s paid out for housekeeping on 23 January 1742.[112] This volume is in fact a master account book for several different households, recording payments for housekeeping to Ant Smedley, Bet Morley, and Sarah Morley.[113] The Parkinson volume—whose entries describe the distribution of the Smedley estate, the marriage of the Morley daughters, the establishment of new households, but also the continuing presence of those households in the family network of transactions—is a good illustration of how accounting practices straddled the discontinuities in family, and enabled continuity as the composition of the household economy transformed.

As well as records of financial transactions, these books are the material traces of a series of practices and conversations. Account books 'evince actions, desires, and relationships', and eighteenth-century men worked hard to keep hold of them.[114] In these ways they demonstrate how men necessarily engaged closely with the domestic consumption undertaken by others. Each entry for the money to his wife in Henry Richardson's account book, for example, is surely also a record of an exchange that took place between the couple, during which Mrs Richardson would have presented her bills, summarized her payments, and outlined the household's needs for the month to come. Perhaps this was sometimes the occasion of some discussion and negotiation, during which Henry offered his own views of the items his wife had bought or wished to buy. Given the social value of good accounts and a well-ordered household, Henry may well have wanted reassurance that his new wife could make sound decisions. Sharing in this common culture, Mrs Richardson may have wished to demonstrate her skill in this regard. Certainly in their written form of bills and

---

[109] [Pilkington] Account book, 25 December, 27 December 1731, f. 114.

[110] 'Accts of Wm and Faith Gray', Gray Family Papers, York City Archives, Acc. 24, A2: 'Disbursements 1818, f. 53; 'Receivings 1818', f. 155.

[111] Account book of Thomas Mort, for example, entries for 10 May, 14 January, 31 July, 5 September, 20 September 1704.

[112] Account book of William Smedley, 23 January 1742.

[113] Ibid. 13 February 1742, 16 April 1742, 28 September 1751.

[114] See Smart Martin's rich analysis of the accounts of John Hook, the Virginia merchant, from 1770, in *Buying into the World of Goods*, pp. 67–93. Quote from p. 68.

receipts, the transactions of Mrs Richardson literally passed through Mr Richardson's hands. The volumes of Pilkington, Gray, Mort, and Parkinson are also merely the remains of a much more extensive system of paperwork.

Records from the marriage of the Reverend John Forth and Elizabeth Forth (née Woodhouse), a prosperous couple from York who married in 1791, reveal these practices somewhat more clearly. Elizabeth brought some considerable property to the marriage and the collaborative housekeeping books show the close involvement of both spouses in the domestic arena. John's first account book from the early years of the marriage contained his accounts, concluding with a summary list of annual accounts including the categories of house furnishings, 'Casual Disbursements', clothes, servants' wages, stock, and 'House keeping Account', the latter being the second largest amount at over £230.[115] John's second volume is similar, though contains some accounts by Elizabeth on the inside covers: she counts the glassware after having company in 1791, for example, and notes expenses for washing gloves, mending shoes, buying thread, and 'Mr Forth's dressing Gown making'. Yet still at this early stage, it is John who records all the 'Sundry Disbursements on Account of House Keeping', the butter, bread, soap, fish, and chicken.[116] Subsequent volumes show the couple both engaging in the detailed matters of accounting for the home, whether the volumes were titled as individual or shared accounts. Elizabeth's volume for 1792–3 contains entries by different hands interspersed, such as where John records entries for early December 1792 only for Elizabeth to continue from the 7th of that month.[117] The same pattern can be seen in the joint account book from 1800.[118] These volumes include disbursements for the full range of items consumed by a family, though they are interspersed with many other different kinds of record. Recipes for food and for the prevention of miscarriage, details of certain products, and instructions for 'The Under Servants Work' are included in the account book of 1792–3, for example. The books may well include the handiwork of a housekeeper, though entries such as 'gave Mr Price for churching me after my lying in of Mary', for October 1793, demonstrate that Elizabeth made many entries.[119] In other sections of her records, Elizabeth recorded the same events in a different form:

Mary Forth Born Sep.r 11th 1793.
She was Baptized by her Papa sep.r 19th.
M[r] Price Church'd me Oct.r 12th[120]

Both John and Elizabeth used their account books as a repository for different types of information.

---

[115] Account book of John Forth, 1791–2, York City Archives: Acc 54:2, ff. 32.

[116] Account book of John Forth, 1792–3, York City Archives: Acc 54:3, verso front cover, f. 43.

[117] 'Housekeeping account book of Elizabeth Forth, 1792–3', York City Archives: Acc 54:4, f. 5.

[118] See, for example, 'Housekeeping Account for the Year 1800—John and Elizt: Forth', York City Archives: Acc 54:7.

[119] 'Housekeeping account book of Elizabeth Forth, 1792–3', ff. 60–72, 50. The amount given to Mr Price was 10s 6d.

[120] Extracts from acct bks and diary of Elizabeth Forth, 1793–1815, York City Archives: Acc 54:10, f. 2.

Despite the evident collaboration in compiling these accounts, they nevertheless occupied one part of a larger system managed by John. The couple's practices within this system can be glimpsed through bills dating from early in their relationship. For example, on the reverse side of a bill addressed to Elizabeth for silverware from a York jeweller on 14 June 1791, the following day John made a note of the total and to whom it was owed to be copied into an account book. The same notes were made on other bills, including those addressed to him.[121] This practice was to continue. The housekeeping accounts show John not just making individual entries, but reviewing all entries and noting summaries in his global accounts elsewhere. In the account book of 1792–3, for example, he concludes the entries for December 1793 with the remark, 'Enter'd this Ac^t. In my Account. J. Forth'.[122] These were not abstract entries, of course, and money passed from John's hands to Elizabeth's, with bills passing back again. In their 'Account Book for Housekeeping for the Year 1798—John and Eliz^t: Forth', Elizabeth notes that John gives her a present of two £5 bills, two weeks later recording how she gave him 'all the Money in her Hands amounting to £61:10'.[123] Elizabeth's purchases were variable, but generally modest, including foodstuffs such as eggs and a goose.[124] Unlike Mrs Richardson, Elizabeth Forth left many written accounts. They plainly show that her everyday engagements with the household were critical: it was Elizabeth's labour—along with that of the servants—that kept this household in operation. But an analytical framework of women's creation of a comfortable home is inadequate for an understanding of their joint, and indeed Elizabeth's, activities.[125] John assisted Elizabeth in the compilation of the housekeeping accounts in which such expenses were recorded, at the same time as he oversaw them and managed the larger system of which they were a part.

The accounts of another upper-middling-sort family in York yield similar findings. Comparing the ledger of the solicitor William Gray with the volume from 1812–1844, in which both William and his wife Faith kept accounts, gives a useful window onto the different areas of responsibility the couple had within the house. Margaret Hunt has examined the printed extracts of Faith Gray's writings to demonstrate how the actions of women in some marriages vie with the notion of separate spheres. Faith Gray shared many skills and roles with her husband; her hard work in the family, in support of his business, in religion, and in philanthropy, matched his own.[126] The copies of Faith Gray's accounts in the joint ledger encompass a range of different disbursements: payments to grandchildren, the cleaning of a clock, the purchase of a mustard pot, servants' wages and Christmas boxes, and an upholsterer's bill. The final section of this volume is 'Receivings', running from

---

[121] Receipt for Elizabeth Woodhouse, 14 June 1791, York City Archives: Acc 54: 24B.
[122] Housekeeping account book of Elizabeth Forth, 1792–3, f. 111.
[123] 'Account Book for Housekeeping for the Year 1798—John and Eliz[t]: Forth', York City Archives: Acc 54:5, f. 36.
[124] Extracts from acct bks and diary of Elizabeth Forth, 1793–1815, ff. 4, 15.
[125] Vickery adopts this approach to the Forth's marital home in *Behind Closed Doors*, pp. 224–7.
[126] Hunt, *Middling Sort*, pp. 166–70.

1812 to 1825. These comprise mainly payments from William to Faith for the housekeeping, and these payments are part of a larger accounting system. The section ends with a final total made by William for the year 1825, and then a note made on the occasion of his wife's death in December 1826: 'And, for the future, in consequence of her lamented death, this separate account of sums received ceases, and only that of disbursements will be continued, taken from W. G.ʸ cash book.'[127] With Faith's death, of course, there was no need for William to record the receivings, though he did continue to note the disbursements pertaining to the house in the same manner. There was overlap between the accounts kept by William and Faith, with both documents detailing work on their property and including entries for food and drink. William's ledger encompassed extensive business and personal transactions, and several pages of payments to at least nine servants between 1804 and 1825.[128] The joint accounts kept by Faith were very broad, but included entries more closely tied to the functioning of the house. Alongside many bills for household products and services, then, it is in this volume, rather than William's, that we find recorded the purchase of three damask table cloths in 1813 and twelve wine glasses in 1817.[129] Men's accounts do not provide rounded information about spousal responsibilities, but they do show that men were involved in the household at many different levels. Some men engaged at the local or micro level through consumption, yet men's accounts are particularly voluble on men's global management of the household at the macro level.

In some cases, then, the wife to whom the payment was made 'for the house' kept her own accounts. Significantly, there are some cases in which this role was superseded by the husband. In his retrospective family records, Benjamin Shaw presents his wife Betty as a poor household manager. Finally reaching exasperation, he wrested the task of accounting from her in 1823: 'on the 5 of april I turned tyrant', he declares, and demanded detailed accounts on household expenses for some months to follow.[130] Betty had kept the household accounts for years and Benjamin's intervention was, by his own reckoning, an extreme step. Nevertheless, the act is presented as an assertion of his authority rather than an upturning of gender roles. This connection between male authority and accounts is also striking in the case of the East Riding schoolmaster Robert Sharp. The couple ran a shop from 1828 to 1833, though this was clearly Ann's domain; as Robert himself wrote, 'My wife is an excellent Shopkeeper', while his own efforts were 'sometimes little better than hindrance'.[131] He reports a series of comic events when left alone as shopkeeper. An accident with two ounces of snuff precipitated a sneezing fit, while antics with flour and then treacle meant that 'where these two came in contact, I was tolerably pasted'.[132] Inept in such matters, Robert was evidently competent in other areas. While Ann had the authority to pay suppliers, it seems Robert kept the accounts. Facing legal action from a disgruntled miller who believed he was

[127] 'Accts of Wm and Faith Gray', 'Receivings' 1825, f. 162.
[128] Ledger of William Gray, Gray Family Papers, York City Archives: Acc 24 A1, ff. 123–6.
[129] 'Accts of Wm and Faith Gray', f. 16; 4.41.
[130] *The Family records of Benjamin Shaw*, p. 64.
[131] *Diary of Robert Sharp*, pp. 229, 231.   [132] Ibid. pp. 210, 303.

owed payment, Ann remained resolute: 'my wife says if ever he comes again she will order him out, and if he will not go she says she will turn him out.' '[H]e is but a little fellow', added Robert, 'and she knows she can manage him.'[133] Two weeks later the miller was back with further demands. Sharp reported: 'told him I believed he was paid the whole as I paid him myself; but he was not convinced until I shewed him the account settled by himself. This was a stunner, in fact nothing further could be said by him.'[134] Robert Sharp had much accounting experience. In addition to schoolmaster, he was parish officer responsible for tax assessment and collecting, he acted for the government selling the official stamps required on legal documents, and he was clerk to the village friendly society. Good accounting, he believed, was necessary to effective working relations; he felt it was 'disagreeable' and tiresome to deal with a man who could not keep good accounts.[135] In contrast to Ann's stalwart truculence, her heated words, and the implied threat of physical violence, it is the act of showing the physical account during a meeting at a public house that resolves the dispute and establishes the Sharps' probity. Little wonder that in a discussion of his son's hopeful prospects, Robert Sharp gently underlined the importance of accounts to his son William: 'I know you are qualified to keep all your accounts correctly, which you will of course take a pride in doing.'[136] A labouring man, Benjamin Shaw nevertheless had much in common with Robert Sharp: for both, literacy and numeracy was a source of manly pride.

APPLYING THE ACCOUNTING MODE

Plainly, account books were works of writing and it is worth noting that men often described writing as a task of work or 'business' that occupied them for long periods and that reflected their ability to discipline themselves and order the world around them. Their records often comment on the practice of writing itself. The anonymous bachelor diarist in Bath was occupied with, 'Business which comprehends writing, drawing, and giving directions to others—working myself—and a great variety of articles that must constantly be remember'd to prevent complaint—then my own private employ—reading (just now) Newton's optics—copying some of Worlidge's Etchings—instructing my Painters—writing to my Friends—writing for my own amusement.'[137] Living in central London, John Stede reported in many of his diary entries how he 'wrote mostly', while for the month of March 1754 he 'busied in accts' every day.[138] He frequently spent his time engaging in 'Dom' affairs, activities that usually took the form of religious devotion or keeping accounts, and

---

[133] Ibid. p. 262. [134] Ibid. p. 263. [135] Ibid. p. 229.

[136] Robert Sharp to William Sharp, 25 December 1821, *Diary of Robert Sharp*, p. 9.

[137] 'Bath Diary for 1769', 27 January.

[138] Diary of John Bradley (1723–29, 1754), Nostell Priory WYL1352 1215–1986, West Yorkshire Archive Service, Leeds: NP A3/2/ (1718): for example, 8 and 9 April 1754, and March 1754. David Hunter has convincingly identified John Stede as the author, rather than John Bradley. See David Hunter, 'What the Prompter Saw: The Diary of Rich's Prompter, John Stede', in Jeremy Barlow and Berta Joncus (eds), *The Stage's Glory: John Rich (1692–1761)* (Newark, Delaware: University of Delaware Press, 2010), p. 70. I thank David Hunter for sending me an advance copy of this.

which Stede described as 'necess[aries]'.[139] John Bradley's diary depicts a personal struggle to discipline himself, beginning with a list of the things he must and must not do, and the rather stark declaration: 'Man's Life being one continu'd Warfare, occasion'd by the Depravity of his Nature, and the continual Solicitations and Importunity of his Enemy, it is of the utmost Importance that he be ever on his Guard.'[140] In the light of his frequent reports of personal failure, Bradley's insistence on having 'busied' suggests that writing was a prophylactic against depravity within and solicitations without. Writing was a time-consuming business.

The account book inscribed by Timothy Tyrell junior provides a good example of how numeracy and literacy were brought together in accounts. This book had functioned as an account book of Timothy Tyrell from 1724, and following his death in 1766 another family member continued to keep rental accounts. During the 1760s, though, the book functioned as an exercise account book as well as a working account book, with pages laid out as a student's workbook with spaces in which to enter the answers to the calculations. Many of the accounts pre-date the mathematical calculations, then, but the latter were inserted in the volume with the earlier accounting function continuing. On one page, details of rents received in spring 1763 onwards are written around the calculations concerning the unit cost per yard of a piece of cloth.[141] On the left edge of some of the pages there are headers written in a diminutive and understated hand: examples include a Mouse, a Horse, a Mule, a Goldsmith, a Lady, a Lord. Beneath the header 'a good girl', the page is filled with the demonstrative, 'Timothy Tyrrell/24th January 1768', surrounded by large curlicue flourishes. The book was now in the hands of Timothy Tyrell junior, and it is perhaps his mother—who lived until 1787—who guided her son in this practice. The volume clearly served as a pedagogic tool in the boy's education in writing and arithmetic, and perhaps other members of the family before him. Below his inscription, the student applied his arithmetic learning, adding:

Born January 19th. 1755/
And is now   1768
                               1755
                          ─────────
                               13[142]

Women's account books showed the similar workbook features, though I have not located a working account book from a middling-sort woman. A rare example is Rebecca Steel's account book—'Began February 16th/Rebecca Steel/Her accompt. Book/Anno 1702'. Here, mathematical exercises on addition, subtraction, multiplication, and division are transformed into narrative problems. Answers are given (in the same hand) with calligraphic flourishes of red, green, and gold ink around that have now faded to brown, sometimes metamorphosing into delicate images such as trumpet-blowing cupids.[143] Steel went to great lengths to embellish her

[139] Diary of John Bradley, 26 February 1754.   [140] Diary of John Bradley, f. 1.
[141] [Tyrell], 'Account book', f. 98.   [142] Ibid. f. 57.
[143] Account book of Rebecca Steel, *passim*; quote at f. 1.

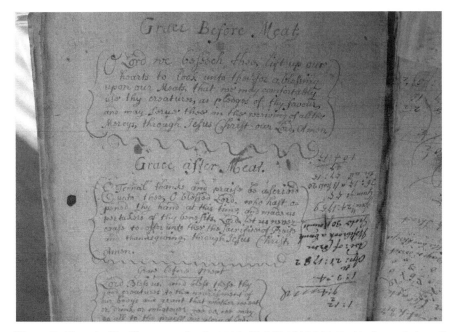

Figure 5: Timothy Tyrell's account book, 1734–66, MS 1945.001. By kind permission of The William Andrews Clark Memorial Library, University of California, Los Angeles.

exercises, many of which concern merchants and were likely drawn from a work such as James Hodder's *Hodder's Arithmetic* (1702) or one of Edward Cocker's many works on penmanship or arithmetic.[144] Steel's book is instructive on how accounts combined numeracy and literacy in works of talented penmanship.

Daniel Renaud's commonplace book shows how writers continued to combine the literary and algebraic later in life. From the front the volume consists mostly of poems, riddles, bon mots, and epigrams, copied from publications including *The Lady's Magazine*, with nothing of a personal note. From the back of the book the material is very different. Here there are notes and hints on algebra and complex calculations. This section begins with an indicative memorandum: 'If numbers are in Direct proportion the product of ye two Extreams will always be equal to ye product of ye Means.'[145] Produced from one of his breeches' pockets, this volume would have stood as testament to Renaud's education, practical knowledge, useful occupation, and impressive range of high-status skills. Indeed, these volumes combined household accounts and many other kind of record. The example from

---

[144] Edward Cocker, *Cockers Arithmetick, being a plain and familiar method suitable to the meanest capacity for the full understanding of that incomparable art* (London, 1678); Edward Cocker, *Cocker's Arithmetick: being a plain and familiar method, suitable to the meanest Capacity for the full understanding of that incomparable art*, 22nd edition (London, 1702); James Hodder, *Hodder's Arithmetick: or, that necessary art made most easie* (London, 1702).

[145] Commonplace book of Daniel Renaud, 1751–63, William Andrews Clark Memorial Library: MS.1977.007, *passim*, quote from f. 1 from the back.

Elizabeth Forth's housekeeping book demonstrated that women mixed different kinds of events in their records; the practice was common to both men and women. Edmund Pilkington's volume combined accounts alongside a list of pupils at the school where he was master, a narrative of family leases, and musical notation.[146] Conversely, accounts were written on other kinds of document, including letters and scraps of paper. Some so-called 'accounts' were kept irregularly, such as the highly selective records of the merchant Christopher Tuthill, which in fact constitute inventories often without numerical value.[147]

The combination of different kinds of record meant that, while account books were used to record regular receipts and disbursements, they also recorded other types of event. Away from his Durham estate and residing in Queen Square, London at the age of 58, Francis Blake's personal account book for 1765 included many non-monetary entries amongst purchases of bread rolls and coffee. Sometimes these are very brief, such as his notes about where he had dinner—'Dined at Ld Mortons' or 'Dined at Home'—or how he had spent his time alone: 'May 5, Trist: Shandy', for example.[148] Such diary-like entries generally occur every few days, but Blake also made entries that increasingly combined accounts with longer and more fulsome descriptions. On 28 October 1765 he notes, 'I sent from Cranwell[?] an Order to my Son to receive #80 of Robert Harigad on or before Martimass day.'[149] In the second extant volume of Blake's accounts, for the years 1769 to 1771, entries gloss purchases with lengthy descriptions that record a busy social life.[150] This includes his retrospective report on 31 December 1770, 'On Xmas day the Gout raged so that I was forced to have a Bed laid on the dining Room Floor, to which I am still confined', and the subsequent comment on 27 January, 'I rode an Airing in the Chaise & ordered the bed out of the Dining Room, for the first Time since Xmas day.'[151] Rather than (or perhaps as well as) entering these details directly into a diary or letter, Blake uses the lined and columned account book as the repository for his notes about the day. Blake's practice of itemizing financial transactions is the prompt for him to also record a number of extra-monetary details about those transactions. In this volume, as in many others, the accounting template was imposed on non-monetary matters.

A different practice was used in Thomas Mort's account book, who used his account book to record all manner of local and household memoranda.[152] The first page indicates how the volume served as combined memorandum and account

[146] See [Pilkington] Account book, *passim*.

[147] The commonplace book of Christopher Tuthill, 1681–1858, William Andrews Clark Memorial Library: MS.1977.003, *passim*. See Chapter 4, pp. 119–21, for a more detailed discussion.

[148] Blake, 'Acct Book from 1 January 1765 to 22 February 1766', 3 February 1765, 8 March 1765, 5 May 1765. See Gordon Goodwin, 'Blake, Sir Francis, first baronet (1707/8–1780)', rev Joseph Gross, *Oxford Dictionary of National Biography*, Oxford University Press, 2004 <http://www.oxforddnb.com/view/article/2577> (accessed 22 July 2005).

[149] Blake, 'Acct Book from 1 January 1765 to 22 February 1766', f. 4, 18 October 1765.

[150] See Chapter 6, pp. 177–8, for fuller discussion of some of these entries.

[151] Francis Blake, 'Accts. from 11th August 1769 to 1st January 1771', William Andrews Clark Memorial Library: MS.1985.002, f. 22, 27 January 1770.

[152] John and Sylvia Tonge, *Astley Hall (Damhouse)* (John and Sylvia Tonge, 2002), pp. 7–10.

book. The page displays 21 monetary entries written horizontally across the page from left to right, beginning with £3 6s 0d paid to Sam Stockton, and ending with £5 10s 0d paid to Sarah Buidock. Squeezed in between two entries horizontally is the correction, 'Mr Wilson . . . dyed Apr: yᵉ 8th & was Buryed Apr: yᵉ 12th'. Additionally, Mort kept notes on the vertical plane: half way down the page, written vertically across three of the values listed horizontally, is the remark: 'my friend Mʳ Wilson dyed Apr: yᵉ: 12 1703 his Wife dyed November: 30th 1704'.[153] Similar combinations of entry continue throughout this closely written book. On 7 January 1706 Mort was invited to a funeral; on 7 December 1708 he wondered if he might re-employ a servant, though only if his brother and sister are willing; and on 8 August 1721, he made a long entry recording the death of that brother, along with a Mr Hamond.[154] A similar kind of horizontal entry appears later, on 19 January 1724, with Mort writing, 'Mr Miles Barret marry'd to Mrs Grace Chaddock', and then detailing when, where and by whom, adding that 'Mrs Elizabeth Wells Bridemaid [*sic*]'. To the right side of the entry, along the spine, Mort added the signpost, 'Mr Barret & Mrs Chaddock married.'[155] The clear pointer to this non-monetary entry suggests that it was used as a repository for varied kinds of information to which Thomas Mort would later return.

Accounts were very often mixed forms of record. This hybridity was due in part to the origins of the practice in 'spiritual accounting', in which men saw God as the source of all credit and debt, and tallied their losses and gains in matters of the soul with the intention of giving a good account of themselves to Him.[156] Adam Smyth argues that in the sixteenth and seventeenth centuries financial accounting was a distinct mode having its own effect on life-writing, and certainly by the late eighteenth century accounting had been cleaved from its spiritual roots.[157] Writing in 1795, the Revd Thornhill Kidd saw book-keeping as tethered firmly to 'this world and its concerns', distracting him from the 'eternal state' on which he wished to focus.[158] Yet even if apparently devoid of a larger Christian framework, accounts from throughout the long eighteenth century show a 'personal' accounting that combined key family events and milestones in a man's personal history with details of monetary value.

A striking case of this form of recording is found in the notebook and account books of Daniel Renaud. Completed alongside the commonplace book considered above, these volumes also show how men refined the records they kept over long periods of time. Daniel Renaud was born on 29 May 1697. Rector of Whitchurch from 1728, he married his wife Christiana Button—born on the same day—on 19 May 1728, and went on to have five children, Mary, David, Ann, Elizabeth, and Daniel. Completed by his successor, the parish registers of Whitchurch recorded his

[153] Account book of Thomas Mort, f. 1, 23 March 1703ff.
[154] Ibid. 7 January 1706, 7 December 1708, 8 August 1721.
[155] Ibid. 19 January 1724.
[156] Muldrew, *Economy of Obligation*, pp. 144–6.
[157] Adam Smyth, *Autobiography in Early Modern England* (Cambridge: Cambridge University Press, 2010), pp. 55–122, esp. pp. 118–21.
[158] 'Memoirs of the late Revd Thornhill Kidd chiefly transcribed from his Letters and Diary', University of Sheffield Special Collections: MS102, p. 10, 18 February 1795.

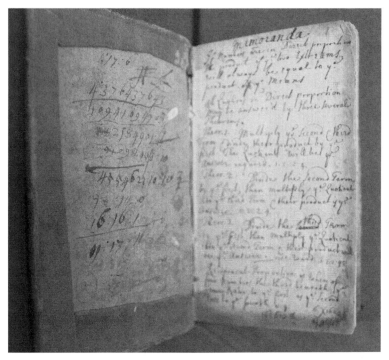

Figure 6: Daniel Renaud, Account book [*c.*1769], William Andrews Clark Memorial Library: MS.1977.008. By kind permission of The William Andrews Clark Memorial Library, University of California, Los Angeles.

burial on 25 June 1772, and Christiana's on 24 May 1787.[159] Renaud was a compulsive record keeper. There are three volumes of his personal records now extant, one notebook (in the Herefordshire Record Office) and two account books (in the William Andrews Clark Memorial Library). Much of the content is overlapping, and the tremendous challenge of identifying the order of compilation is testament to Renaud's complicated system of record keeping. Handwriting is one key. Renaud's Bishop's Transcripts from 1732 and 1770 demonstrate the change in hand as he aged.[160] His will of December 1770 confirms the much less steady and smaller writing of his old age.[161] The Herefordshire notebook was completed from 1732 until at least 1765, and displays the neat, rounded, and large handwriting of the younger man.[162] The manuscripts now at the Clark Library show the younger and later hands: sections

---

[159] Transcript of Whitchurch Parish Registers (1927), Herefordshire Record Office: B39/1. I thank John Harnden for his assistance.

[160] 'A True Transcript of the Marriages, Christnings & Buryins in the Parish of Whitchurch', March 1732 to March 1733 and January 1770 to December 1771, Herefordshire Record Office.

[161] 'The will of Daniel Renaud, 1770', Herefordshire Record Office: Probate series AA20, Box Number 334, June–September 1772.

[162] Notebook of Revd Daniel Renaud, 1730–1769, Herefordshire Record Office: A98/1.

were composed at the same time as the Herefordshire notebook, and the Clark account book (dated 1752–1777) in particular contains much duplicated information entered in the same young hand. If we take Renaud's land at Differnant's Court, for example, the Herefordshire volume recorded the tithes paid for the property, as well as the expenses of the barn and garden wall in 1742, and the 'New Roofing of the House wth Pan tiles & Ceiling [*sic*] &c' in 1746. The last entry on this page recorded the letting of the property in 1750 for 21 years.[163] Later in this volume he gives details of his repairs to the Differnant Estate after buying it from Mr Gwillam in 1739 for £174.[164] The page for Differnant's Court in the Clark account book has much less information, and gives details of repairs separately, but it does record the expiration of the rental in February 1771.[165] One entry gives a clearer suggestion of the order of compilation. Renaud's list of Mr Dusoul's goods, which he purchased in 1736, was noted in both of the volumes. Crucially, the list in the Clark volume gives value to all items, including a candlestick, cravat, and writing paper. The entry in the Herefordshire volume, however, merges the last three into an entry valued at 5s 6d.[166] The Herefordshire volume must surely be the copy, though Renaud continued to update the rougher Clark account book for longer.

The bulk of the second Clark account book dated *c.*1769 was completed later, beginning with record of a Mr Hallings beginning to officiate at a parish in April 1768.[167] The subsequent page is in a younger hand, and entries here appear to start from 1731, but the majority of this volume is clearly made late in Renaud's life.[168] Renaud used this to record significant milestones. '[F]inish'd the Barn at Differnant' and 'Enter'd upon the Criggals' are two such entries.[169] The former refers to the completion of building work on the Differnant Estate, having purchased it in 1739.[170] The latter referred to his purchase of James Workman's lease of the arable land the Criggals for 25 years in September 1742, recorded in the Herefordshire notebook.[171] These are the two properties he bequeathed to his wife, to be passed to his youngest son Daniel upon her death, in his will of 1770.[172] Yet this later volume did not contain only family-related records; it comprised copies of many older documents, as well as records of Whitchurch tithes made by the clerk. This account book consists largely of accounts and copies of legal agreements, but also some miscellaneous items: lists of the men serving on the local manorial court, names of the woods belonging to Whitchurch and the tithes collected for them, a copy of the bond which transferred one of Renaud's properties to his second son

[163] Ibid. f. 16.   [164] Ibid. ff. 38–9.

[165] Daniel Renaud, Account book [1752–1777], William Andrews Clark Memorial Library: MS.1977.009, f. 16v. See ff. 36–7 for details of the repairs to this property listed separately.

[166] Renaud, Account book [1752–1777], f. 39; Notebook of Revd Daniel Renaud, f. 40.

[167] Daniel Renaud, Account book [*c.*1769], William Andrews Clark Memorial Library: MS.1977.008, f. 1.

[168] Ibid. f. 3.

[169] Ibid. f. 39.

[170] Ibid. ff. 38–9.

[171] Notebook of Revd Daniel Renaud, f. 37.

[172] Will of Reverend David Renaud, Clerk of Havant, Hampshire, 9 October 1807: Public Record Office: PROB 11/1469.

Daniel, and a copy of the articles of agreement between the master of the workhouse in Hereford and the Parish of Whitchurch for the maintenance of their poor. This volume served as account book, legal repository, genealogical record and family history, and combined Renaud's role as son, nephew, father, and husband with that of Rector at Whitchurch.

All three documents contain different versions of the Renaud's personal and family memoranda. 'Memoranda relating to Myself &c' in the Herefordshire note-book consists of three pages of 79 lines covering the years 1697 to 1762.[173] 'Memoranda Relating to Myself' in the Clark account book (dated 1752–1777) is a slightly edited version, consisting of 62 lines over two and half pages.[174] Both these volumes have other separate sections of memoranda, for example relating to Renaud's uncle. The second Clark account book combines the personal and other memoranda into one section of 'Memoranda' of 152 lines spread over four and a half pages, which begins with Renaud's small elderly hand.[175] Just as early modern manuals on book-keeping advised that information from the two preparatory books (the waste-Book and Journal) be copied into the Ledger,[176] so Renaud copied out this material several times, making minor changes on each occasion. There are some consistent features of these Memoranda, though, and the set of events are recorded in faux-monetary form. In the version he made most latterly, beginning with his birth in Neuchatel, the memoranda record Renaud's education and early career, followed by his arrival at Whitchurch on 20 April 1728.[177] His uncle arrived in Whitchurch on 7 May '& kept House'.[178] Renaud was soon afterwards married to Christiana on 19 May, they lived at Walcote and had their first baby (Mary). Renaud's uncle married his maid and 'left the Place' on 12 May 1730, and it was later that month that Daniel and Christiana 'Settled at Whitch'.[179] Following a list of the couple's other children, Renaud's record changes. The volume continues to record notable family events—the children's survival of chicken pox, the catching of an 8-foot sturgeon—but now begins to incorporate accounts. Much of this is family-related, a great many entries detailing the costs of the children's education (particularly that of his youngest son, Daniel, who followed in his father's footsteps and was ordained in 1754),[180] but these entries are interspersed with the sale of wood and wheat and the collection of tithes. The second account book ends with

---

[173] Notebook of Revd Daniel Renaud, ff. 86–8.

[174] Renaud, Account book [1752–1777], ff. 68–70.

[175] Renaud, Account book [c.1769], ff. 37–45.

[176] See, for example, Robert Colinson, *Idea Rationaria, or The Perfect Accomptant, necessary for all Merchants and Trafficquers* (London, 1683); William Webster, *An Essay on Book-Keeping, According to the Italian Method of Debtor and Creditor* (London, 1721); James Dodson, *The Accountant, or, The Method of Book-keeping, Deduced from Clear Principles* (London, 1750).

[177] Renaud, Account book [c.1769], f. 37.

[178] Renaud, Account book [1752–1777], f. 66.

[179] Renaud, Account book [c.1769], f. 37.

[180] Ibid. ff. 39–40. Education was an important and large cost for such households, also taking away children's labour from the household economy. See H. R. French and R. W. Hoyle, *The Character of English Rural Society: Earls Colne, 1550–1750* (Manchester and New York: Manchester University Press, 2007), p. 38.

a record that his sons' wives have each been brought to bed of sons of their own.[181] Renaud was importing the form of his parish registers into his personal records, a practice common by this time.[182] He was also registering important family events simultaneously with a process of accounting, adopting the book-keeping method that he employed so vigorously in his life as Rector in order to organize his personal life. In each of his volumes, most space is taken up with monetary accounts of his household, family, and the St Dubricius estate. For such men, book-keeping evidenced 'rational, manly attention to the details of family life'.[183] Accounts evidenced men's engagement with domestic expenditure, sustained the status arising from being a good manager and generated important stores of information.

Daniel Renaud must have kept even more detailed and various accounts, almost certainly on a daily basis. The complicated process involved in such record keeping can be seen from the surviving manuscripts of Edmund Herbert. Herbert, a civil servant who remained unmarried, worked in the Pay Office of the Marine Forces, was a member of Gray's Inn in London, and was made assistant to the Paymaster on 14 July 1740. On appointment, he was given a list of instructions which included, 'to form and draw up general Rules & Instructions proper for the Guidance of the Paymaster', and 'to correspond with the said Paymaster while he is abroad & to receive and adjust the Accompts to be returned by him into my Office at Whitehall'.[184] Given the administrative duties of this post, it is not surprising that he should leave a collection of finely written and carefully maintained personal accounts. What is more surprising, perhaps, is that these accounts include so many personal memoranda: like Renaud, his papers show that Herbert applied the same model of order to his financial accounts and also to his personal and social life.

In the early years of his expense accounts from 1708–1733, Herbert wrote out some transactions at least three times. He would have brought home small individual bills and notes of payments, and from this assemblage he would have begun the records that remain extant today. Probably writing on a daily basis, he recorded these transactions on fragile strips of paper, beginning a new sheet each month. Edmund numbered these strips, and used one side for transactions and the other for memos, this latter category including notes about transactions, travelling, drinking, and acquaintances. One strip notes the death of a Mrs Ellen Perkins on 'Thursd. Yᵉ 18th betw, 5 & 6 in yᵉ morn. in yᵉ 18th yʳ of her Age'.[185] There remain several bundles of these strips, all neatly folded into small packages, with the year and the total expenses written on the front. For each year, these monthly accounts were then copied into different sections of a string-bound volume according to type of expense: for 1708, for example, these included 'Books & pamphlets', 'necessary expenses', 'expenses in generosity', 'expenses in cloaths', 'gain'd [at gam-

[181] Renaud, Account book [*c*.1769], f. 41.
[182] Smyth, *Autobiography in Early Modern England*, pp. 159–208.
[183] Lemire, *Business of Everyday Life*, p. 10.
[184] Herbert Family Papers, Henry E. Huntington Library: Box 3, HE354, f. 2.
[185] Herbert Family Papers, Henry E. Huntington Library: Edmund Herbert's Expense Accounts 1708–1733, Box 11, HE100 (1) 1708, no 18 (November 1708), f. 3.

bling]', 'lost [at gambling]', and a final section of Memoranda.[186] Herbert clearly revisited these second recordings from time to time in later years. Having recorded in the bound volume for 29 June 1708, 'I promis'd to note in my Poct. Book y^t Mrs Jane Atterbury will be married only of a Tuesday or of a Thursday', he later added a small note to the left, 'She was accordingly married to...at Temple Bar Tuesday 12 February 1711/12'.[187] Some of these would then be copied out a third time into a general account book. Men needed to take a long view over their affairs. As such, they had to keep records in such a way that allowed them to be checked much later and copy out their records repeatedly as the system was revised. Herbert's papers demonstrate that he refined his system of record-keeping over his lifetime. Over time, Edmund abandoned keeping accounts according to type, and the monthly accounts were only copied—if at all—into the general account books. This latter, third document, sought to give over a page to a separate person or account: 'Venison', 'Lottery Tickets', 'Sister Herbert', and 'My Dear Father', for example. Besides each single entry Herbert entered a tick, perhaps indicating that it was then entered one further time into another document, no longer extant.[188] At the same time that Herbert was creating monetary records, he was imposing regularity and order on his personal experiences.

The bundles of Herbert's papers are striking material objects, as well as being illuminating texts. For all their volume and extent, they show merely the later stages of accounting and only hint at the tremendous effort of writing, re-writing, and organizing that these practices required. We might see them as the material remains of the 'process of continual achievement' of being middling sort.[189] All large households employed such practices, of course. Managing the considerable household and estate at Cannons, James Brydges orchestrated an extensive paper network. In a letter to his principal secretary, he informs Farquharson that he will send 'a List of Payments' and 'Smyth's weekly Accounts', to be merged with the others in Farquharson's possession. At the same time he also sends the account of a tenant in Bath, together with a list of her goods, and instructs Farquharson to enter the former into 'the Book' and the latter to 'the Inventory'. While he believes some accounts may be in 'my Desk at Cannons', he is not quite sure where the inventory could be, though suspects it lies in the hands of another of his stewards.[190] Fire and flooding were just two real threats to paper records, so accounts were not simply recorded in more than one form but were also produced in multiple sets of duplicates.[191] The size of such a paper industry mirrored the size of the estate and also reflected the disposition of the manager. Chandos was a particularly enthusiastic

[186] Edmund Herbert's Expense Accounts, Box 11, HE100 (1) 1708, *passim*.

[187] Edmund Herbert's Expense Accounts, Box 11, HE100 (1), 1708, f. 17.

[188] Herbert Family Papers, Henry E. Huntington Library: Edmund Herbert's account book, 1705–30, HE99, ff. 37 and 44; f. 38; f. 64; f. 67.

[189] Muldrew, *Economy of Obligation*, p. 299.

[190] Brydges family papers, Henry E. Huntington Library: STB Correspondence, Box 13 (8), James Brydges to James Farquharson, 27 June 1730.

[191] Brydges family papers, STB Correspondence, Box 13 (48), James Brydges to James Farquharson, 26 October 1730.

household manager. Yet the practices of Chandos were related to those of Herbert and others. While Herbert was later assistant to a paymaster, Chandos had himself been paymaster of the queen's forces from 1705 to 1713.[192] Vigilance in household record-keeping was perhaps in these cases a direct result of integration into the bureaucratic processes of government.

Yet men who were further removed from the operations of central government had similarly extensive systems of paperwork. The latest accounts we have for Edmund Pilkington are for October 1732, concluding with the comment, 'Continued this method in a paper book with a blue back'.[193] Similarly, in the account book of the Tyrell family, the later entries from the 1760s are annotated with references to the 'New Book', suggesting calculations were carried over.[194] Henry Richardson's account book of 1748–1753 was almost certainly a final and retrospective version assembled from a rougher volume or loose sheaf of papers. For example, the entry for the purchase of 'a Book of Offices for Thornton Church', for which he paid 2s 6d on 14 March 1748, is followed immediately on the next line by the note 'NB the Church Wardens repaid Me September: 23^d: 1749'. Expectant of the Church Wardens' repayment, Richardson may have left a line blank when he compiled the accounts in March; but the continuation of the pressure and style of the hand and the colour of the ink suggests rather that he has written the March 1748 entries after September 1749.[195] It took a considerable investment of time and effort to create and maintain these paper records. These accounting records also represent a series of carefully executed practices of ordering, a mindset of managing. And, as already discussed, these records suggest that this mindset encompassed more than the monetary. It should not surprise us, of course, that the role of financial manager was complicated by personal relationships, particularly as much of men's work was not only conducted within the house but amongst family members. The same connections were present for women involved in these activities; tradeswomen as well as men operated in commercial and family networks.[196] We have seen how men's engagements with the house were intricately connected to their activities in business, commerce, and farming. Distinctions between 'domestic' and 'business' were murky at best. Participants in the common cause of the household, the records of men and women naturally overlap. As these numeric records developed into a 'standard societal curriculum' in the nineteenth century, they show a landscape 'set within a wider gendered economy, transcending the public/private dichotomy'.[197] In men's global household accounting records, though, the integration of different kinds of information is indicative not simply

---

[192] Joan Johnson, 'Brydges, James, first duke of Chandos (1674–1744)', *Oxford Dictionary of National Biography*, Oxford University Press, 2004 <http://www.oxforddnb.com/view/article/3806> (accessed 5 June 2009).

[193] [Pilkington] Account book, f. 157.

[194] [Tyrell], 'Account book', fol. 77ff.

[195] Richardson, 'A Diary of Disbursements', March 1748.

[196] Hunt, *Middling Sort*, passim; Barker, *Business of Women*, passim; Phillips, *Women in Business*, pp. 95–172.

[197] Lemire, *Business of Everyday Life*, p. 231.

of the connections between these areas but of the manner in which men ordered them within an integrated system of management.

CONCLUSION

Commenting on the blurring of diaries and account books in the long seventeenth century, Craig Muldrew notes that, 'economic events were recorded, not as simple numeric transactions but as *social* exchanges between individuals'.[198] The rational world of economics had not yet been separated from the 'subjective' world of personal emotions and experiences.[199] This chapter has, by contrast, shown that a genre of accounting, well established in print, was in practice used to accommodate an array of different types of information, or aligned with other forms of record in mixed volumes. Continuing a well-developed practice amongst early modern elites, accounts were 'interpretative' and accommodated the social, familial, and personal.[200] These writings did not record all the transactions that took place in households, as the common entries for unspecified 'house use' demonstrate, yet they do document a significant amount of domestic activity. These sources are testament to men's actual and varied activities in the household economy. Yet I remain cautious about how much we can garner about decision-making in household consumption, or men's and women's roles in food preparation, from men's itemizing of the related goods, and particularly pessimistic about an accurate comparative study of men's and women's activities from this material. As evidence of a discourse comprising writing and practices, however, accounting records articulated some central features of men's engagements with the domestic. The mixed form of entry is testament not to the impossibility of separating this information, but to the logic of keeping it together. These household archives recorded personal events as numeric events and alongside information relating to the household economy and wider networks of exchange. These manuscripts show, first, that men engaged with the non-monetary aspects of family life partly through accounting practices. Second, these manuscripts show that while men necessarily engaged with small-scale household consumption, they managed all the resources of the household economy—economic and otherwise—at an overarching or global level. Third, these sometimes extensive and highly skilled manuscripts express the cultural authority of men's management. As the early part of this chapter discussed, men's speech and writing demonstrates that oeconomy was one important resource in defining masculinity. The accounting records of men show that men viewed the family as a unit of oeconomy. Though men struggled with the difficulties of living an oeconomical life, oeconomy was a way of seeing, thinking, and living, and that operated materially through words and practices.

[198] Muldrew, *Economy of Obligation*, p. 64.
[199] Ibid. p. 65. See also, Craig Muldrew, 'The Culture of Reconciliation: Community and the Settlement of Economic Disputes in Early Modern England', *Historical Journal*, 39, 4 (December, 1996), p. 923.
[200] Smyth, *Autobiography in Early Modern England*, pp. 72–104. Quote at p. 104.

4

Keeping House

On 27 February 1748, the West Riding rector Henry Richardson recorded a payment he made to William Hudson of 11d for a 'small hard Brush'.[1] In 1754, the Durham cattle dealer Ralph Ward reported the flagging of the 'fore kitching' in his new house.[2] Much later, in his letters and diary of the 1810s, 20s, and 30s, Robert Sharp, the Yorkshire schoolmaster, noted ordering a pint of ale to accompany the family dinner, commented on the family's acquisition of 'a new Arm Chair, to match with the others', and concerned himself with the things that he and his wife packed in their son's box before sending it off to William in London.[3] And in a richly evocative image, John Darracott, merchant in Bideford, North Devon, in 1730, described how his children, 'Like olive plants surrounded my Table'.[4] Material things of many different kinds litter the writings that men penned in and about their domestic spaces. In men's account and commonplace books, their diaries, and letters, the texture of everyday physical domestic life is palpable. This chapter examines the domestic objects and spaces that were meaningful for men, and explores how men's domestic engagement and domestic authority was legitimized by some of these objects.

Objects are a central part of our understanding of eighteenth-century domestic life. A new culture of 'home' was created partly out of new consumer goods, while the momentous shifts in consumption practices and the nature of commodities was driven in large part by demand for domestic goods.[5] The emphasis in many studies is on the consumption of these new items, often by women, to create a feminized domestic interior. This newly decorated interior has also been identified

[1] Henry Richardson, 'A Diary of Disbursements since January yᵉ first 1748 The First Year after I was Married', West Yorkshire Archive Service, Wakefield: C658, 27 February 1748.
[2] *Two Yorkshire Diaries: The Diary of Arthur Jessop and Ralph Ward's Journal*, ed. C. E. Whiting (Leeds: Yorkshire Archaeological Society, vol. 117, 1951), p. 141.
[3] *The Diary of Robert Sharp of South Cave: Life in a Yorkshire Village, 1812–1837*, ed. Janice E. Crowther and Peter A Crowther (Records of Social and Economic History, New Series 26, For the British Academy, by Oxford University Press, 1997), 1 August 1826, p. 53; 30 January 1833, p. 402; and letters on pp. 1–32.
[4] Diary of John Darracott, 1707–30, William Andrews Clark Memorial Library: MS.1950.010, f. 201.
[5] Jan de Vries, 'Between Purchasing Power and the World of Goods: Understanding the Household Economy in Early Modern Europe', in John Brewer and Roy Porter (eds), *Consumption and the World of Goods* (London and New York: Routledge, 1993), pp. 85–132; Jan de Vries, 'The Industrial Revolution and the Industrious Revolution', *Journal of Economic History*, 54 (1994), pp. 249–70; Jan de Vries, *The Industrious Revolution: Consumer Behavior and the Household Economy, 1650 to the present* (Cambridge: Cambridge University Press, 2008).

as one of the central planks of a middling-sort identity: the 'middle classes invested the home and its furnishings with monetary value and material comforts but they also believed that it expressed social, cultural, emotional and religious attitudes'; this investment in domesticity during the eighteenth century drove changes in the domestic culture of lower and higher social ranks in subsequent decades.[6] Attending to representation rather than practice, others have demonstrated the powerful contemporary connections between women and femininity on the one hand and consumption on the other, though—as we have seen—several historians have also sought to identify the particular kinds of objects associated with men and women respectively.[7] While we might expect—and there is indeed evidence for—differences in some of the things that men and women selected and bought, it is not entirely clear that women consumed more of the material things from which 'home' was made. Rich but scattered comments in a handful of men's diaries may not sustain the view that men were active in the 'acquiring and display' of domestic items.[8] Yet taking consumption to mean purchase and possession, this chapter gives evidence that men were engaged in this new material world of 'home'.[9] Men prided themselves on their knowledge about the quality and design of objects, used objects as markers of memories, shored up relationships—familial and commercial—out of networks of objects, and invested things with emotional significance. And at the centre of domestic ceremonies, men's domestic authority in the family was enacted through the richly symbolic material culture of the table. The meaning of domestic material culture for women has been explored in some detail; this chapter hopes to reconstruct the varied depth of meaning that things held for men.

[6] Margaret Ponsonby, *Stories from Home: English Domestic Interiors, 1750–1850* (Aldershot: Ashgate, 2007), p. 8. See also Leonore Davidoff and Catherine Hall, *Family Fortunes: Men and Women of the English Middle Class, 1780–1850* (1987; London: Routledge, 1992), esp. pp. 357–88; John Smail, *The Origins of Middle Class Culture: Halifax, Yorkshire, 1660–1780* (Ithaca, NY: Cornell University Press, 1995), pp. 164–90.

[7] See, for example, Marta Ajmar, 'Toys for Girls: Objects, Women and Memory in the Renaissance Household', in Marius Kwint, Christopher Breward and Jeremy Aynsley (eds), *Material Memories: Design and Evocation* (Oxford: Berg, 1999), pp. 75–89; Leora Auslander, 'The Gendering of Consumer Practices in Nineteenth-century France', in Victoria de Grazia and Ellen Furlough (eds), *The Sex of Things: Gender and Consumption in Historical Perspective* (Berkeley, CA: University of California Press, 1996), pp. 79–112; G. J. Barker Benfield, *The Culture of Sensibility: Sex and Society in Eighteenth-Century Britain* (Chicago, IL: University of Chicago Press, 1992); Maxine Berg, 'Women's Consumption and the Industrial Classes of Eighteenth-century England', *Journal of Social History*, 30 (1996), pp 415–34; Moira Donald, '"The Greatest Necessity for Every Rank of Men": Gender, Clocks and Watches', in Moira Donald and Linda Hurcombe (eds), *Gender and Material Culture in Historical Perspective* (Basingstoke; New York: Macmillan, 2000), pp. 54–75; Beth Kowaleski-Wallace, 'Tea, Gender and Domesticity in Eighteenth-century England', *Studies in Eighteenth-Century Culture*, 23 (1993), pp. 131–45.

[8] David Hussey, 'Guns, Horses and Stylish Waistcoats? Male Consumer Activity and Domestic Shopping in Late-Eighteenth- and Early-Nineteenth-Century England', in David Hussey and Margaret Ponsonby (eds), *Buying for the Home: Shopping for the Domestic from the Seventeenth Century to the Present* (Aldershot: Ashgate, 2008), p. 68.

[9] See Karen Harvey, 'Barbarity in a Teacup? Punch, Domesticity and Gender in the Eighteenth Century', *Journal of Design History*, 21, 3 (2008), pp. 205–21, for a discussion of how men became increasingly engaged with domesticity through the material culture of drinking over the eighteenth century.

Yet several historians have expanded their categories of material culture to include not just 'consumer goods' or 'new' 'commodities' identified by their novelty or fashionability, but also the 'old' or 'traditional',[10] as well as items that are not simply or always commodities.[11] Indeed, suggesting the only limited relevance of new commodities to the middling-sort men explored in this book, Henry French has found that the middling sort only rarely possessed a distinctive formation of new consumer items.[12] In this chapter I explore different kinds of material culture as it appeared in men's own writing, then, and from the perspectives of the act of purchase, the decision-making prior to purchase, the provision of resources to enable the purchase, the legal ownership of the object, the emotional ownership of the object, the use of the object, and the responsibility for the use and upkeep of the object. Examining this broad range of engagements with a varied material culture shifts the emphasis from 'home' to 'house', and a central theme is material culture to be bought, sold, and improved. Underpinning this chapter is the fact that for the middling sort who are the main focus of this book, including those from business, the trades, professions, and farming, the family remained 'the site of most economic, as well as social, activity'.[13] This overlap between family and economy and an emphasis on property sits somewhat uneasily in a history that emphasizes decorative art, consumer goods, or an emotional investment in personal things.[14] The documents used for this chapter do not uncover individual consumers excited by advertising or searching for the fulfilment of fantasies of pleasure driven by 'modern autonomous imaginative hedonism'.[15] Personal impulses are inarticulate in these records, whereas the unit of the household is palpable.[16] The evidence exposes men striving to manage their property well, to

[10] Lorna Weatherill's work using probate inventories demonstrated the continuation of the older items alongside new consumer goods, for example. See Lorna Weatherill, *Consumer Behaviour and Material Culture in Britain, 1660–1760* (London: Routledge, 1988).

[11] Daniel Roche, *A History of Everyday Things: The Birth of Consumption in France, 1600–1800* (Cambridge: Cambridge University Press, 2000), includes water and light, for example.

[12] Henry French, *The Middle Sort of People in Provincial England, 1600–1750* (Oxford: Oxford University Press, 2007), pp. 141–200. French finds that only the 'chief inhabitants' appear to have more consumer goods, notably for sociability, and these are used so they can make claims to gentility.

[13] Hannah Barker, *The Business of Women: Female Enterprise and Urban Development in Northern England, 1760–1830* (Oxford: Oxford University Press, 2006), p. 6. See also, de Vries, 'Between Purchasing Power and the World of Goods', pp. 85–132; de Vries, *Industrious Revolution*.

[14] See, for example, Neil McKendrick, John Brewer and J. H. Plumb, *The Birth of a Consumer Society: The Commercialisation of Eighteenth-Century England* (Cambridge: Cambridge University Press, 1982), for accounts that emphasize emulation and social status. Sara Pennell takes a very different approach in her micro-study in 'Mundane Materiality: Or, Should Small Things Still be Forgotten?', in Karen Harvey (ed.), *History and Material Culture: A Student's Guide to Approaching Alternative Sources* (London: Routledge, 2009), pp. 173–91.

[15] McKendrick, Brewer and Plumb, *Birth of a Consumer Society*; Colin Campbell, *The Romantic Ethic and the Spirit of Modern Consumerism* (1987; Alcuin, 2005), esp. pp. 77–95. For a useful review of work in this area prior to the late 1990s, see Paul Glennie, 'Consumption within Historical Studies', in Danny Miller (ed.), *Acknowledging Consumption: A Review of New Studies* (London: Routledge, 1995), 164–203.

[16] The most important statement on household-level decisions and consumption is de Vries, *Industrious Revolution*. De Vries concurs that motivations for consumption became increasingly individuated, an argument that is countered somewhat by the argument in this chapter on the continuing emphasis on the unit of the house.

sustain and consolidate this for their families, and in so doing to root themselves and their authority in the physical body of the house.

KEEPING HOUSE

Men's engagement with the house was shaped to a considerable extent by the duties of provisioning and management. Oeconomy equipped men to instruct wives and other dependents in managing the resources of the household, and this included those of the physical house. Xenophon advised men to pay close attention to the items bought for the home and its decoration: the house should not be filled with 'unnecessary Decorations', for example, but be 'built with due Consideration, and for the Conveniency of the Inhabitants'; the husband should teach his wife which are the best rooms for valuable possessions, corn, and wine, and which are 'the most convenient Places for Parlours and Dining-Rooms', 'Bed-Chambers', and the 'Nursery'.[17] Putting into practice the instructions given by her husband, a wife would then, 'receive Goods that are brought into the House, and distribute such a Part of them as [the husband] think necessary for the Use of the Family'.[18] Alongside this moral philosophical sub-genre of oeconomy, didactic books envisaged men not simply as global managers but participants in the mundane and everyday life of the house.[19] Not all men put this into practice, and the involvement of men was dependent on several structural familial and individual factors.

One of the most significant shaping factors for men's involvement with domestic material culture was life-course, and particularly marriage. The York solicitor William Gray (1751–1845) pondered this expected change to his own life in his letters to his father written in his early twenties. As a devout Christian, Gray was adamant that 'the Union between Husband and Wife, the managing a Family, and the bringing up Children', should be done 'in the Nurture and Admonition of the Lord'. 'I would not for a Million of Worlds,' he continued, 'engage myself to an unregenerate Person if she had every Accomplishment [a] Heart could wish; for… I should only have possession of her Body whilst the Devil had possession of her Soul.'[20] By October 1777, William was set to forge his godly union with the twenty-six-year-old Faith Hopwood. In an important letter to his father dealing with 'the State of Life I am entering upon', Gray explained that all their attention was given to things 'of a worldly kind'; he hoped he had support from the Lord, but still, he wrote, 'we are both in need of help'. The husband-to-be had received £300 from his father-in-law to set up home. Mr Hopwood 'has too great a Regard for his Daughter not to make her equal with his other Daughter', 'which is all I desire', added William. Of this, £200 will be spent on furniture; another £300 will

---

[17] Xenophon, *The Science of Good Husbandry: or, The Oeconomics of Xenophon*, trans. Richard Bradley (London, 1727), p. 61.

[18] Ibid. p. 50.

[19] These two sub-genres of oeconomy are discussed at greater length in Chapter 2, pp. 33–50.

[20] Letters of William Gray, sen, Gray Family Papers, York City Archives: Acc 5 & 6, W/6, 21 March 1776, f. 3.

come from the legal partnership, the future profits of which 'will more than maintain my Family'. He tells his father this, not because—as in so many cases—he
requires financial assistance from Mr Gray. Instead, William assures his father
that he will now be able to assist him 'with any Thing you want', and that as a
result his father is now able to prepare a will, leaving a house and personal effects
to his daughter.[21] William's accounts with his father recorded the £27 12s he paid
to Mr Gray between November 1777 and May 1784. On the day that he advised
his father to bequest property to his sister, William also committed £200 to fund
these payments should his father require it. In 1787, he made a note that this
account should be carried over to his second ledger, 'under the title of Contingent
Fund'.[22] Marriage for William Gray meant new financial responsibilities as both
husband and son.

Only one expression of his feelings, this letter nevertheless showed Gray looking
upon marriage as an economic transformation. William preserved his copy, labelled
by him as 'Near October 1777 (mentioning my marriage intended to take place on
the 9th)',[23] and it was perhaps his copy of this important document that sparked
his retrospective assessment of the financial implications of his marriage in 1821,
in his 'Recollections of God's goodness to me in respect of my *temporal concerns*'.
This short narrative is focused on the riches that he has amassed over his life, showing God's goodness working through William's own determination and success.
The comments on his marriage—to a woman he loved and later mourned deeply—
are particularly striking for their focus on money. 'Mean time, I married', he writes
abruptly, receiving 'only £300' from his father-in-law. Yet God was kind and this
amount increased: 'But by the affecting circumstance of ye death of her 3 brothers,
(all in their manhood) it ultimately became enlarged—my wife receiving 1/3 of
her father's property instead of 1/6th.'[24] 'Still', he reflected, 'for some time I could
scarcely sustain ye burden of my very moderate household expenses.'[25] Later, in
February 1822, William paid off his own son's debts when he married, and provided him with a considerable loan, the latter making 'his portion equal with that
of each of my other children'.[26]

Other men—particularly those with sufficient wealth or property—recorded
the material changes that occurred upon marriage. The Reverend John Forth married Elizabeth Woodhouse on 23 June 1791, and soon after a household inventory
for their house was taken. This was an important record of the shared material life
of the couple, recording where and from whom many of their possessions origi-
nated. Some objects were 'old fashioned', some were 'common', many were gifts
from named individuals. Others were bought by the couple as they prepared
for the wedding. The punch ladle was surely the one that John had purchased for
13s 6d from Richard Clark the goldsmith and jeweller just 10 days before the

[21] Letters of William Gray, sen, Acc 5 & 6, W/7, f. 3.
[22] Ledger of William Gray, Gray Family Papers, York City Archives: Acc 24, A1, f. 31.
[23] Letters of William Gray, sen, Acc 5 & 6, W/7, f. 4.
[24] Memoranda of William Gray, Gray Family Papers, York City Archives: D2a, f. 6.
[25] Ibid. ff. 6–7.
[26] Ledger of William Gray, f. 147.

marriage.[27] The twelve mahogany chairs had apparently been purchased by 'M[rs] Woodhouse' (Elizabeth's mother) from John Barber for £15 12s a month earlier, on 13 May 1791.[28] These were surely some of the chairs that were later used in either the drawing room, the parlour, or the best lodging room once the couple were married.[29] Alongside the inventory, John kept an account book containing the section 'Expences in furnishing my house', which included payments to the cabinet maker, silversmith, painter, and upholsterer, and purchases of a 'Tea board' and a 'Napkin Press', and which totalled more than £520.[30] Such evidence for John's global management must be balanced with his involvement in the mundane matters of the household.[31] The couple kept at least three joint account books during their marriage, both making entries on various matters. The volume for 1799, for example, includes notes on getting the pans 'new Tinned', white-washing the house, and making a start on using up 96 Stone of Soap.[32] Expensive furnishings and fittings *and* small-scale improvements came within the compass of John Forth's household role.

'Keeping house' was a significant life-stage for a man even when he and his wife lacked not only a house of their own but much in the way of material possessions. Benjamin Shaw (1772–1841), a mechanic from Preston, married Betty on 23 September 1793, at which point they 'had nothing to go to house with'.[33] Betty was expecting a child, and she had told Benjamin that after the marriage she would live at home until the child was born: 'it would save us some expence, for we had neither furniture, or money, nor friends, & few cloths & she had her little clothes to provide &c'.[34] Soon after the wedding, though, she joined Benjamin in Dolphinholme, and they boarded with a widow. The child was born back at Betty's parents' house in Lancaster, and following her return a new stage began. In Benjamin's recalling of this, the possessions articulated their new state:

> We went to House by our selves & had nothing to put in it, But a bed that my fathers & me at dolphinholme, & Betty had a box of cloaths, & a pair of tings, & a fue pots, &c I made each of us a knife & fork, & 2 Stools, we got a pan, & a looking glass, & a few trifles.[35]

---

[27] Revd Mr Forth, Bill for silverware, 13 June 1791, Munby collection, York City Archives: Acc 54:24a.
[28] Bill for Mrs Woodhouse from John Barber, 13 May 1791, Munby collection, York City Archives: Acc 54: 24e.
[29] 'An Inventory of the Linen, Plate, china, Glass, Delf, and Pottery Ware, Household Goods, and sundry Fixtures belonging to the Rev.[d] M[r] Forth and M[rs] Forth at Slingsby, Taken 3rd December 1791', Munby collection, York City Archives: Acc 54: 1. Mahogany chairs were also in abundance in the later inventory, 'An Inventory of the Household Furniture, Plate, Linen, China, Glass, £c. belonging to the Rev[d] M[r] Forth at Ganthorp, taken 10th June 1806', Munby collection, York City Archives: Acc 54: 1.
[30] Account book of John Forth, 1791–2, Munby collection, York City Archives: 54:2, ff. 1–2.
[31] The roles of Elizabeth and John Forth as suggested by their account books is discussed in Chapter 3, pp. 83–5.
[32] 'Housekeeping Account for the Year 1799—John and Elizt: Forth', Munby collection, York City Archives: 54:6, ff. 4, 28, 52.
[33] *The Family Records of Benjamin Shaw, Mechanic of Dent, Dolphinholme and Preston, 1772–1841*, ed Alan G. Crosby (Record Society of Lancaster and Cheshire, 1991), p. 30.
[34] Ibid. pp. 30–1.   [35] Ibid. p. 32.

Some months later, in 1795, Benjamin found work in Preston; three weeks later Betty joined them and, as he wrote in 1826, they 'took 2 rooms at the corner of dale Street, where we have lived 31 years'.[36] Shaw's comments articulate how 'keeping house' encompassed mundane material domestic things.

The evidence of Gray, Forth, and Shaw is compelling on the connection between a man's role as oeconomist and marriage. Yet while a man may have only become 'ripe for domestication' and entry to a culture of home on the verge of marriage, his role as oeconomical housekeeper began not with the legal change of marital status but with the possession—in some sense—of a house.[37] This was the force of Shaw's phrase, 'We went to House by our selves', and it was echoed by many other men. Thomas Naish had been married and living with his wife for some years when he described how, in 1701 he 'parted from my father and mother and went my selfe to house keeping'.[38] Naish was familiar with the need for upkeep and repairs, being the son of the Clerk of the Fabric, responsible for the material condition of the exterior and interior of the Cathedral, the Close, and other estates of the dean and chapter at Salisbury.[39] Daniel Renaud and his wife Christiana shared their house with Daniel's uncle, until the latter married in 1730 and, as Daniel noted, 'We began To keep House'.[40] Neither Naish nor Renaud owned their houses, though they were both married. But starting to 'keep house' was not necessarily undertaken by married men. Thomas Mort never married but records equal payments of 2s 6d to James Taylor, Mary, and Ellen, with whom he had 'began to keep house' during his sixties.[41] Much later, the Manchester grocer George Heywood also described his setting up of a house with his business partner and wife as a family beginning: 'We have come to live in our own house today, [...] with beginning house keeping we shall have more care upon ourselves but the care will be for our own interest.'[42] In these cases, housekeeping was predicated on a man's possession of a house and on his authority, but it was also a shared practice. Men of the lower-middling sort in particular were used to sharing houses with many others; regardless of emerging domestic ideals centred on a nuclear family, flexible definitions of 'family' were of ongoing relevance.[43]

---

[36] Ibid. p. 33.

[37] Quote from Amanda Vickery, *Behind Closed Doors: At Home in Georgian England* (New Haven, CT: Yale University Press, 2009), p. 88.

[38] *The Diary of Thomas Naish*, ed. Doreen Slater (Wiltshire Archeological and Natural History Society), 1964, vol. 20, p. 46. The subdean post was granted in 1694. See ibid. p. 8.

[39] Ibid. p. 2.

[40] Daniel Renaud, Account book [*c.*1769], William Andrews Clark Memorial Library: MS.1977. 008, f. 37.

[41] Account book of Thomas Mort, 26 March 1703–13 September 1725. Henry E. Huntington Library: L3A1 [new location S10 K3]: 19 November 1705.

[42] Diary of George Heywood, John Rylands Library, Manchester: Eng. MS 703, fol. 77, quoted in Hannah Barker, 'A Grocer's Tale: Gender, Family and Class in Early Nineteenth-Century Manchester', *Gender & History*, 21, 2 (August 2009), p. 350.

[43] Barker, 'A Grocer's Tale', pp. 350–1. See also Hannah Barker and Jane Hamlett, 'Living above the Shop: Home, Business, and Family in the English "Industrial Revolution"', *Journal of Family History*, 35, 4 (2010), p. 319.

An unmarried tradesman from Lancaster, William Stout's sense of housekeeping similarly concerned the physical stuff of the household rather than a status or rite of passage. In early 1691, he reported, 'my trade increasing and shop too little, I had thoughts of adding my bedroom to the shop, and also of house keeping'. It was at this point that his sister Elin, who had already been helping him, offered to be his 'house keeper', and so he rented a parlour, the cellar beneath it, and three bedrooms above, all for 50s per annum.[44] In 1734, Stout began 'to keepe house, and dwell in the roomes over the shop, and to take my brother Leonard's two youngest daughters, Margret and Mary, to be my house keepers'.[45] From c.1739–1742 he was joined by Mary Bayley, a servant of whom Stout wrote, 'I have kept house…with good content'.[46] For Stout, each new stage in housekeeping usually coincided with a physical move but always involved the arrival of a new female presence in the house. With rooms and female assistance, single men could keep house.

Though they may seem fine distinctions, it is important to distinguish 'keeping house' from 'housekeeping'. Housekeeping connoted domestic tasks that serviced the bodily needs of the family. For the East Riding schoolmaster Robert Sharp, 'housekeeping' meant practical domestic tasks, often food preparation, and he performed it reluctantly when left alone in the house: on Sunday 25 June 1826 when a sore foot, no church service, and his daughter's absence prompted the statement, 'so I was the Housekeeper', followed by detailed comments on the peas and new potatoes enjoyed at dinner; and on Sunday 15 April 1827, when his wife and daughter had been away since Friday, he remarked, 'I am still Housekeeper alone, excepting two Cats', preparing the bacon and eggs for his own dinner.[47] Sharp's descriptions of this kind of housekeeping were derisory: as he wrote in May 1833 when Ann was in Skipton, 'I am now my own Housekeeper an office of which I am not much enamoured; I care not how soon I am quit of the situation.'[48] For such men, 'housekeeping' was an unpleasant activity performed out of necessity. 'Keeping house', by contrast, integrated demarcated architectural space and gendered relationships of household management. While it is true that the dynamic uses of space in the house may, as they did in the seventeenth century, have 'mitigated, moderated and even rendered irrelevant patriarchal prerogatives of control', the unit of the middling-sort house correlated with the idea of male household authority and governance.[49] In this context, it is not surprising that beginning to 'keep house'—however facilitated—was such a significant moment.

As with 'housekeeping' and 'keeping house', uses of the words 'house' and 'home' show a discerning lexicon associated with the domestic. For the Devon

---

[44] *The Autobiography of William Stout of Lancaster, 1665–1752*, ed. J. D. Marshall (Manchester: Chetham Society, 1967), vol. 14, 3rd series, p. 102.

[45] Ibid. p. 215.

[46] Ibid. p. 232.

[47] *Diary of Robert Sharp*, pp. 44, 125.

[48] Ibid. p. 413. See also Chapter 2 above, pp. 72.

[49] On rank and authority governing access to domestic space, see Amanda Flather, *Gender and Space in Early Modern England* (Woodbridge: Boydell Press, 2007), pp. 42, 73. Quote from p. 59.

merchant John Darracott, 'my house' comprised wife, children, furniture, relations, friends, and riches.[50] For Richard Kay, the unmarried doctor living with his parents, engaging in 'Business at Home' refers to seeing patients, though being 'employed in Domestic Affairs', 'carrying on some concerns about Home', or being 'employed mostly in common Concern about Home' suggested other sorts of activity.[51] Being 'at home' meant he was present in the house. When Kay reported that he 'kept House, & much by the Fireside', this was on account of his bad teeth; two days later he was still suffering: 'I'm Housekeeper to Day upon Account of my Teeth'.[52] In these cases, 'keeping house' suggests a degree of compulsion; 'home' and 'house' also appear somewhat interchangeable. Whether through their occupation, sociability, or leisure, reports of men spending some considerable time in the domestic interior were very common. This is little surprise, given that many occupations and work tasks took place within the house.[53] Yet even for those men whose work necessarily took place away from their residence, the house was a venue for meaningful activity. John Stede's diary, 'Wherein an Account is taken of the Spending of my Time; Where, How, and with Whom', itemizes his departure and arrival from and to 'hous' and 'home'. Identified as the author by David Hunter, Stede was the prompter of John Rich, who staged *The Beggar's Opera*, and 'Hous' in his diary referred to Rich's Lincoln's Inn Fields theatre.[54] 'Home' was where Stede slept, dined, and spent some considerable time each day. On 12 September 1723, for example he notes, 'Rose […] 7.40. wrot 9 p t; drest and to Hous. 10.15, busied there 12:55. home, busied & din'd 3 + chatted littled & dozed 6:30'.[55] On 9 March 1754, time at home totalled 3 hours and 10 minutes, from rising at 6.50 a.m. until he left for the theatre at 10 a.m., with the time fully accounted for in his diary.[56] Similarly, Robert Sharp's outline of his typical Sunday from 8 a.m. to 10 p.m. traced his movements during which he returns home at 1 p.m. for 'Dinner' and to read.[57] Francis Blake's account book also includes several recordings of dining or simply being 'at Home'.[58] In common with Richard Kay's comment, Blake remarked that some time spent at home was because of ill-health; five consecutive references in May 1765 read 'at home, by yᵉ Gout'.[59] Keen to work, Benjamin Shaw felt that some of his time within doors was enforced: Shaw 'became Soletary,

[50] Diary of John Darracott, ff. 200–2.

[51] Diary of Richard Kay, Chetham's Library: A.7.76: 24 November 1737; 5 October 1742; 26 November 1737; 25 April 1737.

[52] Ibid. 25 January 1744/5; 27 January 1744/5.

[53] Flather discusses the dynamic spatial division of labour in the seventeenth-century house in *Gender and Space*, pp. 75–93.

[54] David Hunter, 'What the Prompter Saw: The Diary of Rich's Prompter, John Stede', in Jeremy Barlow and Berta Joncus (eds), *The Stage's Glory: John Rich (1692–1761)* (Newark, DE: University of Delaware Press, 2010), p. 70.

[55] Diary of John Bradley (1723–29, 1754), Nostell Priory WYL1352 1215–1986, West Yorkshire Archive Service, Leeds: NP A3/2/ (1718), 12 September 1723.

[56] Quoted in Hunter, 'What the Prompter Saw', p. 73.

[57] *Diary of Robert Sharp*, Wednesday 6 June 1827, pp. 138–9.

[58] There were 10 such references in March 1765 alone. See Francis Blake, 'Acct Book from 1 January 1765 to 22 February 1766', William Andrews Clark Memorial Library: MS.1985.002: March 1765.

[59] Ibid. 14–18 May 1765.

& was mostly at home' due to a leg injury.[60] Being at home through injury was a 'confinement',[61] though as with Kay and Shaw it was the experience of illness rather than the house itself that imposed limits. Rarely do men express feeling trapped by domestic space. 'Home' and 'house' had a variety of meanings for men. Houses were to be managed, but the house was also a setting for professional work, sociability, retirement, convalescence, and everyday ablutions. By the end of the eighteenth century, 'home' meant more than a dwelling; it was a multi-faceted state of being, encompassing the emotional, physical, moral, and spatial.[62] 'House' was different, incorporating property management, a particular set of ordered relationships, and an architectural unit.

PROPERTY

In 'keeping house', men managed goods and people over which they exercised proprietorship, even if legally they did not own them. As Rachel Weil has written of the seventeenth century, '[t]he image of a man passing on property to his children seems to stand for the bond between a parent and child in this period, in much the same way that the image of a mother nursing a child at the breast might do in another'.[63] Indeed, as the discourse of oeconomy combined classical and patriarchal models of governance throughout the long eighteenth century, though shifting in focus from the large landowner transforming to the smaller householder, Weil's account holds just as true for the eighteenth century.[64] To some extent this was part of a larger shift towards a capitalist economy in which land and objects became commodified. For some, land was 'a long-term resource', while for others it became 'a commodity to be assessed in terms of price and rent, to be purchased out of the profits of trade and commerce'.[65] While this combination of attitude towards land underpinned what French and Hoyle describe as 'not English Individualism but north-west European individualism', they argue that even in one small village people assumed both instrumental and sentimental attitudes towards land, sometimes buying land to provide for future generations.[66] More widely, the 'paradigm of property in land' remained a significant feature of law, society, and culture.[67] There also occurred a related shift, in which 'things'—not simply commodities—were

[60] *Family Records of Benjamin Shaw*, p. 37.

[61] *Diary of Robert Sharp*, Monday 7 May 1827, p. 130. Sharp. here refers to a friend with a knee injury.

[62] See Karen Harvey, 'Men Making Home: Masculinity and Domesticity in Eighteenth-Century England', *Gender & History*, 21, 3 (2009), pp. 520–40.

[63] Rachel Weil, 'The Family in the Exclusion Crisis: Locke versus Filmer Revisited', A. Houston and S. Pincus, *Nation Transformed: England after the Restoration* (Cambridge: Cambridge University Press, 2001), p. 121.

[64] On the transformation in the discourse of oeconomy, see Chapter 2.

[65] H. R. French and R. W. Hoyle, *The Character of English Rural Society: Earls Colne, 1550–1750* (Manchester and New York: Manchester University Press, 2007), p. 300.

[66] Ibid. p. 22. See also p. 300.

[67] John Brewer and Susan Staves, 'Introduction', in John Brewer and Susan Staves (eds), *Early Modern Conceptions of Property* (London and New York: Routledge, 1996), p. 2. See the essays in this volume for a consideration of land, people, and genetic material as property.

elevated as agents, capable of accruing wealth and profit, but also the independence required for political citizenship and power, the show of good taste and the exercise of civility for social status, the shaping of personal identity, and the export of Western values.[68] Ownership enabled the independence that fostered a public-spirited citizen, and this ownership encompassed the land a man might own, his material things, as well as his status as 'proprietor of *himself*'.[69] Proprietorship was profoundly gendered as well as politicized; the house was the place where these two changes—in ideas about land and objects—converged.

Men's accounts pertain to the coherence of the house as a sound and coherent physical unit, and this invites an analysis of material culture that moves away from what Frank Trentmann has described as the ' "soft", decorative, and visible'.[70] This is not to say that men were unconcerned with the look of interior decoration, though in the records used here this is suggested merely by the appearance of bills, such as Joseph Wilson's note of the painter's bill for redecorating the parlour with white and pink walls and blue and green doors.[71] A more common concern was with house repairs. The extensive works on a new house undertaken in the winter of 1754 for the Durham cattle dealer Ralph Ward were frequently noted in his diary, such as the major improvement of flagging the 'fore kitching' on 21 October.[72] Daniel Renaud noted a similarly heavy task in 1742: 'Laid down an Iron plate under the Kitchen chimney Grate given by Mr R. White.' 'The grate', he noted, 'made by Rich^d. David'. Renaud also costed the roofing of the Rectory.[73] William Gray's indexed ledger has a section set aside for the 'Dwelling House'. In this Gray totted up two sets of repair, with a new chimney and ceiling in a small lodging room in 1788, and a new floor, window, door, hearth, and chimney piece in the best lodging room in 1799.[74] In the same ledger, when totalling up his rent accounts for the year 1805–6, he notes the costs of 'Repairs of my own House' costing £4 7s 1d.[75] In Newcastle during the winter of 1815, the reformer and 'devoted family man' James Losh recorded his damp entrance hall and passages being laid with Roman cement, and also the near-completion of 'a very convenient water closet within the house'.[76] Finally, a relieved Robert Sharp, schoolmaster of

---

[68] Frank Trentmann, 'Materiality in the Future of History: Things, Practices, and Politics', *Journal of British Studies*, 48 (April 2009), pp. 291–4.

[69] Matthew McCormack, *The Independent Man: Citizenship and Gender Politics in Georgian England* (Manchester and New York: Manchester University Press, 2005), p. 24.

[70] Trentmann, 'Materiality in the Future of History', p. 287.

[71] Commonplace book of Revd Joseph Wilson *c*.1774–1821, West Yorkshire Archive Service, Leeds: WYL753, Acc 1886, f. 25.

[72] *Two Yorkshire Diaries*, p. 141.

[73] Renaud, Account book [*c*.1769], f. 39; Daniel Renaud, Account book [1752–1777], William Andrews Clark Memorial Library: MS.1977.009, f. 37.

[74] Ledger of William Gray, f. 35a.

[75] Ibid. f. 102a.

[76] T. S. Dorsch, 'Losh, James (1763–1833)', rev. *Oxford Dictionary of National Biography*, Oxford University Press, 2004 <http://www.oxforddnb.com/view/article/37689>, accessed 29 November 2010; *The Diaries and Correspondence of James Losh*, ed. Edward Hughes (Surtees Society, vol. 171, 1962), p. 46. A statue of Losh dressed in a toga now welcomes the visitor to the Newcastle Literary and Philosophical Society. I thank Helen Berry for this information.

South Cave, recorded the long-awaited mending of 'our Sky light' on 8 August 1821, it having been broken for almost a year.[77]

Many of the repairs noted by men fortify and seal the house. This might be significant given the potency of open points or voids, places where danger might enter and protective objects might be concealed.[78] Or perhaps these major structural works were simply sufficiently costly to be entered into men's accounts. These interpretations are not mutually exclusive, of course, and the maintenance of the physical house was a common feature of many men's records. For some wealthier men from more established families, houses that had been in the family for generations surely held a particular value. Descended from prosperous lower gentry, Thomas Mort resided in the fine manor house built by his grandfather. The stone above the door of Damhouse commemorated his parents' presence in the building: 'Erected by Adam Mort and Margret Mort 1650'. His mother had died in that year, when Thomas was five, and his father eight years later when Thomas was 13. The main body of the house during Thomas Mort's life was constructed much earlier than this in the late sixteenth or early seventeenth century.[79] Thus Mort spent his life in an old three-storey manor house, with bay windows and gables, and a distinctive long gallery.[80] As a minor, then, Thomas inherited a house with a visible past and accompanying social responsibilities in adjoining parishes. By the time Mort died, the house had been sold to his cousin Thomas Sutton, with whom he resided at Damhouse. Mort seemed to have a close relationship with Sutton, making him the distinctive bequest of 'all my Books'.[81]

Yet even for those from less wealthy ranks, as collectors of tithes and taxes middling-sort men were acutely aware of the value of buildings and land. This extended to their role as housekeepers. In the manuscripts of men such as Edmund Pilkington, John Forth, and Robert Sharp, calculations on land value, building work, and household repairs are mixed with information on taxes paid and collected. Daniel Renaud's account book reveals how such a volume included calculations on family and professional property. For example, Renaud itemizes the property of his uncle and the route it takes through the family. His expenses 'in Building & Housekeeping' were considerable, totalling £531 13s 9d. The house he built at Hinton between 1722 and 1726, including the garden, outbuildings, and a lawyer's bill, cost £987 15s 9d, and each year from 1730–1740 he received from his nephew an annuity of £18 (totalling £180). In 1739, the year before his death, he instructed Daniel on his bequest to his wife Mary, which included rents from the Hinton house, and on Mary's death in 1749, Daniel recorded his sale of the goods (for over £34) and the sale of the house (for £100).[82] Daniel had invested in the house at

---

[77] *Diary of Robert Sharp*, p. 51.
[78] See Giorgio Reillo's 'Things that Shape History: Material Culture and Historical Narratives', in Harvey (ed.), *History and Material Culture*, pp. 24–46.
[79] John and Sylvia Tonge, *Astley Hall (Damhouse)* (John and Sylvia Tonge, 2002), p. 10.
[80] For more information on the building, see Tonge, *Astley Hall* and English Heritage 'Heritage Gateway', <http://www.heritagegateway.org.uk/gateway/> (accessed July 2009), Astley Hospital, List Entry Number: 1163258.
[81] 'Will of Thomas Mort of Damhouse 1736', Lancashire Record Office.
[82] Renaud, Account book [1752–1777], fols 66, 67.

Figure 7: Exterior of Damhouse. Photograph by Karen Harvey. Reproduced with kind permission of Morts Astley Heritage Trust.

Hinton and stood to inherit from its sale: his uncle's will bequeathed the 'Messuage ffarm' at Hinton and his land at Wappenham to his wife Mary, and in the event of her death to his nephew and subsequently to his eldest son David. Mary and Daniel were to be the executors.[83] It may be because David did receive the farm at Hinton that his father left him only 'All My Books, Manuscripts' at his death.[84] Alternatively, Renaud left property to his younger son Daniel because his first-born was already in possession of two livings as curate of Aconbury and Dewsall.[85] Renaud's occupation as Rector meant that he was responsible for the church estate, though, and related calculations are included in the volume of accounts. He penned detailed records on a large new barn to house the yield from the church land around Whitchurch, and also listed the personal goods of his deceased neighbour, Mr Dusoul in 1735, including his night gown, seven best shirts, four old shirts, and two cravats.[86] Renaud's writings concern a mix of life-events and forms of property of small and large value. The recording of different kinds and scale of expenditure in these records—the flagging of a kitchen, the building of a new barn, the value of a recent crop, the cost of a watch repair—all pertained to property and income. Such items were bound to be included somewhere in a household's

---

[83] Will of David Renaud of Hinton, Northamptonshire, 17 April 1738, Public Record Office: PROB 11/706.

[84] 'The will of Daniel Renaud, 1770', Herefordshire Record Office: Probate series AA20, Box Number 334, June–September 1772. Also see Will of Reverend David Renaud, Clerk of Havant, Hampshire, 9 October 1807: PROB 11/1469.

[85] Personal communication from John Harnden, Herefordshire Record Office, 29 June 2009.

[86] See Chapter 3, p. 93.

accounts, though it was no means inevitable that they would belong to the man. Their appearance in the accounts of middling-sort men fulfilled the expectations of oeconomy as defined by Xenophon as, 'the just and regular Distribution of a Man's Goods, or the wise Management of his Possessions, or of his Household'.[87] While the economic meaning was important, the notion of property and its wise management had increasing rhetorical force.

Practices of property management were undertaken by men within and without the house and underline the porosity of any 'domestic' boundary. The duties of householder, for instance, were somewhat replicated in the relationship of landlord and tenant. For those with extensive property and complex systems of management, surviving letters give a good sense of the involvement that landlords could have in tenants' domestic lives. Few could rival James Brydges' careful attention to the detail of his rented property in Bath. Brydges bought houses for development, and employed the young architect who was to later make his name in Bath, John Wood. Despite his extensive estate at Cannons, Brydges paid close attention to these houses; his letters show not only an impressive knowledge 'of the most quotidian details of construction', but also that 'his knowledge of indoor plumbing was astonishing'.[88] He gave instructions on moveables and decoration too. He set limits on the number of chairs allowed to the housekeeper Mrs Degge ('Six for Every Bed Chamber & ten for every Dining Room'),[89] and decreed that the alterations on her house comprise stucco-panelled walls in the dining room to accommodate 'several Indian Pictures' in his possession, and a stuccoed floor in either 'a reddish Colour like my Lord Burlington's, or else... in imitation of Marble in white & black Square's lozengewise'.[90] Other landed men monitored their rented property in person. Close to the small family estate at Twisell, County Durham, the baronet Francis Blake visited his property in the villages of West Herrington and Letham, commenting on repairs to fences and dwelling houses.[91] Men lower on the social scale could not boast the resources of Brydges and Blake, but they too recorded dealings with tenants over property. William Coleman, tenant to John Bridges, an attorney in Kent, undertook a series of repairs to the farm that he rented for £55 a year. The surviving accounts from 1712 date from Bridges' death, and continue until 1729.[92] The list of repairs conducted by the carpenter, bricklayer, thatcher, gardener, and smith were folded carefully and retained by Mrs Jane

---

[87] *Science of Good Husbandry*, p. i.

[88] John Eglin, *The Imaginary Autocrat: Beau Nashe and the Invention of Bath* (London: Profile, 2005), pp. 148–9. Quotes at pp. 149 and 150.

[89] Letter from James Farquharson to Mrs Degge, Cannons 15 December 1729, Stowe papers, Henry E. Huntington Library: ST57 vol. 34 (1729–30), p. 54.

[90] Letter from James Farquharson to Mr Ferguson, Cannons 4 April 1730, ST57 vol. 34 (1729–30), p. 263.

[91] Francis Blake, 'Accots. from 11th August 1769 to 1st January 1771', William Andrews Clark Memorial Library: MS.1985.002, ff. 2, 68. See also Gordon Goodwin, 'Blake, Sir Francis, first baronet (1707/8–1780)', rev. Joseph Gross, *Oxford Dictionary of National Biography*, Oxford University Press, 2004 <http://www.oxforddnb.com/view/article/2577> (accessed 22 July 2005).

[92] On the family, see Edward Hasted, 'Parishes: Wootton', *The History and Topographical Survey of the County of Kent: Volume 9* (1800), pp. 364–73. British History Online: <http://www.british-history. ac.uk/report.aspx?compid=63576> (accessed 14 July 2009).

Bridges for her daughter, Deborah.[93] The solicitor William Gray collected rents on several properties and calculated the cost of any repairs.[94] For 1805–6, he notes of Mr Richardson's property, there were 'no repairs of any consequence in this last House during this year'.[95] The letters between the Leeds merchant John Micklethwaite and his tenant John Young dating from the later 1790s provide a window onto the negotiations that could take place between tenant and landlord. Over a series of years, John Young made several requests about his accommodation. In 1807, he asked Micklethwaite to evict another tenant in order to allow Young to 'get room for my Family to eat and sleep'.[96] In 1812, the departure of one tenant in the building prompted Young to request a room elsewhere, reporting 'I find we have not sufficient room for my Family'. The main object of the letter, though, was to request that Micklethwaite allow the Youngs to have sole possession of the out kitchen, and to divide the garden, 'as it is almost impossible to Keep the Women Folks in good humours where the Children constantly intermix and frequently Quarrell'.[97] Finally, on 7 April 1816, Young wrote to request a table for the property.[98] Not a landowner like James Brydges seventy years before him, Micklethwaite was nevertheless addressed as a benevolent patrician in a way which mirrored the changing printed works on oeconomy from the latter half of the eighteenth century.[99]

Letters exchanged amongst upper-middling business families belie any distinctions we might wish to draw between financial and familial matters. Family businesses were 'a crucial site for female economic activity', and as such mark out the limits of 'domestic femininity' for these women.[100] At the same time, conversely, family business ensured men's involvement with the family. This is evident from letters exchanged amongst the Birkbecks, a Quaker merchant and banking family with investments in the Yorkshire Dales textile industry.[101] The extensive correspondence of the family spans the period *c.*1720–1830, and the letters between the adult family members from the 1770s straddled the personal and the financial. Reports of business from one brother-in-law to another of their order for plants and demands from a customer for 'the Remainder of his Yarn Hose' concluded with the brisk statement, 'So much for Business—As to our Nursery'. This was followed fast with a detailed and sympathetic discussion of a wife's sore post-

---

[93] Accounts of William Coleman, 1712–29, William Andrews Clark Memorial Library: C692Z [1712–1729]. See fol. 1 for details of the rental agreement between Coleman and Bridges.

[94] Ledger of William Gray, 'Rent Account' for 1805–19, pp. 101–6.

[95] Ibid. f. 35a, p. 102a. Note the rent on his house for the year was £50: ibid. p. 102b.

[96] John Young to John Micklethwaite, 1 July 1807, John Micklethwaite correspondence, Manchester University John Rylands Special Collections: Eng. MS 1138, folder 2/100, verso.

[97] John Young to John Micklethwaite, 1 August 1812, folder 3/123.

[98] John Young to John Micklethwaite, 7 April 1816, folder 3/144, f. 1. Margaret Young wrote on a broader range of matters concerning the house. See Margaret Young to John Micklethwaite, 2 March 1815, folder 3/141, ff. 1–2.

[99] As discussed in Chapter 2, pp. 48–61.

[100] Barker, *Business of Women*, pp. 172, 173. See also pp. 103–66.

[101] See Thomas Kelly, *George Birkbeck: Pioneer of Adult Education* (Liverpool: Liverpool University Press, 1957), pp. 1–19.

partum nipples and painfully swollen breasts.[102] In a letter from Deborah Braithwaite, she shared with her brother-in-law, William, her fears about the possible death of her poorly daughter Etty, a burden made heavier by her own ill health and 'her daddas absence', making it 'very hard for human Nature to bear'. She signed off by explaining that her husband would continue the letter on the other side. In fact, showing no compunction about juxtaposing his words with hers, he began to write directly beneath her heart-wrenching report, detailing visits he had made and orders placed for the family business.[103]

Dating from 1792 to 1828, the family letters to John Micklethwaite include notifications of financial returns, updates on equipment and premises, and discussions of invoices to pay and accounts to complete. Most of these letters integrate family matters, though: the management of a widowed aunt's annuity, the distribution of a father's estate, the placement of sons in school, and exchanges with nephew, niece, son, brother, sister, agent, associate, and invariably the negotiation of various payments to or on behalf of these family members or friends. John Micklethwaite stood at the centre of an extensive web of management. The melding of financial and familial—and the importance of maintaining good family relations for material well-being—is clearest in John's wrangling with his brother Thomas during the late 1790s. We do not have John's replies, but Thomas's letters present his case as one of virtuous desperation. On 21 December 1795 Thomas expresses his disapproval of John entering into a business deal without Thomas's assent. Pointedly, he accused his elder brother of trying 'to take the Bread out of my Mouth'. The reference to the mundane domestic foodstuff—yet rich with meanings about 'existence itself'—neatly expresses the material nature of the tussle and the matter at stake.[104] Over the next two and a half years, Thomas made repeated pleas for what he describes consistently as his property. He expresses exasperation at his brother's 'Shuffling stile' and stresses his own travails, being 'up to the Ears in Debt'.[105] The linguistic strategies being employed by Thomas—consciously or unconsciously—were various. He also invoked higher authorities. On at least two occasions he alluded to legal action, referring to laws that 'will force even *Brothers* to act justly to each other', followed up later with an outright threat of Chancery.[106] Revealing his worry that he had gone too far, this last threat was accompanied by a note written the following day, couched in more conciliatory language, and offering to John a happier picture of a family without conflict:

---

[102] George Braithewaite to William Birkbeck: West Yorkshire Archive Service (Leeds), WYL449 Birkbeck Papers: 8/56 March 20 [1786?], f. 1.

[103] 'Kendal first day morning', Deborah Braithewaite to William Birkbeck, 8/51 verso, *c*.1786.

[104] For the meanings of bread in early modern societies, see Piero Camporesi, *Bread of Dreams: Food and Fantasy in Early Modern Europe* (1980; Polity Press, Cambridge, 1989), trans. David Gentilcore, quote at. p. 17.

[105] See, for example, John Micklethwaite correspondence, folder 1/27 verso and folder 1/29.

[106] Thomas Micklethwaite to John Micklethwaite, 5 December 1797, folder 1/28, 32.

I should think was it me I would have done with it for my own ease & comfort but I fear nothing will have any effect upon you it's a pitty [*sic*] for how happy you might make yourself and the whole of the Family.[107]

We do not know how this conflict was resolved. The penultimate letter from Thomas in this series describes his receipt of a letter from a creditor, and how his reputation now hangs in the balance; accusing John of prioritizing 'your own pecuniary advantages', he announces that he will show the letter to one final external authority—their father.[108] Sibling conflict—particularly between older and younger brothers—was a result of the workings of primogeniture in commercial families.[109] The material life of all family members was dependent in large part on the maintenance of good family relations.

'ARTICLES OF SMALL VALUE'

The mixing of business and household property in middling men's records exemplifies a coherent arena of management, and this was driven by a desire to preserve economic security and provision for existing and future family. Yet as discussed in Chapter 3, men's management was not limited simply to this macro level; nor do the categories of business and household explain all of the expenses laid out by men. Domestic transactions were often mixed with personal items, alerting us to the ways in which oeconomical management united apparently different areas of practice. Thomas Mort's accounts excluded smaller items of foodstuffs, presumably bundled into the 'house use' amounts paid to the servant Harry Whaley, yet some modest purchases were recorded: 2s 6d for a new spring and chain for his watch, 6d for shoelaces and for a number of pans from James Barnes of Wigan.[110] Perhaps Mort's single status encouraged his engagement with shopping, in the same way as it did for the widower George Gitton, whose responsibility for small household items surely reflected the absence of his wife.[111] William Parkinson's account book include payments 'for house keeping' to a number of different women, and excludes many smaller items of domestic consumption. Amongst the large amounts paid for tithes and taxes, though, were payments of 5d for two lemons, 3s for a chine of beef, and 3s 6d for the replacement of a warming pan base.[112] As we saw in the previous chapter, Henry Richardson recorded domestic consumption of many different types. His account book records disbursements for coffee, brandy, 'Gloves &

[107] Note appended (dated 6 December 1797), to Thomas Micklethwaite to John Micklethwaite, 5 December 1797, folder 1/32.

[108] Thomas Micklethwaite to John Micklethwaite, Folder 1/35.

[109] See Susan Staves, 'Resentment or Resignation? Dividing the Spoils among Daughters and Younger Sons', in Brewer and Staves (eds), *Early Modern Conceptions of Property*, p. 196.

[110] Account book of Thomas Mort, 20 February 1704, 4 May 1704, 20 October 1711.

[111] Gitten (whose diary from 1866 remains) is the man who seems the most skilled consumer in Hussey's study, 'Guns, Horses and Stylish Waistcoats?', pp. 67–8.

[112] Account book of William Smedley, Henry E. Huntington Library: HM3119223, 23 January 1742, 16 August 1751, 4 October 1751.

Groceries', 'Soap and Candles', brass knobs, and a 'small hard Brush' in February, a bed and oak chest in April, a lock for the chest, and more soap in May, handkerchiefs, a book, and 'a small Knife and Fork' in August, repairs to an old oak table in September and to his clock face in October, a food hamper for a Christening in November, and 'two ounces of Scotch Snuff for my Wife' in December.[113]

This combination of domestic and personal items was also a feature of elite men's records. Francis Blake's account books survive for 1765–1766 and 1769–1771, largely detailing food, drink, and services consumed outside his London home. Some of these are very small purchases. There are 17 entries for rolls or bread in January 1765 alone, and a single entry for 2s 1/2d of butter on 9 January.[114] But the volumes also detail larger expenses relating to domestic decoration. During the winter of 1769, this widower in his early sixties is engaged in refurnishing his London home. On the 13 December he orders new furniture for the library, and on 15 December pays a workman for ironwork. On 27 January he pays for the new furniture to be brought down from Berwick, and three days later the chairs in the library are mended. On 17 February the cabinet-maker's man came to hang curtains in the new room, and he returned on 13 March to lead the curtains, open two drawers in a bureau, and mend the 'great Chair'.[115] Small items, large items, soft furnishings, and repairs are all present. Moreover, Blake's sometimes full and descriptive entries for these items render them not simply records of financial expenditure. They show a concern for quality and appearance, and an awareness of the condition of specific items of furniture.

For men engaged in farming, commerce, or the professions, this range of personal and domestic purchases were recorded alongside business transactions. The ledger of the attorney William Gray contained many large sums relating to his legal business (such as the £5,500 recorded for the sale of Samuel Elam's property in 1811), and moderate sums in accounts of funds such as the balance of £4 4s for the York Auxiliary Bible Society and of £14 1s 103/4d for the Charity Fund.[116] But this young man also itemized several smaller items purchased during the first few years of marriage under the title of 'Pocket and miscellaneous Expences'. These included two penknives (2s), a sheet of marbled paper (11/2d), a riding cane (6d), a walking stick (8d), an almanac for his wife (6d), the services of the hairdresser (6d), and a pencil (4d).[117] One of his most regular purchases was fruit, such as 1d for an orange on 11 March 1778, 2d for an apple on 11 April 1778, and the small amounts for oranges, cherries, strawberries, gooseberries, plums, and grapes purchased during 1779.[118] The combination of transactions of very different sizes and types is typical of men's records from across the middling sort. This underlines

[113] See Richardson, 'A Diary of Disbursements', see entries for 3, 18, 27 February, 16 April, 4 May, 4, 5 August, 7 September, 13 October, 10 November, 14 December.

[114] Blake, 'Acct Book from 1 January 1765 to 22 February 1766', entries for January 1765.

[115] Blake, 'Accots. from 11th August 1769 to 1st January 1771', entries for 13, 15 December, 27 January 1769, 17 February, 13 March 1770.

[116] Ledger of William Gray, fols 138, 127, 16.

[117] Ibid. fols 20, 25, 33.

[118] Ibid. fols 20, 33.

men's engagement with the household at different levels, but furthermore indicates how the 'domestic' was combined with the 'personal' and 'commercial' in men's records.

An interest in commodities big and small emerges from men's records, but it is not accurate to insist on men of this middling rank as avid consumers. In their comments on material objects, men showed particular areas of interest and know-ledge. Robert Sharp was especially critical of imprudent consumption. A charac-teristic dismissal was made in June 1821: 'Bought a Set of China 1 Doz. Cups, 1 Doz. Saucers[,] Teapot, a milk Jug[,] 2 Basons and 2 Plates, double gilt edged all for 12 Shillings; but as we neither want them nor have any place to put them in for display, we have packed them in a Basket and put them in the Garrett Closet, if this be not encouraging manufacturers I know what is!!'[119] While Finn remarks that Sharp was 'determined to purchase' such items, it seems more likely that this household purchase was dictated by Robert's wife, Ann.[120] Robert sought to disas-sociate himself from such showy items and he was suspicious of the encroachment of 'Fashion' in household furnishing, represented for him by 'an Italian Iron hung by a Brass faced Warming Pan' appearing alongside the more traditional 'Brass Mortar & Pestle', 'Salt Box', and shining bellows.[121] Succumbing to the attraction of a silk handkerchief in November 1830, Robert was no doubt relieved to discover subsequently it was actually made of cotton.[122] Nevertheless, if we extend the anal-ysis wider than 'new' and 'consumer' items, Robert Sharp appears 'an acquisitive consumer of personal and household goods' with developed consumer skills.[123] Running the general store with his wife Ann between the years 1828–33, Robert had good cause to be familiar with the price of things. 'Butter which was 1s. pr. Lb last week', he commented on market day on Saturday 28 May 1831, 'is this day 1s/5d an extravagant price'.[124] Notably for Sharp, material culture was closely entwined with family relationships. In a letter to his son William (who was in London) in February 1813, Robert laid out specific instructions for the purchase of several items on his behalf. Advising William to postpone 'the Hat buying' because he suspected his son might make a poor choice and 'give too much for it', he instead requested some other items: '2 Skeins of Embroidering Silk like the Pat-tern & 4 Quire of wove Letter Paper to sell at 1 Shilling & 4 Quire of Do.—to sell at 1/6'.[125] While the order for silk was perhaps dictated by his wife or daughter, the paper was surely for him. As he said of one periodical, 'I have not yet read it, there-fore I have the pleasure of anticipation, it is on very fine paper', adding, 'I wish the times Gentleman would procure their paper of a little better texture, for they are

[119] *Diary of Robert Sharp*, Wednesday 21 June 1826, p. 43.

[120] Margot Finn, 'Men's Things: Masculine Possession in the Consumer Revolution', *Social History*, 25, 2 May 2000, p. 142.

[121] *Diary of Robert Sharp*, Thursday 9 April 1829, p. 198.

[122] Ibid. Friday 6 April 1827, p. 122; Monday 29 November 1830, p. 288.

[123] Finn, 'Men's Things', pp. 137.

[124] *Diary of Robert Sharp*, Saturday 28 May 1831, p. 312. On the shop the couple ran together, see, *Diary of Robert Sharp*, 'Introduction', p. xxviii.

[125] *Diary of Robert Sharp*, Letter of Robert Sharp to William Sharp, 1 February 1813, p. 1.

frequently much torn'.[126] An avaricious writer and reader, as well as a schoolmaster, Robert was a seasoned consumer of paper.

Though women have been closely associated with the material culture of home, many men engaged in discussions of quality, value, style, and taste.[127] Taste was a profoundly ethical issue, though.[128] Good management stemmed partly from working within the structural realities of one's status, and for middling-sort men, as for women, material culture was judged by notions of thriftiness and prudence. The twenty-three-year-old York attorney William Gray asserted his determination '*not to live above my Income*, whatever it may be'.[129] Even in a rapidly commercializing society, ideas about appropriate consumption of the different ranks endured. The Preston mechanic Benjamin Shaw bemoaned what he saw as his wife's financial intemperance, tracing it back to the early loss of her mother which prevented Betty's instruction in the 'care and and the [*sic*] managment of the small income that is frequently the portion of the Poor'.[130] Observing the labouring poor such as Shaw, Robert Sharp was critical of the rich: when 'the poor are nearly in a state of starvation, it is amazing that things should be in the state they are, some wallowing in all kinds of extravagance and Luxury'.[131] As a rural middling-sort schoolmaster and tradesman, Sharp employed a notion of thrift that was consonant with Shaw's. In fact, Sharp's views were shaped by the radical writer William Cobbett who advised the labouring classes to avoid china and glass, and instead to use only sturdy and durable vessels.[132] Prudent domestic consumption and a return to a traditional English taste could revivify the nation. As argued in Chapter 2, while oeconomy resonated with elite concerns at the beginning of the eighteenth century, by the end of the century it had assumed a new potency as a discourse for and about the labouring class. Nevertheless, Cobbett's words, like those of the middling and landed consumers of domestic wallpaper, can be set within a long-standing debate over ethics and taste, and one in which all social groups were implicated.[133] A delight in things was nevertheless patterned by a deep-rooted concern for probity.

Men—including the very wealthy—consumed low-value and rather mundane items repetitively and alongside larger and intermittent purchases. A proprietorial approach united this consumption with the management of other domestic, personal, and commercial or professional practices. The nature and purpose of some of the documents discussed above—particularly account books—are likely to fore-

---

[126] *Diary of Robert Sharp*, Thursday 21 January 1830, p. 243.

[127] Amanda Vickery, '"Neat and Not Too Showey": Words and Wallpaper in Regency England', in John Styles and Amanda Vickery (eds), *Gender, Taste and Material Culture in Britain and North America 1700–1830* (New Haven & London: Yale University Press, 2006), pp. 201–22.

[128] See John Brewer's brief discussion in *The Pleasures of the Imagination: English Culture in the Eighteenth Century* (London: HarperCollins, 1997), pp. 87–98.

[129] Letters of William Gray, sen, Acc 5 & 6, W4, 21 February 1774, fol. 3.

[130] *Family Records of Benjamin Shaw*, p. 76.

[131] *Diary of Robert Sharp*, 9 October 1826, p. 73.

[132] William Cobbett, *Cottage Economy* (London, 1822), pp. 197–8. See Chapter 2, p. 56.

[133] Vickery, 'Neat and Not Too Showey', *passim*.

ground this kind of engagement. In the context of balancing the books, a concern for tasteful prudence was bound to surface. Yet other evidence shows that the material items of the house held significant personal or emotional meanings for men. In commonplace books, for example, material culture was interwoven with other entries on highly valued subjects. In one mid-eighteenth-century common-place book of unknown authorship, entries on coats of arms, genealogies, inscriptions, and great buildings of note are interleaved with a recipe for linen stained by fruit, notes on the price of tea, and some miscellaneous accounts.[134] A later York commonplace book completed mainly from the 1820s, similarly combines recipes for mouth wash and ginger beer, an entry for furniture bought and their prices (on 6 November 1826), quotes from the Bible and local newspapers, and lists of births, marriages, and deaths.[135] Preserving these details in a commonplace book shows a significance to material culture that outstripped consumption or the management of resources. The lack of generic distinction is itself evidence of the meaningful connections writers made across their lives, and of the meaningful place accorded to objects within that mental landscape.

Objects were not simply the mundane props of everyday life for men, but were also markers of time and occasion and makers of memory. A good example of this is the 'commonplace book' of Christopher Tuthill, inscribed by him in 1681, and typical of the varied form that men's domestic writings took. Christopher Tuthill (1650–1712) was born in Minehead on 24 June 1650. A merchant, he later settled in Youghal, on the south coast of Ireland, later becoming a Bailiff. Though the pedigree of the family gives his date of arrival as 1685, his list of linen taken in 1684 is headed, 'In youghall 10th February'.[136] Married to Mary Hall on 19 May 1685, the couple had five children, Mary dying in January 1695.[137] During the Irish war, Tuthill was on the side of the English, carrying information for them in September 1691. He subsequently rented 'the Town Bog' as a Bailiff, though the land was damaged by Danish soldiers involved in the conflict. Later, he took a further lease of Kilmore, Ballyliney, and Doorless in 1694, and renewed this lease in 1699.[138] By this time Tuthill had married Hannah Rule (in September 1698).[139] Their marriage articles stated that Hannah owned one-third of the estate, and that another third of the estate would be held in Trust for her. Upon Christopher's death, Hannah was to receive the moiety of his third. Shortly after his death,

[134] Ingilby commonplace book (mid-eighteenth century), West Yorkshire Archive Service Leeds: WYL230/3739.

[135] Diary of Christopher Ware of 54 Stonegate, York City Archives: Acc 143.

[136] The commonplace book of Christopher Tuthill, 1681–1858, William Andrews Clark Memorial Library: MS.1977.003, f. 4.

[137] *Pedigree of Tuthill of Peamore, Co. Devon, of Kilmore and of Faha, Co. Limerick, with Genealogical Notes of the Family, compiled by Lt. Col. P. B. Tuthill, Summersdale, Chichester*. Reprinted from *Miscellanea Genealogica et Heraldica* (London: Mitchell, Hughes & Clarke, 1908), p. 19.

[138] Ibid. p. 19. See also *The Council Book of the Corporation of Youghal from 1600 to 1659, from 1666 to 1687 and from 1690 to 1800. Edited from the original, with Annals and Appendices by Richard Caulfield LL.D., F.S.A., Guildford, 1878*, National Library of Ireland: Ir 94145 c 4; quote from entry for 22 July 1691. I thank Justin Homan Martin for his assistance.

[139] *Pedigree of Tuthill of Peamore*, p. 19.

a deed granted one part of this portion to Christopher and Hannah's son John, his eldest son having died aged 4 in 1695.[140]

Such eventful lives may be a spur to write them down. From one end the Tuthill volume consists of select autobiographical details and those relating to his family.[141] The volume then narrates Tuthill's imprisonment as a Protestant in Ireland in 1689 and 1690.[142] Rather incongruously, this section is immediately followed by a recipe for pickled salmon. From the other end of the book, Tuthill entered his 'accounts'. These were not double-entry accounts, but sometimes simple lists of things without numerical value. Tuthill took frequent stock of his domestic possessions, categorizing objects in several different ways. Separate lists were compiled for books and plate in 1681, and linen in 1681 and 1684, all with values noted. This manner of recording objects by type is soon superseded.[143] The next section recorded the 'Acc[t]: Cost off Goods' for separate occasional years, including 1676, 1683, 1688, 1688 (for a second time), 1685, 1684, 1680, and 1689. Finally,

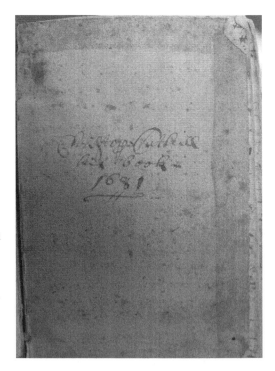

Figure 8: The commonplace book of Christopher Tuthill, 1681–1858, William Andrews Clark Memorial Library: MS.1977.003. By kind permission of The William Andrews Clark Memorial Library, University of California, Los Angeles.

[140] National Library of Ireland: Lands Index for County Cork, Grantors names Index, vol. 23, p. 7, no. 12227; *Pedigree of Tuthill of Peamore*, p. 20.
[141] For a discussion of this section of the volume, see Chapter 5, pp. 139–40.
[142] Commonplace book of Christopher Tuthill, f. 4–5.
[143] Ibid. f. 2–10.

objects were ordered yet again according to who had gifted them. These periodic inventories were perhaps a response to the unpredictable pattern of Tuthill's life, and his desire to take stock before or after a household move. Some of the inventories were taken as a bachelor and around the time of his first marriage to Mary Hall in 1685; others were made around the time of the sailing from Minehead to Youghal, following the later travels of Mary and their children across the Celtic Sea, and immediately prior to Tuthill's first imprisonment. These lists record the movement of goods across the sea, between Minehead and Youghall. Two lists titled '@ *1688* Youghall' are of items sent from Minehead, the first list from his wife including damask napkins and Holland pillowcases.[144] The two lists of goods made in 1699 are in a different hand, much more disciplined than that of the previous writer, and possibly that of his new wife Hannah.[145] Given the risk of losing goods during travel, Tuthill was well advised to make these inventories. Yet this motivation does not account for his inclusion of the information in this volume alongside other kinds of valuable family record, nor for their listing in several different ways. Tuthill's possessions were being preserved in paper and ink.

Commonplace books were originally compendia of noteworthy extracts which would allow the user to recall significant pieces of information, including philosophical concepts, extraordinary tales, and items of family memoranda. Susan Stabile has demonstrated beautifully how the manuscript commonplace book was used by early American women writers to preserve their memories, in a particularly feminine tradition of remembering.[146] Yet the fixing of memories in writing was clearly important to men too. Tuthill used his book to order, record, and preserve apparently unrelated items of personal relevance. His movements across the sea and into and out of prison made his own and his family's future uncertain, and in this context Tuthill's writing can be seen to determinedly fix things during tumultuous times. We cannot know the particular significance of the seemingly out of place recipe for pickled salmon, but, given the weight that Tuthill must have attached to the written record of his life, imprisonment, and domestic possessions, we can safely speculate that this was for him a similarly meaningful and significant feature of domestic life. Quite simply, this volume allowed a variety of domestic things to be later brought to mind.

Objects were remembered. Objects also aided remembrance. Never succumbing to sentimentality in his writing, Robert Sharp plainly reported buying two dozen lead pencils, half a dozen silver spoons ('for which I gave two pounds'), three hundred quills, two hundred needles, 'and a penknife and a half'.[147] Writing equipment were tools of the trade for a schoolmaster, of course; other items may have aided comfort and were certainly functional.[148] Yet the half a penknife was a new

---

[144] Ibid. ff. 15–16.   [145] Ibid. ff. 2–10, 12–16, 21–3.

[146] Susan M. Stabile, *Memory's Daughters: The Material Culture of Remembrance in Eighteenth-century America* (Ithaca, NY; London: Cornell University Press, 2003), pp. 80–2.

[147] *Diary of Robert Sharp*, Friday 7 July 1828, p. 46; Wednesday 6 September 1826, p. 62; Wednesday 1 November 1826, p. 81; Saturday 9 December 1826, p. 90.

[148] Finn, 'Men's Things', p. 141.

blade to be put into an old haft, probably the one briefly mentioned in August 1829: 'that was Jane's, it is not of much value but a great favourite on account of having belonged to her'.[149] Jane was a daughter of Robert, who had died aged 11 in 1815.[150] Keeping hold of a cheap penknife handle suited Robert's proclivity for prudence, but it was the emotional attachment that made it a favourite. Indeed, when Sharp spoke about things in any detail, it was often in the context of his children, specifically his son William. In South Cave with Ann and their daughter Eliza, Robert's long-distance relationship with his London-based son seems to have been built partly on the exchange of things. These were not always new purchases. William would send his clothes-washing and repairs home to South Cave in Yorkshire via Hull; one delivery appears to have 100 items of clothing, including '4 Night Shirts, 8 Shirts, 36 Collars, 32 Cravats, 2 Pairs Drawers, 4 Silk Handkerchiefs, 5 Night Caps, [and] 9 Pairs Stockings'.[151] These would have been prepared carefully by Ann, as were the clothes that William sent on Saturday 10 February 1827 and which were 'got up in a superior stile and bleached so fine & white that they are inimitable'.[152] William also sent clothes north for his father. Ever thrifty, Robert had made a pair of black breeches and a waistcoat out of some trousers and a coat that William sent in 1825.[153] When a long-missing box finally arrived from William in October 1827, it contained a selection of admirable handkerchiefs and useful second-hand clothes: a coat that Robert planned to use, trousers for 'excellent waistcoats', and 'a Hat which I am told will make a Man of me when I wear it'.[154] William also sent new clothing, such as the fine cravats that Robert received shortly before Christmas in 1826.[155] This father and son exchanged and discussed clothes frequently, though Ann and Eliza also received new and second-hand clothing from William. As Robert said of 'a pair of old Shoes' sent by William to his mother, '[s]ometimes articles of small value are highly prized'.[156]

Other men were cognizant of the domestic manufacture of clothes in their family, and the attachment of each garment to its owner. Residing in the north-east not far from Sharp, the farmer William Burton bought mostly textiles to be made up at home. It is significant, though, that whether raw materials or made-up garments, Burton is careful to pin each item to the wearer, such as the £4 2s paid to Mʳ Leethem in August 1832 for 'New Coat & Pantaloons Self', and the 10s and 81/2d paid to 'Frances Selly for Julia a new Bonnett' the following month.[157] Women were heavily invested in material things, especially textiles, though evi-

---

[149] *Diary of Robert Sharp*, Monday 10 August 1829, p. 216.
[150] Ibid.
[151] Ibid. Annotation to Letter from Robert to William, 29 September 1825, p. 28.
[152] Ibid. Saturday 10 February 1827, p. 106.
[153] Ibid. Letter from Robert to William, 11 July 1825, p. 23.
[154] Ibid. Wednesday 17 October 1827, p. 166.
[155] Ibid. Wednesday 13 December 1826, p. 90.
[156] Ibid. Thursday 25 January, p. 101.
[157] Account book and diary of gentleman farmer William Burton (1832–4), West Yorkshire Archive Service, Leeds: GA/C/38, WYL22, entries for 27 August 1832, 18–24 September 1832.

dently men's relationships could also be bonded by clothing.[158] One particularly poignant example can be found in the autobiography of Samuel Millar (1762–1819), a Scottish merchant, sailor, and eventual shipowner. Having accompanied his father on board ship in 1817, Millar's son David was dying of a fever. In his final moments David asked, 'O Dear Father give me a kiss'. Samuel describes regret and guilt at having to refuse: he could not kiss him on the lips because his son is bleeding at the mouth, 'his Hearts Blood coming from'. Once dead, Samuel dressed his dead son in a linen shirt and white cotton night cap, before cutting 'a few locks of hair from his Head to Keep in Rememberance of that good Boy'.[159] A white linen shirt denoted cleanliness, respectability, and purity.[160] In Samuel Millar's elegiac story, the white shirt restored to the boy—and to his father's memory—his intact and clean body.

Clothing was a high-value and frequent category of expenditure in men's accounting records. Some men spent a significant proportion of their disbursements on new clothing, though clothing repairs also feature very frequently. Thomas Mort's accounts for the year 1703/4 contain more than 30 separate entries for garments and accessories: most were for new bespoke items (including 8 pairs of shoes, 5 pairs of stockings, and a wig), and 11 were for repairs (such as mending 'my old black wastcoat' and re-soleing a shoe).[161] A mature bachelor such as Mort perhaps had proportionately more to spend on such items than men with families. Yet married men also spent notable amounts on clothing, in a period that supposedly witnessed the 'great male renunciation' of fashionable sartorial display.[162] Some years later in nearby Bury, the appraisers of yeoman/schoolmaster Edmund Pilkington valued several costly items of household goods, the most valuable items of furniture being a clock and a dresser, each valued at £4 10s. Pilkington's will has little detail of the decorative features of the house, though his account book helps build a fuller picture: the milano fabric bought for a bedhanging in February 1732, and then hung by the tailor (along with some quilting) two months later, the clock case and clock bought for £4 19s on 14 March 1732, and a 'White Chamber Pot', stools, and feather bed bought in April.[163] Nevertheless, the clock and dresser head the inventory, suggesting, perhaps, that they were visible in prominent positions on entering the house. Yet even these prize possessions were outdone by the value of Pilkington's 'Wearing Apparel and Watch', valued at £5.[164]

---

[158] Amanda Vickery, 'His and Hers: Gender, Consumption and Household Accounting in Eighteenth-century England,' in Ruth Harris, Lyndal Roper, and Olwen Hufton (eds), *The Art of Survival: Gender and History in Europe, 1450–2000: Essays in Honour of Olwen Hufton, Past & Present*, Supplement 1, 2006, pp. 12–38. Also appears in the book *Behind Closed Doors: At Home in Georgian England*, pp. 106–28.

[159] Diary of Samuel Millar, Henry E. Huntington Library: HM 47403, pp. 304–5.

[160] Beverly Lemire, *The Business of Everyday Life: Gender, Practice and Social Politics in England, c.1600–1900* (Manchester and New York: Manchester University Press, 2005), p. 115.

[161] Account book of Thomas Mort, entries for the year 1703/4, quote from 5 February.

[162] David Kuchta, *The Three-Piece Suit and Modern Masculinity: England, 1550–1850* (Berkeley, CA: University of California Press, 2000).

[163] [Edmund Pilkington] Account book, William Andrews Clark Memorial Library: MS.1976.001, 22 February 1731; 18 April 1732, 14 March 1731, 25 and 16 April 1732.

[164] 'Will and inventory of Edmund Pilkington, Yeoman, 24th February 1755', Lancashire Record Office: WCW 1755.

Even for labourers, contemporary recommendations expected husbands to take 42 per cent of the annual household clothing budget (compared to the 28 per cent taken by the wife).[165] The household budget of Henry Richardson matched this for the sample year 1748, the first year of his marriage, though with his wife receiving a somewhat smaller percentage: the total expenditure of £216 6s 6d divided with 19 per cent on Mrs Richardson, 37 per cent on Mr Richardson, and 44 per cent on children or non-identified recipients.[166] For this northern Rector, fine clothing was one important part of self-presentation; damaged or inferior garments had undoubtedly negative connotations. Dreaming of his rector's gown on the night of 18 January 1700, both the wife and maid-servant of Thomas Naishe (b.1669) of Salisbury reported it being 'bad' and 'full of montrous holes'. Naish prayed that this did not mark some evil to come, and asked for the Lord's assistance so, 'I may never dishonour my profession, or bring shame on my function, or scandal upon my religion'.[167] For an individual man, dress could express probity and virtue. In the case of fathers, sons, and other household members, fitting out a boy or young man or exchanging appropriate garments might be seen as a middling-sort variation of the dynastic concerns that gentry men expressed in their domestic consumption.[168]

As seen above, the shaping of father–son relationships with objects is clear in the writings of Robert Sharp. Robert's diary was itself the documentary remains of his relationship with his son, having been written the diary expressly for him. The diary itself—sent to William in regular instalments—was one of the many written items linking father and son, alongside the letters, books, and newspapers. Not surprisingly, perhaps, while his daughter Eliza, who was resident with her parents in the early years of the diary, is hardly mentioned, William is a frequent character in the entries. Yet William features in the diary most often through a small range of objects. All of these were themselves contained in William's box, which regularly journeyed back and forth between South Cave and London. In December 1821 a box for William contained partridges, apples, gingerbread, and stockings.[169] In the same year, the Christmas box contained William's shirts, a newspaper, a goose pie, a pork and beef pie, homemade sausages, black puddings and mince pies, and 'five Gold Guineas'.[170] Preparing the box in South Cave was a busy ceremony that often involved the entire family: a 'throng' prepared William's Christmas box on Saturday 16 December 1826, with 'All busy making Minced tarts and a Pork pie for

[165] John Styles, *The Dress of the People: Everyday Fashion in Eighteenth-century England* (New Haven: Yale University Press, 2007), pp. 338, 348.

[166] Richardson, 'A Diary of Disbursements', calculation based on entries for the year 1748.

[167] *The Diary of Thomas Naish*, ed. Doreen Slater (Devizes: Wiltshire Archeological and Natural History Society, 1964), vol. 20, 19 January 1700, p. 42.

[168] William Parkinson spends regular amounts on clothes for the Morley sons in his charge, William and Joseph. See Account book of William Smedley, for example, June 1747 and March 1750. See also discussion of William Stout's clothing of his nephew in Chapter 6, p. 181.

[169] *Diary of Robert Sharp*, Letter from Robert to William, 25 December 1821, p. 9.

[170] Ibid. Letter from Robert to William, 25 December 1821, pp. 10–13.

William'.[171] The items sent to South Cave by William also caused great anticipation.[172] In 1825 William sent home on separate occasions a hymn book, pocket books, and mint lozenges; a printed catalogue, mint drops, and novels; and lozenges, tobacco, ginger, and a selection of books. On this last occasion, Robert reported his daughter's disappointment that 'there was not the smallest token for Eliza'.[173] Meat was often included in the box, and Robert made several excursions to obtain hams for William in 1826. Failing to do so, Robert states, 'however I hope the Box will be fitted up to his satisfaction'.[174] The passage of boxes was so busy, that at one point Robert commented, 'This Box, which we now send, will go inside of the last, and the last will go in the inside of the next we send, so that they will fit one into another like the Sentences in the Agricultural Report, which Cobbett compares to a nest of Pill Boxes'.[175] The largest was perhaps 'the great military Box' he filled with William's clothes and silk handkerchief in September 1825.[176] The range of gifts, tokens, foodstuffs, and books through which the family remained connected to this absent son and brother reveals the myriad domestic items that shored up men's familial relationships. In his letters and diary Robert Sharp revealed the careful attention that he paid to this traffic in things.

In discussing household things in letters—and indeed packaging things with the letters—male writers showed how material culture was part of their ongoing relationships. Writing from Paris in June 1762, as his wife Elizabeth prepared to leave England to join him, Laurence Sterne gave specific instructions on the objects she should pack. Initially requesting only watch chains, pins, needles, and a string bottle-screw,[177] he wrote a subsequent letter focusing primarily on equipment for hot drinks. 'Bring your silver coffee-pot', he began, continuing:

> I had like to have forgot a most necessary thing, there are no copper tea-kettles to be had in France, and we shall find such a thing the most comfortable utensil in the house—buy a good strong one, which will hold two quarts—a dish of tea will be of comfort to us in our journey south—I have a bronze tea-pot, which we will carry also, as China cannot be brought over from England, we must make up a villainous party-coloured tea equipage to regale ourselves.[178]

The letter ends with the parting comment: 'Memorandum: Bring watch-chains, tea-kettle, knives, cookery books, &c./You will smile at this last article—so adieu.'[179] Sterne alludes to a private joke that he shared with Elizabeth, the content

---

[171] Ibid. Saturday 16 December 1826, p. 91. For the same 'throng' preparing to send William's things, see also Thursday 3 December 1829, p. 236, Thursday 2 June 1831, p. 313.

[172] For example, see, ibid. Saturday 3 March, p. 112.

[173] Ibid. pp. 14, 21, 25.

[174] Ibid. Saturday 15 July 1826, p. 48; Sunday 3 December 1826, p. 88; Wednesday 13 December 1826, p. 90. Quote at p. 90. For other entries on meat for William, see, for example, pp. 177, 198.

[175] Ibid. Letter from Robert to William, 25 December 1821, p. 11.

[176] Ibid. Letter from Robert to William, 29 September 1825, p. 28.

[177] *Letters of the Late Rev. Mr Laurence Sterne, To his most intimate Friends*, 3 vols (London, 1775), vol. 1, p. 166.

[178] Ibid. pp. 170–1.   [179] Ibid. p. 175.

of which we might only guess at. But to be sure, everyday things sustained men's social and familial relationships and enabled intimacy.

'OLIVE PLANTS AROUND MY TABLE'

Sterne's joke may have alluded to his unfamiliarity with kitchen matters, though we cannot be sure. Robert Sharp was more assuredly self-mocking about his culinary ineptitude. For example, he described how one Richard Thornton entered with the intention of purchasing vinegar for his cold beef dinner, but on finding Robert serving in the family shop changed his order: 'when he saw me he asked for Ink', Robert explained, 'imagining I suppose that I was more used to Ink than Vinegar'. Thornton's intimation that Robert was unfamiliar with cooking ingredients is matched by Sharp's own snipe at Thornton's own culinary ineptitude: 'Rd. did not find out his mistake till he poured the Ink upon his Beef, he thought it looked black, then he recollected he had asked for Ink, thus was he baulked of Beef & Vinegar'.[180] Nevertheless, men's attention to the details of food and cooking implements, read alongside the printed sources discussed in Chapter 2, caution against the assumption that all men were ambivalent about food preparation. Tuthill's recipe for pickled salmon was one example of a man's safekeeping of a culinary recipe. Medicinal recipes, historically overlapping with food recipes, certainly appear with some regularity in men's commonplace books. Household accounts abutted a recipe for 'A cure for the most desperate toothache' and 'A Receipt for Rheumatic Pains', while descriptions of war with America were punctuated by a recipe 'To make the Green Oil Good for Bruises' and 'Directions for Cleaning Brown Tea Urns &c'.[181] In contrast, women's cookbooks combined recipes for medicine and beauty with those for food. The cookbook of Margrett Greene includes entries 'To Take Red Pimples of the Face' and 'Lady Wreckleys receipt for a Cancer in the breast', for example.[182] As the title of this last recipe indicated, recipes were often circulated between women. Sara Pennell has described this as 'a crucial medium of female association, conversation and friendship', comparing this lightly to the model of knowledge exchange within the gentlemanly culture of natural philosophical practice undertaken by male members of the Royal Society.[183] The men's writings used in this book do not reveal such extensive networks, but they do provide a tantalizing

---

[180] *Diary of Robert Sharp*, Friday 5 February 1830, p. 246.

[181] For pickled salmon see, Commonplace book of Christopher Tuthill, July 1688, f. 27–8; for teeth and rheumatism see Diary of Joshua Sagar of Horbury (1790), RL Arundale Collection, West Yorkshire Archive Service, Wakefield: C1039 (add. Ad), 23 March 30; for bruises and tea urns see, 'R. Mathews Commonplace book' (*c*.1780s), Henry E. Huntington Library: HM694, fol. 4, 16.

[182] Cook book of Margrett Greene, 1701, William Andrews Clark Memorial Library: MS.1980.004, fol. 16, 60.

[183] Sara Pennell, 'Perfecting Practice? Women, Manuscript Recipes and Knowledge in Early Modern England', in Victoria E. Burke and Jonathan Gibson (eds), *Early Modern Women's Manuscript Writing: Selected Papers from the Trinty/Trent Colloquium* (Aldershot: Ashgate, 2004), pp. 242, 247. Quote at p. 242.

glimpse of what may have been the limited exchanges between men on these matters, or the participation of men in the networks of women.[184] Margrett Greene's book was, in fact, also inscribed 'John Craven'.[185]

As a ship's captain, Samuel Millar necessarily concerned himself with matters of health, food, and diet. His remarkable memoir written in *c.*1819, but based on records made from 1775, records the foodstuffs that he is able to obtain for his shipmen and also the meals enjoyed by merchants on land. In Buenos Aires he finds the eggs make very good pudding, the milk very good, the butter good but dear, and the cheese 'worse than any of our Scots Cheese'.[186] Millar is similarly voluminous on the tarnished elegance of the objects on the breakfast table of 'one of the first Rate Merchants': milk is served in 'a large dirty Pitcher', and drunk from 'some White Basons some half Broken and some not over Clean', while tea was taken from 'a Tin Tea Pot that 10 years ago might perhaps been a good one but now it had only a half Spout together with small Tea cup and Broken Saucer'.[187] The material decline is matched by a moral and sexual one: whereas in the West Indies a merchant was expected to have either 'a White Woman for his Wife' or 'what he call his girl', here in South America the merchants 'did not much mind if there is not such a thing as 6 Families slave or Women of any kind to be seen in any Merchant's house'.[188] The worn and broken crockery laid on this table reflected the degeneration of the man to whom it belonged.

This description was particularly significant given the importance attached to occasions of domestic sociability in eighteenth-century English home. Carole Shammas argued that the eighteenth-century home became a centre for non-market-oriented sociability organized by women from the 1720s, opposed to the sociability outside the home engaged in by men.[189] Female work patterns became oriented towards home consumption and sociability, and women acquired autonomy from using tea objects as 'tools of domesticity'. 'Domesticity', indeed, was 'largely a female cause'.[190] Such claims were qualified somewhat by Lorna Weatherill's finding that men and women consumed in equal measure books and utensils for hot drinks.[191] Tea-drinking does appear to have been a domestic activity over which women often presided.[192] Despite the undeniably strong cultural association of women and china, though, some sources suggest that the typical ceramic consumer was a man.[193] Contemporary producers of fine objects clearly recognized

---

[184] Pennell's account includes references to male participation. See ibid. p. 242.

[185] Cook book of Margrett Greene, 1701, f. v64.

[186] Diary of Samuel Millar, pp. 213–14.

[187] Ibid. p. 214.

[188] Ibid. p. 215.

[189] Carole Shammas, 'The Domestic Environment in Early Modern England and America', *Journal of Social History*, 14 (1980), pp. 3–24.

[190] Ibid. pp. 5, 16. See also Chapter 1, p. 9.

[191] Lorna Weatherill, 'A Possession of One's Own: Women and Consumer Behaviour in England, 1660–1740', *Journal of British Studies*, 25 (1986), pp. 131–56.

[192] Kowaleski-Wallace, 'Tea, Gender and Domesticity', pp. 131–45.

[193] Elizabeth Kowaleski-Wallace, *Consuming Subjects. Women, Shopping, and Business in the Eighteenth Century* (New York: Columbia University Press, 1997), p. 58.

the importance of appealing to male consumers.[194] More prosaically, men's demand for the lowly and ubiquitous clay smoking pipe certainly boosted the production of domestic ceramic goods after the seventeenth century.[195] Prominent men established themselves as fashion leaders in fine ceramic ware. George Washington's collecting habits drew American taste towards the Chinese and French.[196] In this influential family, it was George Washington—'a careful household manager', and known to English writers as such—who did the ordering of ceramics.[197] Set against this Atlantic context, Millar's comments on the Buenos Aires merchant's table become a pointed criticism of poor male management.

Recorded in men's eighteenth-century domestic writings are different occasions of domestic dining and drinking, something of a continuation of seventeenth-century practices in which '[m]en were prominent participants in domestic hospitality'.[198] Thomas Naish hosted the Pipe feast for 18 members of the society on 17 July 1709, 'at my house'.[199] Between April and June 1798, Richard Hey (brother of the vicar Samuel Hey at Steeple Ashton, and uncle of the Yorkshire vicar Samuel Sharp), recorded the many occasions of tea drinking, dining, and socializing in mixed groups, sometimes 'with us' at his home in Hertingfordbury and sometimes elsewhere.[200] For Robert Sharp, domestic sociability involved tea, ale, dinner, and, occasionally, wine, at public houses, friends' homes, and his own house. In this case, this sociability was usually male-only, though Sharp would also dine at women's houses and have mixed company to tea at his own house.[201] Though reported infrequently, these occasions must nevertheless have been accompanied in practice by daily acts of family-centred commensality.

Given men's engagement with domestic material culture as property, through provisioning and as constituting family relationships, these occasions of domestic sociability were rich with meaning. The connection between property, ritual, and authority is particularly clear in the images of men gathered with family and friends around a table. One of the most expressive of these images was penned by John Darracott, in the confessional account of his life to God, written between 1707 and 1730. 'John Darracott jun.' was a merchant from an important local family in the busy port town of Bideford, North Devon. He died in 1733 and was buried on

---

[194] Moira Vincentelli, *Women and Ceramics: Gendered Vessels* (Manchester: Manchester University Press, 2000), p. 112; Sarah Richards, *Eighteenth-Century Ceramics: Products for a Civilised Society* (Manchester and New York: Manchester University Press, 1999), p. 39.

[195] Carole Shammas, *The Pre-Industrial Consumer in England and America* (Oxford: Clarendon, 1990), p. 187.

[196] Susan Gray Detweiler, with Christine Meadows, *George Washington's Chinaware* (New York: Harry N Abrams, 1982), p. 9.

[197] Ibid. p. 9. One English author included an article titled 'General Washington's Economy' in his commonplace book: see 'R. Mathews Commonplace book', fol. 141–2 and Chapter 2, pp. 66–7.

[198] Flather, *Gender and Space*, esp. pp. 98–9. Quote at p. 133.

[199] *Diary of Thomas Naish*, p. 66.

[200] Diary of Richard Hey, West Yorkshire Archive Service, Wakefield, Samuel Sharp family papers: C281, 23/3 (April–June 1798).

[201] On mixed sociability, see, for example, *Diary of Robert Sharp*, Friday 29 December 1826 and Tuesday 31 May 1831, pp. 94, 313.

Figure 9: 15–17 Allhalland Street, Bideford, North Devon. Photograph by Denzil Bath.

28 May of that year.[202] On 1 January 1730, reviewing his life 20 years following his marriage, and aged around 40, he describes his life in the ten years after his marriage in 1710:

> I was most Happily married To yᵉ most vertuous of wives a scene of pleasure usher'd in my married Estate I had Riches to Command of & friends & Relations served[?] my house and a Hopefull ofspring Like olive plants surrounded my Table.[203]

Darracott's household family is made up of riches, friends, relations, children, and things, all circling what Darracott describes indubitably 'my Table' in 'my house'. The possessive determiner places Darracott at the centre of this image, not least because this is intended as Protestant confessional writing concerned with the individual soul. Indeed, the final reference to the non-native olive plants is taken from the Psalm 128.[204] At the centre and in 'Command', it is Darracott's duty to tend to

---

[202] Bideford parish registers, Devon Record Office: Burials 1679–1733. I thank staff at the record office.

[203] Diary of John Darracott: fol. 200–1.

[204] *The book of Psalms, with the argument of each Psalm, And A Preface Giving Some General Rules For The Interpretation Of This Sacred Book. By Peter Allix D. D. late Treasurer of Salisbury.* The second edition, (London, 1717), p. 205. See *Eighteenth Century Collections Online*, <http://find.galegroup.com.eresources.shef.ac.uk/ecco/>, Gale Document Number: CW118057407 (accessed 29 November 2010).

this house, including the plant-like children, as a husbandman. At the close of the narrative, and following a series of deaths, those left are gathered again in a thoroughly oeconomical scene: 'Bless me & yᵉ Remains of my Children & make my house sett To Grow and prosper.'[205] Imagining his children around his table, Darracott employed the richly symbolic religious motif of communion at the Lord's table, and his own diary contains numerous references to being a guest at God's Table. Tables were the setting for men's physical and spiritual care of the family: 'how many there be', John Flavell asked, 'whose very tables, in respect of any worship God hath there, do very little differ from the very cribs and mangers at which their horses feed?'[206]

Tables also held secular meanings. As the phrase 'bed and board' suggested, food was both one crucial element of the marital relationship as well as an expectation from temporary lodging. Evidently, the table was a symbol of a householder's authority. Household manuals presented tables as sites of performance for the carving of meat and a master's table as open expressions of his authority.[207] Poorer households may have only one chair alongside other forms of seating, the head of the household presumably taking the former.[208] In households of varying sizes, the table served as an important object, enabling not just ritual commensality but also the monitoring and the regulated distribution of food and drink. Food and its material culture were 'an ordering tool and a template of a particular variety of order'.[209] In James Brydges' house, Cannons, tables served as instruments of control. In a remarkable volume of instructions for the household composed in the early 1720s, the Usher of the Halls was deputed to observe servants carefully at mealtimes, ensuring that 'perfect order be kept', and that if a person is 'rude or misbehaves himself, He is to turn him out of the Hall & not to suffer him to have any Diner that Day nor till he had Acknowledged his Offence publickly before all the Servants'.[210] Alcohol consumption was carefully regulated for each table in the section, 'Regulation for the Allowance of Strong Beer and Ale': the Chaplain's table receiving what they requested, the Officer's table enjoying two bottles of ale ordinarily, or two bottles of strong beer and four bottles of ale when the family was at Cannons, and the servants in the Servants' Hall allowed 28 gallons of ale each week.[211] The same gradations of hierarchy were observable in the objects that diners used at table. The 'Necessaries' deemed wanting by the steward at the Chaplain's Table ran to 18 wine glasses, 8 beer glasses, 1 silver tankard, 4 silver beakers, 12 silver knives,

[205] Diary of John Darracott, fol. 201–2.

[206] John Flavell, *Husbandry Spiritualized: or, the Heavenly Use of Earthly Things* (Leeds, 1788), p. 245.

[207] See, for example, Hannah Woolley, *The Queen-like Closet* (1684).

[208] Flather, *Gender and Space*, pp. 63–4.

[209] Sara Pennell, 'The Material Culture of Food in Early Modern England, *c.*1650–1750', in Sarah Tarlow and Susie West (eds), *The Familiar Past? Archaeologies of Later Historical Britain* (London and New York: Routledge, 1999), p. 47.

[210] Bound volume by Lionell Norman, steward to James Brydges, Stowe Papers, Henry E. Huntington Library: HEH ST44, Part I, 'The Steward's Instructions', p. 10.

[211] Ibid. Part I, 'Regulation for the Allowance of Strong Beer and Ale', p. 22.

forks, and spoons, 12 pewter dishes, 60 pewter plates, and 12 pewter cheese plates. The Servants' Hall tables were equipped with 36 spoons, 5 pint horns, 3 half pint horns, and 6 wooden trenchers.[212] Subsequently Brydges instructed a steward to start a daily record of guests dining at all tables, to be presented to him each Monday morning.[213] Brydges even used provisions to discipline members of the household. Following 'rude and affronting Language' spoken by the confectioner during a dispute about wine at the Officer's table, Brydges withheld wine from that table for a month in 1721.[214] Brydges' estate at Cannons was over 200 miles from Darracott's more humble residence on the Devon coast at Bideford, and these men were further separated by several gradations of rank. Yet for both the table was a significant feature of their oeconomical management, practised and imagined.

In popular printed literature throughout the period, the table was the focus for the domestic sociability orchestrated or presided over by the male housekeeper. The ballad 'The Old Oak Table' depicted a man dreaming that his table told its own history and then complained that it would one day be cut up for firewood. On waking, the man celebrated the continuing role of this articulate object, as long as 'each friend that my humble cheer will partake,/Shall be welcome around my oak table'.[215] Such scenes emphasized the sturdy and organic material of the wood, as well as the gathering of the group around—almost its growth out of—the table. Family members were thus easily imagined as crops to be nurtured, as they were in Darracott's text. Chairs were another item of sturdy furniture imagined to root men to the house. William Stout remembered his father 'sitting in his chair by his house fire' when he called all his children together to exhort them to live godly lives just a few days before his death.[216] Laurence Sterne remembered his father dying in 1731 while in his arm chair.[217] In 1750 Richard Kay reported visiting 'Brother Joseph Baron' while ill, and finding him unable to sit up in bed, though Kay still 'in an officious Manner seated him in his ~~easy~~ Chair with his Gown on'.[218] Another writer reported how he 'went into the Parlour and sat down in my Father's Armchair' following an accident to his hand.[219] In the ballad 'The Old Home down in the Farm', the narrator reflects on his own ageing while his own mother and father are dying; the passing of life is clearly articulated as the narrator imagines someone else seated in his father's chair.[220] Robert Sharp reported a fascinating

[212] Ibid. Part II, 'The Steward's Instructions', pp. 5, 6.

[213] Audit book for Cannons, Stowe Papers, Henry E. Huntington Library: ST24 vol. 1, Audit book for 16 January 1720–27 April 1724, f. 29, Canons 19 June 1721.

[214] Ibid. f. 7, London 3 April 1721; f. 15, London 17 April 1721. In fact, the wine is allowed again after only 14 days.

[215] 'The Old Oak Table' (London: Printed and Published by H. Such, 123, Union Street, Borough. SE, no date), Sheffield University Special Collections: Hewins Ballads, 529(A).

[216] *Autobiography of William Stout*, p. 73.

[217] 'Memoirs of the Life and Family of the late Rev. Mr Laurence Sterne', in *Letters of the Late Rev. Mr Laurence Sterne*, 3 vols (London, 1775), vol. 1, p. 16.

[218] Diary of Richard Kay, 24 June 1750.

[219] 'Bath Diary for 1769', Henry E. Huntington Library: HM62593, 21 February.

[220] 'The Old Home down in the Farm', Written and composed by Gustavus Dubois. Sung by H. J. Howard. Music published by C. Sheard & Co., 192, High Holborn, WC (H. P. Such, Printer, 183, Union Street, Borough, SE), Sheffield University Special Collections: Hewins Ballads, 555/556(K).

exchange in which a chair prompted a tense exchange over a man's provisioning for a house. Having been invited to sit down in a shop, a customer began pondering on the virtues of marriage and furniture. 'I have not got an Arm Chair yet', he reflects, 'I should like one like this it is so easy...an Arm Chair I will have.' The shopkeeper replied, 'well you must buy one when you get your furniture', at which the customer is affronted: 'I fancy I have as good *fonniterry* as a deal of folks', he insists, 'I laid out eight pounds to furnish my house so I will leave you to judge whether I should not have some capital *fonniterry*!!!'[221] As represented by Sharp, a 'great chair' was a must for a man of comfortable social status. While sitting was not positively associated with relaxation in the middle decades of the eighteenth century, and chairs were not for reclining but for activity, the 'arm chairs' and 'easy chairs' connote the steady and comfortable authority of men in the house.[222] By 1822, William Cobbett prescribed wooden, solid, manly, and English furniture for the labourers of England. 'Oak-tables, bedsteads and stools, chairs of oak or of yew-tree' were to populate the rooms of these men in a return to a traditional English taste 'for things solid, sound, and good; for the *useful*, the *decent*, the *cleanly* in dress, and not for the showy'. Instructively, given the repeated references to fathers and sons in men's discussions of domestic objects, Cobbett favoured things that could be passed down through the male line: 'A labourer ought to inherit something besides his toil from his great-grandfather'.[223] Just as women were linked corporeally to particular things—to fine china and petite desks—sturdy tables and chairs were exemplary masculine objects, synecdoches for men's bodies.[224]

CONCLUSION

Men engaged with objects as property, inheritance, symbols, makers of memory and relationships, as well as commodities. The varied types of material culture considered in this chapter constitute not the familiar terrain of the eighteenth-century world of goods, but instead a rather eclectic assortment of things that were important for the British men who left these documents. These things included the mundane and the everyday. The engagement of men with these kinds of goods and provisions was not the same as for women, servants, and their other housekeepers: these men knew the price of butter and bought the bread rolls, but none of the records used in this study show a man buying all the household items required for daily sustenance. Yet we cannot say that these men consumed only the large items that were purchased infrequently; on the contrary, these men were engaged with

---

[221] *Diary of Robert Sharp*, Wednesday 19 May 1830, p. 260.
[222] Glenn Adamson, 'Reading the Absent Object: The Case of the Missing Footstool', in Harvey (ed.), *History and Material Culture*, pp. 192–207.
[223] Cobbett, *Cottage Economy*, p. 197.
[224] Dena Goodman, 'Furnishing Discourses: Readings of a Writing Desk in Eighteenth-Century France', in Maxine Berg and Elizabeth Eger (eds), *Luxury in the Eighteenth Century* (Basingstoke: Palgrave, 2002), pp. 71–88; Beth Kowaleski-Wallace, 'Women, China and Consumer Culture in Eighteenth-century England', *Eighteenth-Century Studies*, 29, 2 (1995–6), pp. 153–67.

household consumption at most levels and positioned physically and imaginatively within the centre of the house by sturdy objects. Perhaps the objects of some of these men survive in descendants' living rooms, bric-a-brac shops, or beneath the ground; none of these middling-sort men were rich or remarkable enough to have their possessions preserved in museums. Yet, just as 'women mapped their lives through intimate domestic spaces and objects, forming links to the past and ensuring connections with posterity', so the manuscript sketches in which men recorded their lives were punctuated with meaningful things.[225]

The evidence considered in this chapter suggests that men viewed domestic material culture in distinctive ways. The social imagining of men's rights to property made their relationship with material culture one with considerable ideological import. Reflecting their good taste and oeconomy, the possession and management of domestic objects created and maintained authority. Domestic sociability around a table succinctly captured a man's authority and rootedness in the house, as well as his proprietorial engagement with domestic things. As examined earlier, such management had a continuing public significance in printed works throughout this period.[226] Men's oeconomical engagement with the material culture of the household also featured in public debates about men's wider political authority, a point that will be addressed in the final chapter of this book.[227] The housekeeping of the male householder remained a motif in the assessment of men's manly skills throughout the long eighteenth century. This was because in their careful management of property and personal investment in meaningful domestic things, men of the middling sort grounded their identities in the material culture of their domestic lives.

---

[225] Stabile, *Memory's Daughters*, p. 73.
[226] See Chapter 2, pp. 44–63.
[227] See Chapter 6, pp. 182–7.

5

Identity and Authority

It is apparent from the discourse of oeconomy, men's domestic practices, and men's own personal writings that the house served as a prism through which men were viewed, that their household management reinforced their social authority, and that their activities in the house were a focus for their private reflections on themselves and the people around them. The house was a principal aspect of an authoritative style of masculinity. This raises questions about the relationship between both personal identity and household authority that have received considerable attention in recent years. There are many possible sources of a person's identity, but work on the eighteenth century has pointed towards the emergence of individualism and the related appearance of a new kind of personal identity based on a 'self'. Charles Taylor's landmark study of philosophical and political thought has been complemented by works that have sought to locate this 'self' in an ever-expanding range of written materials, to specify the nature of this 'self', to establish a clear chronology for its development and—for some—to situate this new self in the modern home.[1]

The nature of personal identity is closely tied to the nature of domestic relations. Keith Wrightson has usefully summarized work on the early-modern family as three well-established narratives of concomitant changes: nuclearization, individualism, and emotionalism. The 'narrowing or contracting of the functions of the family and a more pronounced emphasis upon the cultivation of personal relationships within the nuclear core' had considerable impact on authority in the family: the 'greater personal autonomy' accorded to individuals lessened the authority of the domestic patriarch.[2] In other ways, individualism arguably made the unit of the household less significant to increasingly individual identities. Craig Muldrew envisages the locus of trust and social credit, for example, moving from the household to the self, from 'traditional hierarchy and local courts' to 'the liberal self-disciplined autonomous self'.[3] Such claims emphatically do not imply that individuals experienced a new equality or freedom within the family. As discussed in Chapter 1, arguments have been made for a new kind of patriarchy

---

[1] Charles Taylor, *Sources of the Self: The Making of Modern Identity* (Cambridge, MA: Harvard University Press, 1989).

[2] Keith Wrightson, 'The Family in Early Modern England: Continuity and Change', Stephen Taylor, Richard Connors, and Clyve Jones (eds), *Hanoverian Britain and Empire: Essays on Memory of Philip Lawson* (Woodbridge: Boydell, 1998), p. 3.

[3] Craig Muldrew, *The Economy of Obligation: The Culture of Credit and Social Relations in Early Modern England* (Basingstoke: Macmillan, 1998), p. 331.

perpetuated through internalized values and self-regulation rather than explicit rules and expressions of power. Fathers could be severe and authoritarian whilst also feeling love and joy.[4] Indeed, an internalized self is an important component of these arguments: the nature of personal identity, the autonomy of the individual, and the limits of the self were entwined with the practice of power and control.

There is a consensus amongst historians and literary scholars that the eighteenth century was a period of major change in this regard. Particular forms of writing have been central to the study of the new form of identity built around a 'self'. Michael Mascuch examines the genre of 'unified, retrospective, first-person prose narrative' as evidence for a new form of self.[5] This narrative form enabled the qualities of the 'self' that were key to the new individualist identities: a person's sense of autonomy, agency, and sovereignty over themselves and their destiny.[6] Human narratives of this kind are structured by parts of birth, life, and death, but they bring together these events within 'the tightly woven structure of an overarching authorial intention', usually manifest in a plot.[7] This argument develops Taylor's claim that modern identity was predicated on a 'disengaged, particular self, whose identity is constituted in memory', an identity that can only be found in and through a process of 'self-narration'.[8] For Mascuch this genre has many origins, but its full realization did not appear until the publication in 1792 of James Lackington's memoirs.[9] Significantly, though women did write in this tradition in the eighteenth century, they were working within what Mascuch describes as an 'essentially masculine and middle-class' paradigm of the 'upwardly mobile, self-made subject'.[10] Dror Wahrman furnishes a similar if more precise chronology, arguing that the important change in identity was its coalescence on an interior self as one outcome of the anxiety arising from the American Revolution. Though counter trends continued, it was at this stage that 'identity became personal, interiorized, essential, even innate. It was made synonymous with self'.[11] Wahrman does not examine whether this self was gendered, but does give new foundations for inwardly-turned gender and racial identities.

Mascuch and Wahrman present a relatively smooth development of an authoritative individualist self. Adam Smyth's important study of the 'generic unfixity

---

[4] Anthony Fletcher, *Growing up in England: The Experience of Childhood, 1600–1914* (New Haven and London: Yale University Press, 2008), pp. 129–48.

[5] Michael Mascuch, *Origins of the Individualist Self: Autobiography and Self-identity in England, 1591–1791* (Cambridge: Polity Press, 1997), p. 7.

[6] Ibid. pp. 19–23.

[7] Ibid. p. 200.

[8] Taylor, *Sources of the Self*, pp. 288–9.

[9] Mascuch, *Origins of the Individualist Self*, p. 6.

[10] Ibid. pp. 199–200.

[11] Dror Wahrman, *The Making of the Modern Self: Identity and Culture in Eighteenth-Century England* (New Haven and London: Yale University Press, 2004), p. 276; Dror Wahrman, 'The English Problem of Identity in the American Revolution', *The American Historical Review* 106, 4 (2001), pp. 1236–62. See also Dana Rabin, 'Searching for the Self in Eighteenth-century English Criminal Trials, 1730–1800', *Eighteenth-century Life*, 27, 1 (2003), pp. 85–106.

and experimentation' in sixteenth- and seventeenth-century life-writing amply demonstrates the varied ways in which people in the past represented their lives, though eighteenth-century scholarship tends to prioritize the coherent autobiographical narrative of a newly authoritative and interiorized self.[12] One important exception is the work of Felicity Nussbaum. Nussbaum shows how the category of a manly authoritative and autonomous self was produced in autobiographical writing. If men wrote on the basis of an 'I' that could observe, compile, order, and write itself, then women operated within the notion of 'a private second-sphere subjectivity, an interiority that is defined as subordinate to man in its difference from him'.[13] While men could step outside themselves with rational distance, women were forever interior and in the private. The emerging manly identity was used to sustain both gender and class hierarchies.[14] Autobiographical writing was undertaken by 'the newly literate body of writers that emerged between the working class and the aristocracy', and the practices and technology of writing and self-reflection became 'a property that gathered political and economic power to it'.[15] Nevertheless, Nussbaum also stresses the instability of the autobiographical subject, insisting that some writing challenged this gender- and class-related notion of self. From within their secondary domestic sphere, for example, women writers contested ideologies and imagined 'alternative identities'.[16] Nussbaum also employs a more expansive category of 'autobiographical writing', encompassing texts 'that have ill-defined beginnings, middles, or ends, and that do not explicitly assign moral significance to the events they record', such as those diaries and journals that consist of 'repetitive serial representations of particular moments held together by the narrative "I"'.[17] Nussbaum's inclusion of these kinds of text resists the teleology that can come from trying to trace the origins of a particular genre. It is this tendency that has developed in more recent work, with the canon of autobiography revised to include works by other authors (women, labourers, and other previously marginalized groups), and those 'hybrid' documents that exist between novels and autobiographies.[18]

Whether in narrative autobiography or more irregular writing, many agree that a new kind of personal identity emerged from the private domestic and feminine realm. This was first tangible in domestic novels. In mid-eighteenth-century novels, female narrators voiced a new private middling self, while the interior spaces of these domestic novels served as metaphors for the interior lives of

---

[12] Adam Smyth, *Autobiography in Early Modern England* (Cambridge: Cambridge University Press, 2010). Quote at p. 14.

[13] Felicity A. Nussbaum, *The Autobiographical Subject: Gender and Ideology in Eighteenth-Century England* (Baltimore, MD: Johns Hopkins University Press, 1989), p. xviii.

[14] Ibid. see pp. xvii, 50, 53.

[15] Ibid. pp. 50, 53.

[16] Ibid. p. 153.

[17] Ibid. pp. 17, 18.

[18] Rudolph Dekker, 'Introduction', in Rudolph Dekker (ed.), *Egodoments and History: Autobiographical Writing in its Social Context since the Middle Ages* (Hilversum: Verloren, 2002), pp. 7–20, esp. 13.

individuals.[19] Indeed, psychological privacy was an important new development in which both men and women partook and which allowed for 'simultaneous self-assertion and self-concealment'.[20] Bringing this back to the materials of the eighteenth-century house, its furniture and its boxes, Amanda Vickery has concluded that although not accessible to all, 'some veil of privacy was essential to human integrity'.[21]

For some this represents the development of a specifically 'domestic individualism', in which the individual was located 'in his or her interiority, in his or her removal from the marketplace'.[22] Gillian Brown has argued that in nineteenth-century America this contrasted with an older eighteenth-century tradition of masculine possessive individualism. Instead, this new form of individualism was associated with the 'feminine sphere of domesticity', and moreover signifies 'a feminization of selfhood in service to an individualism most available to (white) men'.[23] Developing this argument, Michael McKeon links a growing distinction between the political subject and the ethical subject to changes in the public and private division: as the domestic began to function allegorically (as in political patriarchalism) it explicated general political issues through the political subject, but as a more fully-formed domesticity emerged in the mid-eighteenth century this exemplified more abstract ethical principles through the ethical subject, or subjectivity.[24] The continuing connections of the private to the public had been shaped partly on the grounds of a new basis for personal identity.

Given the apparent connections between autobiographical writing and a loosely-defined middle-class or bourgeoisie, the middling-sort home might seem a likely place to find newly interior selves. However, Margaret Hunt's study of middling family life has already pinpointed 'the obstacles placed in the way of the pursuit of "possessive individualism"'.[25] With regards to domestic authority in particular, Hunt notes that early-eighteenth-century men such as William Fleetwood continued to conceive of the household 'in terms of duties of members towards one another, particularly the duty of inferior members of the household (servants, children, and women) toward the head'. Individualism trumped such duties only rarely, and in order for the relative success of the 'patriarchal family group'.[26] Rudolph Dekker has commented that 'the connection between the rise of

---

[19] Christine Roulston, *Virtue, Gender and the Authentic Self in Eighteenth-Century Fiction: Richardson, Rousseau and Laclos* (Gainesville: University of Florida Press, 1998).

[20] Patricia Meyer Spacks, *Privacy: Concealing the Eighteenth-Century Self* (Chicago; London: University of Chicago Press, 2003), p. 195.

[21] Amanda Vickery, 'An Englishman's Home is his Castle? Thresholds, Boundaries and Privacies in the Eighteenth-Century London House', *Past and Present*, 199 (2008), p. 173.

[22] Gillian Brown, *Domestic Individualism: Imagining Self in Nineteenth-Century America* (Berkeley, LA; Oxford: University of California Press, 1990), p. 3.

[23] Ibid. pp. 2, 7.

[24] Michael McKeon, *The Secret History of Domesticity: Public, Private, and the Division of Knowledge* (Baltimore, MD: Johns Hopkins University Press, 2005), pp. 437, 466.

[25] Margaret Hunt, *The Middling Sort: Commerce, Gender and the Family in England, 1680–1780* (Berkeley: University of California Press, 1996), p. 11.

[26] Ibid. p. 26.

autobiography, the rise of individualism, and the rise of the bourgeoisie is no longer as obvious as it seemed'.[27] Certainly, in the families discussed by Hunt there were two contrasting value systems, one which prioritized individual economic success, and another which emphasized duty towards family and kin. It was only some time after 1780, when business and investment was detached from the family and situated within larger organizations, that family and business were divided.[28] In the context of everyday household life, Hunt implies, middling-sort family members acted in the context of shared corporate identities, as much as individuals. Indeed, the foremost historian of nineteenth-century middle-class masculinity has observed that in the eighteenth century, 'the most authoritative forms of manliness and civility demanded the *repression* of the self'.[29]

This chapter decouples personal identity from an individualist 'self', and examines the role that the domestic played in the construction of a manly personhood. Importantly, it examines not the new printed autobiography but men's manuscript writing of both narrative and non-narrative form written in and about the domestic, revisiting some of the documents encountered in earlier chapters. Not all writing is about the self, or even personal identity, but a wide range of forms enables us to infer different kinds of identity. Foregrounding issues of form and genre, I discuss three clusters of case studies. The first consists of a set of irregular miscellaneous documents dating from *c.*1681–1853 that seem to elude categories commonly employed by historians or archivists. These raise challenging questions about what men wrote, what it meant to them, what it should mean to us, and (more profoundly) about chronologies and characterizations of identities and the self. These texts do, however, make sense in the light of Charles Taylor's argument for the 'affirmation of everyday life' in thought and writings from the seventeenth century onwards.[30] The second cluster, written between *c.*1743 and 1826, are more recognizably first-person autobiographical writings (usually in something approaching narrative form); they were not descendents of the miscellaneous texts, but a different genre that emerged as miscellaneous texts continued to be written. The third cluster—compiled between 1707 and 1750—are a subset of those first-person autobiographical writings, which allow us to consider more clearly the religious dimensions of the topic, and crucially the way that male writers situated themselves in the house spatially, socially, and emotionally when writing. The chapter shows that men's—as well as women's—identities were rooted in the domestic. Yet while the single-authored documents tell us about individuals, the analysis steers between the development of a female domestic subjectivity and a modern manly individualistic self. The house was critical to private and public constructions of self-identity for men as they constructed a family self. Given that a softening of

---

[27] Dekker, 'Introduction', p. 15.
[28] Hunt, *Middling Sort*, p. 29.
[29] John Tosh, 'The Old Adam and the New Man: Emerging Themes in the History of English Masculinities, 1750–1850', in Tim Hitchcock and Michelle Cohen (eds), *English Masculinities, 1660–1800* (London: Longman, 1999), p. 2.
[30] Taylor, *Sources of the Self*, p. 232.

domestic authority has been tethered to individualism, this masculine family self has important implications for our vision of the eighteenth-century house and family.

FRAGMENTED SELVES?

The authorship of the 'Commonplace book of Christopher Tuthill' is apparently clear in the unequivocal inscription, 'Christoff Tuthill, his Book, 1681'. Begun at the age of 31, four years before his marriage to Mary Hall, the merchant Tuthill created a compendium of personal, political, and domestic material, significant items that could be easily brought to mind with this manuscript record. From one end, the volume contains accounts of Tuthill's household possessions.[31] Completed from the other end, the book lays out elements of Tuthill's eventful life, written not in England but in Ireland, to where Tuthill had moved in 1684 or 1685. It begins, 'I Christoff Tuthill son of Georg Tuthill ... who was son of Christoff Tuthill of Barpole in Munton parish near Taunton ... my mother was young of 2 Child & Daughter of ...'. Following this outline of his parental pedigree, Tuthill goes on to give details of his own birth, on 24 June 1650 in 'Mynhead in Somerset'. He explains that he was married to Mary, the daughter of John Hall, and gives details of where she was from.[32] He notes the birth of his children, including the times of delivery, and their baptismal dates, and he describes the arrival of small pox first to his wife (she survives), and then his young daughter (who dies).[33]

A 'commonplace book' might reasonably include notes of favourite aphorisms, important pieces of news, or the author's attempts at poetry. Filled with details about household possessions and family genealogy, Tuthill's volume is a specifically *domestic* commonplace book that entwines the author and his family. For Tuthill this was a record of *his* life, written in 'his Book' and in the first person, which demonstrated how that life was constructed from the household, its things, its people, and its history. Yet the catalogue entry 'Christopher Tuthill's commonplace book' is somewhat misleading; this is not the 'life in quotations' of some earlier elite commonplace books.[34] The section of the narrative begun by Christopher Tuthill is continued, if in a less fulsome manner, by four successive generations of Tuthill men, through the eighteenth century and up until 1858. The volume thus employs a monetary template, showing the author's domestic managerial role, but also presents events retrospectively in both continuous narrative and periodic description. Moreover, the story being told here is not a simple autobiographical one; the author is positioned in two family lines: the historic, diachronic, and

---

[31] The commonplace book of Christopher Tuthill, 1681–1858, William Andrews Clark Memorial Library: MS.1977.003, from back ff. 2–16, straddling the years 1670–1699. See Chapter 4 for more detailed discussion.

[32] Commonplace book of Christopher Tuthill, f. 3.

[33] Ibid. ff. 4–5.

[34] Smyth, *Autobiography in Early Modern England*, pp. 123–58. Quote at p. 157.

genealogical family as well as the synchronic family. 'Household-family' was one important way of conceptualizing family, emphasizing the economic unit of management under one roof; but the concept of the 'lineage-family'—with an emphasis on persistence over time, patrilineal descent, and property—was also profoundly important as a useful though sometimes contested frame of reference.[35]

Men built up paper archives comprising several kinds of document which were then later used to produce a final version of a record; many of the documents used in this study were themselves written from an archive collected over many years.[36] As discussed in Chapter 3, Daniel Renaud assembled an impressive archive. In contrast to this volume of material, Renaud's will is a very concise document, but it does provide a tantalizing glimpse of the space in which Renaud undertook much of his writing business in the Rectory on the bank of the River Wye. Having bequeathed guineas to his children and grandchildren for mourning, he instructs

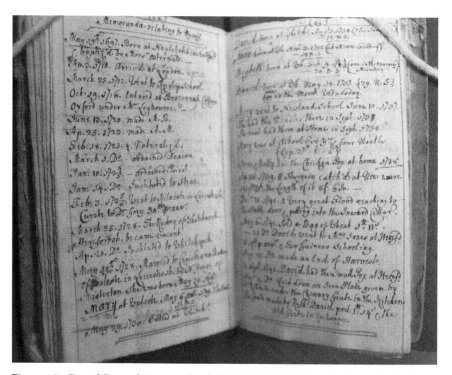

Figure 10: Daniel Renaud, Account book [1752–1777], William Andrews Clark Memorial Library: MS.1977.009, 'Memoranda relating to Myself'. By kind permission of The William Andrews Clark Memorial Library, University of California, Los Angeles.

---

[35] Naomi Tadmor, *Family and Friends in Eighteenth-Century England: Household, Kinship and Patronage* (Cambridge: Cambridge University Press, 2001), pp. 73–102.
[36] See Chapter 3 for a fuller discussion.

his wife that she will find them 'bound up in blue Papers & discreted in a Secret Drawer in My Bureau next to the Window in the White Room'.[37] It was perhaps seated at the bureau next to the window in this white room in around 1769, that Daniel Renaud set about writing the 'Memoranda' in his second account book, recounting events as far back as 1697. This final section of the volume applies a monetary format to details about Renaud's history, from his own birth to those of his children. It also includes notes of notable expenses and remarkable events. It is assembled from records made over many years, kept, filed, and then selected and copied out into the later edited form.

One of Renaud's sources was his earlier vellum-bound account book. In this volume, the 62-lined 'Memoranda relating to Myself', framed with red ink margins around the pages, was begun at a much earlier date than the 152 lines of 'Memoranda' in his second account book. Renaud must have also assembled this longer account from several other sources. It is striking that these different versions of personal and family history were started at different times, but also all updated later in Renaud's life. The 'Mem. Relating to My Brothers' in the first account book, for example, compiles family dates that run through the death of Renaud's parents to the late 1760s.[38] Many men sought to perfect and shape the written account of their lives, and this working over was achieved not just in autobiographical narrative but in other forms of writing. Smyth has shown how early modern financial accounting was as much an influence on life-writing as Puritan self-scrutiny, and this is evident in the later case of Renaud.[39] Of interest to me here are the additional themes of gender, family history, and household authority. Significantly for the current discussion, the different chronological sketches of Renaud's life encompassed his education and career, his co-resident family (kin and servants), and his extended family in England and Switzerland. It describes not only himself and his children but also his parents, brothers, nephews, uncle, grandsons. They also register clearly his investment in certain life events which mattered to him. While the later 'Memoranda relating to Myself' may have been stripped of the material on his uncle and servants, this retrospective account is one of several lives, embedded in this family network.[40] In common with Tuthill's book, Renaud's account book was also updated after his death in 1772, a different hand recording in 1777 that the local parish tither had been let to a Mr Green.[41] The personal history related by Renaud placed him in a web of familial relationships stretching backwards and forwards in time.

Edmund Pilkington's 'account book' shares many features with Renaud's, though Pilkington's is a rather more disorganized volume. Pilkington became the first

---

[37] 'The will of Daniel Renaud, 1770', Herefordshire Record Office: Probate series AA20, Box Number 334, June–September 1772.
[38] Daniel Renaud, Account book [1752–1777], William Andrews Clark Memorial Library: MS.1977.009, f. 71.
[39] Smyth, *Autobiography in Early Modern England*, pp. 57–122.
[40] Daniel Renaud, Account book [*c*.1769], William Andrews Clark Memorial Library: MS.1977.008, pp. 37–41; Renaud, Account book [1752–1777], pp. 68–70.
[41] Renaud, Account book [1752–1777], *c*.1769, f. 29.

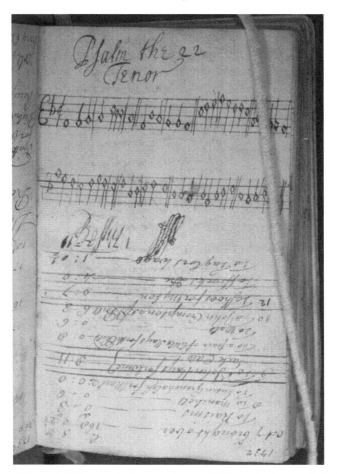

Figure 11: [Edmund Pilkington] Account book, William Andrews Clark Memorial Library: MS1976.001, disbursements for October 1732 and musical notation. By kind permission of The William Andrews Clark Memorial Library, University of California, Los Angeles.

Usher at the re-opened Bury Grammar School in 1730, the opening of which and Pilkington's appointment were announced in the *Universal Spectator and Weekly Journal*, on Saturday 16 May of that year.[42] The school was established by the Rev. Roger Kay, and Pilkington remained Usher for 25 years.[43] The list of scholars from 1730 that appear in Pilkington's account book probably constitute the first cohort

[42] *Universal Spectator and Weekly Journal* (London, England), Saturday, 16 May 1730, no. 84, p. 3. See *17th–18th Century Burney Collection Newspapers*, <http://find.galegroup.com.eresources.shef.ac.uk/bncn>, Gale Document number: Z2001495587 (accessed 9 September 2010).

[43] I. B. Fallows, *Bury Grammar School: A History c.1570–1976* (Bury, Estate Governors of the Bury Grammar Schools, 2001), p. 165. I thank Alan Crosby and Kathryn Stout for their assistance.

of the refounded school.[44] Shortly after taking up the post, Edmund married Margaret, on 23 December 1731, their first two children following soon: Edmund in 1733 and Thomas in 1734.[45] Four further children came later—Robert, George, Elizabeth, and Mary.[46]

Pilkington's extant volume is complicated and imperfect, bearing none of the marks of compulsive record-keeping that Renaud's several volumes appear to display. Pilkington used his volume to record musical scores and to keep accounts from well before his years as schoolmaster, and into the early years of marriage, with accounts beginning in October 1722 and ending in 1732. These were daily accounts typical of many middling men's records, though missing the many everyday purchases necessary for a household of any size. From one end of the volume Pilkington entered accounts, continuing in varied form for around 150 pages, while from the other end musical notation was recorded. At one point, in the centre of the volume, the two forms of content meet on the same page. The disbursements for October 1732—'To a pair of little Stays for the Child 0:8', To Shoes for My Son 0:7, To ffrocks &c. 4:0, To Taylor's Wage 1: 0 1/2'—are written across the musical lines and beneath Pilkington's notation of the tenor part for the 22nd psalm.[47] There are other complications with this volume, because the ordering of disbursements changes over time. The accounts begin in October 1722, and include amongst them payments to individuals for named tasks. Later, though, separate pages are given over to single individuals: the page of receipts from Robert Unsworth, the school usher, includes 'Writing first lay book 1–0' and 'a Second lay book 1–0'.[48] Receipts and disbursements were recorded on separate pages, but these pages are interwoven. For example, receipts from the period October to 7 December 1730, totalling £15 6s 6d, conclude with the note, 'This Acc[t] is carried & Continued 2 leaves further'.[49] Facing this is a list of disbursements from 1 to 14 October, which continues for five pages until receipts from 11 December to 27 January resume.[50] Yet ten years after starting the volume, Edmund's accounting practice remains imperfect. Accounts for the year ending 18 October 1732 conclude with his puzzlement at ending up with the excess sum of 6 shillings in his pocket: 'how I got y[e]: 6 shillings I know not'.[51] Perhaps becoming a father just ten days previously had something to do with his miscalculation, but Pilkington's design for this volume, such as it was, had not quite served its purpose.

Pilkington's accounts are irregular, then, and mixed with musical notation. The writing takes a third form, though, to record changes in the property lease for his home. Prompted by the death of his father in 1729, Pilkington abandoned the

[44] [Edmund Pilkington] Account book, William Andrews Clark Memorial Library: MS1976.001, f. 66–9.

[45] Bury St Mary Parish Registers (microfilm), Lancashire Record Office. Thanks to Alan Crosby for his assistance.

[46] All six children are listed in his will. See 'Will and inventory of Edmund Pilkington, Yeoman, 24th February 1755': Lancashire Record Office, WCW 1755.

[47] [Pilkington] Account book, f. 156.

[48] Ibid. f. 38. See Fallows, *Bury Grammar School*, p. 185, on Unsworth.

[49] [Pilkington] Account book, f. 46.   [50] Ibid. ff. 47–52.   [51] Ibid. f. 157.

tabular accounting in favour of a prose narrative.[52] Identifying when Pilkington wrote this section reveals how he used the volume in practice. The author records that his father took a lease of the house, including the 'Barn, Orchard and Gardens, Meadow, Midlesfield, Moan Ground and Calfcroft', on 18 May 1691. 'And Now', he continued, 'in the year 1730 I Edmund Pilkington son of the s^d Edm^d renew'd the said Lease', adding two names: 'my Self aged thirty and upwards and Cozen Roger Kay of Widdall Gent aged 35'.[53] The subsequent four pages tell of his renewal of two further leases, one also in 1730, though this account is given in the past tense. Thus, Pilkington has added to this narrative at least twice already. Pilkington also provides a short narrative of the ownership of land and leases stretching back to his grandfather, concluding with the statement that 'both these new Leases boar date the second day of June in ye said year 1730'.[54] A line is all that divides this from an account of another lease renewal, for Owlerbarrow, though this time five years later in 1735.[55] Pilkington has now added to the narrative on a third occasion. To this lease he adds two lives, those of his 2-year-old son Edmund, and his 9-month-old son Thomas. About one month later, he describes, he wished to add his wife's name to the lease; thus noting 'Margaret my Wife aged 26' added to the lease. The new lease is dated 15 August 1735.[56] By the time of this third entry, though, Edmund was completing another account book altogether. He left off his accounts in this volume in 1732, then, but to continue the narrative about the lease renewals Pilkington returns to this volume almost three years later to complete the narrative about property with the addition of his wife's name. Already recorded in the legal documents, Pilkington was duplicating these details in his family record. A third document records the changing family ownership of property, a beautifully written will in Pilkington's own hand. Pilkington enjoyed a comfortable living, with goods valued at £156 11s following his death in 1755.[57] Having dealt with the lease renewals, copied the details into his account book, he then gave instructions that his house would pass to his eldest son Edmund upon Margaret's death, and that Edmund would additionally receive all his other leaseholds and tenements. These several documents articulate Pilkington's provision for his wife and children.

Books could be used for many years, rewritten over long periods and in different forms, articulating personal histories in different versions. Writings such as those by Daniel Renaud and Edmund Pilkington show the process of this revision, and if we accept that writing reflects and constructs personal identity, such records raise pointed questions: what kind of a self created such a document? What kind of self does such a document create? Mascuch regards such jumbled manuscript writing as

---

[52] Fallows, *Bury Grammar School*, p. 165.
[53] [Pilkington] Account book, f. 73.
[54] Ibid. f. 74.
[55] Ibid. f. 76.
[56] Ibid. ff. 76–7.
[57] 'Will and inventory of Edmund Pilkington'.

a precursor to the modern autobiographical genre. His discussion of the writings of Samuel Ward, from 1595 to 1630, demonstrates the variety of entries that a man would make in his works. Mascuch describes Ward's 'diary' as containing a vast array of writings without 'intrinsic structure and design', and his writings as a whole as 'open, permeable, amorphous' and a 'heterogeneous mass'.[58] For Mascuch, Ward is part of a first phase of commonplacing lists of information to be used for religious reflection; a second phase began with the Restoration, during which those lists were expanded into historical records and sometimes copied into volumes of family archives.[59] Within this second phase Mascuch sees the roots of modern autobiography, and it is precisely here that we might position Tuthill, Renaud, and Pilkington as part of this heterogeneous style of self-writing, precursors to the modern autobiographical and individualist self. These works would be late examples, though. Instead, the continuation of such 'heterogeneous mass' suggests that these documents are part of the wider 'discursive field' encompassing 'other possible forms of autobiographical textuality and personal self-identity', which Mascuch leaves outside of his analysis.[60] Such texts were not failed autobiography: Nussbaum's perceptive analysis argues convincingly that these processes of revision were an integral part of the reproduction of eighteenth-century identity.[61] So the examples discussed here may loosen ties between a particular form of writing (autobiography) and a particular form of identity (the individualist self). The personal identities articulated in these eighteenth-century writings are not individualistic, and we must certainly think about the chronology of writing and identity anew.

The final example in this cluster of irregular documents is catalogued the 'Diary of Joshua Sagar'. Joshua Sagar, the son of Joshua Sagar and Ann Riley, was baptized on 9 February 1759.[62] As with Tuthill's volume, this book is identified clearly by the author: the first two leaves are crammed with handwritten notes, most of which are financial calculations, but amongst them Joshua Sagar has signed his name no less than six times. Such repeated signing was certainly not uncommon for personal manuscript volumes, but the insistence that this is Sagar's book is notable because this is in fact a printed volume, the thirty-sixth edition of *The Newcastle Memorandum-Book, or, A Methodical Pocket-Journal…Calculated to answer the Immediate Purposes of Gentlemen and Tradesmen in all Parts of Great-Britain, Respecting their Daily Transaction and other Occasional Business*, printed for the year 1789.[63]

---

[58] Mascuch, *Origins of the Individualist Self*, pp. 85, 86.

[59] Ibid. p. 96.

[60] Ibid. pp. 86, 210, 7.

[61] Nussbaum, *Autobiographical Subject*, pp. 15–29. Adam Smyth makes precisely the same point for the sixteenth and seventeenth centuries. See *Autobiography in Early Modern England*, pp. 215–16.

[62] Parish Registers of St Peter, Horbury, 1751–1767, T651, West Yorkshire Archive Service, Wakefield. No record of a marriage or burial has been located. I thank Jennie Kiff at WYAS, Wakefield.

[63] Diary of Joshua Sagar of Horbury (1790), RL Arundale Collection, West Yorkshire Archive Service, Wakefield: C1039 (add Ad). The printed volume's full title is *The Newcastle Memorandum-Book, or, A Methodical Pocket-Journal for the Year M.DCC.LXXXIX. Calculated to answer the Immediate Purposes of Gentlemen and Tradesmen in all Parts of Great-Britain, Respecting their Daily Transaction and other Occasional Business*, 36th edn (Newcastle, 1788).

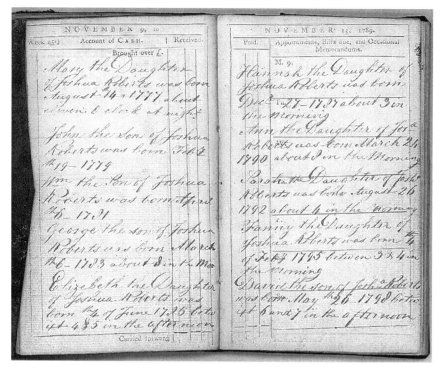

Figure 12: Diary of Joshua Sagar of Horbury (1790), RL Arundale Collection, West Yorkshire Archive Service, Wakefield: C1039 (add Ad), 9–15 November. By permission of West Yorkshire Archive Service.

This is the only extant copy of that years' edition.[64] Following the inscriptions, and in the same hand, a series of entries were made from 1787 to 1791. Sagar was paid large amounts for wool, and was possibly a wool merchant. For example, on 2 March, he was paid £11 2s 3d for 23st 6lb of short wool.[65] Certainly, several family members worked in the cotton and wool industries when the 1841 census was taken, including a Joshua Roberts, wool spinner, aged 59.[66] While Sagar wrote the details of entries on the left hand-page, and used the right-hand page to give further details, this book was not used quite as was intended by the publisher: an entry for 2 March 1791, for example, is made in the space for 1 January 1789. By 5 January the accounts are not within the columns, but across them. They continue until the page for 23 March, by which point Sagar has been completing the book for seven years (an entry here is dated 1787). From this point the entries start to change, including 'A cure for the most desperate toothache', 'A Receipt for

[64] According to the English Short Title Catalogue, last accessed February 2009.
[65] Diary of Joshua Sagar, vii, page January 1.
[66] *Index to the 1841 Census vol. 3 Horbury* (Wakefield and District Family History Society, nd), West Yorkshire Archive Service, Wakefield: 1841/3, p. 47.

Rheumatic Pains' (30 March), 'For a Cough' and 'To Make the Teeth White' (5 April), 'Directions to make a Microscope' (19 April), and 'Grubs on Gooseberries' (20 April).[67]

In common with several domestic manuscripts, the volume has two further periods of compilation. The first of these dates from around 1840, when a series of entries are made relating to gardening: there are several entries to dahlias, for example, on 24 May, 14 December, and 20 December. The second period dates from 1853, when one author makes calculations on the ages of the family members born to Joshua Roberts in the late eighteenth century. Parish records show that Roberts married Hannah Sagar (Joshua Sagar's elder sister) on 8 June 1777. Joshua signed his name neatly, while Hannah simply left her mark.[68] It seems likely that Joshua Sagar's book passed to Hannah Sagar or directly to her son David Roberts. He was the tenth in the list of births in the volume, recorded as the 'Son of Joshua Roberts Gardener, and Hannah his wife bapt^d, 17 June 1798' in parish records,[69] and is listed in the 1841 and 1851 censuses as a gardener living in Horbury.[70] Like Tuthill's volume, Sagar's is completed by his descendents, though in this case the middle-aged nephew continued the volume of the deceased uncle.[71]

In its first phase of compilation during the 1790s, though, this book was a domestic miscellany used for recording monetary items and also recipes for medicinal, cosmetic and technological use, and husbandry. While there is nothing in Sagar's book, or in the books like it, that prove that these writers thought of themselves as 'objects of their own making',[72] the insistent signing of the document suggests a strong connection to the person. Catherine Field regards similar works authored by women as 'a significant genre of self-writing'. In manuscript recipe books, Field sees a fluid but directed process of self-fashioning, arguing that in the signatures and annotations by their owners/compilers, their amalgamation of instructions on an impressive range of topics, and their emphasis on the 'individual practice and experience of receipts', such books constructed a sense of women's individual and authoritative self.[73] As noted above, Nussbaum distinguishes women's autobiographical writing from men's, interpreting this as outside the masculinist force of the category of the autonomous, rational, and private autobiographical self.[74] Yet expanding our categories of self-writing to include a range of material written by both men and women,

---

[67] See also Chapter 4, p. 126.

[68] Records of Banns of Marriages in the Chapelry of Horbury, WYAS, Wakefield: WDP 135/1/3/1, fiche 10669, p. 50. Hannah Sagar was born in 1757. See Parish Registers of St Peter, Horbury, 1751–1767, WYAS, Wakefield: T651.

[69] 'Register of the Christenings and Burials within the Parochial Chapelry of Horbury in the Diocese of York, no. 5', WYAS, Wakefield: Microfilm WDP 135/1/1/5, fiche 10638, p. 93.

[70] *Index to the 1841 Census vol. 3 Horbury*, p. 47; *Index to 1851 Census, vol. 22, Horbury, Surnames Hi to Z* (Wakefield and District Family History Society, 1998), WYAS, Wakefield: 1851/20, p. 23.

[71] See Chapter 6, below, for a more detailed discussion of genealogy.

[72] Mascuch, *Origins of the Individualist Self*, p. 131.

[73] Catherine Field, 'Many Hands Hands: Writing the Self in Early Modern Women's Recipe Books', in Michelle M. Dowd and Julie A. Eckerle (eds), *Genre and Women's Life Writing in Early Modern England: Reimagining Forms of Selfhood* (Aldershot: Ashgate, 2007), pp. 50, 56.

[74] Nussbaum, *Autobiographical Subject*, p. xxi.

we can see how men's and women's domestic writings show overlapping con-cerns. Women and men both recorded recipes, for example. The commonplace book of Ann Bromfield contains copies of letters, poems, recipes for black pud-ding, mince pies, and pickled walnuts, a calendar of birth dates, and an essay on friendship. The volume is signed 'Ann Bromfield Ann Bromfield' on the flyleaf, and a later writer has explained below, 'my G^t G^t Grandmother, married W. Moore'.[75] It is a significant difference between men's and women's manu-script (rather than printed) works of this kind, that men did not usually frame recipes with these statements of the authority of experience. Still, the personal stamp made by both men and women on these volumes is a sign of self-identity. Nevertheless, as in Field's study, we need to ensure that any analysis balances individual self-expression and the connections with family and friends.[76] In the case of Sagar, as with many works by women, the books are authored by several hands over time. Any 'self' fashioned by such documents is a family self syn-chronically, but also diachronically.

There were tensions in fashioning an individual self-identity while being thor-oughly embedded in the family, and several scholars have highlighted the tensions that existed for women in particular. An analysis of the almanacs of Karoline von Hessen-Darmstadt (1721–1774), from an Austrian princely family, reveals Karo-line's experimentation with a range of ego-documents (letters, diaries, and essays), and also the complicated intertwining of Karoline's 'public' role as politician with her 'personal side' or 'Self'.[77] Of two books used later in her life, there was one in which she '"itemizes" events', and in which she registered her public role and her personal identity together, thus presenting her 'fragmented' self.[78] This might point to a struggle for women in particular, and certainly others have argued that women faced particular difficulties in reconciling their social and domestic identities with the forging of an individual personhood in the process of writing. Bringing us to everyday practice and social relations, Margaret Hunt makes the point that 'some people (women, servants, slaves) were simply expected, liberal theory or no, to be significantly less "individualistic" than others'.[79] Women could play a critical role in the domestic record-keeping, nevertheless, contributing to the literate and spe-cifically middling-sort project of '"the family of the text"'.[80] Well into the nine-teenth century, the role of family archivist in the comfortable middle class household was often assumed by women, certainly amongst Quaker communi-ties.[81] In the cases of John and Elizabeth Forth, and William and Faith Gray, family

---

[75] Commonplace book of Ann Bromfield, [1740–1748]: William Andrews Clark Memorial Library: MS.1968.002.

[76] Field, 'Many Hands Hands', p. 59.

[77] Helga Meise, 'The Limitations of Family Tradition and the Barrier between Public and Private: Karoline von Hessen-Darmstadt's "Schreib = Calender" between Almanac and Diary', in Dekker (ed.), *Egodocuments and History*, pp. 107–24; quotes at p. 115, 119.

[78] Ibid. pp. 114, 121.

[79] Hunt, *Middling Sort*, pp. 81–2.

[80] Ibid. p. 86.

[81] Sandra Stanley Holton, *Quaker Women: Personal Life, Memory and Radicalism in the Lives of Women Friends, 1780–1930* (Abingdon: Routledge, 2007).

domestic writings were thoroughly collaborative works.[82] So just as women took part, so men made very important contributions to this shared project, and the nature of *their* mixed writings suggests just as complicated an interweaving of public and private as in some women's records. The formation of a modern male individualist self, impermeable to the family, would be as much an historical inaccuracy as would the claim that women have lacked individual selves because of their familial roles.[83]

Moreover, men accrued authority from their domestic writings. Apparently messy and disorganized at times, these writings—and their revisions—spoke of men's attempts to impose order on life. Their style of writing often had clear roots in the practice of commonplacing. Ann Moss believes that by the eighteenth century, commonplacing had been rendered outmoded as a marker of status, partly because 'politeness' and 'good taste' undermined the collection and display of knowledge and wealth.[84] Yet commonplacing experienced a resurgence following the publication of John Locke's new method in 1690, designed to improve the mind and memory as the very seat of the self. Locke's own commonplace books—comprising entries 'from miscellanea and memoranda to receipts and lists of books, from medical notes and moral and theological maxims to accounts of debts'—became a model for the 'intellectual, moral, and social edification' of the self.[85] The assorted contents of men's domestic miscellanea were not the precursors of an autobiographical subject, then, but rather the manifestation of a long-standing system of recording and ordering that improved—rather than narrated or reflected upon—the self of the author.

Such edifying domestic practices were—certainly amongst the middling sorts—more easily accessible to men than to women. As noted above in the case of Joshua Sagar's diary, the parish record of the marriage of Joshua Roberts and Hannah Sagar, the children of whom are recorded in the manuscript, shows the bachelor's steady and neat signature, and the spinster's simple mark: a shaky cross, like that of almost all the other women in the register.[86] In this household in the village of Horbury on the outskirts of Wakefield, as in many others further afield, men's ability to write was connected to their social authority and greater access to education. Masculine authority in the house was not predicated on an autonomous 'I' created through the writing of autobiography: this practice was conducted by only very few. Rather, male authority was grounded in an individual self that was embedded in but also shaped through writing about the family. Ordering family

---

[82] See Chapters 3 and 4 for a more detailed discussion.

[83] See Alison Mackinnon, 'Fantasizing the Family: Women, Families and the Quest for an Individual Self', *Women's History Review*, 15, 4 (2006), pp. 663–75, for a useful comment on these issues in relation to women.

[84] Ann Moss, *Printed Commonplace-Books and the Structuring of Renaissance Thought* (Oxford: Clarendon Press, 1996), pp. 275–6. See also Chapter 1, p. 21.

[85] Lucia Dacome, 'Noting the Mind: Commonplace Books and the Pursuit of the Self in Eighteenth-Century Britain', *Journal of the History of Ideas*, 65, 4 (2004), pp. 614, 615.

[86] Records of Banns of Marriages in the Chapelry of Horbury, WDP 135/1/3/1, fiche 10669, p. 50.

life through domestic records attracted social status that accrued both to the family but also to the person of the author.[87]

AUTOBIOGRAPHICAL NARRATIVES

Many of the documents considered in this book are of the type of varied miscellanea discussed above. Yet some men also wrote first-person autobiographical writings in narrative form. Indeed, telling stories through narrative in particular was closely linked to masculinity in several ways; the frequent analogies between writing and reproduction, and also associations made between editing or an inability to write with castration, suggest how a narrative line was consonant with a coherent male identity.[88] It was in first-person autobiographical narratives that writers most obviously planted the authorial self firmly in the family.

Autobiographies, along with many account books, commonplace books, and diaries, invariably began with a section on the writer's parental family, reflections on their childhood, and (if relevant) the parents of his wife, followed by their conjugal family. This familial context was present in the narrative of William Stout, for example, a Lancaster tradesman who completed his autobiography in the years approaching 1742. Just as many of the extant domestic writings discussed above were assembled from others and subsequently improved, it is evident that Stout compiled this work from a number of notes and documents.[89] His annual reporting of his 'account of all my effects, reale and personall', totalling in 1713 £19,321 14s 11d, is a brief indication of the many pages of detailed accounting this tradesman kept or had kept on his behalf.[90] Stout was conscious and proud of his literary abilities, and it is perhaps for this reason that he discusses his childhood in such detail. Education is a prominent theme of his representation of his early life, with his parents placing great emphasis on the formal schooling of their sons and the home education of their daughter in reading, knitting, spinning, and needlework. Other gendered divisions existed in Stout's childhood home: it was his mother who was 'full imployed in housewifery', while also joining her husband and servants in agricultural labour.[91] The responsibilities of Stout's parents necessitated that his mother was also assisted by her daughter in housework; and it was this sister— Elin—who was 'early confined to waite on her brother, more than she was able', later to wait on all the younger children, and who subsequently became William Stout's own housekeeper.[92] She was later followed by his two young nieces Margret and Mary.[93] Stout did not marry and does not describe his domestic arrangements in any considerable detail, though he does note the frequent occasions on which he

---

[87] See also Chapter 3, pp. 72–9.
[88] See Raymond Stephanson, *The Yard of Wit: Male Creativity and Sexuality, 1650–1750* (Philadelphia, PA: University of Pennsylvania Press, 2004).
[89] J. D. Marshall, 'Introduction', *The Autobiography of William Stout of Lancaster, 1665–1752*, ed. J. D. Marshall (Manchester, Chetham Society, 1967), 3rd series, vol. 14, pp. 17–18.
[90] Ibid. p. 168.   [91] Ibid. pp. 68–9. Quote at p. 68.
[92] Ibid. pp. 68–9, 102–3. Quote at p. 68.   [93] Ibid. p. 215.

begins to 'keep house'.[94] Indeed, rooted in his early domestic experiences, the formation and reformation of his own household is a consistent thread running through Stout's writing.

A rather different story is told by the Preston mechanic Benjamin Shaw (1772–1841) in his exceptional autobiography. The full title of the work indicates the range of content in this document: 'Benjamin Shaw' Family Records &c A short Account of Benjamin Shaw and his Family &c with some Short Scetches of his ancestors written by himself in 1826 partly for his own use & Partly for his Children'.[95] This detailed and characterful family history that stretches back to the 1690s is an astonishing achievement for a labourer who taught himself to write and who struggled with acute poverty. It was compiled 'from memory partly, & partly from a few notes kept by me, for my own use, mostly of the latest dates, mentioned, &c'.[96] Later in the work, though, Shaw adds that, 'the few notes that I have by me, from my birth until the present time', will assist in his account 'of myself, & family'.[97] Shaw had access to documents stretching back over a long period of his family history, and some of these notes survive. His short and densely written six-page document 'Memorable Events', contains brief notes that fed into the autobiography. The headings 'Memorable Events', 'Marriages', and 'Memorandums' are misleading, as each list contains a wide variety of different events: dates of employment, deaths, miscarriages, premises burning down, election results, and rain storms. Completed in different inks and showing development in the handwriting, this was kept by Shaw over several years as a contemporary record.[98] By contrast, Shaw's autobiography was a retrospective account grounded in his own modest paper archive.

Shaw's writing began as a domestic practice: forced through injury to be 'mostly at home' in late 1798, Shaw 'excercised [*sic*] my spare time in reeding [*sic*] of which I was very fond … [with] a few Book [*sic*], of my own'.[99] His literary and numeracy skills are presented as an important component of his manly working-class respectability.[100] Shaw discusses his early life with detail and frankness; his was a tough upbringing, and Shaw struggled to find and retain work throughout his life, latterly becoming a mechanic in Preston. Shaw's story follows the autobiographical mould, beginning as far back as he can remember or document, detailing both his mother's and father's side of the family, and describing his own childhood and youth in the household. He recalls the berry trees in the larger house that his family moved to once the third child was born,[101] being spoilt as a child by his

---

[94] Ibid. pp. 103, 215. See Chapter 4 for a more detailed discussion of men 'keeping house'.

[95] *The Family Records of Benjamin Shaw, Mechanic of Dent, Dolphinholme and Preston, 1772–1841*, ed. Alan G. Crosby (Record Society of Lancaster and Cheshire, 1991), vol. 130, p. 1.

[96] Ibid. p. 1.

[97] Ibid. p. 21.

[98] Benjamin Shaw, 'Memorable Events' (1817–40), Lancashire Record Office: DDX/1554/3. I thank Alan Crosby for his assistance.

[99] *Family Records of Benjamin Shaw*, p. 37.

[100] Shani D'Cruze, 'Care, Diligence and "Usfull Pride" [*sic*]: Gender, Industrialisation and the Domestic Economy, *c*.1770 to *c*. 1840', *Women's History Review*, 3, 3 (1994), p. 335.

[101] *Family Records of Benjamin Shaw*, p. 21.

paternal grandparents,[102] nursing his younger siblings and running other errands, and then escaping again to his grandparents' where he 'lived like a prince': 'no wonder', he reflected, 'that when I went to my grandfathers I should think it the happiest part of my life'.[103] Shaw reiterates that sentiment a short while later, stating more emphatically that the times in his early teens when he would spend Saturday nights staying with his grandparents were 'the happiest part of my life'.[104] The record of these memories, bittersweet in view of Shaw's later experiences, is remarkable coming from the hand of a man of this background.

Shani D'Cruze has noted that Shaw situated himself in the context of household, his family and kin, focusing on 'his close affective relationships'.[105] Stemming from his experiences of poverty, perhaps, though in common with men such as Stout, Shaw devotes a great deal of attention to his experience of work.[106] He began work in the family before the age of 8—when with household jobs he 'was kept bussyly employed'—and by the age of 10 he began to work with his father at turning.[107] Work and home are entwined, then, as are family and politics. In a comment about his early life, one of several in which he identified with his own father struggling to manage a family, he describes how 'my sister Hannah was born—my father began to feel the effects of a growing family, for the times were very bad then on account of the war, and stagnation with trade—this year [1775] was fought the battle of Bunker Hill'.[108] Shaw's early life is rooted in a family economy: the family is hired and sacked en masse by a mill owner, for example.[109] His own struggles to maintain the family are clear. An early sign of what will come is the honest confession of his response during his wife's first labour: 'Sometimes I thought how foolish I had been—& wished that she might die I think that if she had died, I should have greatly rejoiced, for we were so poor, & such a dark prospect before us, that it was quite discourageing [*sic*] however it was not so to be'.[110] Childhood memories, experiences of work, the shared struggles of the family, political events, notable military conflicts, and personal confessions: these events all mark time but do not fit neatly into a category of 'unified, retrospective first-person prose narrative [that] uniquely totalizes its subject'.[111] Freed from the imposition of the individualistic self, Shaw emerges as a complex person for whom personal identity is shot through with the corporate identity of family, private memories, and public events.

Considerably wealthier and more prolific than Benjamin Shaw was William Gray (1751–?1845), an attorney in York, son of a linen weaver and mantua maker. Gray wrote numerous accounts, letters, and memoranda, and also two autobiographical works. The four-page narrative titled 'Hedon' is a moving remembrance of his early childhood. This piece does not open with a description of parents and family, but instead with a one-page description of 'my father's house'. Situated on

---

[102] Ibid. p. 22.   [103] Ibid. p. 23.   [104] Ibid. p. 24.
[105] D'Cruze, 'Care, Diligence and "Usfull Pride"', p. 316.
[106] See Ibid. pp. 315–45.   [107] *Family Records of Benjamin Shaw*, p. 23.
[108] Ibid. p. 21.   [109] Ibid. p. 26.   [110] Ibid. p. 32.
[111] Mascuch, *Origins of the Individualist Self*, p. 23.

the street running north from the Market Place, 'about half way down it, on the *right*', Gray begins, was the house in which he was born. He then embarks on a memory trip around the house:

> The House (itself a small one) was in two compartments; that to the right forming a working shop, and back shop; the left the sitting family room, & behind it a kitchen: then, a back yard & garden. The stair case, I think, was ascended through a door from the back part of the sitting room—about half way up, to the left, we passed a small lodging room, and then reached the chamber over the sitting room…In that room, I was born, and in that room my mother died, when I was 10 years old.[112]

Gray does not linger in any part of the house or garden, until the tour concludes in what for him is evidently the most meaningful room in the house, literally the domestic place from which he first emerged. The room also marked an ending for Gray: as we learn in his second narrative, his father was soon to remarry 'a homely, narrow minded woman…[who] was far from kind to me'.[113]

Gray continued to revisit the houses of neighbours as memory-stores of their residents: Neddy Collinson's house '[n]early opposite to my father's house', for example, in which the 'family lived in comfort and plenty' and where Gray 'commenced my reading career' on account of Collinson being 'a bit of a reading man'.[114] 'Hedon' is not a comprehensive account of a childhood, though it does contain some noteworthy details of boys being tied to bedposts at home and driving dame-school teachers to distraction. It reads as a rather spontaneous attempt on the part of Gray to retrospectively record his most significant early experiences—his birth, childhood home, neighbours, schooling, and character—and to hint at their role in forming the now mature man. In the final incident Gray describes, he receives a gift of half a crown from his godfather at the age of six. Taking care of it for him, his mother told him, 'I must write it down in my prayer book'. 'Accordingly I wrote in a very scrawling hand, "Margaret Gray owes W^{m}. Gray 18 pence"'. His mother having kindly explained that he had 'put it down short', he added beneath, '"And a Shilling." That prayer book I had many years'.[115] The keen adult reader, writer, and accountant here confirmed that even as a young boy he was an aspiring record-keeper and keeper of books.

Gray's second autobiographical narrative stands in some contrast to this personal memoir. This eight-page work 'Recollections of God's goodness to me in respect of my *temporal concerns*', written in 1821, is a thoroughly spiritual autobiography written by a deeply devout man. It begins rather conventionally, with a description of Gray's parents, his early education, childhood and working life, marriage, and (in brief) his more recent financial good fortune. Framed by tales of his childhood begging and his present 'comparative ease & affluence', the account supports Gray's concluding thanks to God.[116] Lest the imagined reader think the

[112] William Gray, 'Hedon', Gray Family Papers, York City Archives: Acc 5, 6, 24, 235/D2a, f. 1.

[113] William Gray, 'Recollections of God's goodness to me in respect of my *temporal concerns*', Gray Family Papers, York City Archives: Acc 5, 6, 24, 235/D2b, f. 3.

[114] Gray, 'Hedon', f. 2.   [115] Ibid. f. 2.

[116] Gray, 'Recollections of God's goodness', f. 7.

piece self-serving, Gray insists, 'I review this not, I hope in a way of boasting or self complacency, but to record the kindness & beneficence of ye giver of all good things, to me, his undeserving creature'.[117] The short work stands in a long tradition of spiritual autobiography. Gray does not include the intimate personal early memories, nor does it present Gray as the maker of his own life; it insists on God's Providence, confirmed by a narrative of Gray's relentless improvement. Significantly, Gray employs a metaphor of domestic space to illustrate this upward climb. His laborious and menial job as a young man was 'domestic drudgery', a situation in which he 'seemed lost to all hope of rising in life'. The transformation came with the 'commencement of my clerkship—not indeed in any *ambitious* way; but my release from kitchen slavery, & admission into ye parlour, cheered me with ye expectation that my future days would, at least, be comfortable'.[118]

Though Gray struggled to, 'scarcely sustain ye burden of my very moderate household expenses', he was able to provide amply for 'my basket & my store'.[119] Both works talk about the houses of William's past. Yet Gray's two documents— the traditional Protestant autobiography and the thoroughly personal and secular rendering of an early life—caution against easy conclusions about the author's identity. These two autobiographies underline the truism that individuals are complicated and identity multi-faceted. They offer not an autonomous and individualistic self, but an author who reflected on individual personal experiences driven largely by events outside the compass of their control.

The unique autobiography of the Scottish sailor and eventual shipowner Samuel Millar (born in 1762 or 1763) presents a similar picture. 'Memores and Vicissitudes of S M written by himself' is a 328-page manuscript autobiography of Millar's eventful life. His experiences of several conflicts while on board ship, his early brushes with love, his marriage and family, the tragic death of his beloved son, and of other men in his charge—are all described in urgent and gripping style. Likely to have hailed from a dissenting family, and thus difficult to trace in parish or other formal records, Millar's travels were nevertheless reported in the press. His voyage to New York aboard the Mercury of Kirkaldy was noted in *The Caledonian Mercury* in January 1800, for example, a voyage that he notes he took without his wife because she spent 'the whole passage so sick' on his last Atlantic crossing.[120] Similarly, Millar's volume notes how he was 'taken by the Enemies of Great Britain' many times during his maritime career; his capture by the French off Barbados in 1804, one of six captures he listed later in 1815, made it into *The Lancaster Gazette & General Advertiser* of Saturday 24 March.[121] Millar's manuscript provides a rich and personal background to these short printed newspaper reports.

---

[117] Ibid. f. 7. [118] Ibid. f. 4. [119] Ibid. f. 7.

[120] *The Caledonian Mercury*, Monday 20 January, 1800; See *19th Century British Library Newspapers*, <http://find.galegroup.com.eresources.shef.ac.uk/bncn>, (accessed November 2011), Gale Document Number: BB3205303098. Diary of Samuel Millar, Henry E. Huntington Library: HM 47403 f. 89.

[121] *The Lancaster Gazette & General Advertiser*, Saturday 24 March 1804. See *British Newspapers*, <http://find.galegroup.com.eresources.shef.ac.uk/bncn>, Gale Document number: R3208730763 (accessed June 2010). Diary of Samuel Millar, f. 231.

Written as a single narrative without paragraph breaks or consistent sentence breaks, but without corrections or crossings out, Millar's autobiography was a singular feat of writing. It was surely based on previous drafts, and was certainly a narrative constructed from a selection of other documents. Millar itemized some of these: the parents' 'Family Bible in the house that kept a Register of all our names', the 'box of Various Manuscripts and papers' that came into his possession some years prior to starting the 'Memores', and the 'Different Manuscripts and papers by me from the Year Seventeen Hundred and Seventy Five to the Year ____'; in other words, from about the age of 13 until the present time of writing, and most likely the conclusion of the work (in 1819).[122] Millar's 'Memores' are highly specific about monetary values, the dates of political events, weather conditions, the detail of food and drink served at mealtimes, and his own emotional responses. Millar's collection of papers must have been rich compendia of records of many different kinds, because his diary merges political and maritime issues with the domestic matters of both his blood and ship family. These documents were the archives from which he assembled the narrative. At some point during the 'Memores'—probably around the beginning of 1815—Millar's narrative is no longer about the past, but about the present. So while the bulk was assembled and written retrospectively, a large section was written contemporaneously. The work thus encompassed many different forms and practices of writing.

The composition of the extant manuscript autobiography was an achievement not simply because of the impressive synthesis of a number of other documents, but also because of the conditions in which some of these documents were used and produced. Millar only describes in detail one of the manuscripts written by himself, his pocket book. He took this with him on board ship, and on two occasions the pocket book was nearly lost. Facing strong weather on 28 December 1796, Millar's thoughts turned to his father, his father's death, and to his advice to Samuel that he should do to others as he wished them to do to him and that life events were part of God's plan. With his mind thus on the family past, his thoughts turned to the survival of the record of his own life: 'A thought Struck me I should take my pocket Book and fasten it inside my Jacket Pocket' to inform anyone who subsequently found him or the vessel how long they had been lost. Going to locate the pocket book beneath deck, Millar found it missing from his trunk, which had been smashed as the cellar filled with water; he found the book and the papers it contained scattered about the cellar with his clothes.[123] Later, in 1807, another incident left him dripping wet on deck, having lost 'all most all of my Clothes Books papers and every valuable thing belonging to me'.[124] It was a struggle to write on board ship, and the effort put into this endeavour shows Millar's determination to ensure the survival of the paper records.

Millar discusses his reasons for undertaking such a challenging exercise early in his narrative. He began planning the memoirs forty years earlier, he writes, and had

---

[122] Diary of Samuel Millar, f. i. [123] Ibid. pp. 64–5. Quotes at p. 65.
[124] Ibid. p. 136.

'often thought of keeping Manuscripts' between leaving school and going to sea. He gives an account of the various sources from which his narrative is constructed and thus underlines the veracity of his narrative.[125] He also explains that he began writing the narrative while 'under a very Long Quarantine' in the Mediterranean: 'not knowing what to do with myself I thought I could not be better imployed than to write [an] account of my Life'.[126] Millar framed this explanatory preface with genealogical bookends. The first noted that while 'in my Memoirs I take little or no notice of Parents', he wished that here 'be it known to all whom it may concern that my Parents might be of the Plebisain Race still they had wherewith to bring up a large family and give a good Education to all of us'.[127] If the memoirs were rooted in this improving environment of Millar's childhood family, then part of their intention was to give an account of his life to his own family: the second bookend notes, 'I have wrote only to shew my family'—and also to provide 'a Guide to some of my young boys ^ sons [...] to prevent them from trusting to [*sic*] much to fair promises.'[128] In between, Millar confirmed that not only did he hail from good and honest parents, but that his grandfather owned land, and that, 'who knows if I was to trace my Pedgree Two of Three Hundred Years backwards but I might find some one or other of them in that High and Honourable line'.[129] Millar was part of a family that included generations in the past, present, and future.

Millar becomes a character of his own making in his reports of adventures at sea and interludes on shore, though it was God who was his 'guide in manhood'.[130] But Millar always situated himself surrounded by his family, even when at sea. Millar's repeated references to 'my little family' are threaded through the writing, pulling it together, tying it to the opening frame, and also providing the narrative drive: the voyages and landings at exotic destinations are interludes, hung between the main quest to get back to his family. The nature of his engagement with this family was complex. Driving his career was a very real and urgent financial imperative: his prayer during one of his many captures was that he would be able to continue to work 'for the maintenance of my little family', and though in 1816 he pondered if the time had now come that he might be 'intitled to a little Ease' with his family, he considered that whilst God kept him healthy and strong he would be happy to 'persevere for a livelihood for my family'.[131] '[H]ope is the Anchor of the Soul', he explained, and it was his hope to retire with enough to support his family.[132] The harsh economic realities of maintaining a household disrupted this hope, so when in December 1817 his resources 'could not keep my house', he was forced to board another ship.[133]

Millar had another reason for leaving Kirkaldy after a visit of just a few weeks, and this was his 'getting Melancholy', something he experienced intermittently following the death of his son on 29 May 1817. On the occasion of him leaving his family to go back on board ship, Millar expressed regret.[134] He clearly felt too unwell to stay with his family. Observant and communicative about his emotional

---

125 Ibid. f. i.   126 Ibid. f. ii.   127 Ibid. f. i.   128 Ibid. f. ii–iii.
129 Ibid. f. ii.   130 Ibid. p. 230.   131 Ibid. pp. 231–2, 256.
132 Ibid. p. 256.   133 Ibid. p. 315.   134 Ibid. p. 315.

state, Millar also possessed a lively imagination and remarked on the often unpleasant reminders of things that 'come Forcibly on my Mind'.[135] The emphasis was not so much on an individualized internal self, but rather on his family and his prolonged absences from it; Millar's family served as an emotional compass. Millar's lively account presents him as an individual character in a story; the 'Memores and Vicissitudes of S M written by himself' is assuredly a story about himself. As in some earlier writing, here was a self-conscious examination of a self before individualism, a self which was real and substantive but which is not autonomous.[136] At the same time, Millar insisted on the power of Providence and all that this suggested about the limits to his own agency, and he relied on dates to mark time and provide structure rather than a tightly woven structure or plot driving the narrative forward. Indeed, if anything drives this narrative forward it is Millar's family, pulsing through and pulling his story along.

The discussion so far has highlighted the complicated and hybrid nature of some men's written documents, in which the autonomy and agency of the individual is present but also limited, by God, family, or both. Those studies which tether autobiography to new forms of identity are almost exclusively concerned with print, while none of the documents used in this chapter were prepared for publication. Their lack of generic clarity may be a result of their personal and more circumscribed purpose. Yet men's (and indeed women's) domestic writings did have an audience, often written for circulation amongst family and friends and for God. Nor can the manuscripts be dispatched as the hand-written and inferior versions or precursors to the fully formed printed autobiographies: as already noted, these manuscripts were kept well into the nineteenth century. Finally, the weaving of family life and men's familial roles through an autobiographical account was common to both manuscript and print. A striking and late example is William Cobbett's *Advice to Young Men* (1829), in which he addressed both middle- and upper-class readers about their roles in family, society, and politics. A short introductory autobiography gave the reader a résumé of Cobbett's main achievements. The description of his thoroughly active life concludes with the final item, 'bred up a family of seven children to man's and woman's state'.[137] Throughout the guidance that Cobbett provides his readers on a series of male role and life-stages, he inserts a series of autobiographical sections as exegeses. His recourse to personal experience is most striking in the chapter, 'To a Father'. In this, Cobbett talks in detail about his own experiences as a new father and his approach to bringing up his children; this, he explains, grew out of his own experiences of childhood.[138] Cobbett's corpus situated men in a civil society.[139] In this work, he drew on his own

---

[135] Ibid. p. 136.
[136] See Geoff Baldwin, 'Individual and Self in the Late Renaissance', *Historical Journal*, 44, 2 (2001), pp. 341–64, *passim*, and pp. 345, 363–4.
[137] William Cobbett, *Advice to Young Men, and (incidentally) to Young Women, in the Middle and Higher Ranks of Life. In a series of letters, addressed to a youth, a bachelor, a lover, a husband, a father, a citizen, or a subject* (London, 1829), p. 5.
[138] Ibid. see for example, pp. 200, 227, 246–9, 261–8.
[139] See Chapter 2, pp. 56–7.

personal experiences of the family to explicate his advice on right living in this society. In common with some of the other writings considered in this discussion, Cobbett's is a public presentation of an authoritative male author thoroughly embedded in the family. It was also, to a large extent, a fictionalized account. As Cobbett was writing this work, his marriage and his relationships with his children were disintegrating.[140] It is indicative of the cultural force of the image of the man in the house that, regardless of these troubles, Cobbett raised up a fictionalized version of his own domestic experiences as a beacon to his readers.

WRITING, SECLUSION, AND THE HOUSE

In his diary for 30 April 1843, the lay preacher John Young sought to underscore a passage from Matthew 10:36—'man's enemies are those of his own household'. He echoed the sentiment with a comment from the *Westminster Review*: 'the greatest and most formidable opponent a man has to engage who wishes to give his life to the noble pursuit of wisdom is *The Demon of Domestic arrangements, and habits*'.[141] Young's struggle was to locate a private space for reflection within his house, while increasingly domestic retreat was aligned with femininity.[142] The alignment of the space of the domestic interior and the space of the mind or self in the eighteenth century was arguably of particular relevance to women. The association between these two spaces and the space of the female body has been located in a range of materials, too.[143] By the time that Young was writing, some argue, a public political and masculine subjectivity stood against a private ethical feminine subjectivity that had become thoroughly politicized as a wellspring of virtue.[144] Undoubtedly, some men articulated a tension between *their* need for retreat on the one hand and the house on the other. The feminized dressing rooms and closets of eighteenth-century literature support arguments for an increasingly domesticated

---

[140] Leonora Nattrass, *William Cobbett: The Politics of Style* (Cambridge: Cambridge University Press, 1995), p. 201.

[141] *The Diary of John Young: Sunderland Chemist and Methodist Lay Preacher, covering the years 1841–1843*, ed. G. E. Milburn (Leamington Spa: Surtees Society, 1983), vol. 195, Sunday 30 April 1843, pp. 85–6.

[142] Brown, *Domestic Individualism*, p. 1.

[143] See, for example, Tita Chico, *Designing Women: The Dressing Room in Eighteenth-century English Literature and Culture* (Lewisburg: Bucknell University Press, 2005); Karen Harvey, 'Gender, Space and Modernity in Eighteenth-Century England: A Place called Sex', *History Workshop Journal*, 51 (2001), pp. 158–79; Karen Harvey, 'Spaces of Erotic Delight', in Miles Ogborn and Charles Withers (eds), *Georgian Geographies: Essays on Space, Place and Landscape in the Eighteenth Century*, (Manchester: Manchester University Press, 2004), pp. 130–50; Karen Lipsedge, '"Enter into Thy Closet": Women, Closet Culture, and the Eighteenth-Century', in John Styles and Amanda Vickery (eds), *Gender, Taste and Material Culture in Britain and North America 1700–1830* (New Haven and London: Yale University Press, 2006), pp. 107–22; Spacks, *Privacy*, *passim*; Cynthia Wall, 'Gendering Rooms: Domestic Architecture and Literary Acts', *Eighteenth-Century Fiction*, 5, 4 (July 1993), pp. 349–72.

[144] Sharon Harrow, *Adventures in Domesticity: Gender and Colonial Adulteration in Eighteenth-Century British Literature* (New York: AMS Press, 2004), p. 7.

and privatized notion of femininity, although these spaces were as often open and sociable as they were closed and solitary.[145] Susan Stabile sees the practices of writing and personal identity of upper-middle-class women writers in Philadelphia as firmly ensconced in the architectural spaces of the house. More particularly, the powerful poetic connections between writing, family memory, and the house was a female practice that contrasted with the public and political concerns of men in the new republic.[146] The profoundly corporeal and emotional connection to the house forged by these Philadelphia women is absent from the men's writing that I have examined, though we know that men had strong connections to the physical house in many ways.[147] In first-person retrospective narratives, such as William Gray's 'Hedon', men's accounts of their lives were situated in the physical and emotional space of home. This final section of the chapter will explore two further works, dating from the first half of the eighteenth century, in which the authors were rooted in the family both emotionally and spatially. The purpose of these works was to give thanks to God and precipitate self-improvement. Highly self-reflective, these writers underscored how improvement of the inner self was firmly situated in a domestic setting. Often overlooked by historians of the home, men's Christian faith was a profoundly important factor in their personal lives throughout this period, and particularly to the house.[148] Part of the Protestant confessional genre that was central to the development of a modern Western individualist self, each of these writers presented himself to God as a family self positioned in the space of the house.

Richard Kay (1716–1751), a Lancashire doctor and committed Nonconformist, kept a diary from 1737 to 1750. From his childhood, he lived most of his life with his parents and siblings at Baldingstone House near Bury. Tucked away on a shelving hill amongst trees, Baldingstone is a two-storey stone house dating from the early seventeenth century.[149] When the diarist's yeoman grandfather died in

---

[145] Chico, *Designing Women*, p. 14. See also Lena Cowen Orlin, *Locating Privacy in Tudor London* (Oxford University Press, Oxford, 2007), pp. 296–326.

[146] Susan M. Stabile, *Memory's Daughters: the Material Culture of Remembrance in Eighteenth-century America* (Ithaca, NY; London: Cornell University Press, 2003).

[147] For a fuller discussion, see Chapter 4.

[148] Hannah Barker's work pays due attention to this in her analysis of the concerns of eighteenth- and nineteenth-century male diarists. See her 'Soul, Purse and Family: Middling and Lower-Class Masculinity in Eighteenth-Century Manchester', *Social History*, 33, 1, pp. 24–31; idem, 'A Grocer's Tale: Gender, Family and Class in Early Nineteenth-Century Manchester', *Gender & History*, 21, 2 (August 2009), pp. 340–57. See also Chapter 2 of this book, pp. 46–51.

[149] See English Heritage 'Heritage Gateway', <http://www.heritagegateway.org.uk/gateway/> (accessed July 2009), Baldingstone House, List Entry Number: 1356839. The first son, Richard (the diarists's uncle), took ownership in 1705, although the will of Richard Kay (d.1697) shows that he bequeathed the house to his second son Robert (the diarists's father, then aged 13). See 'An Inventory of the goods & Chattels of Richard Kay late of Baldingstone in Walmersley in the parish of Bury in the County of Lancaster', 4 April 1697, Lancashire Record Office: WCW 1697 Richard Kay; Dr W. Brockbank and Rev F. Kenworthy, 'Introduction', *The Diary of Richard Kay, 1716–51 of Baldingstone, near Bury: a Lancashire Doctor*, ed. Dr W. Brockbank and Rev. F. Kenworthy (Manchester: Chetham Society, 1968), vol. 16, 3rd series, p. 2; W. Hewitson, 'Baldingstone House and the Kays', *East Lancashire Review*, (no date), Bury Library: Bury RIS Misc File, A78.4, p. 10.

Figure 13: Baldingstone House with Georgian sash windows (*c*.1890): Bury Archive Service, b13175. By kind permission of Bury Archives.

1697, Baldingstone was a significant local house with small buildings to the rear to form a courtyard and at least three cottages. His grandfather's will, made at the property in 1696, totalled £806 17s.[150] Richard Kay the elder bequeathed the main house to his eldest son (also Richard), while other property on the land, including the three cottages, went to the second son, the diarist's father (Robert). For some years, the brothers and their wives lived on the same estate, with the elder son undertaking global housekeeping for this extended family.[151]

From 1713, though, the diarist and his father were to live in the main house. At this date, the house retained its near century-old structure: a six-roomed building of a roughly symmetrical linear structure with a central door and window, with two further sets of mullioned windows to either side. The door opened onto a central room, with two rooms either side and three further rooms above. In the inventory of the diarist's grandfather (taken in the same year as the will), the lower floor comprised the 'Entry Chamber', containing desks and books, flanked by a 'Kitchen' containing little more than a cheese press and also 'the House', with its cupboard, table, chairs, stools and cushions. Above was the 'Parlour' housing

---

[150] Will of Richard Kay, 25 January 1696.
[151] See 'Extracts from the Journals of Mr Richd Kaye of Baldingstone & Chesham in the Par. of Bury Co. Lanc. now in the poss^n of Mrs Kay of Bury. Jan. 20. 1848. R.R.R.', Chetham's Library: C.6.34–77 Raines Collection, vo. 31, ff. 430–1.

two beds and linen chests, a 'further Chamber' with a bed, desk, and chest, along with barley and corn sacks, and 'the Middlemost Chamber' with two further beds, a desk, and chest.[152] Given that all three upper rooms were for sleeping, it is likely that the stairs were located in an aisled hall running along the length of the rear of the house, a characteristic of domestic architecture of this size in the region.[153] It is unclear whether any of these goods remained in the house during the lifetime of the diarist Richard Kay, though it is likely; however, no inventory was made for his father and Richard himself died intestate less than a year later.[154] The only tantalizing glimpse is offered in the will of his father Robert, who left his wife £100 and the choice of his household goods, plate, linens, and furniture.[155]

We can be more confident about the architectural space of the house. Baldingstone has been extended several times. At some point during the eighteenth century, two wings were added at right angles to the main house, and the front extended.[156] Tell-tale Georgian sash windows in an early photograph—and now replaced with mullions—show the changes to the front of the property. The new spaces would have been invaluable to the family of Robert and Elisabeth and their six children, the many visiting patients of the father and son doctors, and the several overnight guests—sometimes six at a time—that the family hosted on many occasions.[157] The extensions also enabled the further subdivision of Baldingstone House, a development taking place across the countryside. The newly created domestic spaces were one aspect of a widespread desire for 'privacy'.[158] 'Privacy', here, has many different meanings, both spatial and psychological.[159] For Richard Kay, it is not difficult to see the attraction of a place of quiet seclusion. Writing in the house as a man from the age of 21 until his death aged 35, living with his two younger sisters Rachel and Elisabeth, his parents, patients, visitors, and their children, Kay must have taken some relief in taking himself off to his 'closet'. Indeed, it was through his 'Closet duties' that he hoped to 'disentangle & disengage my Self from those Encumbrances whatever I meet with'.[160] His writing and self-reflection—his attention to his self—were only made possible by the architectural changes to Baldingstone house.

Looking out through the low windows of his comfortable room onto rolling fields pressing in on all sides, and having spent the last three days engaged in husbandry, Richard Kay admitted that 'Husbandry be both an ancient and honourable Employment', but rather loftily declared that the pursuit was better suited to

---

[152] 'An Inventory of. the goods & Chattels of Richard Kay'.
[153] McKeon, *Secret History of Domesticity*, p. 256.
[154] Admon for Richard Kay, 2 December 1755, Lancashire Record Office: WCW 1755.
[155] Will of Robert Kay, Yeoman, Lancashire Record Office: WCW 1752.
[156] Jean Bannister, 'Home of a Doctor Diarist', *Bury Times*, Friday 19 July 1974, p. 7.
[157] See Marjorie Lilian Kay, 'Transcript of the diary of Richard Kay', Private collection. See, for example, 3 February 1747, 29 December 1747. I am very grateful to Jonathan Kay and his father for access to this transcript.
[158] McKeon, *Secret History of Domesticity*, pp. 212–68.
[159] For an excellent discussion of the different meanings of privacy, see Orlin, *Locating Privacy*.
[160] Diary of Richard Kay, Chetham's Library: A.7.76: 6 December 1737.

persons of 'weaker Capacities and of meaner Extract and Education than myself'.[161] His concern was for writing, reflection, God, and medicine, encompassed in his oft-repeated occupation in 'Domestick Affairs' and 'Business at Home'. Here was a man whose preference was for domestic seclusion and the opportunity for reflection that this allowed, rather than the more conventional route for men through husbandry and management. Kay engaged in different types of writing, keeping records of the sermon's heard at the local Dissenting chapel, as his uncle appears to have done in what is now known as the 'Kay Note Book'.[162] Kay also wrote a diary, but his concern during his seclusion was his 'little Manuscript'. He first mentions this book when it was already underway, commenting that he required direction from God, and declaring himself 'determined what Method to take in order that I may both amend and enlarge the same'.[163] The book was composed of 'chief Requests' that Kay then arranged into alphabetical order to create 'a Directory which may the better enable me to suit the remarkable [*sic*] Passages I shall at any Time hear or read or come into my Thoughts to the various Subjects I have there been meditating upon'.[164] The content can be distinguished from many of the examples discussed above, but the general method of production and revision is very similar. Kay's work consisted of '107 sheets all writ by my Self in Little Hand Writing', and, as Kay explained, was written as 'a young Man, perhaps before I enter much into worldly Business, but to be sure before I enter into a married Relation of Life to give my Thoughts & Endeavours for the better & more full Discharge of it'. There is slippage between himself and the manuscript, because in Kay's description it is not clear where his person ends and the book begins. Kay's writing as a good work and the work of God in creating him are thus indistinguishable: 'as thou hast hitherto dealt faithfully with me both in the Discovery & Discharge of what I have already done, so I trust yea do Sincerely beg of thee that as thou art begun a good Work in me, thou wou'd'st carry on, perfect, finish & compleat the same, & that so as will be most for thy Glory & for the Good & Comfort both of my own Self & Soul, & of all about me.'[165] Kay's writing was a parallel work to complete, and by implication one that—like God's good work in him—concerned himself and those about him.

Kay worked on his book for many years; it was written not as a continuous narrative, but was expanded and corrected over time. As he explained in 1738, 'I have purposed within my Self this winter by God's Grace and Assistance to write over and to enlarge some little upon my little Manuscript.'[166] The speech that Kay delivered to his parents as he handed them his manuscript shows how the writing sprang from a religious impulse, and also how his 'private Proceedings' were positioned by Kay in a secluded space.[167] Kay wrote and presented his work in his closet, the place where he regularly retired for 'closet Duties & closet Employments' while seated

---

[161] Diary of Richard Kay, 30 April 1737.
[162] Brockbank and Kenworthy, 'Introduction', *Diary of Richard Kay*, p. 3.
[163] Diary of Richard Kay, 27 April 1737.
[164] Ibid. 4 November 1737.   [165] Ibid. 4 November 1737.
[166] Ibid. 11 October 1738.   [167] Ibid. 11 April 1740.

at his 'Escrutore'.[168] Closets could be small annexes to larger rooms, though Kay's closet had a fire and on one occasion may have accommodated five people for 'a Dish of Tea'.[169] Kay described the continual revisions to the work that he had undertaken in his closet, noting that the sheets 'bear Date from the 21st Year of my Age & since then what has been my Study about them has only been here & there to bring them into fewer & better Words'. When Kay finally presented the book to his parents in the closet, his speech approached an hour in length. He handed the book to his father and requested that he record his errata; the book remained an ongoing good work to be perfected by his father. Once again, though, it was not clear whether the 'further Improvements' mentioned by Kay referred to his life or his work.[170] Unfortunately, Kay was not able to improve the book on the basis of his father's responses as soon as he would have liked, because (perhaps still stunned by that hour-long speech) twelve months later his parents had still not yet returned the corrected volume.[171] Though Richard's uncle was an important figure at the Dissenting chapel on Silver Street in Bury, it seems likely that Richard's serious-minded Nonconformity outstripped that of his parents.

Kay's little manuscript was titled 'Entrance upon the World; or Self-Employment in Secret'.[172] The subtitle was lifted from 'one little Book' that Kay bought in 1738 at a book auction, 'Self Employment in Secret', likely to have been an edition of John Corbet's book of the same title, first printed in 1681.[173] The first substantive section of the book consists of Corbet's reflections on the state of his soul, written intermittently over a period beginning some twenty years prior to the publication. The second part is titled 'Notes for My Self' and consists of maxims and thoughts.[174] This dense book, rooted in traditions of spiritual autobiography and the closely focused self-examination that this involved, was for Kay—as no doubt for many other young men—an inspiration to find a space in which to conduct their own writings. But while Kay was writing from religious impulse, the finished item was delivered not to God but to his temporal family, his parents. Kay's attention is closely trained on 'my Self', but he asks for blessings on 'all this our House & Family', 'all us the Children of this House & Family very comfortably & very mercifully both in our Vocations & Relations'.[175]

Kay's diary remains accessible, but his little manuscript does not survive in any form. The lost manuscript would have borne some resemblance to John Darracott's 'diary', kept between 1707 and 1730. Darracott was one of a large extended

---

[168] Ibid. 16 November 1737.   [169] Ibid. 24 February 1749.
[170] Ibid. 11 April 1740.   [171] Ibid. 11 April 1741, p. 41.
[172] Ibid. 11 April 1740, p. 33.
[173] Ibid. 13 April 1738, p. 22. *Early English Books Online*, <http://eebo.chadwyck.com> shows editions of 1681, 1684, 1690, and 1700 (hereafter 'EEBO'). *English Short Title Catalogue*, <http://estc.bl.uk> shows four further editions were published in 1773, 1786, 1795, and 1800 (both accessed 19 January 2009).
[174] John Corbet, *Self-Imployment in Secret* (London, 1681), pp. 36–47. See *EEBO*, <http://eebo.chadwyck.com> (accessed 19 January 2009).
[175] Diary of Richard Kay, 20 June 1739, 22 June 1739.

family of prosperous and well-connected merchants in the coastal town of Bideford, North Devon. In the late seventeenth century, Bideford was a busy port enriched particularly by the trade in Virginian tobacco. John Darracott himself inherited £100 and property on central Allhalland Street from his maternal grandfather in 1697, John Frost, the mayor of Bideford.[176] Probably a three-room and cross-passage house during Darracott's ownership, this was situated at the corner of Conduit Lane, a main thoroughfare from the busy Quay behind. Remodelled in the early eighteenth century, this would have been a smart if modest building, possibly housing a shop on the ground floor, and situated opposite the 'Merchant House'.[177] Of Darracott's family we know little other than the brief details given in the volume, such as that his son John was 'Entomb[ed] in ye Great Sea' during a voyage to Virginia.[178] Such rich descriptions are rare in the diary, though. The document is singularly concerned with Darracott's repeated covenants with God, his sufferings, and what he described as his 'backsliding'. It shows the outcome of the secret self-employments that took place in Kay's closet.

While Kay clearly perfected his manuscript over time, presumably writing some retrospectively, Darracott's writing straddled the diary and autobiographical form: some entries are retrospective essays, some are annual summaries, and some urgent statements of the renewal of his holy vows on the day they were made. This was a personal representation of the writer's life as directed by providence. As in the seventeenth-century religious narrations seen by Mascuch as part of the pre-history of autobiography, God (rather than the writer) is the author of this life, and the emphasis is on devotion to God than on 'unique self-identities'.[179] Darracott's joys and sufferings are emphatically not the result of human action. He certainly experienced considerable and repeated sorrow over the many deaths in his family. Having buried fourteen family members in thirteen years, Darracott described his anguish and confusion in the winter of 1727:

> I am of *man* y^t hath seen afflictions afflictions of divers sorts variety of afflictions Losses, Crosses disappointments Sickness & *Deaths* of... my near & Dear-Relations— They are all Gone to Glory before me & I left alone... to bear ye miseries of mortality. Last august & Last Septemb^r Dyed my Dear Bro^r Rich^r. & my *dearest dearest* Spouse— They are Gone Gone To Glory—Lord, Why! Why! art thou displeased & angry wth thy poor Creature?... thou hast stript me of my Riches thou hast now Taken away ye desire of my Eyes. Lord Stay thy hand.[180]

---

[176] Frank J Gent, *The Trial of the Bideford Witches* (1982; Crediton, MMI, 2001), p. 2. Gent's work is also a useful introduction to the history of early-modern Bideford. See also John Watkins, LLD, *An essay towards a history of Bideford, in the county of Devon* (Exeter, [1792]). See *Eighteenth Century Collections Online*, <http://find.galegroup.com.eresources.shef.ac.uk/ecco/>, Gale Document number: CW3301803897 (accessed 12 August 2010).

[177] I thank Tim Wormleighton at North Devon Record Office. See National Monuments Record 'Images of England', <http://www.imagesofengland.org.uk/>, number 375714 (accessed July 2009).

[178] Diary of John Darracott, 1707–30, William Andrews Clark Memorial Library: MS.1950.010, f. 20.

[179] Mascuch, *Origins of the Individualist Self*, p. 70.

[180] Diary of John Darracott, pp. 175–6.

While Darracott's preoccupation was apparently with the state of his own soul, Darracott also presents himself as part of a family unit. He reports on the fortunes of this family frequently: '[M]y family hath been blest wth health & Strength this year' and 'I desire to offer my self and my family entirely to y^r divine providence', he wrote in 1717. In the face of such loss, he asks God to hold the family together fast: 'Lord bless me and my family, make no breaches in ye midst of us.'[181] In November later that year, Darracott thanks God for 'giving me and my family so much health & Strength and no Deaths amongst my Little ones', but he also describes the 'Losses in my Estate' and the 'Reproches [*sic*] and troubles on all Sides'.[182] It is very difficult to extricate the spiritual, bodily and architectural features of Darracott's house, and in fact they are thoroughly integrated. Management, order, and health were connected, and Darracott included the health of the family in his sphere of responsibility.[183] His comment that his 'dwelling' is 'desolute' in January 1722 refers to the 'many of my dead friends & neighbours' but also 'thou and thy Children', as well as, perhaps, the material domestic space.[184] Whichever was the case, it was in this year that Darracott leased his house on Allhalland Street to the merchant Nathaniel Watson for £190.[185] Some months later Darracott gave hopeful thanks: 'Bless us y^t our Concerns may be settled y^t so we & our houshold may serve God Chearfully'.[186] The following years seem to have gone well. In a short narrative penned on 1 January 1730, Darracott described himself in his house surrounded by friends, relations, and healthy offspring; 'Clouds & thick darkness Tempest & Storms beat upon my Soul' and his wife and several children die, but having weathered the storm together, at the close of the narrative he and the remaining children regroup.[187] Darracott presented a particularly pronounced combination of inward self-scrutiny with a family self. This family self was evidently shared by his children: the book closes with the announcement that, 'My Dear Father John Darracott departed this Life 16 May 1733, ... he Left me & [illeg] Bro^s. & Sisters be = hind wthout ... any Fr^d. ... & to y^e protection of God only'.[188] Darracott left four sons and two daughters aged between 8 and 23.

---

[181] Ibid. ff. 71, 73, 83.   [182] Ibid. ff. 84–5, 85.

[183] Lisa Smith, 'The Relative Duties of a Man: Domestic Medicine in England and France, ca. 1685–1740', *Journal of Family History*, 31, 3 (2006), pp. 237–56, esp. 247. See also Alun Robert James Withey, 'Health, Medicine and the Family in Wales, *c.* 1600–*c.*1750' (Unpublished PhD thesis, Swansea University, 2009).

[184] Diary of John Darracott, f. 109.

[185] Lease from John Darracott to Nathaniel Watson, North Devon Record Office: B156/B/2/7, 1722. The lease also included a messuage on Maiden Street. The house on Conduit Lane, Allhalland Street, had been in the possession of the tenant, John Bullhead.

[186] Diary of John Darracott, f. 113.

[187] Ibid. ff. 201–2. Quote at f. 201.

[188] Ibid. f. 203.

CONCLUSION

In his book *Circles and Lines: The Shape of Life in Early America* (2004), John Demos discusses how people wrote their stories using either circles or lines, arguing that the latter became more common in ego-documents after 1750.[189] Demos claims that the new linear model or metaphor was male, while the traditional metaphor of the family as a little circle became associated with the feminine world of home.[190] Yet, the image of the family circle as it appeared in men's writings had men at its centre and was to be found in a range of types of material across the period. This image was present in representations of the table examined in the previous chapter, could be found in early visions of the 'happy Cottager surrounded by a faithful, affectionate Wife, and pretty tatling Offspring', and was also deployed in William Cobbett's fantasy of the noble labouring man with 'a blooming family about him'.[191] These representations certainly presented men as tender and caring.[192] Yet in common with Joanne Bailey's analysis of court records, though, I find little evidence of a particular late-eighteenth-century language of sensibility in these writings.[193] This chapter has used examples from across the century. Letters from the later period are more expressive than the account books and miscellaneous domestic writings sampled throughout the century, but not only is the different register tied to the different genre, there are also significant continuities in both genre and register. One continuity suggested by the different examples from across the century discussed in this chapter is of the range of shapes employed in men's writing about the house. Eighteenth-century English men used both circles and lines in their writing. They conveyed their stories of childhood, marriage, and family life in autobiographical narrative, but they also pictured themselves within a present here-and-now family group and recorded this in periodic forms. These documents are not always voluminous on men's personal feelings about the house and family. Nevertheless, the multi-faceted investments that men made in the 'house', and in some cases the integrated manner in which men described the physical architecture, family relations, and the spiritual and emotional house, demonstrates

---

[189] John Demos, *Circles and Lines: The Shape of Life in Early America* (Cambridge, MA; London: Harvard University Press, 2004), pp. 60ff.

[190] Ibid. p. 76.

[191] *The Woman's Advocate: or, The Baudy Batchelor out in his Calculation* (London, 1729), p. 12; William Cobbett, *Cottage Economy* (London, 1822), p. 9.

[192] Joanne Bailey, 'Reassessing Parenting in Eighteenth-century England', in Helen Berry and Elizabeth Foyster (eds), *The Family in Early Modern England* (Cambridge: Cambridge University Press, 2007), p. 221.

[193] Joanne Bailey also finds no evidence of the language of romance and sentiment, nor of domesticity: the latter was, she argues, 'restricted to print rather than spouses' self-representations'. See Joanne Bailey, *Unquiet Lives: Marriage and Marriage Breakdown in England, 1660–1800* (Cambridge: Cambridge University Press, 2003), p. 201. Bailey here deploys a particular meaning of 'domestic' that overlaps with sensibility and which posits the home as a repository of expressive emotion. In the later article in Berry and Foyster, she finds that letters do register the key concepts of 'sensibility' and 'domesticity'. ('Reassessing Parenting', p. 232).

that the 'house' was a significant physical and psychological space for the construction of men's identities. The powerful psychological connections between writing, the domestic, space, and memory—what Stabile refers to as 'the material culture of remembrance'—may have been distinctively feminine in eighteenth-century America, but this does not apply to the English case.[194] Men in eighteenth-century England used domestic space to mark out their lives, sometimes using it mnemonically for thoughts or life-stages. Though this chapter has touched on the anxieties for some men of too close an association with the domestic, what is more striking is their presentation of self ensconced within the family group. Men's self-identities were grounded in the physical and emotional space of the house and the social relationships of family. The house literally and metaphorically generated masculine identities.

Rather than a model of feminine domestic individual identity or masculine market individual identity, then, these varied writings present a version of identity that exists on two continuums, from self to family and from house to society. This chimes with work on self and emotion in early America and which rethinks categories of identity and the separation of an autonomous self from society. Focusing on sensibility in particular, studies show how the inner emotional world of (male) citizens of the early Republic connected directly to the social and political realm.[195] Returning to a major theme of this book, oeconomy referred to management of the house and the world, but also of the emotions. If a man can 'regulate yourself', then the sins of '*Pride, Covetousness, Gluttony, Idleness, Impurity, Anger* and *Envy*' will be replaced with humility, moderation, and fortitude.[196] Controlled self-improvement, undertaken through the process of reflection and writing, was consonant with the oeconomical project of order through management. In this way, a man's innermost self and private consciousness was ever and always coupled with his actions in society. Inner self and outer world came together.

Often silent on men's personal feelings about the home, men's writings were even less voluble on their authors' attitudes to household government. It is not at all easy to detect whether these men were disciplinarians or benevolent patriarchs. Perhaps the silence on this issue is indisputable evidence of an absence of strict discipline and deference. Yet the documents themselves articulated and represent an important aspect of men's autonomy—and authority of self—and with it their authority in the house. Narratives of consolidating individualism have gone hand in hand with changes in domestic patriarchy: individualism dismantled the authority of the domestic patriarch by establishing the autonomy of other people in the household. Yet the masculine family self confounds these couplings: masculine

---

[194] Stabile, *Memory's Daughters*, p. 24.
[195] Nicole Eustace, *Passion is the Gale: Emotion, Power and the Coming of the American Revolution* (Chapel Hill: University of North Carolina Press 2008); Sarah Knott, 'Sensibility and the American War for Independence', *American Historical Review* 109, 1 (2004), pp. 19–40.
[196] Philippe Sylvestre Dufour [pseud Jacob Spon], *Moral Instructions for Youth: Or, a Father's Advice to a Son. Translated from the French, At first only for particular, and now publish'd for general Use. Being an attempt to season the growing generation with Virtuous Principles* (London, 1742), p. 42.

personal identity was rooted in both the house and the world and these men represented the family themselves. The accumulating force of the 'patriarchal notion of political entitlement' by the nineteenth century suggests why the shaping of men's personal identity as a family self was to soon become vital to male authority both within and without the house.[197]

[197] Matthew McCormack, ' "Married Men and the Fathers of Families": Fatherhood and Franchise Reform in Britain', in Trev Lynn Broughton and Helen Rogers (eds), *Gender and Fatherhood in the Nineteenth Century* (Basingstoke: Palgrave Macmillan, 2007), pp. 43–54; quote at p. 52.

6

Conclusion: Oeconomy and the Reproduction of Patriarchy

Through oeconomical practices that straddled the house and the world outside, and in rooting personal identity in the house and family, individual men accessed authority both within and without the house. This was a specifically manly form of authority, shaped and practised in the house but also exercised outside. Oeconomical authority was not coterminous with masculinity, though it was gendered and did foreground many culturally vaunted manly values. Practised and proven by individual men, oeconomy was a discourse through which men as a group could access a particular kind of authority. Indeed, these practices were shared, transmitted, and reproduced between men within families, and this became increasingly significant for middling-sort men. These practices were also reproduced between men of different social groups, though, and the authority of individual men in their houses was shored up by this fraternity of oeconomy.

This concluding chapter examines the implications of oeconomy as a model and practice of domestic patriarchy. As earlier chapters of this book have shown, men engaged in the house in practical ways that constituted acts of management and authority. Studies of family life have suggested that domestic patriarchy shifted in the eighteenth century to become less authoritarian, more hidden and internalized, but any attempt to understand 'domestic patriarchy' must deal with material practices as well as intangible norms and the manner in which patriarchy was actively re-created (and, indeed, contested) and manufactured.[1] Importantly, relations between men were just as important to the construction and maintenance of male authority as relations between women. Men's most pressing concern in the family, Linda Pollock demonstrates, may well have been threats from other men, as was noted in Chapter 1.[2] To the issue of gender, though, we must add age and social status to our discussion of patriarchy. As this chapter will discuss, for men acutely aware of the labour involved in establishing the family, it was imperative that sons continued the line. As in earlier periods, the system of patriarchy served to maintain social stratification, and the good conduct of domestic patriarchy

---

[1] See Chapter 1, pp. 2–8, for a more detailed discussion of changes in domestic patriarchy.

[2] Linda Pollock, 'Rethinking Patriarchy and the Family in Seventeenth-Century England', *Journal of Family History*, 23, 1 (1998), p. 22. See Chapter 1, p. 4.

helped shore up social status.[3] The material nature of relationships between men of different life-stages and social ranks are the focus of the first half of this chapter.

The second half of the chapter will turn to the public force of these relationships, drawing together the discussion of the political resonance of oeconomy in Chapter 2 with the focus throughout this book on the middling sort. What was the political significance of the oeconomical house for the middling sort? By the early nineteenth century, a specifically private domesticity had become a vital political discourse (to the working class for Anna Clark, to the middle class for Dror Wahrman) after the late 1820s and 1830s.[4] Before then, Wahrman argues, there was nothing particularly middle class about domesticity.[5] Indeed some work insists upon a shared culture of the home between social groups. Lawrence Klein's account of 'polite culture' embodied in new social spaces, objects, codes of conduct, and domesticity was seemingly accessible to all. Amanda Vickery's study of Lancashire gentry families detected important overlaps with upper middling families, and her most recent study considers 'genteel and middling' homes together, taking in both country house piles and London townhouse lodgings.[6] The lack of attention to rank and class in such studies is intriguing given the rapidly changing social structure in which houses sat. Politeness was a flexible discourse, though it is not at all clear that it served as the most important for the middling sort, and for middling-sort masculinity in particular.[7] For commercial men, at least, politeness stood alongside other values like vigour, fraternity, and prudence.[8]

Other studies are clear that a specifically middling-sort culture of the home was born of a desire to consolidate and ascend socially, culturally, and economically. Christopher Flint makes the clearest statement yet of domesticity serving as a political ideology of the middling sort prior to the last two decades of the eighteenth century.[9] Margaret Hunt's thoroughgoing study reconstructs the public value of a middling-sort domesticity for the families of that social rank, a domesticity that comprised hard work as well as comfort. Such works excavate the roots

---

[3] Michael J. Braddick and John Walter, 'Introduction. Grids of Power: Order, Hierarchy and Subordination in Early Modern Society', in Michael J. Braddick and John Walter (eds), *Negotiating Power in Early Modern Society: Order, Hierarchy and Subordination in Britain and Ireland* (Cambridge: Cambridge University Press, 2001), pp. 1–42.

[4] Anna Clark, *Struggle for the Breeches: Gender and the Making of the British Working Class* (Berkeley, LA; London: University of California Press, 1995); Dror Wahrman, *Imagining the Middle Class: The Political Representation of Class in Britain, c.1780–1840* (Cambridge: Cambridge University Press, 1995), pp. 377–408.

[5] Ibid. pp. 379–81.

[6] This is the phrase used to describe the main social focus throughout Amanda Vickery, *Behind Closed Doors: At Home in Georgian England* (New Haven, CN: Yale University Press, 2009). See also Lawrence Klein, 'Politeness and the Interpretation of the British Eighteenth Century', *Historical Journal*, 45 (2002), pp. 869–98.

[7] Karen Harvey, 'The History of Masculinity, *circa* 1650–1800', in Karen Harvey and Alexandra Shepard (eds), 'Special Feature on Masculinities', *The Journal of British Studies*, 44, 2 (2005), p. 307.

[8] John Smail, 'Coming of Age in Trade: Masculinity and Commerce in Eighteenth-Century England', in Margaret Jacob and Catherine Secretan (eds), *The Self Perception of Early Modern Capitalists* (New York: Palgrave Macmillan, 2008), pp. 236–40.

[9] Christopher Flint, '"The Family Piece": Oliver Goldsmith and the Politics of the Everyday in Eighteenth-Century Domestic Portraiture', *Eighteenth-Century Studies*, 29, 2 (1995–6), pp. 127–52.

of the middle-class domestic ideology explored by Davidoff and Hall for the period from 1780, an ideology that rendered the home an important middle-class space for women, a possession of middle-class men, and a functioning site of business relationships.[10] As I have sought to underline throughout this book, the social and economic role of the house—rather than the domesticity of the home—was an important feature of middling-sort status and particularly crucial to notions of middling-sort masculinity. There is some significant evidence of this already. John Smail has characterized commercial masculinity as a combination of 'prudential masculinity' (thrift and sound judgement) and 'chivalric masculinity' (nobility and honour), together with an emphasis on marriage and the financial and domestic contributions of a wife, a framework of less relevance for the landed or labouring.[11] Honour and credit were fastened to men in their good conduct as householders. As Henry French has demonstrated, middle-sort social identity was based on the assumption 'that "inhabitants," and particularly "chief inhabitants" comprised the *male* heads of financially independent households in the settlement'.[12] Put simply, definitions of household with social and political weight had men woven into their fabric.[13] For middling-sort men—whether of the 'chief inhabitants' or major merchants in the work of Henry French and John Smail, or from the broader social stratum discussed by Peter Earle and Margaret Hunt—keeping the house together and well ordered was the best security of economic stability and public status.

This chapter brings together the print and domestic manuscripts that have been examined throughout this book. More exploratory than previous chapters, it considers the reproduction of oeconomical practices between different generations of middling-sort families as a process of status building. I will then move towards some tentative conclusions about men of other social groups and the possibilities of a shared discourse of oeconomy. The closing case study ties back to Chapter 2, showing the relevance of oeconomy to the judgement of men's actions in the realm of public politics. Though the household was not part of E. P. Thompson's analysis of social power and class struggle in the 'field of force' between eighteenth-century 'Patricians and Plebs', Thompson recognized that the household was central to the creation and maintenance of both patriarchy and paternalism.[14] Order in the house sustained social stratification. As Gerda Lerner observes, 'Class differences were, at their very beginnings, expressed and constituted in

---

[10] Margaret Hunt, *The Middling Sort: Commerce, Gender and the Family in England, 1680–1780* (Berkeley, LA: University of California Press, 1996), pp. 193–215; Leonore Davidoff and Catherine Hall, *Family Fortunes: Men and Women of the English Middle Class, 1780–1850* (1987; Routledge, London, 1992).

[11] Smail, 'Coming of Age in Trade', pp. 240–6.

[12] Henry French, *The Middle Sort of People in Provincial England, 1600–1750* (Oxford: Oxford University Press, 2007), p. 107.

[13] Naomi Tadmor, 'The Concept of the Household-Family in Eighteenth-Century England', *Past and Present*, 151 (1996), p. 120.

[14] E. P. Thompson, *Customs in Common* (Harmondsworth: Penguin, 1993), pp. 18–19. Originally published as E. P. Thompson, 'Patrician Society, Plebeian Culture', *Journal of Social History*, 7, 4 (1974), pp. 382–405.

terms of patriarchal relations.'[15] It was precisely here, in the public estimation of social rank, that the long-lasting dividends of oeconomy for men were inestimable.

CREATING A FAMILY LINE

A common motif of eighteenth-century novels was failure in the male line.[16] For a father who sought security for himself and his family, establishing a family line was critical and allowed the inheritance of things besides property and goods. For an expanding middling sort seeking to enlarge networks, only by consolidating around a corpus of shared values would they be able to assess the 'character and ability of each other's sons and apprentices'.[17] The writings produced by middling-sort men were one aspect of the creation a corporate identity that would transcend time and reinforce the 'lineage-family' as distinguished by credit, probity, and order.[18] Several of the volumes examined in earlier chapters demonstrate this practice in action. Men such as Benjamin Shaw and Samuel Millar wrote for their offspring and descendents, while the books of Joshua Sagar and John Darracott were taken up and added to by later generations. The frequent loss of children made this process all the more poignant. Christopher Tuthill's account book—combining key events in his family story, lists of births, marriages, and deaths, recipes, and inventories— is a very good example of how telling stories about one's ancestors, one's self, and one's offspring was literally bound up with the practical tasks they performed daily as household managers. Yet, as discussed in Chapter 5, the book was completed from 1681 to 1854 by five successive generations of men, passed from father to son, until John Tuthill sailed for New York in 1852. This volume is a patrilineal text, a written manifestation of the reproduction of the male line.[19]

In the case of printed works, the connection between fathers and sons forged by writing was also evident. Two years before Dudley North's *Observations and Advices Oeconomical* (1669) was published, his son John explained how the work connected three generations of Norths: 'I hope my Father will bee pleased to follow the steps of my Grandfather in the Vertue of imparting, if not to the world, yet to

[15] Gerda Lerner, *The Creation of Patriarchy* (Oxford: Oxford University Press, 1986), p. 213. Quoted in Elizabeth Kowaleski-Wallace, *Their Fathers' Daughters: Hannah More, Maria Edgeworth, and Patriarchal Complicity* (New York; Oxford: Oxford University Press, 1991), p. 4.

[16] Brian McCrea, *Impotent Fathers: Patriarchy and Demographic Crisis in the Eighteenth-Century Novel* (Newark: University of Delaware Press, 1998), *passim*, and p. 18. McCrea links this to a demographic crisis amongst the aristocracy, though demographic change affected all social ranks, and the burgeoning group of novel readers were the upp.er-middling sort.

[17] Craig Muldrew, *The Economy of Obligation: The Culture of Credit and Social Relations in Early Modern England* (Basingstoke: Macmillan, 1998), p. 58.

[18] On the concept of the 'lineage-family' see, Naomi Tadmor, *Family and Friends in Eighteenth-Century England: Household, Kinship and Patronage* (Cambridge: Cambridge University Press, 2001), pp. 73–102.

[19] See the commonplace book of Christopher Tuthill, 1681–1858, William Andrews Clark Memorial Library: MS.1977.003.

his owne posterity, those note's [,] observations, or discourses hee has made in his life time, when I haue heard & haue reason to think that many of such a nature doe lye dormant in his hands.'[20] A few years later, in 1685, another son received a volume of instructions fast upon his father's death and, again, the volume (later published in English in 1742 as *Moral Instructions for Youth*) tied three generations of men. Initially, the book bodied forth the absent father: it was 'written in his Spirit and Manner, and agreeable to his Sentiments and Advices'. After losing his father, but gaining the book, the son devoted himself to it: 'I read it over and over, and endeavour'd to live it over too, that I might in some degree...approve myself the very Son of such a Father.' Soon the book would be passed down again, 'now it having pleased God to give me a Son'.[21] This book was part of an ongoing repro-duction of the male line as well as the particular style of masculinity advocated in its pages.

Making sense of the written family histories considered in Chapter 5, we should recognize how they could be invaluable to an emergent social group who lacked traditional markers of status. This was certainly one motivation for the memorial-ization of families in Renaissance Italy. In Venice, families created and projected a group ideology through a range of public documents, but newer and less estab-lished families seeking to confirm their social status in Florence lacked this option and instead engaged in private memorialization in *ricordanze*: 'veritable family annals, in which the head of the family noted ordinary events on a day-to-day basis in journals or account books'.[22] Written by heads of household, indeed intended to be kept locked away from women, these books seem to have emerged out of the record-keeping of merchants.[23] Their purpose was to prove status and lineage through a family identity constructed out of a shared history and memory.[24] Such readings are pertinent to the interpretation of the writings of eighteenth-century English middling-sort men examined in this book. The middling sort lacked a shared group ideology that could be publicly memorialized, and these families were concerned to prove their social as well as financial worth. There are sugges-tions that the tradition of family history began with aristocratic men—not women—leaving records to their sons, though women in some families played a

---

[20] Bodleian, MS North, *c*10, p. 17. Quoted in Dale B. J. Randall, *Gentle Flame: The Life and Verse of Dudley, Fourth Lord North (1602–1677)* (Durham, NC: Duke University Press, 1983), p. 86. Dud-ley North described his own poems themselves as children to whom he, the parent, had given birth. 'Dedication', in Randall, *Gentle Flame*, p. 128.

[21] Philippe Sylvestre Dufour [pseud Jacob Spon], *Moral Instructions for Youth: Or, a Father's Advice to a Son. Translated from the French, At first only for particular, and now publish'd for general Use. Being an attempt to season the growing generation with Virtuous Principles* (London, 1742), pp. i–ii.

[22] James Grubb, 'Memory and Identity: Why the Venetians Didn't Keep Ricordanze', *Renaissance Studies*, 8 (1994), pp. 375–87; quote from Christine Klapisch-Zuber, *Women, Family, and Ritual in Renaissance Italy*, trans. Lydia Cochrane (Chicago and London: The University of Chicago Press, 1985), p. 95.

[23] See review by Giovanni Ciappelli in *Journal of Modern History*, 64 (1992), p. 817.

[24] See Giovanni Ciappelli, 'Family Memory: Funcions, Evolution, Recurrences', in Giovanni Ciap-pelli and Patricia Lee Rubin, *Art, Memory, and Family in Renaissance Florence* (Cambridge: Cambridge University Press, 2000), pp. 26–38.

role in memorializing the family past.[25] My research for this study suggests that such documents kept by middling-sort women were rarely created, certainly rarely saved, though. In contrast, the varied documents composed by male oeconomists made manifest not just good management and financial probity, but a store of other cultural resources such as literacy, numeracy, self-discipline, and lineage. In creating families existing in the past but also the future, the domestic manuscripts explored in this book shored up middling-sort family status for the long term.

SHARED MODELS OF HOUSEHOLD GOVERNMENT

As discussed in Chapter 2, oeconomy slowly reoriented as a discourse to serve as political legitimization for middling-sort men. Throughout this book I have emphasized how the words and practices of middling-sort men articulated household management. Yet oeconomy had been established as a mode of household management for the landed elite, and these elite household managers continued to deploy oeconomy into the eighteenth century. I wish to suggest here that the adaptability of oeconomy to different social status groups was one reason for its endurance, and that men's adherence to its general principles across the social hierarchy gave oeconomy considerable force. Nevertheless, as this section will explore, management of the household was necessarily undertaken using strategies specific to rank.

The sharing of practices of household management between the middling sort and landed elite has been raised in previous chapters, notably in the way that merchants' relationships with tenants echoed those of landowners such as James Brydges (1674–44), first Duke of Chandos.[26] Indeed, born to rich merchants and landed gentry, and having enlarged the house Cannons in Herefordshire, Chandos is a good example of a keen oeconomist. Brydges established complex systems during the 1720s in order to ensure that his management reached into the farthest corners of his estates and dealings, far exceeding 'the Family' of 136 people living in and around the main house of Cannons.[27] With regards to the main house, intricate instructions were composed for the steward, the usher of the halls, and the butler, designed to ensure that members of the family and also visitors were subject to the household system. The Steward's Instructions required him to 'take particular care that all the Servants be present at the Performance of Divine Worship', 'nor that any of the Inferiour Servants go abroad out of call in the day time'. Servants of

[25] Michael Mascuch, *Origins of the Individualist Self: Autobiography and Self-identity in England, 1591–1791* (Cambridge: Polity Press, 1997), pp. 93–4. On women and family history see, for example, Alice Friedman, *House and Household in Elizabethan England: Wollaton Hall and the Willoughby Family* (Chicago, IL; London: University of Chicago Press, 1989); Sandra Stanley Holton, *Quaker Women: Personal Life, Memory and Radicalism in the Lives of Women Friends, 1780—1930* (Aldershot: Routledge, 2007).

[26] See Chapter 4, pp. 110–15, 130–1.

[27] Bound volume by Lionell Norman, steward to James Brydges, Stowe Papers, Henry E. Huntington Library: HEH ST44, Part I, pp. 26, 27–32.

gentlemen or other strangers were to be 'decently entertain'd', and not to 'become the occasion of any Irregularities'.[28] According to the 'Storekeeper's Usher of the Hall's Instructions', the usher was to 'take particular notice of every Stranger who comes': if they were of 'the meaner sort', they were not to 'loiter about the House'; if they were 'honest substantial Men, & not looked idle Fellows', they could be 'asked to dinner, or to drink before they go away, & more especially this to be observed towards Tenants'; finally, if these strangers were 'of the better sort & come to see the Duke', the usher was to take them 'into the Tapestry Room'.[29] A weekly Audit Board was also established to review accounts, at whose first meeting these four important personages met to consider a single bill from Ives the Glazier for £1 2s 16d.[30] Chandos also regulated the tenants off his Cannons estate, notably in Bath where his female lodging-house keepers served as the urban stewards, managing the tenants who sat in Brydges' chairs and slept in his beds.[31] To allow this, hundreds of letters between Brydges' principal secretary and stewards traversed the south of England on matters large and small.[32] As a large landowner, then, Brydges' authority touched many different men and women. The degree of Brydges' fanaticism was perhaps exceptional, but like all men of his social group oeconomy was practised by him and the others who deployed authority in his name.

The case of Brydges shows the implementation of oeconomy as it had been laid out in printed works of the late seventeenth century. But by the 1720s, oeconomy was being sold to those well below Brydges' rank to the expanding middling sort. One of the responsibilities shared by landed and middling oeconomists was that of management. Titled landowners, merchants, professionals, businessmen, and tradesmen had people to manage. The appropriate behaviour for men in this hierarchy of management was a topic of much concern in the printed work on oeconomy. The stated purpose of much of this advice was to retain the social order. Thus, the 'superior Obligation' of a man in this position was to treat his servant with 'that Mildness and Gentleness, which tempering and mitigating the Irksomeness of Servitude, may move him to serve you with Chearfulness'.[33] The popular work *The Oeconomy of Human Life* devoted a chapter to 'Masters and Servants', which exhorted that 'the state of servitude [...] is the appointment of God, and hath many advantages'.[34] In return for a servant's fidelity, the master was to be a benevolent patrician, who must be 'reasonable in [his] commands, if thou expectest a ready obedience'.[35] The axes of class and age were central to this book's vision of social order, and benevolence turned the middling-sort man into a patrician. The

---

[28] Ibid. 'Steward's Instructions', p. 1.
[29] 'Storekeeper's Usher of the Hall's Instructions', Stowe Papers, Henry E. Huntington Library: STB Miscellaneous papers, Box 1 (7), ff. 1–4.
[30] Audit book for Cannons, Stowe Papers, Henry E. Huntington Library: ST24 vol. 1, f. 1.
[31] John Eglin, *The Imaginary Autocrat: Beau Nashe and the invention of Bath* (Profile, London, 2005), pp. 151–6.
[32] Brydges family papers, Henry E. Huntington Library: STB Correspondence, Boxes 13–23.
[33] Dufour's *Moral Instructions for Youth*, p. 78.
[34] *The Oeconomy of Human Life. Translated from an Indian Manuscript. Written by an Ancient Bramin*, 4th edn (London, 1751), p. 69.
[35] Ibid. p. 70.

Figure 14: 'Masters and Servants', from *Oeconomy of Human Life* (1795) Huntington Library: RB124104, p. 89. Reproduced by kind permission of The Huntington Library, San Marino, California.

appropriate treatment of servants was one aspect of a more general education in household management, and the house was the training ground for benevolence, or how to be manly in a starkly hierarchical society. Indeed, just as the figure of the benevolent and manly middling-sort friend on the street *required* the figure of the beggar—'[e]lite manliness was in part defined by the existence of an unmanned pauper hoard'—so a good oeconomist required someone to manage.[36]

---

[36] See Tim Hitchcock, 'Tricksters, Lords and Servants: Begging, Friendship and Masculinity in Eighteenth-century England', in Laura Gowing, Michael Hunter and Miri Rubin (eds), *Love, Friendship and Faith in Europe 1300–1800* (Basingstoke: Palgrave Macmillan, 2005), p. 192. Robert Sharp described a master getting a gardener a place at a sugar-refinery, while also paying him £5 a year, as 'a very Gentlemanly action to an old Servant'. *The Diary of Robert Sharp of South Cave: Life in a Yorkshire Village, 1812–1837*, ed. Janice E. Crowther and Peter A. Crowther (Records of Social and Economic History, New Series 26, For the British Academy, by Oxford University Press, 1997), Thurs 18 March 1830, p. 251.

Models of management and household order were widely shared, I contend, but with considerable resources at their disposal, landed men had many more tools available. Brydges was sufficiently wealthy and powerful to toy with legal action against a Captain Herbert Russell who stalled in paying a legal fine on Brydges' land: 'I woud have you without more ado, bring an action against him, he is a very surly obstinate fellow, & I will make an example of him', he wrote to his principal secretary and steward James Farquharson.[37] Francis Blake could similarly bring his resources to bear in publicly reinforcing his authority. Being made aware of 'a violent Trespass committed upon my Estate' on 12 November 1769, Blake noted in his account book, 'I must punish him for to deter him & others especially in Eatall, from repeating the like'. He subsequently added, 'I punished him thus, made him ask pardon in the Public Newspapers'.[38] Other techniques could be used by all managers. On discovering that a servant had been, 'reporting false and scurrilous things of me, and making me & my Domestic Concerns the common subjects of his Discourse and all in a disadvantageous Light', Blake responded swiftly: 'I was forced to dismiss upon Acc^t. of Lying and scurrilous Reports he had raised of me as if I starved him, when the Truth is that beside Bread & washing he cost me 1^s p day.'[39] Some pages later, Blake returns to record his own benevolence, reporting that he gave the servant money for subsistence, 'till the Boy was provided for or set out for the north which he might either do by Sea or with my Horses by land, & either way at my Expense; but not to stay in my Family again'.[40]

Elite men bound members of their 'family' using various instruments, including money, benevolence, and legal documents. Susan Whyman's discussion of primogeniture in the elite late-Stuart Verney family, demonstrates fathers' considerable control over their sons' marriages, mainly through the use of strict settlement. This, says Whyman, fostered 'a dynastic mindset'; thus, 'sons were bound to their fathers' wishes by hoops of steel forged out of shared values'.[41] Sir Francis Blake's negotiations over his son's marriage in 1770 demonstrate both the hard control of the contract (the 'hoops') and the soft control of the 'shared values'. Seeking to make a match for his son, Blake met the father of the likely bride: 'We discoursed chiefly about my Son's Conduct which he was very inquisitive after, & I did what I could to remove all Impressions to his Prejudice, for I found there were some & especially concerning his Want of economy.'[42] Emphasizing his own frugality, he added, 'I dined at home on green Pease'.[43] Protracted negotiations then ensued

[37] Brydges family papers, Henry E. Huntington Library: STB Correspondence, Box 13(52), 1 November 1730, f. 3.

[38] Francis Blake, 'Accots. from 11th August 1769 to 1st January 1771', William Andrews Clark Memorial Library: MS.1985.002, inside front cover, dated Sunday 12 November 1769.

[39] Blake, 'Accot. from 11th August 1769 to 1 January 1771', 30 December 1765, f. 57; 31 December 1765, f. 45.

[40] Francis Blake, 'Acct Book from 1 January 1765 to 22 February 1766', William Andrews Clark Memorial Library: MS.1985.002: 30–31 December 1765, f. 57.

[41] Susan Whyman, *Sociability and Power in Late-Stuart England: The Cultural Worlds of the Verneys, 1660–1720* (Oxford: Oxford University Press, 1999), p. 143.

[42] Blake, 'Accots. from 11th August 1769 to 1st January 1771', 2 July 1770, f. 47.

[43] Ibid. 2 July 1770, f. 47.

over the marriage settlement, what Blake called 'the Treaty'.[44] Throughout the process, Blake also sought to exert more informal pressure on his son to change his behaviour: he 'upbraids' him for continuing a connection with a Mrs Hereford, for example, and instructed him to 'smooth Things over' when the negotiations seemed to be stalled.[45]

As discussed above, lineage was a preoccupation of middling-sort men, who also shared Blake's concerns about the marriage of sons. The bachelor diarist from Bath, for example, felt under considerable pressure from his father concerning the matter of his possible marriage.[46] Yet, as Thompson argued, different social groups possessed their own specific 'grids of inheritance' through which to transmit property but also social status.[47] The practices and discourse discussed in previous chapters shows the kinds of tools available to middling-sort men. The managerial and oeconomical practices of middling-sort householders ensured family continuity and reproduction through the male line, in the absence of legal techniques such as entail and strict settlement. These men may have lacked 'hoops of steel', but they could certainly inculcate 'shared values' through their domestic practices. In reproducing oeconomy, these men could utilize training, the status of financial manager, as well as informal moral pressure.

Training was likely to be most effective for boys and young men. Between 1778 and 1785, William Martin was Manager of the Aire and Calder Navigation, a network of waterways linking towns in the north-east of England. He was described by one of his correspondents as a 'Man of business with matters to be carried on Clear', while another correspondent flattered him as a 'Man of Abilities' with whom he had hoped to enjoy 'a little more discourse abᵗ philosophy and other valuable subjects'.[48] Significantly, William Martin commissioned research into all of the births, marriages, and deaths recorded under the name of 'Martin' in the register of Old Brampton in Derby.[49]

His skills were called into use when Martin was required to educate his son in financial probity. William Martin's son attended Eton, apparently arranged with just one peremptory letter in July 1778.[50] In 31 July 1783, a Mary Hird wrote from the school to William Martin. Mary's counsel about wise spending had not been heeded by Master Martin, she advised, and she requested that his father intervene. She had sent his box ahead, and included his half year's account, 'that you may look it over with him'. She continued, 'I must beg the favour of you to give him such instructions relating to those necessaries he may have occasion for here, as it is not in my power to prevent his having what I may think unnecessary—I

[44]　Ibid. 2 August 1770, f. 52.
[45]　Ibid. 10 June 1770, f. 44; 12 July 1770, f. 49.
[46]　See Chapter 3, p. 68.
[47]　E. P. Thompson, 'The Grid of Inheritance: A Comment', in E. P. Thompson, *Persons and Polemics: Historical Essays* (London: Merlin, 2003), pp. 358, 360.
[48]　Will Staines to William Martin, 28 November 1785, West Yorkshire Archive Services, Wakefield: C695 1/14; Robᵗ Beighton to William Martin, 19 June 1778, C482/1, f. 2, f. 1.
[49]　Ibid.
[50]　Letter from W[illia]m Langford to William Martin, 16 July 1778, C482/2.

find my advice of little service, therefore I cannot take upon me to be answerable for his conduct in these matters. Some articles in the Tradesmans [sic] Bills were without my knowledge.' Sending Martin 'respectful compliments', and signing off 'Your most humble Servt', Hird asked the father to school the son in money management.[51] William Martin was well qualified to provide his son with this instruction; the management of his own extensive accounts is mentioned by several business associates in their letters to him.[52] With their discussion of various intellectual 'abilities' and this stress on good accounting, Martin's letters show the fusion of prudence and chivalry of 'commercial masculinity'.[53] Master Martin was experiencing an issue of wider concern. In the same year that Hird wrote to Martin, a brief 'set of maxims…respecting oeconomy' were published for boys away at school: 'It were well if Parents and Masters would attend to the conduct of Children in these particulars', the author explained, 'It is the epidemical madness of this age to spend on Monday the allotment for the present week, and to mortgage on Tuesday the allowance for the next.'[54] Master Martin was financially dependent on his father while he was at school; and under the law of necessaries, fathers were responsible for sons' debts until they reached the age of 21.[55] It was therefore imperative that sons were sufficiently schooled in accounting.[56]

The role that the early-modern household played in trade and exchange diminished with the institutionalization of credit, but credit continued to operate informally within families into the nineteenth century.[57] This was the context for many of the written exchanges about financial matters between fathers and their grown sons, during which fathers sought to exert their authoritative role as financial manager. The more privileged young men remained financially dependent on fathers not only through childhood but also while at university,[58] and this dependence continued well into a son's adult life. Nevertheless, sons were not always as biddable as fathers might hope. The Rev. George Alderson (1768–1834), rector at Birkin, near Pontefract, came to know this too well. Alderson was rector at Birkin in the West Riding of Yorkshire from 1770, until his death in July 1835.[59] He had two sons and a daughter, Margaret. His son George went into partnership with a Dr Jefferson, who wrote to Alderson on 19 August 1801, without George's knowledge, to request that he intervene: 'Your son George owes me money', he stated;

[51] Letter from Mary Hird to William Martin, 31 July 1783, C482/4.
[52] See, for example, Elias Wright to Jonathon Smyth, 21 August 1783, C1063/3/8; Will Staines to William Martin, 28 November 1785, C695 1/14.
[53] Smail, 'Coming of Age in Trade', pp. 229–52, esp. p. 244.
[54] *School dialogues, for boys. Being an attempt to convey instruction insensibly to their tender minds,… By a lady*, Vol. 2 (London, [1783]), pp. 98, 99.
[55] Margot Finn, *The Character of Credit: Personal Debt in English Culture, 1740–1914* (Cambridge; New York: Cambridge University Press, 2003), pp. 273–4.
[56] See Chapter 3 for a fuller discussion of accounting.
[57] Finn, *Character of Credit, passim*.
[58] On male youths at university, see ibid. pp. 273–4.
[59] CCEd Record ID 148744; 'George Alderson (CCEd Person ID 83072)', *The Clergy of the Church of England Database 1540–1835*, <http://www.theclergydatabase.org.uk> (accessed August 2008).

'Will you have the goodness to advance for him, & assist me with 20l or 30l, by Saturday.'[60] Alderson replied, 'I sincerely believe your Feelings originate from good Principles', and he duly paid £20.[61] Alderson apparently then wrote to his son, who tried to restore his father's confidence in him: 'you shall have the Books produced to you and I hope every thing then may be formally closed'.[62] These financial difficulties were resolved by the time that Alderson was called upon to assist with the financial difficulties of his other son.

William was rector at Everingham in the East Riding from July 1829.[63] A collection of memos kept by George Alderson records the money he lent to William in the years between 1819 and 1827.[64] For the year 1828, an acknowledgement from William, on a strip of paper just 8 inches by 2 inches confirmed, '12th April 1828. I hereby acknowledge to have rec^d of my Father the Sum of 45£'s which I promise to pay & to be accountable for to him the first opportunity.' On the reverse, George reinforced: 'Son W^{ms} Acknowledgement For 45£ lent To him 12th April 1828.'[65] William had considerable debts, though, and by January 1832 he began 'to feel the situation of his Family most acutely'.[66] A note of George Alderson's, dated 23 January 1832, made reference to the money due 'on Acc.^{t} of Everingham Rectory', William's house. The problems continued: a final letter from early November 1833 conveys George Alderson's exhaustion at his son's financial mismanagement, as well its implications of moral shortcomings:

> Dear W^m
> Writing lessons of any kind is at my Period of Life become very irksome and unpleasant but much more so when I am urged to do it on Business which solely results from y^r own Misconduct, Folly, Imprudence and Want of Attention.[67]

George Alderson died a year after writing this letter to his adult son; fathers might remain responsible for sons' finances for life. The persistence of family-based credit bound these men together, and through the web of family finance men of older generations sought to manage younger men.

Family-based credit operated not just between fathers and sons. The Lancaster tradesman William Stout remained unmarried and without children, but he took a close interest in the housekeeping of his nephews, William and John Stout. William was an apprentice in his uncle's shop for many years, being supported as

[60] Letter from J. Jefferson, 19 August 1801, in Papers of Rev Samuel Sharp and family 1584–1865, West Yorkshire Archive Services, Wakefield: C281 16/5.

[61] Draft of reply to J. Jefferson, 21 August 1801, C281 16/5.

[62] Letter from father to son, no date, C281 16/5.

[63] 'William Alderson (CCEd Person ID 122865)', *The Clergy of the Church of England Database 1540–1835*, <http://www.theclergydatabase.org.uk> (accessed August 2008).

[64] Account of money given to son William and Jonathan Smith of Leeds, 1819–c.1828, West Yorkshire Archive Services, Wakefield: C281 16/6, 2.

[65] Ibid. 16/6, 1.

[66] As quoted in letter from George Alderson to William Alderson, 21 January 1832, West Yorkshire Archive Services, Wakefield: C281 16/8.

[67] Letter from George Alderson to William Alderson, 6 November and 7 November 1833, C281 16/8.

long as—Stout made clear—'he would be governed by my advice'.[68] Much to Stout's disappointment, though, William resisted his uncle's instructions and proved to be 'idle and prodigall'.[69] Stout found the sight of his nephew's 'ill management and conduct' so unbearable, that he was forced to retreat into reading, writing, and lonely garden walks at sunrise and sunset.[70] Despite William's seeming ungratefulness and truculence, though, Stout continued to bail him out—to the tune of £930 by 1732.[71]

William Stout achieved greater success with his younger nephew, John. In 1730, he promised to buy the 16-year-old an estate worth £40 a year, 'if he was industrious and frugall'.[72] Against Stout's wishes, John's parents set him up as an apprentice with a draper; Stout found that he had to pay not only the £40, but also the cost of John's clothes for the duration of the apprenticeship.[73] Once the apprenticeship was concluded, Stout advanced John a considerable loan to set up shop in Lancaster.[74] Though Stout tried to guide both his nephews in oeconomy, he felt that only John was sufficiently responsive to exhortations about frugality and management. Craig Muldrew has contrasted Stout's successful management of his own trade with the failure of his nephew, seeking to illustrate how easy it was for a household (in this case, young William's) to lose credit.[75] Yet the fraternity of oeconomy that Stout sought to foster rendered the boundaries between these men's households imprecise. For Stout, their households were his business. As he declared authoritatively, 'I inspected the house-keeping of my nephew William Stout'.[76] He examined their moral and economic management and sought to discipline them in exchange for financial support.[77] Stout exercised 'patriarchal manhood', a form of masculine identity that was an aspiration to men with or without co-resident offspring. Yet it is not necessary to describe Stout as acting as a surrogate father for his young nephews.[78] Oeconomy required management that was easily elided with a paternal identity, but fatherhood as either a biological or social identity was not essential for an oeconomist.

Though the discourse of oeconomy changed during this period, its roots were in a model of estate management.[79] The middling sort utilized older languages for

---

[68] *The Autobiography of William Stout of Lancaster, 1665–1752*, ed. J. D. Marshall (Manchester, Chetham Society, 1967), 3rd series, vol. 14, p. 200.

[69] Ibid. p. 206.

[70] Ibid. p. 201.

[71] Ibid. p. 210.

[72] Ibid. p. 206.

[73] Ibid. pp. 206–7.

[74] Ibid. p. 223.

[75] Muldrew, *Economy of Obligation*, pp. 171–2.

[76] *Autobiography of William Stout*, p. 232.

[77] For a later example of an uncle managing a nephew, see T. Micklethwaite to John Micklethwaite 7 May 1824, John Micklethwaite correspondence, Manchester University John Rylands Special Collections: Eng MS 1138, folder 5/207.

[78] Helen Berry and Elizabeth Foyster, 'Childless Men in Early Modern England', in Helen Berry and Elizabeth Foyster (eds), *The Family in Early Modern England* (Cambridge University Press, Cambridge, 2007), p. 183.

[79] See Chapter 2 for a full discussion of how the discourse of oeconomy changed.

their own purposes. Henry French argues that the middling sort appropriated a language of landed gentility in their bid for social status, not because they wanted to be landowners, but because this was the language through which social authority was expressed.[80] John Smail's study of the honour code underpinning merchants' credit networks similarly notes that, 'non-elites were appropriating the forms and language of an aristocratic honor that was already being rationalized and civilized'.[81] Both French and Smail have noted the importance of both prudence and domesticity to the middling sort, distinguished by contemporaries from those above and below.[82] Oeconomy was not simply derivative of an older model of estate management, but was melded with increasingly important modes of record-keeping associated with their stewards and other servants and with the arenas of business and commerce. If by the nineteenth century the household was governed by the rules of the commercial world,[83] then a large part of the labour of this re-shaping was performed by middling men keeping their own accounts and by those compiling the accounts of their masters. In this context, we might view the volumes of family histories and accounts as evidence not only of the good oeconomist, but also of a particular kind of middling-sort cultural inheritance that men sought to bequeath to their successors.

FROM THE HOUSE TO THE NATION

Throughout this book I have emphasized that the notion of the middling-sort house conflated the public and private. Oeconomy was not domesticity, but embodied a different culture of the domestic. Thus, according to Xenophon, oeconomy 'breeds good Men'; men who can govern and are thus 'worthy the Command of Kingdoms'.[84] The evidence used in this book has been about, or emerged from, the house, but in this final section of the book I will explore the public resonance of the house using a case study drawn from the genre of visual political satire. At the same time that it represents the political nation, this public material takes us to the heart of the house, the kitchen.

Kitchens are perhaps the most studied room in the history of the interior. And the dull metalware pots and pans used and displayed there have given rise to as large a volume of work as the ceramic and silver items involved in tea-drinking in the parlour. As we might expect, a good portion of this work is about women: their networks, agency, and creativity. But this gendering of the kitchen is actually rather recent. Architectural historians show that the medieval hall (the area for food prep-

---

[80] French, *Middle Sort of People*, pp. 201–9, 258–67.

[81] John Smail, 'Credit, Risk, and Honor in Eighteenth-Century Commerce', *Journal of British Studies*, 44 (2005), p. 454.

[82] French, *Middle Sort of People*, p. 25; Smail, 'Coming of Age in Trade', p. 246.

[83] Beverly Lemire, *The Business of Everyday Life: Gender, Practice and Social Politics in England, c.1600–1900* (Manchester: Manchester University Press, 2005).

[84] *The Science of Good Husbandry: or, the Oeconomics of Xenophon*, trans. Richard Bradley (London, 1727), pp. 39, 87–8.

aration *and* consumption) was one important theatre for the performance of manly status. The emergence of the 'kitchen' and its demotion to the hidden reaches of the house was coterminous with its feminization in some ranks, though in the early-modern middling-sort house the kitchen was neither separated nor gendered in any straightforward way.[85] Hidden or not, though, kitchens were the heart of a household, crammed with functional items that were as expressive as any other domestic object. The kitchen in early modern England was 'a contested, highly populated space', but—containing the hearth and its fire—rightly seen as 'the structural and psychological centre of the household'.[86] We can also say that the kitchen was the most 'homely' room in the eighteenth-century sense of the word, to mean unadorned functionality.[87]

The series of prints I wish to explore were published early in the reign of George III, which began on 25 October 1760 during the Seven Years' War. This inaugurated a period of dramatic change in the personnel of government. The King replaced many leading ministers and members of the Royal Household.[88] Notoriously, he brought John Stuart, 3rd Earl of Bute (his tutor and previously confidante of his father) into his administration, and Bute rose in office quickly. The role of this 'favourite' was to be inextricably linked with George III's reassertion of royal independence. William Pit resigned as prime minister on 5 October 1761, and the Duke of Newcastle as first Lord of the Treasury on 26 May 1762.[89] Bute had become the head of government in eighteen months. As Paul Langford has identified, this was a crisis about 'the management of the State.'[90] It was also expressed through the discourse of oeconomy.

During the same phase, Earl Talbot was appointed Lord Steward of the Royal Household in March 1761, inaugurating a series of changes in the Royal Kitchen, and both Bute and Talbot feature in a series of prints depicting this space. In 'A Catalogue of the Kitchin Furniture of John Bull, Esq[r]. leaving of House-keeping now Selling by AUCTION' (1762), Talbot with his richly embroidered coat and wand of office stands next to a clerk, instructing him to sell off the nation's cookware, and declaring of the kitchen staff, 'why let 'em starve'. The verses beneath reinforce the visual remarks on poverty and neglect, exhorting, 'BRITONS whose bags are continually swelling [to] let Hospitality reign through your Dwelling'. In contrast to the urgent faces of the hungry servants to the left, a young and handsome Bute stands on the right. He discusses with the Princess of Wales whether he

[85] Amanda Flather, *Gender and Space in Early Modern England* (Woodbridge: Boydell Press, 2007), pp. 61–2.

[86] Sara Pennell, '"Pots and Pans History": The Material Culture of the Kitchen in Early Modern England', *Journal of Design History*, 11, 3, 1998, p. 202.

[87] See Chapter 5, p. 153, for another use of this word.

[88] B. W. Hill, *British Parliamentary Parties, 1742–1832: From the Fall of Walpole to the First Reform Act* (London: George Allen & Unwin, 1985), pp. 90–4. Bute took the Treasury following Newcastle's resignation over policy in the Continental war.

[89] Frank O'Gorman, *The Long Eighteenth Century: British Political and Social History, 1688–1832* (London: Arnold, 1997), pp. 201–3.

[90] Paul Langford, 'The Management of the Eighteenth-Century State: Perceptions and Implications', *Journal of Historical Sociology*, 15, 1, March 2002, p. 103.

Figure 15: 'A Catalogue of the Kitchin Furniture', Huntington Library: Print Pr 211.1 33 BM 3990. Reproduced by kind permission of The Huntington Library, San Marino, California.

should purchase one item of the kitchen furniture wrenched from its setting and now abandoned prominently on the floor.[91] Neither displayed nor in use, John Bull's end to house-keeping had rendered these pots and kettles bereft, emptied of what Sara Pennell has identified as their voluble 'social capital'.[92]

The new system in the Royal Kitchen is presented as one of extreme frugality. In 'The Kitchen Metamorphoz'd' (1762), we see Talbot, again with coat and wand, as dinner is being prepared in the Royal Kitchen. Here the scene of deprivation is even more pronounced, with the expanse of floor filled with so little, its extent contrasting with the paltry herring and a half being proffered by the cook.[93] The title of 'A Miserable Cold Place. Alteration and Oh-Economy', underlines the bleakness of what should be a warm, full, and busy space. The empty hearth—and in the

---

[91] 'A Catalogue of the Kitchin Furniture of John Bull, Esqr leaving of House-keeping now Selling by AUCTION' (1762), Henry E. Huntington Library Art Collection: HM Pr Box 211.1/33.

[92] Sara Pennell, 'Mundane Materiality, or, Should Small Things be Forgotten? Material Culture, Micro-Histories and the Problem of Scale', in Karen Harvey (ed.), *History and Material Culture: A Student's Guide to Approaching Alternative Sources* (Aldershot: Routledge, 2009), p. 180.

[93] 'The Kitchen Metamorphos'd' (1762), Henry E. Huntington Library Art Collection: HM RB379995, p. 7.

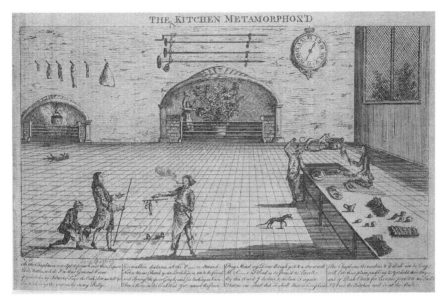

Figure 16: 'Kitchen Metamorphos'd', Huntington Library: RB379995, p. 7. Reproduced by kind permission of The Huntington Library, San Marino, California.

other prints too—underlines the lack of warmth and provision; the moaning 'Oh-Economy' gives the print one of its humorous kicks. And this is a particularly Scotch oeconomy. Indeed, this image (and 'A Catalogue of the Kitchin Furniture') was published in the collection of prints, *The Scots scourge; being a compleat supplement to the British antidote to Caledonian poison* ([1765?]), wherein oeconomy was defined as 'A pitiful manner of furnishing the royal kitchen, and a profuse method of expending the money of the Kingdom'.[94] In these three engravings, the Royal Kitchen resonates with issues of nation and race, political competition, men's management and their duties of benevolence in government.

The language of oeconomy was also used to target Bute's handling of the ongoing Seven Years' War, and in particular his proposals for peace with France. In 'The Pe**e-Soup-makers, Or, A New Mess at the B-d—d Head' (August 1762), together with the Duke of Bedford, Bute the Scot prepares a bland and cheap meal, too insipid for the English palate. The weakness of the Scot's food is run together with his conciliatory position on France, and next to Pitt Bute appears as a weak and a poor oeconomist. Images of a specifically 'Scotch Oeconomy' were one aspect

---

[94] *The Scots scourge; being a compleat supplement to the British antidote to Caledonian poison: in two volumes. Containing fifty-two anti-ministerial, political, satiric, and comic prints, during Lord Bute's administration, down to the present time*, 3rd edition, 2 vols (London, [1765?]), vol. 1, p. 18. See *Eighteenth Century Collections Online*, Gale Document Number CW108647027, <http://galenet.galegroup.com/servlet/ECCO> (accessed June 2009).

Figure 17: 'A Miserable Cold Place. Alteration and Oh-Economy', Huntington Library: RB379995, p. 7. Reproduced by kind permission of The Huntington Library, San Marino, California.

that the attacks upon Bute and Talbot shared; selling off the nation's kitchen possessions and offering only limp soups at a time of war conformed to widespread prejudices about the Scottish.[95] In the 'crescendo of abuse' against Bute in prints during the early 1760s, a number of different issues were linked: his Scottishness, his close relationships with the Princess Dowager (the new King's mother) and thus his influence with the King, his negotiations with the French, and finally a crisis over the Cider Tax in March 1762, portrayed as a general tax and a threat to liberty and property.[96] Oeconomy thus raised issues about the common good, national identity, and international strength.

Another important context for these prints comprised important changes in political culture. During the 1760s and 1770s, radicals increasingly located 'the balanced constitution's essential repository of virtuous "independence" further down the socio-political scale: in the citizenry itself.'[97] Parliamentary politics would henceforth involve a larger and more broadly constituted public, and at the same time ideals of republicanism became moved to the foreground, centred on a citizenry defined by '[the] personal value of "independent" sincerity, egalitarianism,

[95] Herbert M. Atherton, *Political Prints in the Age of Hogarth. A Study of the Ideographic Representation of Politics* (Oxford: Clarendon, 1974), pp. 209–15.

[96] M. Dorothy George, *English Political Caricature to 1792: A Study of Opinion and Propaganda* (Oxford: Clarendon Press, 1959), p. 121.

[97] Matthew McCormack, *The Independent Man: Citizenship and Gender Politics in Georgian England* (Manchester and New York: Manchester University Press, 2005), p. 80.

patriotism and simple virtue'.[98] Independence—long thought essential for citizenship—could now be furnished by 'small freehold property, a receptive sensibility and simple virtues such as rurality, industry and abstemiousness. As such, independence began to be equated less with property and rank, and more with masculinity itself.'[99] Significantly for this study, one important aspect of this was the reworking during the 1770s, 1780s, and 1790s of the character of 'the man of simplicity' as an anti-aristocratic figure, whose 'independence' was rooted partly in a domestic (country) retreat.[100]

The prints from the early 1760s were part of this changing political sphere, and they suggest how oeconomy—as well as independence—was a substantive part of the reorientation of political participation. Men had long been involved in physic and cookery recipes, and this continued well into the eighteenth century. But if the medieval hall had expressed men's status, the eighteenth-century kitchen meant something quite different. In the 1720s, the kitchen was at the core of the project to increase the household's wealth—and as a consequence the nation's wealth—through careful management. By the 1760s, though, this form of oeconomy held less appeal to those engaged in public political debate. As we saw in Chapter 2, from mid-century civic ideals of male domestic management were changing. First they were appropriated in a more explicitly national discourse of public-spirited households. Elite estate patricians were then eclipsed by citizens practising domestic management in a more public-spirited way. The kitchen was now part of a household that was not simply an economic unit in a larger economy, but was also part of a society and a nation; men's household management was seen in that context. The print culture of the 1760s suggests there may have been an important shift in how people understood the relationship between men and the house, and the public political significance of this relationship. A middling-sort evolution of oeconomy that had begun in lay political theory decades earlier, now informed critiques of the monarchy and central government.

CONCLUSION

By the beginning of the eighteenth century, Wendy Wall comments, 'domesticity had largely vanished as a key term in political debates about government and nationality'.[101] In contrast, I have argued that in the eighteenth century, oeconomy elevated the skills and virtues required to be a benevolent citizen, and that middling-sort men's right to citizenship was firmly grounded in their own material practices in (not just possession of) a house. As Matthew McCormack and others have recently shown, the 'public' and 'private' have, since at least the eighteenth century, been 'continuous and mutually constitutive' for political

---

[98] Ibid. p. 100.   [99] Ibid. p. 100.   [100] Ibid. pp. 109–15.
[101] Wendy Wall, *Staging Domesticity: Household Work and English Identity in Early Modern Drama* (Cambridge: Cambridge University Press, 2002), p. 16.

masculinities.[102] By the third quarter of the eighteenth century, the domain of oeconomy and nation were one and the same. The language used to describe the actions of men in both realms overlapped; politicians were represented serving in the nation's kitchen as they performed their work as ministers of the realm at war. The events of the 1760s show the political significance of men's provisioning and their activities in managing the moral and economic resources of the household. Talk of soup and kitchen furniture foregrounded the material aspects of the house, fusing mundane domestic activity with governance in the house and the nation. The influences of ancient household theory and political patriarchalism could still be detected, and hierarchy and order were enduring concerns. But oeconomists were now tasked to secure and increase wealth and to acquire and exercise the skills and virtues of the good governor and citizen. The discourse of oeconomy had already transformed and was becoming not a language of political governance for the elite, but a language of political engagement for the middling sort. The authority of male household managers derived not from God, land, or title but from those practices that were reproduced between fathers and sons, uncles and nephew, practices that were being adapted by a growing social group to establish new lineages and social and political status. Through everyday domestic practices of financial and property management, men not only expressed and maintained their domestic authority but also reproduced authority across the generations.

This chapter has tentatively suggested the emergence of a secular fraternity of oeconomy reproduced between men of different generations and between the elite and the middling social ranks. Commenting on the nineteenth century, Broughton and Rogers have astutely identified that, 'the implicit hierarchalism in paternalist discourse associated uneasily with the other idealized forms of masculine identification, such as those of brotherhood or fellowship, thereby generating conflict rather than resolution'.[103] Tensions between men are evident in the requests of younger sons to their older brothers, the tired counselling of fathers to their sons, and the treatment of tenants and servants by wealthier men. Men of different ages and ranks were patently not a homogenous group united in a patriarchal alliance. And yet there were gendered and manly practices and discourses that could work rhetorically and practically to bind men together; the good management of a house was certainly one of the most important. A fraternity of oeconomy was consolidated over this period, and embedded in the everyday material practices of the house.

*

The centrality of the home and a privatized, feminine domestic ideology has been placed at the heart of the construction of middle-class identity in the second half

---

[102] Matthew McCormack, 'Introduction', in Matthew McCormack (ed.), *Public Men: Masculinity and Politics in Modern Britain* (Basingstoke: Palgrave Macmillan, 2007), p. 4. See also Matthew McCormack and Matthew Roberts, 'Conclusion: Chronologies in the History of British Political Masculinities, *c.* 1700–2000', in McCormack (ed.), *Public Men*, p. 189.

[103] Trev Lynn Broughton and Helen Rogers, 'Introduction: The Empire of the Father', in Trev Lynn Broughton and Helen Rogers, (eds), *Gender and Fatherhood in the Nineteenth Century* (Basingstoke: Palgrave Macmillan, 2007), p. 18.

of the eighteenth century. By contrast, I have excavated a different domestic culture, that of the house well managed. *The Little Republic* has discussed a longstanding discourse of oeconomy which transformed during the eighteenth century to become a significant component of middling-sort identity, a language of citizenship and political engagement. Men's engagement with the house was not in the manner of a distant patriarch, who retired to the 'refuge' of home. The house was not a haven from the political world; on the contrary, it was central to the establishment of a secure manly and social status. Men acted within the domestic environment as general managers, accountants, consumers, and as keepers of the family history in paper and ink. And it is their records in paper and ink that have taken me into these men's houses and—I believe—into men's heads. For all their richness, these records provide a mediated and partial view of the domestic, one created by men themselves not by women, wives, children, and servants. But in setting out on this project my aim was precisely to understand what men thought and felt about their own and other men's domestic lives, to reconstruct the terms on which men engaged in the domestic, to identify the meanings given to men's presence, and to examine whether the domestic could be a site of manly authority. The authority and status that accrued to a man and his family who used the language or practices of oeconomy could be considerable, yet this authority arose from small acts of power patterning peoples' lives in their houses.

Bibliography

MANUSCRIPT PRIMARY SOURCES

Chetham's Library
Diary of Richard Kay, A.7.76.
'Extracts from the Journals of Mr Richd Kaye of Baldingstone & Chesham in the Par. of Bury Co. Lanc. now in the poss^n of Mrs Kay of Bury. Jan. 20. 1848. R.R.R.', C.6.34-77 Raines Collection, vol. 31, ff. 430–40.

Devon Record Office
Bideford parish registers, Burials 1679–1733.

Henry E. Huntington Library
Account book of Thomas Mort, 26 March 1703–13 September 1725, L3A1 [S10 K3].
Account book of William Smedley, HM3119223.
Bath Diary for 1769, HM62593.
Brydges family papers, mssSTB.
Diary of Samuel Millar, HM 47403.
Herbert Family Papers, mssHE 1–419.
R. Mathews Commonplace book (c.1780s), HM694.
Stowe papers, mssST.

Herefordshire Record Office
Notebook of Revd Daniel Renaud, 1730–1769, A98/1.
'The will of Daniel Renaud, 1770', Probate series AA20, Box Number 334, June–September 1772.
Transcript of Whitchurch Parish Registers (1927), Herefordshire Record Office: B39/1.

John Rylands Library, University of Manchester
John Micklethwaite correspondence, Eng MS 1138.

Lancashire Record Office
Admon for Richard Kay, 2 December 1755, WCW 1755.
'An Inventory of the goods & Chattels of Richard Kay late of Baldinsgtone in Walmersley in the parish of Bury in the County of Lancaster', 4 April 1697, WCW 1697.
Parish Registers Bury St Mary.
Benjamin Shaw, 'Memorable Events' (1817–40), DDX/1554/3.
Will of Robert Kay, Yeoman, WCW 1752.
'Will of Thomas Mort of Damhouse, 1736'.
'Will and inventory of Edmund Pilkington, Yeoman, 24th February 1755', WCW 1755.

Lichfield Record Office
Admon of Joseph Morley, 14 October 1740, B/C/11.
'Will of William Smedley, 21 April 1742', B/C/11.

North Devon Record Office
Lease from John Darracott to Nathaniel Watson, B156/B/2/7, 1722.

Private Collection
Marjorie Lilian Kay, 'Transcript of the diary of Richard Kay', Private collection.

Public Record Office
Will of David Renaud of Hinton, Northamptonshire, 17 April 1738, PROB 11/706.
Will of Reverend David Renaud, Clerk of Havant, Hampshire, 9th October 1807, PROB
    11/1469.

University of Sheffield Special Collections
'Memoirs of the late Revd Thornhill Kidd chiefly transcribed from his Letters and Diary',
    MS102.
Hewins Ballads, 529(A).

West Yorkshire Archive Service, Leeds
Account books of (unidentified) merchant, WYL24 1773–1814.
Birkbeck Family Papers, WYL449.
Diary of John Bradley (1723–29, 1754), Nostell Priory WYL1352 1215–1986, NP A3/2/
    (1718).
Account book and diary of gentleman farmer William Burton (1832–4), GA/C/38,
    WYL22.
Ingilby commonplace book (mid-eighteenth century), WYL230/3739.
Ingilby commonplace book 1723–7, WYL230/3591.
'Commonplace book of Revd. Joseph Wilson *c.*1774–1821', WYL753, Acc 1886.

West Yorkshire Archive Service, Wakefield
Commonplace book, C86.
Diary of Richard Hey, Samuel Sharp family papers, C281, 23/3 (April–June 1798).
Correspondence of William Martin, C482, C695, C1063.
Land Tax returns for Hampsthwaite, 1781–1832, QE13/5/21.
Parish Registers of St. Peter, Horbury, 1751–1767, T651.
Records of Banns of Marriages in the Chapelry of Horbury, WDP 135/1/3/1.
'Register of the Christenings and Burials within the Parochial Chapelry of Horbury in the
    Diocese of York, no. 5', Microfilm WDP 135/1/1/5.
Henry Richardson, 'A Diary of Disbursements since January ye first 1748 The First Year
    after I was Married' (1748–53), C658.
Diary of Joshua Sagar of Horbury (1790), RL Arundale Collection, C1039 (add. Ad).
Papers of Rev. Samuel Sharp and family 1584–1865, C281.

William Andrews Clark Memorial Library
Francis Blake, 'Acct Book from 1 January 1765 to 22 February 1766', MS.1985.002.
Francis Blake, 'Accots. from 11th August 1769 to 1st January 1771', MS.1985.002.
Commonplace book of Ann Bromfield, [1740–1748], MS.1968.002.
Accounts of William Coleman, 1712–29, C692Z [1712–1729].
Diary of John Darracott, 1707–30, MS.1950.010.
Cook book of Margrett Greene, 1701, MS.1980.004.
[Edmund Pilkington] Account book, MS1976.001.

Daniel Renaud, Account book [1752–1777], MS.1977.009.

Daniel Renaud, Account book [*c*.1769], MS.1977.008.

Commonplace book of Daniel Renaud, 1751–63, MS.1977.007.

Account book of Rebecca Steel, MS. fS8135 M3 H531 1702.

[Timothy Tyrell, 1755–1832], 'Account book with mathematical exercises' (1725–1768), MS. 1945.001.

The commonplace book of Christopher Tuthill, 1681–1858, MS.1977.003.

York City Archives

Gray Family Papers, Acc 5, 6, 24 & 235.

Munby collection, Acc 54.

Diary of Christopher Ware of 54 Stonegate, York City Archives: Acc 143.

PRINTED PRIMARY SOURCES

The Account Book of Richard Latham, 1724–1767, Records of Social and Economic History, New series; 15, ed. Lorna Weatherill (Oxford: Published for the British Academy by Oxford University Press, 1990).

John Adams, *The flowers of ancient history. Comprehending, on a new plan, the most remarkable and interesting events, as well as characters, of antiquity*, 3rd edition (London, 1796).

Joseph Addison, *Interesting anecdotes, memoirs, allegories, essays, and poetical fragments, tending to amuse the fancy, and inculcate morality* (London, 1794).

The Autobiography of William Stout of Lancaster, 1665–1752, ed. J. D. Marshall (Manchester: Chetham Society, 1967), vol. 14, 3rd series.

Anne Battam, *The lady's assistant in the oeconomy of the table: a collection of scarce and valuable receipts*, second edition (London, 1759).

Cæsar Beccaria, *A Discourse on Public Oeconomy and Commerce* (London, 1769).

Biographia classica: the lives and characters of all the classic authors, the Grecian and Roman poets, historians, orators, and biographers (London, 1740).

The book of Psalms, with the argument of each Psalm, And A Preface Giving Some General Rules For The Interpretation Of This Sacred Book. By Peter Allix D. D. late Treasurer of Salisbury. 2nd edition, (London, 1717).

Richard Bradley, *A Complete Body of Husbandry, Collected from the Practice and Experience of the most considerable Farmers in Britain* (London, 1727).

Richard Bradley, *The Country Housewife and Lady's Director* (Dublin, 1727).

Richard Bradley *The Country Housewife and Lady's Director, in the Management of a House, and the Delights and Profits of a Farm*, 6th edition (London, 1736).

Richard Bradley, *The Country Housewife and Lady's Director*, ed. Caroline Davidson (1727; London: Prospect Books, 1980).

R[ichard] Bradley, *The Weekly Miscellany For the Improvement of Husbandry, Trade, Arts, and Sciences* (London, 1727).

Robert Brown, *The Compleat Farmer; or, the Whole Art of Husbandry* (London, 1759).

Ludwig Wilhelm Brüggemann, *A view of the English editions, translations and illustrations of the ancient Greek and Latin authors* (Stettin, 1797).

William Cobbett, *Cottage Economy* (London, 1822).

William Cobbett, *Advice to Young Men, and (incidentally) to Young Women, in the Middle and Higher Ranks of Life. In a series of letters, addressed to a youth, a bachelor, a lover, a husband, a father, a citizen, or a subject* (London, 1829).

Edward Cocker, *Cockers Arithmetick, being a plain and familiar method suitable to the meanest capacity for the full understanding of that incomparable art* (London, 1678).

Edward Cocker, *Cocker's Arithmetick: being a plain and familiar method, suitable to the meanest Capacity for the full understanding of that incomparable art*, 22nd edition (London, 1702).

N[oel] Chomel, *Dictionaire Oeconomique: or, The Family Dictionary*, Revised by Richard Bradley (London, 1725).

Robert Colinson, *Idea Rationaria, or The Perfect Accomptant, necessary for all Merchants and Trafficquers* (London, 1683).

The Complete Family-Piece: and, Country Gentleman, and Farmer's, Best Guide, 2nd edition (1736; London, 1737).

Cookery Reformed; or, the Ladies Assistant (London, 1755).

John Corbet, *Self-Imployment in Secret* (London, 1681).

Daniel Defoe, *The Family Instructor*, 2nd edition (London, 1715).

Daniel Defoe, *The great law of subordination consider'd; or, the insolence and unsufferable behaviour of servants in England duly enquir'd into* (London, 1724).

Daniel Defoe, *The behaviour of servants in England inquired into* (London, [1726?]).

The Diary of John Young: Sunderland Chemist and Methodist Lay Preacher, covering the years 1841–1843, ed. G. E. Milburn (Leamington Spa: Surtees Society, 1983), vol. 195.

The Diary of Richard Kay, 1716–51 of Baldingstone, near Bury: a Lancashire Doctor, ed. Dr W. Brockbank and Rev. F. Kenworthy (Manchester: Chetham Society, 1968), vol. 16, 3rd series.

The Diary of Thomas Naish, ed. Doreen Slater (Wiltshire Archeological and Natural History Society), 1964, vol. 20.

Robert Dodsley, *L'Economia della Vita Umana Di Roberto Dodsley, In Inglese, con Traduzione in Lingua Italiana* (Leeds, 1797).

James Dodson, *The Accountant, or, The Method of Book-keeping, Deduced from Clear Principles* (London, 1750).

Philippe Sylvestre Dufour [pseud Jacob Spon], *Moral Instructions for Youth: Or, a Father's Advice to a Son. Translated from the French, At first only for particular, and now publish'd for general Use. Being an attempt to season the growing generation with Virtuous Principles* (London, 1742).

William Ellis, *The country housewife's family companion: or profitable directions for whatever relates to the management and good oeconomy of the domestick concerns of a country life* (London, 1750).

William Ellis, *The Modern Husbandman* (London, 1750).

The Family Records of Benjamin Shaw, mechanic of Dent, Dolphinholme and Preston, 1772–1841, ed. Alan G. Crosby (Record Society of Lancashire and Cheshire, 1991).

England's Happiness Improved: or, an Infallible Way to get Riches, Encrease Plenty, and promote Pleasure (London, 1697).

Robert Filmer, *Patriarcha: or The Natural Power of Kings* (London, 1680).

John Flavell, *Husbandry Spiritualized* (London, 1669).

John Flavell, *Husbandry Spiritualized: or, the Heavenly Use of Earthly Things* (Leeds, 1788).

Hannah Glasse, *The House-Keepers's Pocket Book, and Complete Family Cook* (London, 1783).

Oliver Goldsmith, *The Vicar of Wakefield* (1766, Harmondsworth: Penguin, 1982, 1986).

The good housewife, or, Cookery reformed: containing a select number of the best receipts…from the papers of several gentlemen and ladies eminent for their good sense and oeconomy (London, 1756).

James Hodder, *Hodder's Arithmetick: or, that necessary art made most easie* (London, 1702).

Husbandry Moralized; or, Pleasant Sunday Reading for a Farmer's Kitchen (Dublin; [No date, 1772, 1797?]).

Index to the 1841 Census vol. 3 Horbury (Wakefield and District Family History Society, n. d.).

Index to 1851 Census, vol. 22, Horbury, Surnames Hi to Z (Wakefield and District Family History Society, 1998).

Samuel Johnson, *A Dictionary of the English Language*, 4th edition (London, 1777).

Henry Kent, *The directory: containing an alphabetical list of the names and places of abode of the directors of companies persons in publick business* (London, 1736).

[Dorothy Kilner,] *Dialogues and Letters in Morality, Oeconomy, and Politeness, for the Improvement and Entertainment of Young Female Minds* (London, 1780).

Lady, *Maxims and Cautions for the Ladies: Being a Complete Oeconomy for the Female Sex* (London, 1752).

[William Lawson], *A New Orchard & Garden: Or, The best way for Planting, Graffing, and to make any ground good for a rich orchard* (London, 1683).

Edward Laurence, *The Duty of a Steward to His Lord* (London, 1727).

Letters of the Late Rev. Mr. Laurence Sterne, To his most intimate Friends... To which are prefix'd, Memoirs of his Life and Family, 3 vols (London, 1775).

John Mair, *Book-Keeping Methodiz'd: or, A Methodical Treatise of Merchant-Accompts, according to the Italian Form*, 2nd edition (Edinburgh, 1751).

G[ervase] Markham, *Country Contentments; or the Husbandman's Recreations. Containing The Wholesome Experience, in which any ought to Recreate himself, after the Toyl of more Serious Business*, 11th Edition (London, 1683).

Gervase Markham, *The English House-Wife, containing The inward and outward Vertues which ought to be in a Compleat Woman*, 9th edition (London, 1683).

'The Married Man's Answer to the Batchelor's Estimate', in Henry Carey, *Cupid and Hymen: a voyage to the isles of love and matrimony* (London, 1748).

Miscellaneous Reflections upon the Peace, And its consequences. More especially on a just, as well as real and national Oeconomy (London, 1749).

National Oeconomy Recommended, as the only means of retrieving our trade and securing our liberties (London, 1746).

Dudley North, *Observations and Advices Oeconomical* (London, 1669).

The Oeconomist: or, Edlin's Weekly Journal, 1 September 1733.

The Oeconomy of Female Life. By a lady (London, 1751).

The Oeconomy of Human Life. Translated from an Indian Manuscript. Written by an Ancient Bramin. To which is prefixed an account of the manner in which the said manuscript was discovered. In a Letter from an English Gentleman now Residing in China to the Earl of E**** (London, 1751).

The Oeconomy of Human Life. Translated from an Indian Manuscript. Written by an Ancient Bramin, 4th edition, (London, 1751).

John Plaw, *Rural Architecture* (London, 1794).

Elizabeth Raffald, *The Experienced Housekeeper, for the use of Ladies, Housekeepers, Cooks, &c.* (London, 1789).

John Richards, *The Gentleman's Steward and Tenants of Manors Instructed* (London, 1760).

Jean-Jacques Rousseau, 'A Dissertation on Political Economy', *The Miscellaneous Works of Mr. J. J. Rousseau*, vol. 2 (1755; London, 1767).

The Science of Good Husbandry: or, The Oeconomics of Xenophon, trans. Richard Bradley (London, 1727).

Thomas Sheridan, *A General Dictionary of the English Language. One main Object of which, is, to establish a plain and permanent Standard of Pronunciation* (London, 1780).

Adam Smith, *An Inquiry into the Nature and Causes of The Wealth of Nations* (London, 1776).

Laurence Sterne, *The Life and Opinions of Tristram Shandy, Gentleman*, ed. Melvyn and Joan New (1759–67; Penguin, 1978, 2003).

Reverend Dr [Jonathan] Swift, *Directions to Servants in General* (London, 1745).

Jean-Baptiste Say, *A Treatise on Political Economy* (1803; Philadelphia: Lippincott, Grambo & Co. 1855), 6th edition, trans. C. R. Prinsep, ed. Clement C. Biddle.

School dialogues, for boys. Being an attempt to convey instruction insensibly to their tender minds, . . . By a lady, Vol. 2 (London, [1783]).

The Scots scourge; being a compleat supplement to the British antidote to Caledonian poison: in two volumes. Containing fifty-two anti-ministerial, political, satiric, and comic prints, during Lord Bute's administration, down to the present time, 3rd edition, 2 vols (London, [1765?]).

Sarah Trimmer, *The oconomy of charity; or, an address to ladies concerning Sunday-Schools* (London, 1787).

John Trusler, *The distinction between words esteemed synonymous in the English language, pointed out, and the proper choice of them determined*, 2nd edition (London, 1783).

Two Yorkshire Diaries: The Diary of Arthur Jessop and Ralph Ward's Journal, ed. C. E. Whiting (Leeds: Yorkshire Archaeological Society, vol. 117, 1951).

The Universal Family-Book: or, a Necessary and Profitable Companion for All Degrees of People of Either Sex, (London, 1703).

[Ned Ward], *The Batchelor's Estimate of the Expences of a Married Life. In a Letter to a Friend. Being an Answer to a Proposal of Marrying a Lady with 2000l. Fortune*, Third edition (London: Printed for T. Payne at the Crown in Ivy-Lane, near Pater-noster Row, 1729).

John Watkins, LLD, *An essay towards a history of Bideford, in the county of Devon* (Exeter, [1792]).

William Webster, *An Essay on Book-Keeping, According to the Italian Method of Debtor and Creditor* (London, 1721).

George Wheler, *The Protestant Monastery: or, Christian Oeconomicks* (London, 1698).

The Woman's Advocate: or, The Baudy Batchelor out in his Calculation: Being the Genuine Answer Paragraph by Paragraph, to the Batchelor's Estimate. Plainly Proving that Marriage is to a Man of Sense and Oeconomy, both a Happier and less Chargeable State, than a Single Life (London: J. Roberts, 1729).

Josiah Woodward, *The Necessary Duty of Family Prayer*, 6th edition (1722).

Hannah Woolley, *The Queen-like Closet: or, Rich Cabinet, stored with all manner of Rare Receipts for Preserving, Candying and Cookery . . . to which is added A Supplement, presented to all Ingenious Ladies and Gentlewomen*, 5th edition (1670; London, 1684).

Xenophon, *Xenophon's Treatise of Housholde*, trans. Gentian Hervet (London, 1532).

Xenophon, *Oeconomicus: A Social and Historical Commentary*, trans. Sarah B. Pomery (Oxford: Clarendon Press, 1994).

Xenophon Memorabilia and Oeconomicus, The Loeb Classical Library, trans. E. C. Marchant (London, 1923).

Arthur Young, *Rural Oeconomy: or, Essays on the Practical Parts of Husbandry* (London, 1770).

INTERNET SOURCES

The Clergy of the Church of England Database 1540–1835, <http://www.theclergydatabase.org.uk>
Early English Books Online, <http://eebo.chadwyck.com>
Eighteenth Century Collections Online, <http://find.galegroup.com.eresources.shef.ac.uk/ecco/>
English Heritage 'Heritage Gateway', <http://www.heritagegateway.org.uk/gateway/>
English Short Title Catalogue, <http://estc.bl.uk>
National Monuments Record 'Images of England', <http://www.imagesofengland.org.uk>.
Old Bailey Proceedings Online, <http://www.oldbaileyonline.org>.
Oxford Dictionary of National Biography, Oxford University Press, 2004, <http://www.oxforddnb.com>.

UNPUBLISHED RESEARCH

Julie Day, 'Elite Women's Household Management: Yorkshire, 1680–1810' (PhD thesis, University of Leeds, 2007).
Margaret Hunt, 'English Urban Families in Trade, 1660–1800: The Culture of Early Modern Capitalism', (PhD thesis, New York University, 1986).
William Van Reyk, 'Christian Ideals of Manliness During the Period of the Evangelical Revival, *c.*1730 to *c.*1840' (University of Oxford DPhil thesis, 2007).
Jonathan White, 'Luxury and Labour: Ideas of Labouring-class Consumption in Eighteenth-century England' (PhD thesis, University of Warwick, 2001).
Alun Robert James Withey, 'Health, Medicine and the Family in Wales, *c.* 1600–*c.*1750' (PhD thesis, Swansea University, 2009).

CHAPTERS AND ARTICLES

Glenn Adamson, 'The Case of the Missing Footstool: Reading the Absent Object', in Karen Harvey (ed.), *History and Material Culture: A Student's Guide to Approaching Alternative Sources* (London: Routledge, 2009), pp. 192–207.
Doohwan Ahn, 'Xenophon and the Greek Tradition in British Political Thought', in James Moore, Ian Macgregor Morris, Andrew J. Bayliss (eds), *Reinventing History: The Enlightenment Origins of Ancient History* (London: Centre for Metropolitan History, Institute of Historical Research, School of Advanced Study, University of London, 2008), pp. 33–55.
Joanne Bailey, 'Favoured or Oppressed? Married Women, Property and "Coverture" in England, 1660–1800', *Continuity and Change*, 17, 3 (2002), pp. 1–22.
Geoff Baldwin, 'Individual and Self in the Late Renaissance', *Historical Journal*, 44:2 (2001), pp. 341–64.
Hannah Barker, 'Soul, Purse and Family: Middling and Lower-Class Masculinity in Eighteenth-century Manchester', *Social History*, 33, 1 (2008), pp. 12–35.
Hannah Barker, 'A Grocer's Tale: Gender, Family and Class in Early Nineteenth-Century Manchester', *Gender & History*, 21, 2 (August 2009), pp. 340–57.
Hannah Barker and Jane Hamlett, 'Living above the Shop: Home, Business, and Family in the English "Industrial Revolution"', *Journal of Family History*, 35, 4, (2010) pp. 311–28.
Judith Bennett, 'Feminism and History', *Gender and History*, 1 (1989), pp. 251–72.

Helen Berry and Elizabeth Foyster, 'Childless Men in Early Modern England', in Helen Berry and Elizabeth Foyster (eds), *The Family in Early Modern England* (Cambridge University Press, Cambridge, 2007), pp. 158–83.

Joanna Bourke, 'Housewifery in Working-class England, 1860–1914', *Past and Present*, 143 (1994), pp. 167–97.

Frank E. Brown, 'Continuity and Change in the Urban House: Developments in Domestic Space Organisation in Seventeenth-century London', *Comparative Studies in Society and History*, 28 (1986), pp. 558–90.

Ida Bull, 'Merchant Households and their Networks in Eighteenth-century Trondheim', *Change and Continuity*, 17 (2), 2002, pp. 213–31.

Peter Burke, 'The Cultural History of Dreams', in Peter Burke, *Varieties of Cultural History* (Cambridge: Polity Press, 1997), pp. 22–42.

Barbara Burman and Jonathan White, 'Fanny's Pockets: Cotton, Consumption and Domestic Economy, 1780–1850', in Jennie Batchelor and Cora Kaplan (eds), *Women and Material Culture, 1660–1830* (Basingstoke: Palgrave Macmillan, 2007), pp. 31–51.

James P. Carson, '"The Little Republic" of the Family: Goldsmith's Politics of Nostalgia', *Eighteenth-Century Fiction*, 16, 2 (2004), pp. 173–96.

Bernard Capp, 'Separate Domains? Women and Authority in Early Modern England', in Paul Griffiths, Adam Fox and Steve Hindle (eds), *The Experience of Authority in Early Modern England* (Basingstoke: Macmillan, 1996), pp. 117–45.

Miranda Chaytor, 'Household and Kinship: Ryton in the Late Sixteenth and Early Seventeenth Centuries', *History Workshop Journal*, 10 (1980), pp. 25–59.

Irene Cieraad, 'Dutch Windows: Female Virtue and Female Vice', in Irene Cieraad (ed.), *At Home: An Anthropology of Domestic Space* (New York: Syracuse University Press, 1999), pp. 31–52.

Nicholas Cooper, 'Rank, Manners and Display: The Gentlemanly House, 1500–1750', *Transactions of the Royal Historical Society*, 12 (2000), pp. 291–300.

David Cressy, 'Kinship and Kin Interaction in Early Modern England', *Past and Present*, 113 (1986), pp. 38–69.

John Crowley, 'From Luxury to Comfort and Back Again: Landscape Architecture and the Cottage in Britain and America', Maxine Berg and Elizabeth Eger (eds), *Luxury in the Eighteenth Century* (Basingstoke: Palgrave, 2002), pp. 135–50.

Lucia Dacome, 'Noting the Mind: Commonplace Books and the Pursuit of the Self in Eighteenth-Century Britain', *Journal of the History of Ideas*, 65, 4 (2004), pp. 603–25.

Kathleen Davies, 'Continuity and Change in Literary Advice on Marriage', in R B Outhwaite (ed.), *Marriage and Society: Studies in the Social History of Marriage* (London: Europa, 1981), pp. 58–80.

Shani D'Cruze, 'Care, Diligence and "Usfull Pride": Gender, Industrialization and the Domestic Economy, c.1770 to c.1840', *Women's History Review*, 3 (1994) pp. 315–45.

Moira Donald, 'Tranquil Havens? Critiquing the Idea of Home as Middle-Class Sanctuary', in Inga Bryden and Janet Floyd (eds), *Domestic Space: Reading the Nineteenth-Century Interior* (Manchester: Manchester University Press, 1999), pp. 103–20.

Donald D. Eddy, 'Dodsley's "Oeconomy of Human Life," 1750–1751', *Modern Philology*, 85, 4, (May 1988), pp. 460–79.

Catherine Field '"Many Hands Hands": Writing the Self in Early Modern Women's Recipe Books', in Michelle M. Dowd and Julie A. Eckerle (eds), *Genre and Women's Life Writing in Early Modern England: Re-imagining Forms of Selfhood* (Aldershot: Burlington; VT: Ashgate, 2007), pp. 49–64.

Margot Finn, 'Women, Consumption and Coverture in England, *c*.1760–1860', *Historical Journal*, 39, 3 (1996), pp. 703–22.

Margot Finn, 'Men's Things: Masculine Possession in the Consumer Revolution', *Social History*, 25, 2 (2000), pp. 133–54.

Christopher Flint, '"The Family Piece": Oliver Goldsmith and the Politics of the Everyday in Eighteenth-Century Domestic Portraiture', *Eighteenth-Century Studies*, 29, 2 (1995–6), pp. 127–52.

Henry French, 'Social Status, Localism and the "Middle Sort of People" in England 1620–1750', *Past and Present*, 166 (2000), pp. 66–99.

Alice T. Friedman, 'Architecture, Authority, and the Female Gaze: Planning and Representation in the Early Modern Country House', *Assemblage*, 18 (1992), pp. 41–61.

Jane Garnett, 'Political and Domestic Economy in Victorian Social Thought: Ruskin and Xenophon', in Stefan Collini, Richard Whatmore, Brian Young (eds), *Economy, Polity, and Society: British Intellectual History 1750-1950* (Cambridge: Cambridge University Press, 2000), pp. 205–23.

Dena Goodman, 'Furnishing Discourses: Readings of a Writing Desk in Eighteenth-Century France', in Maxine Berg and Elizabeth Eger (eds), *Luxury in the Eighteenth Century* (Basingstoke: Palgrave, 2002), pp. 71–88.

Hannah Greig, 'Eighteenth-century English Interiors in Image and Text' in Jeremy Aynsley and Charlotte Grant (eds), *Imagined Interiors: Representing the Domestic Interior since the Renaissance* (London: V&A Publications, 2006), pp. 102–12.

Robbie Gray, 'Self-made Men, Self-narrated Lives: Male Autobiographical Writing and the Victorian Middle Class', *Journal of Victorian Culture*, 6, 2 (2001), pp. 286–312.

Gay L. Gullickson, 'Love and Power in the Proto-industrial Family' in Maxine Berg (ed.), *Markets and Manufacture in Early Industrial Europe* (London: Routledge, 1991), pp. 205–26.

Karen Harvey, 'Barbarity in a Teacup? Punch, Domesticity and Gender in the Eighteenth Century', *Journal of Design History*, 21, 3 (2008), pp. 205–21.

Karen Harvey, 'Men Making Home: Masculinity and Domesticity in Eighteenth-Century England', *Gender & History*, 21, 3, (2009), pp. 520–40.

Karen Harvey and Alexandra Shepard, 'What Have Historians Done with Masculinity? Reflections on Five Centuries of British History, *circa* 1500–1950', introduction to a 'Special Feature on Masculinities?' in *The Journal of British Studies*, 44, 2 (2005), pp. 274–80.

Karen Harvey, 'The History of Masculinity, *circa* 1650–1800', *The Journal of British Studies*, 44, 2 (2005), pp. 296–311.

W. Hewitson, 'Baldingstone House and the Kays', *East Lancashire Review*, (no date), Bury Library: Bury RIS Misc File, A78.4.

Tim Hitchcock, 'Tricksters, Lords and Servants: Begging, Friendship and Masculinity in Eighteenth-century England', in Laura Gowing, Michael Hunter and Miri Rubin (eds), *Love, Friendship and Faith in Europe 1300–1800* (Basingstoke: Palgrave Macmillan, 2005), pp. 177–96.

W. G. Hoskins, 'The Rebuilding of Rural England, 1560–1640', *Past & Present*, 4 (1953), pp. 44–59.

Martha Howell, 'The Gender of Europe's Commercial Economy, 1200–1700', *Gender and History*, 20, 3 (November 2008), pp. 519–38.

David Hussey, 'Guns, Horses and Stylish Waistcoats? Male Consumer Activity and Domestic Shopping in Late-Eighteenth- and Early-Nineteenth-Century England', in David Hussey and Margaret Ponsonby (eds), *Buying for the Home: Shopping for the Domestic from the Seventeenth Century to the Present* (Aldershot: Ashgate, 2008), pp. 47–69.

Matthew Johnson, 'The Englishman's Home and it's Study', in Ross Samson (ed.), *The Social Archaeology of Houses* (Edinburgh: Edinburgh University Press, 1990), pp. 245–57.

Lawrence Klein, 'Politeness and the Interpretation of the British Eighteenth Century', *Historical Journal*, 45 (2002), pp. 869–98.

Sarah Knott, 'Sensibility and the American War for Independence', *American Historical Review* 109, 1 (2004), pp. 19–40.

Beth Kowaleski-Wallace, 'Tea, Gender and Domesticity in Eighteenth-century England', *Studies in Eighteenth-Century Culture*, 23 (1993), pp. 131–45.

Beth Kowaleski-Wallace, 'Women, China and Consumer Culture in Eighteenth-century England', *Eighteenth-Century Studies*, 29, 2 (1995–6), pp. 153–67.

Paul Langford, 'The Management of the Eighteenth-Century State: Perceptions and Implications', *Journal of Historical Sociology*, 15, 1 (March 2002), pp. 102–6.

Edmund Leites, 'Confucianism in Eighteenth-Century England: Natural Morality and Social Reform', *Philosophy East and West*, 28, 2 (April 1978), pp. 143–59.

Judith S. Lewis, 'When a House Is Not a Home: Elite English Women and the Eighteenth-Century Country House', *Journal of British Studies*, 48 (April 2009), pp. 336–63.

Karen Lipsedge, '"Enter into Thy Closet": Women, Closet Culture, and the Eighteenth-Century', in John Styles and Amanda Vickery (eds), *Gender, Taste and Material Culture in Britain and North America 1700–1830* (New Haven; London: Yale University Press, 2006), pp. 107–22.

Matthew McCormack, '"Married Men and the Fathers of Families": Fatherhood and Franchise Reform in Britain', in Trev Lynn Broughton and Helen Rogers (eds), *Gender and Fatherhood in the Nineteenth Century* (Basingstoke: Palgrave Macmillan, 2007), pp. 43–54.

Matthew McCormack and Matthew Roberts, 'Conclusion: Chronologies in the History of British Political Masculinities, *c.* 1700–2000', in Matthew McCormack (ed.), *Public Men: Masculinity and Politics in Modern Britain* (Basingstoke: Palgrave Macmillan, 2007), pp. 188–91.

Michael McKeon, 'Historicizing Patriarchy: The Emergence of Gender Difference in England, 1660–1760', *Eighteenth-Century Studies*, 28, 3 (Spring, 1995), pp. 295–322.

Michael McKeon, 'The Secret History of Domesticity: Private, Public, and the Division of Knowledge', in Colin Jones and Dror Wahrman (eds), *The Age of Cultural Revolutions: Britain and France, 1750–1820* (London; Berkeley, CA: University of California Press, 2002), pp. 171–89.

Michael Mascuch, 'Social Mobility and Middling Self-identity: The Ethos of British Autobiographers, 1600–1750', *Social History*, 20 (1995), pp. 45–61.

Helga Meise, 'The Limitations of Family Tradition and the Barrier between Public and Private: Karoline von Hessen-Darmstadt's "Schreib = Calender" between Almanac and Diary', in Rudolph Dekker (ed.), *Egodocuments and History: Autobiographical Writing in its Social Context since the Middle Ages* (Hilversum: Verloren, 2002), pp. 107–24.

Craig Muldrew 'Class and Credit: Social Identity, Wealth and the Life Course in Early Modern England', in Henry French and Jonathan Barry (eds), *Identity and Agency in England, 1500–1800* (Basingstoke: Palgrave Macmillan, 2004), pp. 147–77.

David Aaron Murray, 'From Patrimony to Paternity in The Vicar of Wakefield', *Eighteenth-Century Fiction*, 9, 3 (1997), pp. 327–36.

Susan Moller Okin, 'Women and the Making of the Sentimental Family', *Philosophy and Public Affairs* (1982), 11, 1, pp. 65–88.

Sara Pennell, '"Pots and Pans History": The Material Culture of the Kitchen in Early Modern England', *Journal of Design History*, 11, 3 (1998), pp. 201–16.

Sara Pennell, 'The Material Culture of Food in Early Modern England, *c.*1650–1750', in Sarah Tarlow and Susie West (eds), *The Familiar Past? Archaeologies of Later Historical Britain* (London and New York: Routledge, 1999), pp. 35–50.

Sara Pennell, 'Consumption and Consumerism in Early Modern England', *Historical Journal*, 42, 2 (1999), pp. 549–64.

Sara Pennell, 'Perfecting Practice? Women, Manuscript Recipes and Knowledge in Early Modern England', in Victoria E. Burke and Jonathan Gibson (eds), *Early Modern Women's Manuscript Writing: Selected Papers from the Trinty/Trent Colloquium* (Aldershot: Ashgate, 2004), pp. 237–58.

Sara Pennell, 'Mundane Materiality, or, Should Small Things be Forgotten? Material Culture, Micro-histories and the Problem of Scale', in Karen Harvey (ed.), *History and Material Culture: A Student's Guide to Approaching Alternative Sources* (Aldershot: Routledge, 2009), pp. 173–91.

Linda Pollock, 'Rethinking Patriarchy and the Family in Seventeenth-century England', *Journal of Family History*, 23, 1 (1998), pp. 3–27.

Mary Poovey, 'Between Political Arithmetic and Political Economy', in John Bender (ed.), *Regimes of Description: In the Archive of the Eighteenth Century* (Stanford, CA: Stanford University Press, 2005), pp. 61–78.

Giorgio Reillo, 'Things that Shape History: Material Culture and Historical Narratives', in Karen Harvey (ed.), *History and Material Culture: A Student's Guide to Approaching Alternative Sources* (London: Routledge, 2009), pp. 24–46.

Kate Retford, 'From the Interior to Interiority: The Conversation Piece in Georgian England', *Journal of Design History* 20, 4 (2007) pp. 291–307.

Kate Retford, 'Patrilineal Portraiture? Gender and Genealogy in the Eighteenth-century English Country House' in John Styles and Amanda Vickery (eds), *Gender, Taste, and Material Culture in Britain and North America, 1700–1830* (London: The Yale Center for British Art & the Paul Mellon Centre for Studies in British Art, 2006), pp. 315–44.

Kate Retford, 'Sensibility and Genealogy in the Eighteenth-century Family Portrait: The Collection at Kedleston Hall', *Historical Journal*, 46, 3 (2003) pp. 533–60.

Michael Roberts, '"Words they are Women, and Deeds they are Men": Images of Work and Gender in Early Modern England', in Lindsey Charles and Lorna Duffin (eds), *Women and Work in Pre-Industrial England* (London: Croom Helm, 1985), pp. 122–80.

Marie-Claire Rouyer-Daney, 'The Representation of Housework in the 18th-Century Women's Press', in Isabelle Baudino, Jacques Carré and Cécile Révauger (eds), *The Invisible Woman: Aspects of Women's Work in Eighteenth-Century Britain* (Aldershot: Ashgate, 2005), pp. 27–36.

Gordon J. Schochet, 'The Significant Sounds of Silence: The Absence of Women from the Political Thought of Sir Robert Filmer and John Locke (or, "Why can't a woman be more like a man?")', in Hilda Smith (ed.) *Women Writers and the Early Modern British Political Tradition* (Cambridge: Cambridge University Press, 1998), pp. 220–42.

Carole Shammas, 'The Domestic Environment in Early Modern England and America', *Journal of Social History*, 14 (1980), pp. 3–24.

Carole Shammas, 'Anglo-American Household Government in Comparative Perspective', *William and Mary Quarterly*, 52 (1995), pp. 104–44.

Carole Shammas, 'Carole Shammas Responds', *William and Mary Quarterly*, 52 (1995), pp. 163–6.

Alexandra Shepard, 'Manhood, Credit and Patriarchy in Early Modern England *c.* 1580–1640', *Past and Present*, 167 (2000), pp. 75–106.

Alexandra Shepard, 'From Anxious Patriarchs to Refined Gentlemen? Manhood in Britain, *circa* 1500–1700', *The Journal of British Studies*, 44, 2 (2005), pp. 281–95.

John Smail, 'Credit, Risk, and Honor in Eighteenth-Century Commerce', *Journal of British Studies*, 44 (2005), pp. 439–56.

John Smail, 'Coming of Age in Trade: Masculinity and Commerce in Eighteenth-Century England', in Margaret Jacob and Catherine Secretan (eds), *The Self Perception of Early Modern Capitalists* (New York: Palgrave Macmillan, 2008), pp. 236–40.

Lisa Smith, 'The Relative Duties of a Man: Domestic Medicine in England and France, ca. 1685–1740', *Journal of Family History*, 31, 3 (July, 2006), pp. 237–56.

Tim Stretton, 'Coverture and Unity of Person in Blackstone's *Commentaries*', in Wilfrid Prest (ed.), *Blackstone and His Commentaries: Biography, Law, History* (Oxford: Hart, 2009), pp. 111–28.

Naomi Tadmor, 'The Concept of the Household-family in Eighteenth-century England', *Past and Present*, 151 (1996), pp. 110–40.

E. P. Thompson, 'The Grid of Inheritance: A Comment', in E. P. Thompson, *Persons and Polemics: Historical Essays* (London: Merlin, 2003), pp. 263–300.

John Tosh, 'The Old Adam and the New Man: Emerging Themes in the History of English Masculinities, 1750–1850', in Tim Hitchcock and Michelle Cohen (eds), *English Masculinities, 1660–1800* (London: Longman, 1999), pp. 217–38.

John Tosh, 'Masculinities in an Industrializing Society: Britain, 1800–1914', *Journal of British Studies*, 44 (2005), pp. 330–42.

Frank Trentmann, 'Materiality in the Future of History: Things, Practices, and Politics', *Journal of British Studies*, 48 (2009), pp. 291–4.

Nicola Verdon, '… subjects deserving of the highest praise: Farmers' Wives and the Farm Economy in England, *c.*1700–1850', *Agricultural History Review*, 51, 1 (2003), pp. 23–39.

Amanda Vickery 'Women and the World of Goods: A Lancashire Consumer and her Possessions, 1751–81', in John Brewer and Roy Porter (eds), *Consumption and the World of Goods: Consumption and Society in the Seventeenth and Eighteenth Centuries* (London: Routledge, 1993), pp. 274–301.

Amanda Vickery, 'His and Hers: Gender, Consumption and Household Accounting in Eighteenth-century England,' Ruth Harris, Lyndal Roper, and Olwen Hufton (eds), *The Art of Survival: Gender and History in Europe, 1450–2000: Essays in Honour of Olwen Hufton, Past & Present*, Supplement 1 (2006), pp. 12–38.

Amanda Vickery, '"Neat and Not Too Showey": Words and Wallpaper in Regency England', in John Styles and Amanda Vickery (eds), *Gender, Taste and Material Culture in Britain and North America 1700–1830* (New Haven, London: Yale University Press, 2006), pp. 201–22.

Jan de Vries, 'Between Purchasing Power and the World of Goods: Understanding the Household Economy in Early Modern Europe', in John Brewer and Roy Porter (eds), *Consumption and the World of Goods* (London and New York: Routledge, 1993), pp. 85–132.

Jan de Vries, 'The Industrial Revolution and the Industrious Revolution', *Journal of Economic History*, 54 (1994), pp. 249–70.

Dror Wahrman, 'Percy's Prologue: From Gender Play to Gender Panic in Eighteenth-century England', *Past & Present*, 159 (1998), pp. 113–60.

Dror Wahrman, 'The English Problem of Identity in the American Revolution', *The American Historical Review* 106, 4 (2001), pp. 1236–62.

Dror Wahrman, 'Change and the Corporeal in Seventeenth- and Eighteenth-Century Gender History: Or, Can Cultural History be Rigorous?', *Gender and History*, 20, 3 (2008), pp. 584–602.

Cynthia Wall, 'Gendering Rooms: Domestic Architecture and Literary Acts', *Eighteenth-Century Fiction*, 5, 4 (1993), pp. 349–72.

Cynthia Wall, 'A Geography of Georgian Narrative Space', in Miles Ogborn and Charles Withers (eds), *Georgian Geographies: Essays on Space, Place and Landscape in the Eighteenth Century* (Manchester: Manchester University Press, 2004), pp. 114–29.

Lorna Weatherill, 'A Possession of One's Own: Women and Consumer Behaviour in England, 1660–1740', *Journal of British Studies*, 25 (1986), pp. 131–56.

Rachel Weil, 'The Family in the Exclusion Crisis: Locke versus Filmer Revisited', in Alan Houston and Steven C. A. Pincus, (eds), *A Nation Transformed: England after the Restoration* (Cambridge: Cambridge University Press, 2001), pp. 100–24.

Keith Wrightson, 'The Family in Early Modern England: Continuity and Change', Stephen Taylor, Richard Connors, and Clyve Jones (eds), *Hanoverian Britain and Empire: Essays on Memory of Philip Lawson* (Woodbridge: Boydell, 1998), pp. 1–22.

BOOKS

Susan Dwyer Amussen, *An Ordered Society: Gender and Class in Early Modern England* (New York: Columbia University Press, 1988).

Herbert M. Atherton, *Political Prints in the Age of Hogarth. A Study of the Ideographic Representation of Politics* (Oxford: Clarendon, 1974).

Joanne Bailey, *Unquiet Lives: Marriage and Marriage Breakdown in England, 1660–1800* (Cambridge: Cambridge University Press, 2003).

Hannah Barker, *The Business of Women: Female Enterprise and urban Development in Northern England, 1760–1830* (Oxford: Oxford University Press, 2006).

G. J. Barker Benfield, *The Culture of Sensibility: Sex and Society in Eighteenth-Century Britain* (Chicago: University of Chicago Press, 1992).

John Barrell, *The Birth of Pandora and the Division of Knowledge* (Basingstoke: Palgrave Macmillan, 1992).

William James Booth, *Households: On the Moral Architecture of the Economy* (Ithaca; London: Cornell University Press, 1993).

Michael J. Braddick and John Walter (eds), *Negotiating Power in Early Modern Society: Order, Hierarchy and Subordination in Britain and Ireland* (Cambridge: Cambridge University Press, 2001).

John Brewer and Susan Staves (eds), *Early Modern Conceptions of Property* (London and New York: Routledge, 1996).

Gillian Brown, *Domestic Individualism: Imagining Self in Nineteenth-Century America* (Berkeley, LA; Oxford: University of California Press, 1990).

Trev Lynn Broughton and Helen Roger (eds), *Gender and Fatherhood in the Nineteenth Century* (Basingstoke: Palgrave Macmillan, 2007).

Richard Bushman, *The Refinement of America: Persons, Houses, Cities* (New York: Vintage, 1993).

Colin Campbell, *The Romantic Ethic and the Spirit of Modern Consumerism* (1987; Alcuin, 2005).

Philip Carter, *Men and the Emergence of Polite Society in Britain, 1660–1800* (Harlow: Longman, 2001).

Roger Chartier (ed.), *A History of Private Life: Volume III - Passions of the Renaissance*, trans. Arthur Goldhammer, general editors Phillipe Aries and George Duby, (London: Belknap Press, 1989).

Tita Chico, *Designing Women: The Dressing Room in Eighteenth-century English Literature and Culture* (Lewisburg: Bucknell University Press, 2005).

Christopher Christie, *The British Country House in the Eighteenth Century* (Manchester: Manchester University Press, 2000),

Anna Clark, *Struggle for the Breeches: Gender and the Making of the British Working Class* (Berkeley; Los Angeles; London: University of California Press, 1995).

J. C. D. Clark, *English Society 1660–1832: Religion, Ideology and Politics during the Ancien Regime* (1985; Cambridge: Cambridge University Press, 2000).

Lisa Forman Cody, *Birthing the Nation: Sex, Science, and the Conception of Eighteenth-Century Britons* (Oxford: Oxford University Press, 2005).

Deborah Cohen, *Household Gods: The British and their Possessions* (New Haven, Conn.: Yale University Press, 2006).

C. H. Collins Baker and Muriel I. Baker, *The Life and Circumstances of James Brydges First Duke of Chandos, Patron of the Liberal Arts* (Oxford: Clarendon Press, 1949).

John E. Crowley, *The Invention of Comfort: Sensibilities and Design in Early Modern Britain and America* (Baltimore: Johns Hopkins University Press, 2001).

Leonore Davidoff and Catherine Hall, *Family Fortunes: Men and Women of the English Middle Class, 1780–1850* (1987; London: Routledge, 1992).

Rudolph Dekker (ed.), *Egodocuments and History: Autobiographical Writing in its Social Context since the Middle Ages* (Hilversum: Verloren, 2002).

John Demos, *Circles and Lines: The Shape of Life in Early America* (Cambridge, MA; London: Harvard University Press, 2004).

David Dewing (ed.), *Home and Garden: Paintings and Drawings of English, Middle-class, Urban Domestic Spaces 1675 to 1914* (London: Geffrye Museum, 2003).

H. T. Dickinson, *Liberty and Property: Political Ideology in Eighteenth-Century Britain* (London: Weidenfeld and Nicolson, 1977).

Peter Earle, *The Making of the English Middle Class: Business, Society and Family Life in London, 1660–1730* (London: Methuen, 1989).

John Eglin, *The Imaginary Autocrat: Beau Nashe and the Invention of Bath* (London: Profile, 2005).

Amy Erickson, *Women and Property in Early Modern England* (London: Routledge, 1993).

Nicole Eustace, *Passion is the Gale: Emotion, Power and the Coming of the American Revolution* (Chapel Hill: University of North Carolina Press 2008).

B. Fallows, *Bury Grammar School: A History c.1570–1976* (Bury, Estate Governors of the Bury Grammar Schools, 2001).

Margot Finn, *The Character of Credit: Personal Debt in English Culture, 1740–1914* (Cambridge; New York: Cambridge University Press, 2003).

Amanda Flather, *Gender and Space in Early Modern England* (Woodbridge: Boydell Press, 2007).

Anthony Fletcher, *Gender, Sex and Subordination in England, 1500–1800* (New Haven; London: Yale University Press, 1995).

Anthony Fletcher, *Growing up in England: The Experience of Childhood, 1600–1914* (New Haven and London: Yale University Press, 2008).

Christopher Flint, *Family Fictions: Narrative and Domestic Relations in Britain, 1688–1798* (Stanford, CA: Stanford University Press, 1998).

Elizabeth Foyster, *Manhood in Early Modern England: Honour, Sex and Marriage* (Harlow: Addison, Wesley, Longman, 1999).

Henry French, *The Middle Sort of People in Provincial England, 1600–1750* (Oxford: Oxford University Press, 2007).

H. R. French and R. W. Hoyle, *The Character of English Rural Society: Earls Colne, 1550–1750* (Manchester and New York: Manchester University Press, 2007).

M. Dorothy George, *English Political Caricature to 1792: A Study of Opinion and Propaganda* (Oxford: Clarendon Press, 1959).

Mark Girouard, *Life in the English Country House: A Social and Architectural History* (1978; Harmondsworth: Penguin, 1980).

Natasha Glaisyer and Sara Pennell (eds), *Didactic Literature in England, 1500–1800: Expertise Constructed* (Aldershot: Ashgate, 2003).

Erving Goffman, *The Presentation of Self in Everyday Life* (1959; Harmondsworth: Penguin, 1974).

D. R. Hainsworth, *Stewards, Lords and People: The Estate Steward and his World in later Stuart England* (Cambridge: Cambridge University Press, 1992).

Julie Hardwick, *The Practice of Patriarchy: Gender and the Politics of Household Authority in Early Modern France* (Pennsylvania: Pennysylvania State University Press, 1998).

Karen Harvey, *Reading Sex in the Eighteenth Century: Bodies and Gender in English Erotic Culture* (Cambridge: Cambridge University Press, 2004).

Karen Harvey (ed.), *History and Material Culture: A Student's Guide to Approaching Alternative Sources* (London: Routledge, March 2009).

Douglas Hay and Nicholas Rogers, *Eighteenth-Century English Society: Shuttles and Swords* (Oxford: Oxford University Press, 1997).

Sandra Stanley Holton, *Quaker Women: Personal Life, Memory and Radicalism in the Lives of Women Friends, 1780–1930* (Abingdon: Routledge, 2007).

Margaret Hunt, *The Middling Sort: Commerce, Gender and the Family in England, 1680–1780* (Berkeley: University of California Press, 1996).

Susan Jenkins, *Portrait of a Patron: The Patronage and Collecting of James Brydges, 1st Duke of Chandos (1674–1744)* (Aldershot: Ashgate, 2007).

Matthew Johnson, *An Archaeology of Capitalism* (Oxford: Blackwell, 1996).

Robert W. Jones, *Gender and the Formation of Taste in Eighteenth-Century Britain: The Analysis of Beauty* (Cambridge: Cambridge University Press, 1998).

Elizabeth Kowaleski-Wallace (ed.), *Their Fathers' Daughters: Hannah More, Maria Edgeworth, and Patriarchal Complicity* (New York; Oxford: Oxford University Press, 1991).

Elizabeth Kowaleski-Wallace, *Consuming Subjects. Women, Shopping, and Business in the Eighteenth Century* (New York: Columbia University Press, 1997).

David Kuchta, *The Three-Piece Suit and Modern Masculinity: England, 1550–1850* (Berkeley, CA: University of California Press, 2002).

Peter Laslett, *Family Life and Illicit Love in Earlier Generations: Essays in Historical Sociology* (Cambridge: Cambridge University Press, 1977).

Peter Laslett and Richard Wall (eds), *Household and Family in Past Time: Comparative Studies in the Size and Structure of the Domestic Group over the last Three Centuries* (Cambridge: Cambridge University Press, 1972).

Beverly Lemire, *The Business of Everyday Life: Gender, Practice and Social Politics in England, c.1600–1900* (Manchester: Manchester University Press, 2005).

Kenneth A. Lockridge, *On the Sources of Patriarchal Rage: The Commonplace Books of William Byrd and Thomas Jefferson and the Gendering of Power in the Eighteenth Century* (New York: New York University Press, 1992).

Matthew McCormack, *The Independent Man: Citizenship and Gender Politics in Georgian England* (Manchester and New York: Manchester University Press, 2005).

Matthew McCormack (ed.), *Public Men: Masculinity and Politics in Modern Britain* (Basingstoke: Palgrave Macmillan, 2007).

Elizabeth McKellar, *The Birth of Modern London: The Development and Design of the City, 1660–1720* (Manchester: Manchester University Press, 1999).

Neil McKendrick, John Brewer and J. H. Plumb, *The Birth of a Consumer Society: The Commercialisation of Eighteenth-Century England* (Cambridge: Cambridge University Press, 1982).

Michael McKeon, *The Secret History of Domesticity: Public, Private, and the Division of Knowledge* (London; Baltimore, MD: Johns Hopkins University Press, 2005).

Brian McCrea, *Impotent Fathers: Patriarchy and Demographic Crisis in the Eighteenth-Century Novel* (Newark: University of Delaware Press, 1998).

Michael Mascuch, *Origins of the Individualist Self: Autobiography and Self-identity in England, 1591–1791* (Cambridge: Polity Press, 1997).

Doreen Massey, *Space, Place and Gender* (Cambridge: Polity Press, 1994).

Shawn Lisa Maurer, *Proposing Men: Dialectics of Gender and Class in the Eighteenth-century English Periodical* (Stanford, CA: Stanford University Press, 1998).

Tim Meldrum, *Domestic Service and Gender, 1660–1750: Life and Work in the London House* (Harlow: Pearson, 2000).

Simon Middleton and Billy G. Smith (eds), *Class Matters: Early North America and the Atlantic World* (Philadelphia, PA; Oxford: University of Pennsylvania Press, 2010).

Pavla Miller, *Transformations of Patriarchy in the West: 1500–1900* (Bloomington: Indiana University Press, 1998).

John Moreland, *Archaeology and Text* (London: Duckworth Academic, 2001).

Ann Moss, *Printed Commonplace-Books and the Structuring of Renaissance Thought* (Oxford: Clarendon Press, 1996).

Craig Muldrew, *The Economy of Obligation: The Culture of Credit and Social Relations in Early Modern England* (Basingstoke: Macmillan, 1998).

Mary Beth Norton, *Founding Mothers and Fathers: Gendered Power and the Formation of American Society* (New York: Alfred A. Knopf, 1996).

Felicity A. Nussbaum, *The Autobiographical Subject: Gender and Ideology in Eighteenth-Century England* (Baltimore, MD: Johns Hopkins University Press, 1989).

Lena Cowen Orlin, *Private Matters and Public Culture in Post-Reformation England* (Ithaca; London: Cornell University Press, 1994).

Lena Cowen Orlin, *Locating Privacy in Tudor London* (Oxford: Oxford University Press, 2007).

Mark Overton, Jane Whittle, Darron Dean, Andrew Hann, *Production and Consumption in English Households, 1600–1750* (London: Routledge, 2004).

Ruth Perry, *Novel Relations: The Transformation of Kinship in English Literature and Culture, 1748–1818* (Cambridge: Cambridge University Press, 2004).

Nicola Phillips, *Women in Business, 1700–1850* (Woodbridge: Boydell, 2006).

J. G. A. Pocock, *The Machiavellian Moment: Florentine Political Thought and the Atlantic Republican Tradition* (1975; Princeton, NJ: Princeton University Press, 2003).

Mary Poovey, *Genres of the Credit Economy: Mediating Value in Eighteenth- and Nineteenth-Century Britain* (Chicago: Chicago University Press, 2008).

Dale B. J. Randall, *Gentle Flame: The Life and Verse of Dudley, Fourth Lord North (1602–1677)* (Durham, N C: Duke University Press, 1983).

Caroline Robbins, *The Eighteenth-Century Commonwealthman: Studies in the Transmission, Development and Circumstance of English Liberal Thought from the Restoration of Charles II until the War with the Thirteen Colonies* (1959; New York: Athenaeum, 1968).

Christine Roulston, *Virtue, Gender and the Authentic Self in Eighteenth-Century Fiction: Richardson, Rousseau and Laclos* (Gainesville: University of Florida Press, 1998).

David Sabean, *Property, Production, and Family in Neckarhausen, 1700–1870* (Cambridge: Cambridge University Press, 1990).

Raffaella Sarti, *Europe at Home: Family and Material Culture, 1500–1800* (trans. Allan Cameron; New Haven: Yale University Press, 2002).

Charles Saumerez Smith, *Eighteenth-Century Decoration: Design and the Domestic Interior* (London: Weidenfeld and Nicolson, 1993).

Gordon J. Schochet, *The Authoritarian Family and Political Attitudes in 17th-Century England* (1975; New Brunswick, NJ: Transaction, 1988).

Carole Shammas, *The Pre-Industrial Consumer in England and America* (Oxford: Oxford University Press, 1990).

Carole Shammas, *A History of Household Government in America* (Charlottesville; London: University of Virginia Press, 2002).

Alexandra Shepard, *Meanings of Manhood in Early Modern England* (Oxford: Oxford University Press, 2003).

Robert B. Shoemaker, *Gender in English Society, 1650–1850: The Emergence of Separate Spheres?* (Harlow: Longman, 1998).

John Shovlin, *The Political Economy of Virtue: Luxury, Patriotism, and the origins of the French Revolution* (Ithaca, NY; London: Cornell University Press, 2006).

John Smail, *The Origins of Middle Class Culture: Halifax, Yorkshire, 1660–1780* (Ithaca, NY: Cornell University Press, 1995).

Ann Smart Martin, *Buying into the World of Goods: Early Consumers in Backcountry Virginia* (Baltimore, MD: Johns Hopkins University Press, 2008).

Adam Smyth, *Autobiography in Early Modern England* (Cambridge: Cambridge University Press, 2010).

Michael Snodin and John Styles, *Design and the Decorative Arts, Britain 1500–1900* (V & A Publications, London, 2001).

Marie Louise Stig Sørensen, *Gender Archaeology* (Cambridge: Polity Press, 2000).

Patricia Meyer Spacks, *Privacy: Concealing the Eighteenth-Century Self* (London: University of Chicago Press, 2003).

Susan M. Stabile, *Memory's Daughters: The Material Culture of Remembrance in Eighteenth-century America* (Ithaca, NY; London: Cornell University Press, 2003).

Susan Staves, *Married Women's Separate Property in England, 1660–1833* (Cambridge, MS: Harvard University Press, 1990).

Lawrence Stone, *The Family, Sex and Marriage in England, 1500–1800* (1977; Harmondsworth: Penguin, 1979).

Kristina Straub, *Domestic Affairs: Intimacy, Eroticism and Violence between Servants and Masters in Eighteenth-Century Britain* (Baltimore, MD: Johns Hopkins University Press, 2009).

Naomi Tadmor, *Family and Friends in Eighteenth-Century England: Household, Kinship and Patronage* (Cambridge: Cambridge University Press, 2001).

Charles Taylor, *Sources of the Self: The Making of Modern Identity* (Cambridge, MS: Harvard University Press, 1989).

E. P. Thompson, *Customs in Common* (Harmondsworth: Penguin, 1993).

Peter Thornton, *Authentic Décor: The Domestic Interior, 1620–1920* (1984; London: Seven Dials, 2000).

John and Sylvia Tonge, *Astley Hall (Damhouse)* (John and Sylvia Tonge, 2002).

John Tosh, *A Man's Place: Masculinity and the Middle-Class Home in Victorian England* (New Haven, CN; London: Yale University Press, 1999).

Keith Tribe, *Land, Labour and Economic Discourse* (London: Routledge, 1978).

Randolph Trumbach, *The Rise of the Egalitarian Family: Aristocratic Kinship and Domestic Relations in Eighteenth-Century England* (New York; London: Academic Press, 1978)

Ted Underwood, *The Work of the Sun: Literature, Science, and Political Economy, 1760–1860* (Basingstoke: Palgrave Macmillan, 2005).

Amanda Vickery, *The Gentleman's Daughter: Women's Lives in Georgian England* (New Haven, CN: Yale University Press, 1998).

Amanda Vickery, *Behind Closed Doors: At Home in Georgian England* (New Haven, CN: Yale University Press, 2009).

Jan de Vries, *The Industrious Revolution: Consumer Behaviour and the Household Economy, 1650 to the Present* (Cambridge: Cambridge University Press, 2008).

Dror Wahrman, *Imagining the Middle Class: The Political Representation of Class in Britain, c.1780–1840* (Cambridge: Cambridge Univeristy Press, 1995).

Dror Wahrman, *The Making of the Modern Self: Identity and Culture in Eighteenth-Century England* (New Haven, CN: Yale University Press, 2004).

Wendy Wall, *Staging Domesticity: Household Work and English Identity in Early Modern Drama* (Cambridge: Cambridge University Press, 2002).

Lorna Weatherill, *Consumer Behaviour and Material Culture in Britain, 1660–1760* (London: Routledge, 1988).

Rachel Weil, *Political Passions: Gender, the Family and Political Argument in England, 1680–1714* (Manchester: Manchester University Press, 1999).

Susan Whyman, *Sociability and Power in Late-Stuart England: The Cultural Worlds of the Verneys, 1660–1720* (Oxford: Oxford University Press, 1999).

Raymond Williams, *Cobbett* (Oxford: Oxford University Press, 1983).

John P. Zomchick, *Family and the Law in Eighteenth-Century Fiction: The Public Conscience in the Private Sphere* (Cambridge: Cambridge University Press, 1993).

Index

Printed in the USA/Agawam, MA
December 11, 2014

603463.015